Formed by Difference

Leading Multicultural Organizations with Integrity

Dr. M. M. Elmendorf

FORD MOUNTAIN PUBLISHING, LLC

Contents

Dedication

This work is dedicated first to God, whose patience and grace made it possible. Any wisdom here reflects His instruction; all flaws are mine alone.

For those who have ever felt like a foreigner in their own workplace — and for the leaders wise enough to notice.

For every team formed by difference — shaped not despite its tensions, but through them.

May these pages return dignity to those who have quietly carried it for others.

Preface

This book draws from extensive qualitative research in multicultural organizational leadership. The study employed interviews, observations, and document analysis across multiple contexts over several years. The goal was to understand how diverse teams navigate complexity, build trust, and sustain mission over time. Every insight in these pages emerged from listening to real leaders and team members facing real challenges in multicultural environments. All identifying details have been removed or altered to protect confidentiality.

While the research was conducted in specific organizational settings, the patterns observed transcend any single context. These dynamics appear wherever people from different cultural backgrounds work together toward shared purpose. The frameworks and practices offered here aren't theoretical constructs—they emerged from the lived experience of leaders who graciously shared their struggles, insights, and hard-won wisdom. The integration of contemporary research, historical examples, and biblical teaching reflects a conviction that we need multiple sources of insight to navigate the complexity of multicultural leadership.

A Caveat on Worldview

I need to be honest about something.

This book emerged from research, yes—from careful observation, systematic analysis, and rigorous method. But it also emerged from a lived experience and conviction. I am a follower of Jesus Christ. I believe Scripture is true, authoritative, and relevant to every dimension of life—including how we lead, work together, and build organizations that honor human dignity. That conviction shapes how I see the world.

When I observe patterns of trust, justice, empowerment, or cultural bridge-building, I see echoes of kingdom values. When I see exploitation, exclusion, or dehumanization, I see violations of what God intended for human community.

I've tried to write honestly about what I observed without imposing my faith on you. The frameworks, practices, and insights in this book are offered not as doctrinal requirements but as practical wisdom that has proven effective in diverse settings. They can be understood, evaluated, and implemented based on their merit, regardless of your spiritual commitments.

That said, I won't pretend to write from a neutral position—no researcher does. My faith shapes how I interpret what I observe. It informs my conviction that every human being carries the image of God and deserves dignity, that leaders are called to stewardship rather than exploitation, that justice and mercy aren't optional extras but core requirements of faithful leadership.

If you don't share my faith, I hope you'll still find the practical frameworks useful. Many have. If you do share it, I hope you'll see this as an invitation to integrate your deepest convictions into your leadership rather than compartmentalizing them. Either way, I ask that you evaluate what follows not by my credentials or theological commitments, but by whether it helps you lead more effectively, build healthier teams, and create organizations where diverse people can flourish together.

A Fair Warning

I love learning. I love history. I love stories.

As such, this book is filled with stories from history and the Bible that encapsulate the themes and lessons of the chapters, and it is my hope that by reading these stories, you may gain greater insight on the chapter's details.

As such, this book is NOT MEANT TO BE READ IN ONE SITTING. Please, do not do that to yourself or to your organization, or your loved ones. This book is meant to be digested slowly, with the reader mulling over each chapter for a goodly bit before moving to the next.

And in that line of thought, it is not (exactly) meant to be read in order, either. While there may be a chapter here and there where there are references to previous chapters, it is possible to read them out of order by way of table of contents, though in the order you need.

Introduction

Why This Book Exists

Leadership across cultures is one of the most consequential challenges of our time. Organizations everywhere are becoming more diverse—not just demographically, but in the lived experiences, values, and worldviews people bring to their work. This diversity creates unprecedented opportunity for innovation, resilience, and kingdom impact. But it also introduces friction, misunderstanding, and complexity that can derail even the most well-intentioned teams.

This book exists because the gap between diversity as aspiration and diversity as lived reality is often painful. Leaders find themselves navigating invisible cultural currents they were never trained to see. Team members from minority backgrounds carry burdens their colleagues don't recognize. Organizations espouse values of inclusion while inadvertently perpetuating systems that favor certain voices and marginalize others.

For Christian leaders, this challenge carries particular weight. We serve a God who calls people from every nation, tribe, and tongue into one body (Revelation 7:9, NIV). We claim the gospel transcends all human divisions. Yet our organizations often struggle to reflect that reality. Cultural intelligence isn't just a leadership competency—it's a theological imperative rooted in the very nature of God's mission in the world.

Who This Book Is For

This book is written primarily for Christian leaders working in multicultural contexts—whether in nonprofits, churches, educational institutions, businesses, or mission organizations. If you lead a team where people come from different cultural backgrounds, this book is for you.

You might be an executive director navigating cultural tensions on your leadership team. You might be a department manager trying to create space for quieter voices. You might be a founder building an organization with diversity as a core value but uncertain how to translate that value into practice. You might be a team member from a minority background trying to help your leaders understand dynamics they can't see from their position of cultural majority.

The frameworks and practices in this book emerged from extensive qualitative research in multicultural organizations, combined with careful attention to Scripture, historical examples, and contemporary scholarship. While the content is grounded in Christian conviction about human dignity, justice, and community, the practical wisdom offered here has proven effective across diverse settings.

How to Use This Book

This book is organized into four parts, each building on the previous one:

PART ONE: SEEING WHAT'S REALLY HAPPENING

These foundational chapters help you recognize the invisible dynamics at play in multicultural organizations—the three-layer reality of organizational life and the false choice between high performance and human dignity.

PART TWO: BUILDING THE FOUNDATION

These chapters address the core organizational systems required for healthy multicultural leadership—trust, voice, and cultural intelligence. Without these foundations, other interventions rarely succeed.

PART THREE: LEADING FOR THE LONG HAUL

These chapters explore the leadership practices that sustain diverse teams through challenge—from shared leadership and transcendent vision to faith-informed values, navigating scarcity, and managing turnover and transition.

PART FOUR: SUSTAINABLE TRANSFORMATION

These chapters focus on the rhythms, development systems, and long-term faithfulness required to create lasting change rather than short-lived initiatives.

Each chapter follows a consistent structure:
• Opening Scene: Vivid workplace scenario you may find relatable
• Research and Contemporary Practice
• Historical Examples
• Biblical Examples
• Watch For This: Warning signs to recognize
• Try This Week: Specific actionable practices with time estimates
• Reflection Questions: Three levels (Quick Check, Deeper Reflection, Team Discussion)
• Moving Forward: A chapter summary/encouragement to keep on the hard path of choosing to do better each and every day

Multicultural Organizational Health Check

Although there is a separate companion toolkit available (see below for more details), included within this book is an organizational health check based on the topics and frameworks found within this book. It is a useful tool for assessing personal and organizational growth.

Full Companion Toolkit Available

The frameworks, templates, and tools referenced throughout this book are available as a comprehensive companion toolkit. This free resource includes assessment templates and implementation guides to help you apply these principles in your organization.

Access the full toolkit at: https://fordmountainpublishing.com/formed_by_difference_toolkit/

PART ONE: SEEING WHAT'S REALLY HAPPENING

SEEING WHAT'S REALLY HAPPENING

Cross Cultural Work in Practice

Opening Scene

The conference room fell silent when Hannah finished speaking. She had suggested adjusting the project timeline to account for the upcoming Lunar New Year celebrations—a major holiday for half the team. But the silence that followed wasn't agreement. It was the particular quality of quiet that signals discomfort no one wants to name.

Finally, James cleared his throat. "We appreciate the input, but we really need to keep the original deadline. We've already committed to the board." His tone was pleasant, professional. The decision was clearly final. Around the table, several team members nodded. The Asian staff members—representing five different countries and cultural backgrounds—said nothing. Their faces remained neutral, but their body language shifted almost imperceptibly. Shoulders tightened. Eyes dropped to notebooks. The meeting continued, but something had fractured that wouldn't be easy to repair.

Later, in hushed conversations near the coffee machine and in careful emails sent after hours, the real responses emerged. "They never listen." "We're just expected to adapt to their way of doing things." "I told you it wasn't worth bringing up." Hannah wondered if she should have stayed silent. James wondered why people seemed distant for the rest of the week. Neither could quite name what had happened, but both knew something important had been missed.

The Reality of Cross-Cultural Work

Working across cultures isn't just about learning customs or avoiding offense. It's about navigating fundamental differences in how people understand communication, time, authority, conflict, and relationships. These differences operate largely below conscious awareness, shaping behavior in ways neither party fully recognizes.

The opening scene illustrates what researchers call the "cultural iceberg," a term often attributed to Edward Hall. Above the waterline sit visible cultural markers—holidays, food, dress, language. Below the waterline lie invisible but more powerful elements—assumptions about time, communication styles, power dynamics, and decision-making processes. Most cross-cultural friction happens in this invisible territory.

Hannah's suggestion about the Lunar New Year wasn't primarily about holiday logistics. It was a test of whether cultural considerations matter in this organization's decision-making. James's response—polite but firm—sent a clear message: efficiency and board commitments trump cultural accommodation. His tone was kind. His decision was final. And his cultural framework (likely Western, task-oriented, linear-time) shaped that decision in ways he probably didn't consciously recognize.

The Asian team members' silence wasn't passive acceptance. In many Asian cultural contexts, direct disagreement with authority—especially in public settings—signals disrespect and disrupts group harmony. Silence protects both the individual from appearing contentious and the group from public conflict. From their cultural framework, speaking up again would escalate tension unnecessarily. From James's framework, silence meant consent.

This is the daily reality of multicultural organizational life: the same interaction means completely different things to people operating from different cultural frameworks.

The Three-Layer Reality

Every organizational interaction operates simultaneously on three distinct but interconnected layers. Understanding these layers is essential for effective multicultural leadership because problems visible on one layer often have roots in another.

Layer One: The Visible Task

This is what appears on agendas and in job descriptions—the work to be accomplished, deadlines to be met, decisions to be made. Most meetings focus exclusively here. "We need to finalize the budget." "The report is due Friday." "Who will lead the new initiative?"

Layer Two: The Relational Climate

Beneath the visible tasks flow relational dynamics—trust levels, power dynamics, team cohesion, psychological safety. Questions operating here include: Do people feel safe speaking honestly? Do they trust leadership to follow through? Do they believe their contributions matter? Is there residual hurt from previous interactions?

Layer Three: The Cultural Undercurrent

Deepest and least visible are cultural assumptions about communication, authority, time, conflict, and relationships. These shape how people interpret everything happening in layers one and two. The same silence means "I agree" in one cultural framework and "I strongly disagree but won't say so publicly" in another. Here's why this matters:

Problems occurring on Layer One(tasks aren't getting done) often have roots in Layer Two (trust has eroded) or Layer Three (cultural frameworks are clashing without anyone recognizing it).Leaders who address only the visible task layer rarely solve the actual problem.

The Three Layers in the Opening Scene

Let's analyze the meeting through all three layers:

Layer One (Visible Task): Hannah suggested adjusting the timeline for Lunar New Year. James declined, citing board commitments. The task discussion appeared straightforward and resolved.

Layer Two (Relational Climate): Trust fractured in this interaction. The Asian team members learned their cultural considerations don't influence decisions. Hannah learned her voice doesn't carry weight. James remained unaware that relational damage occurred. Future interactions will be shaped by this erosion of trust, even if no one names it.

Layer Three (Cultural Undercurrent): Multiple cultural frameworks clashed invisibly. James operated from a framework prioritizing efficiency, individual decision-making authority, and linear time. The Asian team members operated from frameworks valuing group harmony, indirect communication, and cyclical time that honors cultural celebrations. Neither framework is wrong—but the collision went unrecognized and unaddressed.

Effective multicultural leadership requires attending to all three layers simultaneously. Address only the task and you'll be perpetually confused about why people seem disengaged. Address only relationships without recognizing cultural undercurrents and you'll misinterpret behavior constantly. *Challenge moving forward: as you read the opening scenes in the subsequent chapters,* try to *determine the three layers within the scene.*

What Research Tells Us

Cross-cultural organizational research consistently demonstrates that cultural differences operate largely outside conscious awareness while significantly impacting performance. Hofstede's landmark research identified six dimensions along which cultures vary: power distance, individualism vs. collectivism, masculinity vs. femininity, uncertainty avoidance, long-term vs. short-term orientation, and indulgence vs. restraint. These dimensions shape expectations about leadership, decision-making, communication, and relationships in ways people rarely articulate.

Erin Meyer's work on the Culture Map provides practical frameworks for understanding eight key areas where business cultures differ: communicating, evaluating, leading, deciding, trusting, disagreeing, scheduling, and persuading. Her "good communication" looks completely different across cultures—what seems clear and direct in one framework appears blunt and disrespectful in another.

Amy Edmondson's research on psychological safety shows that team members need to believe they can speak up without risking punishment, humiliation, or marginalization. However, her research was conducted primarily in Western contexts. When applied multiculturally, we must recognize that psychological safety itself is culturally constructed—safety to speak up directly in meetings isn't universal. Some cultural frameworks define safety as the ability to share concerns through private channels without forcing public confrontation.

The Historical View

History offers powerful examples of cross-cultural leadership—both its triumphs and its failures. These stories reveal that the challenges facing today's multicultural organizations are not new; they are as old as human cooperation itself.

The Silk Road Caravanserais

For over fifteen centuries, the Silk Road connected civilizations from China to the Mediterranean. What made this vast trading network function wasn't just commerce—it was an intricate system of cultural navigation. Caravanserais, the inns, and trading posts that dotted the route, became laboratories for cross-cultural leadership.

The most successful caravanserai managers learned to read the three layers instinctively. They understood that a Persian merchant's haggling style meant something different from a Chinese trader's silence during negotiations. They created neutral spaces where Buddhist, Muslim, Christian, and Hindu travelers could coexist peacefully—not by eliminating differences, but by establishing shared protocols that honored them.

When conflicts arose, wise caravanserai leaders rarely addressed only the visible dispute. They understood trade agreements were built on relational trust, and that cultural misunderstandings could destroy months of relationship-building in a single mishandled moment. The Silk Road thrived not despite cultural difference, but because of systems designed to bridge it.

Applying the Three Layers:

- Layer One (Visible Task): The surface-level work of the Silk Road was a commercial exchange—negotiating prices, moving goods, completing transactions, and managing the logistics of long-distance travel. These were the items that appeared on every trader's agenda and the reason caravanserais existed at all.

- Layer Two (Relational Climate): Beneath each transaction flowed the relational trust required to make trade possible at all. Merchants who met repeatedly along the route built reputations and relationships that determined whether deals would be honored. Caravanserai managers had to maintain an environment where diverse travelers felt safe enough to rest, share meals, and conduct business with strangers—a fragile climate that any single mishandled conflict could destroy. The most successful managers understood that protecting the relational climate was as important as facilitating the trade itself.

- Layer Three (Cultural Undercurrent): Deepest of all were the invisible cultural assumptions each traveler brought with them—radically different frameworks for negotiation, time, hospitality, trust, and conflict. A Persian merchant's animated haggling wasn't aggression; it was respect for the process. A Chinese trader's silence wasn't disinterest; it was deliberation. Religious practices around prayer, food, and rest added further complexity. Caravanserai managers who succeeded were those who recognized these invisible frameworks without demanding that any group abandon them—creating shared protocols that allowed different cultural logics to function side by side.

The lesson: The Silk Road's longevity wasn't an accident of geography or commerce alone. It was built on leaders who understood that visible transactions (Layer One) could only flow consistently when relational trust (Layer Two) was cultivated and cultural differences (Layer Three) were honored rather than flattened.

The Jesuit Missions in China

In the late sixteenth century, Matteo Ricci arrived in China with a mission—and a problem. Previous European missionaries had failed spectacularly, dismissed as "barbarians" by Chinese officials who found their cultural ignorance offensive. Ricci took a different approach. He spent years mastering Mandarin, studying Confucian classics, and learning Chinese customs. He dressed as a Chinese scholar, not a European priest. When he finally gained access to the imperial court, he came bearing gifts that demonstrated respect: accurate maps, clocks, and mathematical instruments.

Ricci's cultural intelligence allowed him to see what others had missed. He recognized that Confucian values of respect, harmony, and learning weren't obstacles to his mission—they could be bridges. He framed Christianity in terms that resonated with Chinese philosophical traditions rather than demanding immediate acceptance of foreign frameworks.

His success was remarkable: within decades, Jesuits advised Chinese emperors, translated scientific texts, and built lasting relationships. The lesson isn't about religious agreement—it's about the power of genuine cultural humility. Ricci succeeded because he refused to operate only on Layer One. He understood that lasting influence required deep engagement with Layers Two and Three.

Applying the Three Layers:

- Layer One (Visible Task): The surface-level task Ricci arrived with was clear—sharing his faith with Chinese officials and, ultimately, gaining access to the imperial court. Every previous missionary had attempted this task directly, presenting their message and expecting acceptance. On Layer One, the goal seemed straightforward: make contact, communicate content, complete the mission.

- Layer Two (Relational Climate): Where previous missionaries failed was in neglecting the relational layer entirely. Chinese court culture was deeply relational—trust had to be established over years, and it flowed through demonstrated respect for Chinese learning and authority. By arriving as a cultural student rather than a cultural expert, Ricci built relationships that gave his message a hearing. His gifts weren't bribes; they were relational investments. They communicated: I have come to contribute, not merely to convert. When the relational climate was healthy, the visible task became possible.

- Layer Three (Cultural Undercurrent): Ricci's genius lay in his willingness to go deepest—to understand the invisible cultural frameworks that shaped how Chinese scholars and officials understood knowledge, authority, learning, and truth. Confucian assumptions about hierarchy, harmony, and the nature of wisdom weren't obstacles to navigate around; they were the very architecture through which Ricci's message had to travel. Rather than demanding that Chinese intellectuals adopt a European cultural framework before receiving his message, Ricci translated his message into frameworks they already inhabited. He didn't change what he believed; he changed how he communicated it—and that required operating fluently on Layer Three.

The lesson: Ricci's predecessors failed not because their message was wrong but because they operated only on Layer One, ignoring the relational and cultural layers that determined whether anyone would listen. Ricci's success demonstrates that lasting influence in cross-cultural contexts requires attending to all three layers simultaneously—and usually in reverse order.

The Marshall Plan's Overlooked Dimension

After World War II, the Marshall Plan rebuilt Europe's shattered economies. But its success wasn't primarily about money—it was about cultural intelligence that history books often overlook. American planners initially approached reconstruction with a purely task-oriented mindset: identify problems, allocate resources, measure progress. They were puzzled when their well-funded initiatives met resistance.

The breakthrough came when planners began listening differently. They discovered European nations had vastly different cultural relationships with aid, pride, and national identity. What felt like straightforward help to Americans felt like humiliating dependence to some Europeans. The plan's eventual success required adapting to local contexts: allowing nations to determine their own priorities, framing assistance as partnership rather than charity, and creating structures that preserved national dignity while enabling cooperation. Countries weren't just given resources—they were given voice in how those resources would be used. The Marshall Plan succeeded where other aid efforts failed because its leaders eventually learned to see beyond the visible task of economic reconstruction to the relational and cultural layers beneath.

Applying the Three Layers:

- Layer One (Visible Task): American planners began with a clear and urgent Layer One mandate: rebuild war-shattered European economies, prevent the spread of communism, and restore political stability. The tasks were concrete—infrastructure, food supply, industrial capacity, financial systems. Resources were allocated. Progress was measured. On paper, the plan seemed well-designed.

- Layer Two (Relational Climate): The early resistance planners encountered was a Layer Two problem. The relational climate between American providers and European recipients was fraught with complexity that well-funded task completion could not fix. Many European nations had centuries-old traditions of national pride and self-determination. Receiving aid—however generously offered—activated deep relational dynamics around dignity, dependency, and the power imbalance between giver and recipient. American planners initially misread European hesitation as logistical friction or political obstruction. It was, in fact, a relational signal: the climate of the relationship had to change before the work could succeed. When planners shifted from directing to partnering—giving nations voice in their own recovery—the relational climate improved, and cooperation followed.

- Layer Three (Cultural Undercurrent): Most invisible, and most consequential, were the cultural frameworks each nation brought to the table. American planners operated from a cultural framework that valued efficiency, directness, measurable outcomes, and the assumption that help freely given would be freely received. European nations brought cultural frameworks shaped by historical trauma, colonial memory, national identity, and deeply rooted assumptions about sovereignty and self-determination. What felt culturally neutral to Americans—here are resources, here is a plan, let's measure results—felt culturally loaded to Europeans who understood that accepting a plan designed elsewhere meant ceding agency over their own futures. The breakthrough came when Americans recognized that these weren't personality conflicts or bureaucratic inefficiencies. They were cultural frameworks colliding invisibly—and the plan had to adapt to those frameworks, not the other way around.

The lesson: The Marshall Plan's early struggles and eventual success offer a masterclass in what happens when Layer One thinking collides with Layer Two and Three realities. Task-focused leaders who encounter unexpected resistance should ask: What relational dynamics are we missing? Whose cultural framework are we failing to see?

The Biblical View

Scripture demonstrates cross cultural work in action throughout, particularly in leadership contexts.

Joseph: A foreigner in Pharaoh's court

Joseph's story is often told as a narrative of individual success—from slave to ruler. But it's equally a masterclass in cross-cultural navigation. Sold into Egypt as a teenager, Joseph entered a world completely foreign to his Hebrew upbringing. Egyptian culture, religion, language, and power structures differed radically from everything he knew. Yet Joseph not only survived—he thrived, eventually becoming second only to Pharaoh himself. How?

Joseph learned to operate on all three layers simultaneously. He mastered the visible tasks (managing Potiphar's household, interpreting dreams, administering grain supplies), but he also attended to relational trust and cultural context. He adopted Egyptian dress and customs. He took an Egyptian name and married into Egyptian society. He learned to communicate in ways Egyptians could receive.

Yet Joseph never abandoned his core identity. When his brothers arrived during the famine, he eventually revealed himself and reconciled—bridging his Hebrew past with his Egyptian present. Joseph's genius was holding multiple cultural frameworks without losing himself in the process. For leaders today, Joseph models what it means to become "all things to all people" while maintaining integrity. Cultural adaptation isn't betrayal—it's stewardship of the influence God provides.

Applying the Three Layers:

- Layer One (Visible Task): At every stage of his story, Joseph demonstrated exceptional competence on Layer One. He managed Potiphar's household with such skill that his master "left everything he had in Joseph's care." In prison, he administered affairs so effectively that the warden put him in charge of all other prisoners. Before Pharaoh, he not only interpreted dreams but immediately offered a practical seven-year agricultural strategy. Joseph was never just a visionary—he was a deliverer of results. His Layer One competence opened doors that cultural outsiders rarely accessed.

- Layer Two (Relational Climate): What made Joseph's competence sustainable across radically different environments was his instinctive attention to relational trust. With Potiphar, he built trust through consistent reliability before anything else was asked of him. With the cupbearer and baker in prison, he attended to their distress before offering interpretations—reading the relational room before speaking into it. With Pharaoh, he framed his interpretation not as personal achievement but as divine gift, deflecting the credit in a way that honored the relational dynamic between a servant and a king. Later, with his brothers, he managed perhaps the most complex relational restoration in Scripture—testing, grieving, and ultimately reconciling across years of betrayal and separation. At every stage, Joseph understood that the relational climate determined whether his competence would be trusted or feared.

- Layer Three (Cultural Undercurrent): Most remarkable is Joseph's fluency across cultural frameworks that could not have been more different. Hebrew culture and Egyptian culture differed profoundly in language, religion, governance, and assumptions about honor, identity, and divine agency. Rather than demanding that Egyptians receive him on Hebrew terms, Joseph became culturally fluent in Egyptian frameworks—adopting dress, name, marriage, and customs while retaining his core identity and values. When he spoke to Pharaoh about God's role in the dreams, he translated theological conviction into a framework Pharaoh could receive. When he finally revealed himself to his brothers, he reframed their betrayal through a providential narrative that neither denied the wound nor made reconciliation impossible. Joseph moved between cultural frameworks without losing himself in any of them.

The lesson: Joseph's rise was not simply the result of divine favor or individual talent. It was the result of operating simultaneously on all three layers—delivering visible results, cultivating relational trust, and navigating cultural frameworks with intelligence and humility. For multicultural leaders today, Joseph's story is a reminder that cultural adaptation is not compromise. It is the stewardship of influence.

The Jerusalem Council: When cultural collision demanded resolution

Acts 15 records perhaps the most significant cross-cultural conflict in early church history. The question seemed simple: Must Gentile converts follow Jewish customs? But beneath that visible task-level question churned deep relational and cultural tensions. Jewish believers had centuries of cultural identity tied to circumcision, dietary laws, and Sabbath observance. Gentile believers came from vastly different backgrounds where these practices were foreign or even offensive. Both groups genuinely followed Jesus—but their cultural frameworks clashed dramatically.

The Jerusalem Council's resolution demonstrates sophisticated three-layer leadership. On Layer One, they made a clear decision: Gentiles need not adopt Jewish customs. But the leaders didn't stop there. The Jerusalem Council models what multicultural organizations need today: clear decisions made with relational sensitivity and cultural wisdom.

Applying the Three Layers:

- Layer One (Visible Task): The presenting task before the Jerusalem Council was a doctrinal and practical question that demanded resolution: must Gentile believers be circumcised and observe Mosaic law to be considered full members of the community? This was not a minor administrative matter—it had immediate, practical implications for every Gentile church Paul had planted and every Jewish community that received them. The council had to make a clear, authoritative decision that could be applied across a rapidly expanding movement spanning multiple cultures and geographies.

- Layer Two (Relational Climate): The council's leaders understood that a correct decision delivered poorly could fracture the community as surely as a wrong decision. The relational stakes were enormous: Jewish believers had deep emotional and identity-level investment in practices that had defined their people for centuries. Gentile believers had equally deep convictions about their freedom in Christ. Simply issuing a ruling and expecting compliance would have left the relational wounds unattended. The council's decision to send Paul, Barnabas, Judas, and Silas in person—rather than a letter alone—was a deliberate Layer Two strategy. Trusted relationship-holders would carry the decision, absorb the questions, and embody the unity the council was trying to create. The letter itself acknowledged the distress caused by the conflict, validating the relational experience of those affected before presenting the resolution.

- Layer Three (Cultural Undercurrent): The deepest layer of the Jerusalem Council's work was articulating a principle that could govern an inherently multicultural community indefinitely: unity does not require uniformity. This was not a compromise or a middle ground—it was a fundamental reframing of what Christian community meant across cultural boundaries. Jewish cultural practices were not wrong; they were simply not universally required. Gentile cultural frameworks were not inferior; they were simply different. The council's letter identified a small number of genuinely cross-cultural concerns (avoiding practices associated with idol worship and sexual immorality) while explicitly refusing to burden Gentiles with requirements that were cultural rather than essential. In doing so, the council modeled what every multicultural organization needs: the wisdom to distinguish between what is core and what is cultural, and the courage to protect both without collapsing them into each other.

The lesson: The Jerusalem Council's enduring influence was not primarily the specific decision it made but the three-layer leadership it modeled. Clear decisions (Layer One), delivered relationally (Layer Two), grounded in a unifying cultural principle (Layer Three)—this is the template for navigating multicultural conflict at the highest stakes.

Paul: Becoming all things to all people

No biblical figure navigated cross-cultural complexity more intentionally than the Apostle Paul. A Pharisee's Pharisee, Paul might have demanded that all converts adopt his Jewish-educated framework. Instead, he became history's most culturally adaptive leader. "I have become all things to all people," Paul wrote to the Corinthians, "so that by all possible means I might save some." This wasn't chameleon-like manipulation—it was strategic cultural intelligence rooted in love.

In Athens, Paul didn't begin with the Hebrew Scriptures. He started with Greek philosophy and local religious practices, quoting their own poets before introducing Christ. In Jewish synagogues, he reasoned from Torah. Among Romans, he emphasized citizenship and universal truths. Paul's letters show constant attention to all three layers. He addressed visible problems (task), built and maintained relationships through personal greetings and prayers (relational), and consistently adapted his communication to each culture's values and assumptions (cultural).

For modern leaders, Paul's example challenges the assumption that cultural adaptation compromises conviction. Paul's message remained consistent; his methods were infinitely flexible. He models the hard work of translating truth across cultural boundaries without diluting it.

Applying the Three Layers:

- Layer One (Visible Task): Paul's Layer One task was consistent across every context he entered: share the message of Christ crucified and risen, establish communities of believers, and strengthen those communities through teaching and correspondence. What varied dramatically was not the task but the method. In Thessalonica, he reasoned from Scripture across three Sabbaths. In Lystra, he appealed to creation and conscience when Scripture was not common ground. In Corinth, he planted himself for eighteen months to build a community through sustained presence. Paul's Layer One competence lay not just in his message but in his relentless adaptability in delivering it.

- Layer Two (Relational Climate): Paul's letters reveal a leader who was as attentive to relational dynamics as to theological content—sometimes more so. His closing chapters of greetings, naming individual people and their specific contributions, were not filler. They were deliberate relational investment, signaling to each community that they were known, valued, and connected to a wider network of care. When relational ruptures threatened communities—the factions in Corinth, the conflict between Euodia and Syntyche in Philippi, the tension over Jewish and Gentile table fellowship in Galatia—Paul addressed them directly and pastorally before returning to doctrinal instruction. He understood that a community whose relational climate was fractured could not receive or apply the teaching it needed. Layer Two was not a detour from the task; it was the soil in which the task could take root.

- Layer Three (Cultural Undercurrent): Paul's most remarkable cross-cultural leadership happened at Layer Three—in his ability to enter diverse cultural frameworks and find within them the language, concepts, and values that could carry his message. His speech on the Areopagus is perhaps the clearest example: he did not begin with Abraham or Moses, because those names carried no weight in Greek philosophical culture. He began where his audience already lived—with their religious curiosity, their poets, their own longing for the unknown God—and built a bridge from their framework to his. In Jewish contexts, he reasoned from the shared authority of Torah. Among Romans, he invoked citizenship, law, and universal truth. This was not relativism or compromise. Paul's core convictions remained fixed. What changed was his willingness to inhabit each cultural framework deeply enough to translate those convictions into language that each framework could receive. That is Layer Three work at its most demanding and most effective.

The lesson: Paul's ministry is perhaps the most sustained example in history of all three layers operating simultaneously and intentionally. For multicultural leaders today, Paul's example offers both inspiration and challenge: cultural adaptation is not a betrayal of conviction—it is the labor that conviction requires when it is serious about reaching people who do not already share your framework.

Nuances and Blind Spots

The comfortable silence problem. In many cultural frameworks, silence carries as much meaning as words — signaling respect, disagreement, discomfort, processing time, or deference to authority. When certain team members rarely speak in meetings and leadership interprets this as agreement or a lack of ideas, they're reading silence through only one cultural lens. A single approach to drawing people out will consistently misread the room.

The invisible workload. Some team members carry a heavy "cultural translation" burden — explaining one group's behavior to another, mediating misunderstandings, code-switching constantly. This exhausting labor often goes entirely unrecognized and unrewarded. Leaders must ask honestly: *Who is doing most of the adapting here, and is that distribution fair?*

The "we're past all that" assumption. Leadership believes the organization has moved beyond cultural tension because no one complains publicly. Meanwhile, concerns flow through informal channels leadership never accesses. Absence of visible conflict is not the same as health — it may simply mean people have learned that speaking up isn't worth the cost.

The single-culture standard. Evaluation criteria, meeting structures, communication norms, and decision-making processes often reflect one cultural framework — usually the dominant one — while being presented as neutral or universal. This is one of the most common and consequential blind spots in multicultural organizations, and it's rarely visible to those inside the dominant framework.

The deadline-relationship collision. Recurring tension between "getting things done" and "maintaining relationships" is frequently misread as a personality clash. More often, it's a collision between task-based and relationship-based cultural frameworks — neither of which is wrong. Similarly, when someone seems perpetually late or frustratingly rigid about schedules, the real issue is usually clashing time orientations, not character flaws.

The surface-level diversity trap. Organizations that celebrate visible cultural markers — food, festivals, dress — while leaving invisible elements unaddressed (communication styles, authority expectations, time orientation, conflict approaches) have the form of inclusion without the substance. Deeper cultural dynamics don't disappear because they're unacknowledged; they simply go underground.

The revolving door pattern. When staff from certain cultural backgrounds consistently leave earlier than others, the data is telling you something: the environment works better for some cultural frameworks than others. This pattern is easy to attribute to individual fit or circumstance. It's harder — and more honest — to ask what the organization itself may be making untenable.

Conflict styles and trust are both culturally shaped. Direct confrontation, mediated discussion, indirect communication, face-saving avoidance — all are legitimate approaches in different cultural frameworks. Organizations that recognize only one style as "healthy" will routinely mishandle conflicts that arise from other frameworks. The same is true for trust: task-based cultures build it through competence and reliability; relationship-based cultures build it through personal connection and shared time. Neither is superior, but organizations typically favor one without knowing it — leaving members of the other framework feeling like they can never quite break in.

Try This Week

Day 1–2: Map the Three Layers of One Recent Interaction

Choose a meeting or conversation from the past two weeks that didn't land the way you expected. Write down what happened on each layer:

- *Layer One*: What was the stated task or topic?

- *Layer Two*: What relational dynamics were present — trust, safety, power?

- *Layer Three*: What cultural assumptions might have been operating that no one named?

You don't have to have answers. The practice is learning to ask the questions. Most leaders never get to Layer Two or Three. Getting there — even in retrospect — is the beginning of a different kind of leadership.

Day 3: Ask Before You Decide

In one upcoming decision that affects your team, pause before presenting your conclusion. Instead, open with a genuine question: *"Before I share where I'm leaning, help me understand what's at stake for different people here."*

Then listen — not to confirm your direction, but to genuinely learn what you might be missing. Notice who speaks, who doesn't, and what the silence in the room might be carrying.

Day 4: Name the Invisible Workload

Identify one person on your team who regularly serves as a cultural translator — explaining one group's behavior to another, code-switching to navigate different expectations, or absorbing friction others don't notice. Reach out privately and simply say: *"I've noticed you do a lot of bridging work on this team. I want you to know I see it, and I want to understand more about what that costs you."*

Don't fix anything. Just make the invisible visible.

Day 5: Audit One "Neutral" Practice

Choose one standard practice in your organization — a meeting format, an evaluation process, a communication norm — and ask honestly: *Whose cultural framework does this naturally favor? Who has to adapt most to participate fully?*

You may not change the practice this week. But naming whose framework it reflects is the first step toward making it genuinely inclusive rather than accidentally exclusive.

Weekend: Sit with the Silence

Recall the last time someone on your team went quiet — in a meeting, after a decision, during a difficult moment. Resist the assumption that silence meant agreement. Ask yourself: *What might that silence have been saying that I didn't have the framework to hear?*

If the relationship allows it, follow up this week with a simple, private question: *"When we discussed [topic], I realized I may not have fully understood your perspective. I'd like to, if you're open to sharing."*

Not every silence will become a conversation. But extending the invitation changes the relational climate — and that changes everything.

Reflection Questions

Quick Check (1-2minutes)

- On a scale of 1-5, how often do you consider cultural dynamics when planning meetings or making decisions?

- Can you name the cultural framework(s) that most influence your own leadership approach?

Deeper Reflection(5-10 minutes)

- Recall a recent interaction that didn't go as expected. Looking back through the three-layer framework, what might you have missed?

- Who on your team comes from cultural backgrounds most different from yours? What have you learned about their cultural framework?

- Where does your organization's culture (stated or unstated) favor certain cultural frameworks over others?

Team Discussion(15-30 minutes)

- Share a time when you experienced cultural misunderstanding—either when you were misunderstood or when you misunderstood someone else. What did you learn? How might recognizing the three-layer reality have helped?

Moving Forward

Understanding the three-layer reality helps you see what's actually happening in multicultural organizations. But seeing the problem isn't enough—you need organizational systems that address all three layers simultaneously. The opening scene with Hannah and James didn't have to end that way. Imagine an alternative: James pauses after Hannah's suggestion. Instead of immediately citing board commitments, he asks, "Help me understand what's at stake here." The conversation shifts. Hannah explains that Lunar New Year isn't just a holiday—it's when family obligations peak, when cultural identity matters most, when asking people to work through it sends a message about whose priorities matter.

James still has real constraints. The board deadline exists. But now he sees the full picture. Together, the team explores options: front-loading work before the holiday, adjusting which deliverables need that specific date, communicating proactively with the board about a slight revision. The decision might not change—but the process does. And that process shapes whether people feel seen or invisible. Cross-cultural leadership is not a destination—it's a direction. It's the daily practice of noticing what you've missed, asking what you don't understand, and adjusting how you lead so that people from every background can bring their full contribution to shared purpose.

Cultural Intelligence for Everyone

Opening Scene

The deadline was Friday. Sarah, the project manager, had made this clear in Monday's meeting: "We need the final report by 5 PM Friday. No exceptions—the board presentation is Monday morning."

By Thursday afternoon, Sarah started checking in. Her American and German team members had submitted their sections. The Chinese and Korean team members hadn't. She sent a friendly reminder email: "Just checking—you're still on track for tomorrow?" They replied: "Yes, working on it."

Friday at 4:30 PM, Sarah sent an urgent message: "I need your sections in 30 minutes." At 5:15, they sent apologetic messages asking for an extension until Monday. Sarah was furious—they'd said they were "on track" but clearly weren't. The team members felt blindsided—they'd been working hard all week and thought Sarah understood they needed the weekend to polish their work properly.

Neither party was wrong. Both were frustrated. And both completely missed that they'd been operating from fundamentally different cultural frameworks about time, communication, and what "on track" actually means.

What Cultural Intelligence Actually Means

Cultural intelligence (CQ) is the capability to function effectively in culturally diverse situations. It's not about memorizing cultural facts or being a chameleon who adapts to every context. It's about developing the capacity to recognize when cultural frameworks are operating, understand how they're shaping interactions, and adjust your approach appropriately.

Research distinguishes CQ from cultural knowledge (information about specific cultures) and from emotional intelligence (ability to read and respond to emotions). CQ specifically addresses navigating across cultural difference—recognizing patterns, suspending judgment, and adapting behavior when interacting with people from different cultural backgrounds.

In the opening scene, Sarah had cultural knowledge—she knew her team was international. She likely had emotional intelligence—she could read that people were stressed. What she lacked was cultural intelligence: the ability to recognize that "on track" meant different things in different cultural frameworks, that her communication style might not be eliciting honest status updates, and that her assumptions about deadlines weren't universal.

The Four Dimensions of Cultural Intelligence

According to Earley/Ang/Livermore's framework and the author's own research, cultural intelligence operates across four interconnected dimensions. Strength in one doesn't compensate for weakness in another—all four must develop together.

CQ Drive (Motivation)

Your interest, confidence, and drive to adapt cross-culturally. Do you see cultural difference as obstacle or opportunity? Are you willing to invest energy in understanding unfamiliar frameworks? Do you persist when cross-cultural interactions become frustrating?

- Leaders with high CQ Drive approach cultural challenges with curiosity rather than irritation. They're energized by learning new perspectives rather than exhausted by difference. They see the effort required to navigate cultural complexity as worthwhile investment rather than unnecessary burden.

- Leaders with low CQ Drive avoid cross-cultural situations when possible, become frustrated quickly when misunderstandings occur, and often conclude that "they should adapt to us" rather than examining their own assumptions.

CQ Knowledge (Cognitive)

Your knowledge about how cultures are similar and different—not just facts about specific cultures but understanding of cultural dimensions and how they shape behavior. This includes frameworks like Hofstede's dimensions (power distance, individualism/collectivism, uncertainty avoidance) and Meyer's Culture Map (communicating, evaluating, leading, deciding, trusting, disagreeing, scheduling, persuading).

- Leaders with high CQ Knowledge understand that cultures vary systematically along predictable dimensions. They can anticipate where friction might occur based on cultural frameworks. They recognize that behavior making no sense in their framework may be perfectly logical in another.

- Leaders with low CQ Knowledge either know nothing about cultural variation or, worse, hold stereotypes they mistake for knowledge. They're repeatedly surprised by cross-cultural mis-understandings because they lack frameworks for predicting them.

CQ Strategy (Metacognitive)

Your awareness and planning during cross-cultural interactions. Are you paying attention to cultural dynamics in real-time? Do you check assumptions rather than acting on them? Can you plan for cultural challenges before they occur? Do you adjust your mental models when they prove inaccurate?

- Leaders with high CQ Strategy pause before important cross-cultural interactions to consider what might go wrong. They notice when something feels "off" and investigate rather than dismiss. They consciously monitor their own assumptions and test them against reality.

- Leaders with low CQ Strategy barrel through cross-cultural situations without reflection. They don't notice cultural dynamics until conflict erupts. They assume their interpretations are correct rather than questioning them.

CQ Action (Behavioral)

Your ability to adapt verbal and nonverbal behavior appropriately when relating cross-culturally. Can you adjust communication style—more direct or more indirect—depending on context? Can you modify your approach to time, feedback, decision-making when the situation requires it?

- Leaders with high CQ Action have a wide behavioral repertoire. They can be direct or indirect, formal or informal, fast or deliberate depending on what the situation requires. They adapt naturally without feeling like they're being fake.

- Leaders with low CQ Action have one style that they use regardless of context. They may recognize that adaptation is needed but feel unable to actually modify their behavior. They often experience cross-cultural situations as forcing them to be "inauthentic."

All four dimensions matter. High motivation without knowledge leads to well-intentioned mistakes. Knowledge without strategy means you can't apply what you know in real-time. Strategy without action is analysis paralysis. Action without motivation feels forced and unsustainable.

Common Cultural Dimensions That Create Friction

Understanding key cultural dimensions helps leaders anticipate where misunderstandings are likely to occur.

Communication: Direct vs. Indirect

- Direct communication cultures (common in the US, Germany, Netherlands, Israel) value explicit, clear, literal communication. Say what you mean. Get to the point. Silence is the absence of content.

- Indirect communication cultures (common in Japan, China, Korea, much of the Middle East) value implicit, contextual, diplomatic communication. Meaning is conveyed through context, tone, and what's not said. Silence carries meaning. Face-saving matters.

In the opening scene, Sarah's Asian team members may have been communicating indirectly. "Working on it" might have meant "we're behind but don't want to disappoint you directly." "Yes" to "are you on track?" might have been polite acknowledgment rather than factual status report. Sarah's direct communication style prevented her from reading these signals.

Time: Linear vs. Flexible

- Linear time cultures (common in Northern Europe, US, Japan) treat time as a finite resource to be managed efficiently. Schedules are commitments. Deadlines are firm. Being late signals disrespect.

- Flexible time cultures (common in Latin America, Middle East, much of Africa, Southern Europe) treat time as fluid and subordinate to relationships. Schedules are guidelines. Deadlines are negotiable. Being present matters more than being punctual.

Sarah's Friday deadline was experienced as absolute in her framework but potentially flexible in her team members' frameworks—especially if producing quality work (which honors relationship with colleagues) required more time.

Power Distance: Hierarchical vs. Egalitarian

- High power distance cultures (common in East Asia, Latin America, Arab countries) accept and expect an unequal distribution of power. Hierarchy is natural. Deference to authority is appropriate. Subordinates don't challenge superiors publicly.

- Low power distance cultures (common in Scandinavia, Israel, Australia, US) minimize power differences. Hierarchy is functional, not inherent. Challenge and dissent are acceptable. Leaders are accessible and open to critique.

Sarah's team members from high power distance cultures may have found it inappropriate to tell a superior directly that the deadline wasn't achievable. That would be tantamount to saying she'd set an unreasonable timeline—a challenge to her authority.

Individualism vs. Collectivism

- Individualist cultures (common in US, UK, Australia, Netherlands) prioritize individual achievement, autonomy, and self-expression. Personal opinion matters. Individual accountability is expected.

- Collectivist cultures (common in East Asia, Latin America, Africa) prioritize group harmony, loyalty, and consensus. Group opinion matters more than individual views. Shame and honor are collective.

Sarah's team members from collectivist backgrounds may have been reluctant to stand out by admitting problems when others hadn't. They may have wanted to consult with peers before responding. The individual accountability Sarah expected may have felt culturally inappropriate.

The Historical View

History offers powerful examples of cultural intelligence enabling—or its absence destroying—cross-cultural cooperation.

The Meiji Restoration: Deliberate Cultural Learning

When Commodore Perry's "Black Ships" arrived in Japan in 1853, they revealed how far Japan had fallen behind Western military and industrial technology during its centuries of isolation. The Japanese response—the Meiji Restoration beginning in 1868—represents perhaps history's most deliberate, strategic application of cultural intelligence to national transformation. Japanese leaders recognized they needed to learn rapidly from Western cultures without losing Japanese identity. Their approach was systematic:

- CQ Drive: They sent hundreds of officials, students, and scholars abroad specifically to learn. The Iwakura Mission (1871-1873) took over 100 government leaders on an 18-month tour of the United States and Europe. They were genuinely motivated to understand, not just observe.

- CQ Knowledge: They studied Western legal systems, educational structures, military organization, industrial processes, and political institutions with scholarly rigor. They didn't just collect facts—they developed frameworks for understanding how Western societies functioned.

- CQ Strategy: They selectively adopted what served Japanese purposes while maintaining Japanese values. They took the Prussian constitution as a model (authoritarian but modern) rather than the American (too democratic for their context). They adapted Western education but preserved Japanese moral instruction. They modernized industry while protecting traditional arts.

- CQ Action: Within a generation, Japan transformed from a feudal society to an industrial power. Japanese leaders dressed in Western clothes for some occasions and traditional garb for others. They learned multiple behavioral repertoires and deployed them strategically.

The Meiji example shows cultural intelligence operating at institutional, not just individual, scale. The lesson: organizations, not just individuals, can develop deliberate cultural learning strategies. And cultural intelligence doesn't mean wholesale adoption of foreign ways—it means selective, strategic adaptation that serves your own purposes while remaining genuinely open to learning.

Cyrus the Great: Building an Empire Through Cultural Respect

When Cyrus the Great conquered Babylon in 539 BCE, he faced a standard conqueror's problem: how to rule a vast empire containing dozens of distinct peoples, languages, religions, and customs. Previous empires had solved this through forced assimilation—impose the conqueror's language, gods, and ways on the conquered. Cyrus chose a radically different approach that demonstrated sophisticated cultural intelligence.

The Cyrus Cylinder, discovered in Babylon, records his philosophy: "I am Cyrus, king of the universe, the great king... When I entered Babylon in peace, I took up my lordly residence in the royal palace amidst rejoicing and happiness... I sought the welfare of the city of Babylon and all its sacred centers." Rather than destroying Babylonian culture, he honored it. Cyrus's cultural intelligence showed in all four dimensions:

- CQ Drive: Cyrus was genuinely motivated to understand the peoples he ruled. He didn't view cultural difference as obstacle to overcome but as reality to respect. When he conquered Babylon, he participated in their New Year festival and took the hand of their god Marduk—a Persian king honoring Babylonian religious customs. When he freed the Jews from captivity, he funded the rebuilding of their temple in Jerusalem and returned sacred vessels taken by previous conquerors. This wasn't cynical manipulation—his policies were remarkably consistent across all conquered peoples.

- CQ Knowledge: He understood different peoples organized religion, governance, and social life in fundamentally different ways. He recognized that the Jews' covenant with their God was central to their identity in ways that paralleled but differed from Persian Zoroastrianism. He grasped that Babylonians saw their king as servant of Marduk, Egyptians saw pharaoh as divine, and Greeks organized around city-states. He didn't just know facts about cultures—he understood their frameworks.

- CQ Strategy: Cyrus planned deliberately for cultural integration. Rather than imposing Persian governors everywhere, he often retained local leaders who understood local customs. He allowed peoples to maintain their laws, languages, and religions while requiring only loyalty to the empire and payment of tribute. He positioned himself differently in different contexts—as chosen of Marduk in Babylon, as liberator to the Jews, as legitimate pharaoh in Egypt. He adapted his legitimation strategy to each culture's framework.

- CQ Action: He adapted behavior constantly across cultural contexts. In Persia, he was Zoroastrian king. In Babylon, he honored Marduk. In Jerusalem, he was instrument of Yahweh. He didn't pretend to be Babylonian or Jewish—he remained distinctly Persian—but he adapted his approach to honor each culture's central values. His decrees were issued in local languages. His policies respected local customs. His administration employed people from conquered nations in significant roles.

The Persian Empire became history's first successful multi-ethnic, multi-religious empire. Conquered peoples generally welcomed Persian rule because it was dramatically less oppressive than alternatives. The empire lasted over two centuries—extraordinary stability for its time. When Alexander conquered Persia two hundred years later, he explicitly tried to continue Cyrus's approach of cultural respect. Cyrus didn't abandon Persian identity or values. He remained thoroughly Persian in worldview. But he recognized that effective rule required adapting approach to cultural context. He understood that people would give their best when their core identities were respected rather than threatened.

The lesson for modern leaders: Cultural intelligence doesn't require abandoning your own culture or pretending to be what you're not. It requires genuine respect for difference, strategic thinking about how to bridge frameworks, and willingness to adapt your approach while maintaining your core commitments. Cyrus proved that cultural intelligence isn't just morally right—it's strategically effective. Empires built on forced assimilation fracture under stress. Organizations built on cultural respect develop resilience.

Admiral Zheng He: Chinese Naval Diplomacy Across Cultures

Between 1405 and 1433, Admiral Zheng He led seven massive naval expeditions from China to Southeast Asia, India, Arabia, and East Africa. His treasure fleet—over 300 ships carrying 28,000 men—was the largest naval force the world had seen. Yet remarkably, these expeditions conquered no territory. Instead, they demonstrated sophisticated cultural intelligence in establishing trade relationships and diplomatic ties across radically different cultures.

Zheng He himself embodied cultural complexity: he was Muslim by birth, served a Confucian emperor, commanded Buddhist and Taoist sailors, and navigated Hindu, Islamic, and Christian kingdoms. His success required operating effectively across all these frameworks. His cultural intelligence showed in all four dimensions:

- CQ Drive: Zheng He was genuinely motivated to understand the peoples he encountered. Rather than viewing foreign cultures as inferior or barbaric (despite commanding overwhelming military force), he approached them with curiosity and respect. He brought translators fluent in Arabic, Persian, Tamil, and other languages. He collected information about local customs, religions, trade goods, and political structures. His fleet included scholars whose job was to document cultural practices. This wasn't extraction—it was genuine interest in understanding how different peoples organized life.

- CQ Knowledge: He developed deep knowledge of cultural frameworks across the Indian Ocean world. He understood that Islamic kingdoms from Arabia to Malacca organized trade and diplomacy differently than Hindu kingdoms in India or Buddhist kingdoms in Southeast Asia. He grasped that gift-giving carried different meanings in different contexts—sometimes establishing hierarchy, sometimes creating reciprocal obligation, sometimes demonstrating wealth. He recognized some cultures valued directness, while others required elaborate indirection. He built mental models for predicting how different cultures would respond to Chinese overtures.

- CQ Strategy: He planned deliberately for cultural engagement. Before arriving in ports, his fleet sent advance notice and gifts appropriate to local customs. In Islamic ports, he highlighted his Muslim identity and funded mosque construction. In Hindu kingdoms, he made offerings at temples. In Buddhist lands, he supported monasteries. He wasn't being duplicitous—he was strategically emphasizing different aspects of his complex identity and China's multifaceted civilization, depending on what would create connection. He also planned for conflict: when pirates threatened trade routes or rulers acted aggressively, he used force decisively—but always framed through local cultural understanding of legitimate authority.

- CQ Action: He adapted behavior constantly. In Mecca, he sent offerings to the holy sites. In Calicut, India, he erected a stone tablet in three languages (Chinese, Tamil, Persian) honoring Hindu, Islamic, and Buddhist deities—an extraordinary act of cultural flexibility. When receiving foreign dignitaries, he modified protocol based on their customs. When giving gifts, he matched them to cultural values—exotic animals to some kingdoms, fine silks to others, precious metals to still others. He maintained Chinese identity and imperial dignity while adapting approach to cultural context.

Zheng He established tributary relationships with over thirty states without conquest. Trade flourished. Chinese prestige expanded across the Indian Ocean world. Kings from Arabia to Africa sent delegations to Beijing. The expeditions demonstrated that a massive power could engage weaker states through cultural intelligence rather than force. Tragically, China abandoned these expeditions after 1433, turning inward for centuries. But Zheng He's voyages proved what sophisticated cultural intelligence could accomplish. With overwhelming military superiority, he could have conquered. Instead, he built relationships through cultural respect and strategic adaptation.

The lesson for modern leaders: Power and cultural intelligence aren't opposites—they're complements. Organizations with resources and capabilities can use them to dominate, or they can use cultural intelligence to build genuine partnerships. Zheng He showed that even when you have an overwhelming advantage, cultural intelligence creates better long-term outcomes than cultural arrogance. The treasure fleet is forgotten, but the principle remains: sustainable influence requires understanding and respecting the cultural frameworks of those you seek to engage.

The Biblical View

Scripture demonstrates cultural intelligence in action throughout, particularly in cross-cultural mission and leadership contexts.

Peter's Vision: Transforming Deep Assumptions

Peter faced perhaps the most challenging cultural intelligence development moment in early church history: recognizing that Gentiles were
included in God's kingdom without becoming culturally Jewish (Acts
10:9-48). God gave Peter a vision of unclean animals with the command:
"Get up, Peter. Kill and eat." Peter's response revealed his deeply held
cultural framework: "Surely not, Lord! I have never eaten anything
impure or unclean." God replied: "Do not call anything impure that
God has made clean."

Then Peter was sent to Cornelius's house—a Gentile home he would
have previously avoided as defiling. He acknowledged his transformation: "You are well aware that it is against our law for a Jew to associate
with or visit a Gentile. But God has shown me that I should not call
anyone impure or unclean." This wasn't just learning cultural facts—it
was transforming deeply held assumptions about whose culture God
values. Peter's cultural intelligence grew through:

- CQ Drive: He allowed himself to be challenged even when the
  vision disturbed him. He went to Cornelius's house despite
  discomfort because God directed him.

- CQ Knowledge: He recognized his own cultural blinders—assumptions so deep he'd never questioned them. He learned that
  his cultural framework, however sacred it felt, wasn't the only
  valid one.

- CQ Strategy: He paused to process what God was teaching
  rather than dismissing the vision as indigestion. He reflected on
  its meaning and connected it to the invitation from Cornelius.

- CQ Action: He actually entered Gentile space, ate with Gentiles, baptized Gentiles, and stayed with them several days. He

changed his behavior, not just his beliefs.

The outcome: "The circumcised believers who had come with Peter were astonished that the gift of the Holy Spirit had been poured out even on Gentiles." Peter's cultural intelligence opened the gospel to all nations—the most consequential cross-cultural breakthrough in church history.

Daniel: Maintaining Identity While Mastering Foreign Culture

When Babylonian forces conquered Jerusalem in 605 BCE, they took the brightest young men from Judah's nobility into exile. Among them was Daniel, who would spend his entire adult life navigating Babylonian and later Persian imperial courts while maintaining his Jewish faith and identity. His story (Daniel 1-6) demonstrates sophisticated cultural intelligence in an extremely challenging context.

Daniel faced the classic cultural intelligence challenge: how to function effectively in a dominant culture that conflicts with your core values, without either abandoning your identity or becoming so rigid that you can't engage. His cultural intelligence showed in all four dimensions:

- CQ Drive: Daniel was motivated to understand Babylonian culture even while maintaining Jewish faithfulness. He didn't withdraw into isolated Jewish community or refuse to learn. Instead, he mastered Babylonian language and literature, studied their wisdom traditions, and learned to operate in their political system. When offered the king's food and wine (which would violate Jewish dietary laws), he didn't refuse with contempt—he proposed a respectful alternative and trusted God with the outcome (Daniel 1:8-16). His motivation wasn't to prove Babylonian culture inferior but to serve God faithfully within it.

- CQ Knowledge: He developed deep knowledge of Babylonian frameworks. He learned their language "and literature" fluently enough to surpass native Babylonian wise men (1:17-20). He understood their political system well enough to navigate palace intrigue. He grasped their religious worldview—polytheistic, divination-focused, king-centered—not to adopt it but to understand how Babylonians thought. When interpreting Nebuchadnezzar's dreams, he demonstrated knowledge of Babylonian dream interpretation traditions while providing distinctly monotheistic interpretation (2:27-28). He knew the culture well enough to communicate truth through their frameworks.

- CQ Strategy: Daniel planned strategically for cultural engagement. He accepted a Babylonian name (Belteshazzar) without abandoning his Hebrew identity. He served Babylonian kings faithfully while maintaining Jewish practices. When cultural compliance would violate core convictions (eating unclean food, worshiping false gods), he planned careful responses. His approach to the dietary issue was brilliant strategy: a respectful request, proposed test, trust in God's vindication. When prayer to anyone but the king was forbidden, he didn't hide his prayers to prove a point, but he also didn't parade them provocatively—he simply continued his established practice (6:10). He thought strategically about when to adapt and when to stand firm.

- CQ Action: He adapted behavior constantly while maintaining core identity. He worked in the imperial bureaucracy. He counseled pagan kings with respect even while delivering hard messages. He used Babylonian forms (dreams, visions, court protocols) to communicate Hebrew truth. When interpreting Nebuchadnezzar's troubling dream, he began with culturally appropriate deference: "My lord, if only the dream applied to your enemies" (4:19). He adapted communication style to cultural context while delivering God's message faithfully. Yet he also maintained distinctly Jewish practices that marked him as different—daily prayer toward Jerusalem, dietary restrictions, refusal to worship idols.

The results: Daniel rose to top leadership positions in both Babylonian and Persian empires while maintaining Jewish faithfulness. His cultural intelligence allowed him to influence pagan kings toward recognizing the true God without compromising his convictions. Nebuchadnezzar acknowledged God's sovereignty (4:34-37). Darius issued a decree honoring God (6:26-27). Daniel survived regime changes that destroyed others because he'd built trust across cultural frameworks. Daniel never became Babylonian. He remained distinctly Jewish in faith and practice. But he developed such deep cultural intelligence that he could serve pagan empires with excellence while maintaining covenant faithfulness.

The lesson for modern leaders: Cultural intelligence doesn't require abandoning your convictions or identity. Daniel shows how to master a dominant culture's frameworks while maintaining core commitments. He understood the difference between cultural forms (negotiable) and theological convictions (non-negotiable). He adapted everything that could be adapted while standing firm on what mattered most. This isn't compromise—it's sophisticated cultural intelligence that allows faithful presence in contexts that don't share your values.

Ruth: Cross-Cultural Commitment and Integration

The book of Ruth tells the story of a Moabite woman who married into an Israelite family, was widowed, and then chose to follow her Israelite mother-in-law Naomi back to Bethlehem rather than return to her own people. Ruth's story (Ruth 1-4) demonstrates remarkable cultural intelligence—a foreigner successfully integrating into a culture that historically viewed Moabites with suspicion and hostility, while maintaining her dignity and ultimately becoming ancestor to King David and Jesus Christ.

Ruth faced an extreme cultural intelligence challenge: entering a foreign culture as a poor, widowed, childless woman from a despised ethnic group. She had every disadvantage. Yet she navigated Israelite culture with such skill that she became honored and integrated. Her cultural intelligence showed in all four dimensions:

- CQ Drive: Ruth was deeply motivated to understand and adapt to Israelite culture. Her famous declaration to Naomi reveals this drive: "Where you go I will go, and where you stay I will stay. Your people will be my people and your God my God. Where you die I will die, and there I will be buried" (1:16-17). This wasn't casual interest—it was total commitment to cultural transition. She chose to leave her native Moab, her family, her gods, and her cultural comfort zone to embrace an entirely foreign framework. This level of CQ drive is rare—most people cling to familiar cultural patterns even when living in new contexts. Ruth fully committed to learning and adapting.

- CQ Knowledge: Ruth quickly learned key aspects of Israelite culture. She understood the gleaning laws that allowed the poor to gather leftover grain in fields (2:2)—indicating she'd learned about Israelite social welfare practices. She grasped the cultural significance of the kinsman-redeemer tradition and the protocols around it (3:9). She recognized the importance of respectful approach to authority figures (2:10, 13). She learned enough about Israelite religious culture to sincerely embrace their God. She didn't just know facts about Israel—she understood the values and frameworks that organized Israelite life: covenant loyalty (hesed), family obligation, religious devotion, community interdependence.

- CQ Strategy: Ruth planned strategically for cultural integration. When gleaning, she deliberately chose to work in Boaz's field (2:3)—likely not accident but strategic choice based on what she'd learned about his character and Naomi's family connections. When Naomi instructed her in the cultural protocol for approaching Boaz as kinsman-redeemer (3:1-5), Ruth followed the plan precisely—showing strategic trust in cultural guidance from someone who understood the context. She timed her approach, prepared herself appropriately, and used culturally correct language and gestures. She demonstrated strategic thinking about how to navigate a complex cultural situation with high stakes.

- CQ Action: Ruth adapted her behavior constantly to Israelite cultural norms. She showed appropriate deference and humility: "Why have I found such favor in your eyes that you notice me—a foreigner?" (2:10). She worked diligently, conforming to Israelite work ethic (2:7). She dressed and presented herself according to Naomi's cultural guidance (3:3). She used respectful, culturally appropriate language when speaking to Boaz (2:13; 3:9). She followed proper protocols around relationships and marriage. Yet she didn't become invisible—she maintained enough distinctive identity that people recognized her as "Ruth the Moabite" while respecting her character and conduct.

Ruth won the respect of the community. Boaz praised her publicly: "All the people of my town know that you are a woman of noble character" (3:11). The town elders blessed her marriage with prayers comparing her to Rachel and Leah, the matriarchs of Israel (4:11-12). She bore a son who became grandfather to King David and ancestor to Jesus. A Moabite widow became so integrated into Israelite culture and honored in Israelite community that she entered the messianic line. Ruth didn't cease being Moabite. Scripture continues calling her "Ruth the Moabite" even after her successful integration (2:21; 4:5, 10). Her identity remained, but she gained a second identity as honored member of Israelite community. She bridged cultures without erasing either.

The lesson for modern leaders: Cultural intelligence enables integration without erasure. Ruth shows how someone from outside can learn a new culture deeply enough to thrive within it while maintaining their original identity. She demonstrates that successful cross-cultural navigation requires genuine drive to understand, systematic knowledge acquisition, strategic planning for cultural situations, and consistent behavioral adaptation. But most importantly, she shows that cultural intelligence works both ways—Boaz and the Israelite community also demonstrated CQ by recognizing Ruth's character and receiving her fully despite cultural difference. True cultural integration requires CQ from both the person entering new culture and the community receiving them.

Nuances and Blind Spots

Labeling instead of investigating. When someone's behavior doesn't make sense to us, the instinct is to reach for a shortcut: "They're just difficult" or "That culture is too indirect." Cultural intelligence begins when we replace those labels with curiosity — *What framework might explain what I'm seeing?* The goal isn't to excuse everything, but to understand before you judge.

Stereotyping disguised as cultural knowledge. There's a meaningful difference between cultural intelligence and cultural facts. Knowing holidays, customs, and general tendencies isn't the same as the capacity to function effectively across difference — which requires motivation, flexibility, and honest self-reflection, not just a mental database. Worse, cultural "knowledge" applied too rigidly becomes its own kind of bias: "Asians don't speak up" or "Americans are individualistic" used as explanations rather than as invitations to learn about the actual person in front of you. Individual variation within any cultural group is enormous.

Your own culture is the hardest to see. Cultural frameworks are like water to fish — invisible precisely because they're everywhere. Most leaders have never examined their own cultural assumptions because they experience them as "just how things are." This is why color-blindness claims — "I don't see cultural difference" or "We're all the same" — aren't enlightened. They're a failure to notice the water you're swimming in. Developing genuine cultural intelligence starts with recognizing that your own approach is culturally shaped, not universal.

Repeating yourself louder isn't a strategy. When communication breaks down across cultures, the reflex is often to try the same approach with more force — speaking slower, louder, or more emphatically. True cultural intelligence means asking instead: *Is there a different channel, format, or frame that might actually land?* Different cultural frameworks genuinely prefer different modes — not as quirks, but as legitimate ways of processing and exchanging information.

The asymmetry of adaptation. In most multicultural organizations, adaptation isn't mutual — it's lopsided. Those with less power adapt to dominant culture while dominant culture members rarely adjust at all. This invisible labor is cognitively and emotionally taxing, and it often goes entirely unrecognized and uncompensated. The question every leader should ask regularly: *Who is doing the adapting here, and is that distribution fair?*

Intention doesn't equal impact. Cross-cultural mistakes are often excused with "I didn't mean it that way." But in cross-cultural contexts, impact matters more than intention. The question isn't whether you meant to offend — it's whether you're willing to close the gap between what you intended and how it was received. Defensive reactions to cultural feedback are a reliable sign that CQ development has stalled.

Discomfort is the curriculum. Cultural intelligence doesn't grow in comfortable, familiar settings — it grows when our assumptions are genuinely challenged and new responses are required. Organizations that insulate their leaders from cross-cultural friction don't protect them; they prevent them from developing. The goal isn't to eliminate discomfort but to process it productively.

Not every tension is morally neutral. Cultural intelligence doesn't mean accepting everything. Some cultural frameworks contain practices that genuinely conflict with organizational values or ethical principles. The mark of mature CQ isn't suspension of all judgment — it's the ability to distinguish between cultural *preferences* (where flexibility and mutual adaptation are appropriate) and genuine *value conflicts* (where clarity and firmness are required, but can still be offered with respect).

<hr>

Try This Week

Choose ONE practice to build cultural intelligence:

Practice 1: Explicitly Invite Cultural Perspective (10 minutes in next meeting)

Before making a decision, ask: "Are there cultural considerations I'm missing here?" or "How might this land differently for team members from different backgrounds?" Then make genuine space for actual answers—silence, clarifying questions, invitation of specific people who might have different perspectives. Don't let the question become rhetorical.

Practice 2: Offer Multiple Communication Channels (5 minutes to set up)

For your next important request or announcement, provide multiple ways to respond: verbal (meeting discussion), written (email response), private (one-on-one conversation), anonymous (feedback form). Notice who uses which channel—this reveals cultural communication preferences and may surface input you'd otherwise miss.

Practice 3: Complicate One Stereotype (15 minutes reflection)

Write down one cultural generalization you hold (e.g., "Asians are indirect" or "Americans are always rushing" or "Europeans are more formal"). Then list three specific people from that background who don't fit the pattern. Reflect on what accounts for the variation. The goal isn't abandoning cultural frameworks but holding them loosely enough to see individuals.

Practice 4: Cultural Learning Conversation (20-30 minutes)

Invite someone from a different cultural background to teach you about one aspect of their framework. Be specific: "How do people from your background typically handle disagreement with a boss?" or "What does 'being on time' mean in your cultural experience?" Listen to learn, not to debate, compare, or defend your own approach.

Reflection Questions

Quick Check (1-2 minutes)

- Which of the four CQ dimensions (Drive, Knowledge, Strategy, Action) is your strongest? Which needs most development?

- When was the last time you changed your approach because of a cross-cultural interaction? What did you learn?

Deeper Reflection (5-10 minutes)

- Think about a recent cross-cultural misunderstanding. What cultural dimensions might have been operating? How might higher CQ have helped you navigate differently?

- What aspects of your own cultural framework are hardest for you to see? What would someone from a very different background find strange about how you operate?

- Where in your organization is cultural adaptation asymmetric—some people constantly adapting while others never adjust? What would more equitable distribution of adaptation look like?

- When have you been on the receiving end of low cultural intelligence? What did it feel like? What do you wish the other person had understood?

Team Discussion (15-30 minutes)

- As a team, discuss: "What cultural intelligence mistakes have we made as an organization? What did we learn? What patterns do we see?" Focus on organizational patterns, not individual blame. Identify one specific area where the team's collective CQ needs development and discuss concrete steps to address it.

Moving Forward

Cultural intelligence forms the bridge between good intentions and effective cross-cultural leadership. Trust matters—but trust must be built across cultural frameworks that define trustworthiness differently. Voice matters—but voice must flow through channels that work across cultural communication styles. And cultural intelligence is what enables leaders to build trust and create voice in ways that actually function across difference.

The opening scene with Sarah and her team didn't have to end in frustration. With higher cultural intelligence, Sarah might have recognized that "on track" could mean different things across cultures. She might have created multiple checkpoints rather than assuming a single deadline would be interpreted uniformly. She might have offered private channels for honest status updates rather than relying only on public acknowledgment. She might have asked, earlier in the week, "What would help you meet this deadline?" rather than assuming her communication had been sufficient.

Cultural intelligence isn't about becoming an expert in every culture represented on your team. It's about developing the capacity to recognize when cultural frameworks are operating, stay curious rather than judgmental, and adapt your approach when the situation requires it. This capacity develops through practice, reflection, and willingness to learn from mistakes.

What High Performance Means

Opening Scene

A leader stands before the board, presenting impressive numbers. Enrollment is up. Test scores have improved. Efficiency metrics look strong. The board applauds. In the parking lot afterward, two staff members compare notes.

"Did you notice three people didn't show up today?" one asks.

"Burnout," the other replies quietly. "And two more are actively job hunting. We're hitting numbers—but losing people."

Across town, another organization tells a different story. Staff gather weekly for shared meals. Relationships are warm. People genuinely care about one another. Yet projects regularly miss deadlines, and the organization is slowly losing relevance. "We're a family," the leader says—while privately wondering whether warmth without results truly serves anyone.

Both leaders feel the same tension. Is high performance a trap word—something that forces a choice between results and humanity? The tension is real. The choice is false.

The False Choice

Research consistently points to a truth many leaders sense intuitively but struggle to operationalize: high-performing environments are not the most pressurized or the most sentimental. They are places where people understand what matters, feel safe enough to speak honestly, know how their work connects to a larger purpose, and trust that leadership cares about both outcomes and people. When researchers ask whether high-performance systems actually function inside organizations, responses cluster into telling patterns. Some describe cautious optimism—progress, but incomplete. Others note slow movement in the right direction. Very few express full confidence that the system works smoothly.

These are not declarations of arrival. They are hopeful assessments from people who have seen enough to believe improvement is possible—but not enough to feel secure. Those who leave often offer a more complex picture. Some describe informal systems that sustained the organization for seasons: colleagues training one another, peer-driven development, relationship-based leadership growth that emerged organically. Others point to what never quite materialized—inconsistent leadership, half-built systems, anxiety created by unpredictability, and good intentions that never cohered into durable patterns. What emerges is not failure—but an organization caught between two inadequate models and searching for a third way.

What High Performance Actually Requires

A high-performance work system (HPWS), properly understood, is not a productivity machine. It is a set of practices that respects people and actively invests in their development—enhancing ability, expanding opportunity, and building skills—while fostering trust and shared commitment to purpose. The research is clear about consequences —

and in multicultural organizations, those consequences carry a layer of complexity that leaders can easily underestimate.

When leaders do not develop a HPWS, the effects compound across cultural lines. The absence of an intentional system erodes autonomous motivation and job satisfaction — the internal drives that produce discretionary effort rather than mere compliance. This matters in any organization, but in cross-cultural settings it matters with particular force, because motivation is itself shaped by cultural context. What feels empowering to a staff member from an individualistic background may feel exposing or disrespectful to a colleague shaped by values of harmony, loyalty, and social order. When no intentional system exists, leaders default to whatever motivational framework feels natural to them — which typically reflects their own cultural formation, not the diversity of the team.

The same dynamic affects learning and participation. Hierarchical leadership structures prevent the flexibility a HPWS requires, and in multicultural organizations those hierarchies often run along cultural fault lines that leadership never named or examined. Staff from high-power-distance backgrounds may already assume that speaking up, disagreeing, or asking questions is not their role — and an underdeveloped system reinforces that assumption rather than challenging it. The result is not passive compliance but a kind of organizational silence: knowledge that never surfaces, problems absorbed rather than solved, participation that exists in form but not in substance.

When access to necessary knowledge and skills erodes, that erosion is not evenly distributed. Staff farther from leadership, newer to the organization, or navigating language and cultural barriers lose access first and fastest. Individual and team effectiveness then deteriorates not because people lack ability, but because the system failed to develop the ability that was already there. This often shows up as a persistent gap between the potential a diverse team theoretically offers and the results the organization actually achieves — a gap that leaders sometimes misread as a people problem when it is, in fact, a systems problem.

When leaders do develop a HPWS, the gains are real — and in multicultural organizations, they are also distinctive. Group dynamics strengthen when a shared system creates common language and common practices across cultural difference, rather than simply placing diverse people in proximity and hoping for connection. Growth-commitment cultures emerge when staff from varying backgrounds genuinely perceive that the organization is investing in their development, not merely extracting from their existing capacity. That perception produces a reciprocal response: people think more freely, take constructive risks, solve problems, and invest in the organization's future. But reciprocity follows from consistent, structural investment — it cannot be coaxed from goodwill alone.

Innovation increases through distributed leadership precisely because multicultural teams, when genuinely empowered, bring genuinely different perspectives to problems. This only happens, however, when the system creates the conditions — psychological safety, multiple voice pathways, shared accountability — that allow those perspectives to enter the conversation rather than being filtered through a single cultural default. Teams that develop shared competence, motivation, and opportunity-seeking behavior do so because the system made growth possible for every member, not just those most culturally proximate to leadership. That is the practical difference between a multicultural organization that performs and one that merely appears diverse.

The Four Pillars of Human Performance

Both research and field experience point to four interdependent pillars. When they reinforce one another, people thrive. When one weakens, the whole structure becomes unstable.

1. Clarity — People Know What Success Looks Like and Why It Matters

Clarity goes beyond job descriptions. It answers three essential questions: What are we trying to do? Why does it matter? How will we know if we've succeeded?

Organizations experience clarity along a spectrum. At one end, people articulate direction clearly and understand how their work contributes. At the other, individuals work in parallel without shared understanding—some areas well supported, others left to improvisation. The result is a patchwork of confidence and confusion. Data consistently reveals this gap. Roughly half of staff feel they receive information effectively and on time. A significant portion do not. That gap generates anxiety—and anxiety erodes performance. The clarity gap appears in predictable ways:

- Shifting expectations: New responsibilities assigned without adequate preparation

- Directional uncertainty: Lack of visibility into what comes next

- Opaque personnel decisions: Unexplained departures that fuel fear and speculation

Clarity improves when organizations articulate vision that transcends cultural boundaries—shared values and mission that allow people to return to common ground even amid differing approaches.

2. Consistency — Promises, Policies, and Behavior Align

Consistency is the bedrock of trust. When leaders say one thing and do another—or when policies apply unevenly—trust evaporates. Performance soon follows. Organizations that experience leadership transitions often describe the difference starkly. The change is "night and day." New leadership that brings follow-through and predictability produces a palpable shift in climate. Yet shadows linger. Staff who lived under inconsistent leadership recall unpredictable expectations, emotional volatility, favoritism, and anxiety about shifting rules. Consistency shows up in:

- Follow-through: Input that leads to action

- Predictable access: Leaders who respond and remain available

- Visible presence: Leaders who engage rather than disappear

Inconsistency leaves lasting damage. Frequent structural changes, unexplained role losses, and constant resets teach people to stay silent. Silence prevents feedback. Lack of feedback undermines system building. The cycle reinforces itself.

3. Contribution — People See Their Impact and Have Voice

Contribution is about meaning and agency. Do people know their work matters? Do they help shape how work happens?

Organizations that cultivate contribution create environments where voice feels safe—not risky. At the highest end, people experience genuine participation in direction and decision-making. Contribution gaps emerge through:

- Power distance: Rhetoric of participation without lived access

- Bias patterns: Some voices consistently amplified, others ignored

- Cultural blind spots: Overlooking culturally appropriate decision-making norms

What opens contribution is empowering leadership—leadership that builds self-efficacy and autonomy. When leaders listen and act, staff become more confident that their voice matters.

4. Care — People Are Seen as Humans, Not Roles

Care holds everything together. Without it, clarity becomes manipulation, consistency becomes rigidity, and contribution becomes extraction. Strong cultures of care show up in mutual support, respect, and collaboration that feels natural rather than forced. The data here is sobering. Roughly one in five people do not feel important or secure. That represents a failure no performance system can afford. Care appears—or fails—in:

- Work-life boundaries

- Support during transitions

- Recognition and modeling

Its absence is unmistakable: people committed to mission but disconnected from leadership, colleagues struggling alone, resource scarcity used as excuse rather than constraint requiring choice. One plea captures it simply: help those who are struggling to do their part.

The Dark Side of High Performance

Poorly implemented HPWS does not simply fail to help — it actively causes harm. When systems increase demands without proportionally increasing resources and support, the result is not higher performance but accelerated depletion. This pattern recurs in organizations that have adopted the language of high performance without building the infrastructure to sustain it — where "we hold ourselves to a high standard" functions as cover for under-resourcing, and where "we're a family" makes excessive demands feel unreasonable to resist.

In multicultural organizations, these risks are compounded in specific ways. Unequal workload distribution rarely falls randomly. It tends to settle on staff from backgrounds where declining requests from authority feels like a violation of relational order — people who absorb disproportionate burden precisely because the system makes it easy to load them. When that imbalance goes unacknowledged, it communicates something unmistakable: the organization notices output, not people. Chronic resource strain tells the same story. Responding to scarcity by raising expectations without raising support is a values statement, whether or not leadership intends it as one.

High turnover in multicultural settings carries a disruption cost that goes beyond lost institutional knowledge. Staff who have invested in cross-cultural relationship-building — learning unspoken norms, earning the trust that allows honest communication across cultural lines — take something irreplaceable with them when they leave. Research participants described the cumulative fatigue of reopening to new colleagues again and again as turnover cycled through their organization. What appears as a staffing problem on a spreadsheet is often the visible evidence of a system that has been consuming people rather than developing them.

Persistent uncertainty amplifies all of this. In multicultural organizations, ambiguity fractures along cultural lines, with staff interpreting the same silence or the same announcement through very different frameworks — and arriving at divergent, sometimes contradictory, conclusions about what leadership intends. That interpretive gap widens when communication is inconsistent, producing an environment where proximity to leadership, not quality of communication, determines who feels secure and who does not.

The same practices that build resilience and engagement when implemented well produce strain and withdrawal when implemented carelessly. A performance culture that consumes people's existing capacity without investing in its renewal is not a high-performance system — it is a countdown. And in multicultural organizations, that countdown is often invisible to leaders until the most capable and committed people are already gone.

The Five Forces for Enhancement

From the research emerge five reinforcing forces that translate the four pillars into daily practice. They are not sequential steps but simultaneous conditions — each one strengthening the others, each one, when absent, quietly undermining the rest.

    I. **Consistent leadership action is the foundation everything else rests on.** The research found it to be the single most disruptive variable in organizational health when it was missing. When leaders applied standards unevenly, made commitments they didn't keep, or behaved differently depending on who was watching, people stopped focusing on their work and started scanning for danger. The damage compounded over time — staff who survived seasons of erratic leadership carried that residue forward even after conditions improved, requiring sustained evidence before hope became genuine trust. Consistency is also tested most severely in exceptions, not routines. Anyone can be consistent when it costs nothing. The real measure comes when enforcing a standard is inconvenient, when treating everyone equally disappoints someone with influence. That is when consistency either becomes a value or reveals itself as a performance.

2. **Clear communication is how the Clarity pillar actually gets built across an organization.** But the research found that the most common communication failures were not information that went unsent — they were information that was transmitted but never truly received. Messages traveled; meaning didn't. A second, more corrosive pattern was proximity inequality: those close to leadership experienced clarity, while those farther away received the same announcements without the same context or rationale. Trust then distributed itself along lines of access rather than equity. Perhaps most revealing was the damage done by unclosed feedback loops. When organizations solicited input and made no visible use of it, people learned that voice was performative — the appearance of openness without the substance. This was found to be more damaging than never asking at all.

3. **Compelling vision is the force that keeps the Clarity pillar from becoming merely procedural.** People who understand

why a standard exists behave differently than those who simply comply with it. The research found that the organizations struggling most were not those without mission statements — they were those in which the stated mission had drifted from daily reality, visible in annual reports but absent from budget decisions, hiring criteria, and the language of ordinary leadership. Team members could recite the words but could not explain why they mattered. When that happens, vision becomes decoration, and decoration has no purchase on behavior when things get hard. Lowell's experiment failed for exactly this reason: the founding vision remained as rhetoric while management practice drifted toward extraction. The words outlasted the commitment.

4. **Growth culture is the expression of the Care pillar in its most demanding form — not simply protecting people from difficulty, but investing in their capacity to grow beyond it.** The research was direct about what its absence produced: the highest performers going quiet, the most engaged staff becoming withdrawn, "canaries in the coal mine" signaling system failure before anyone named it. Organizations where growth culture had eroded were consuming people's existing capacity without replacing it — extractive in the precise sense the chapter warns against. Genuine growth culture requires tolerating the inefficiency of development: training takes time that could be spent on immediate production, feedback conversations are uncomfortable, mistakes must be treated as information rather than indictment. Organizations that won't pay that cost never build the capacity they need and eventually find themselves wondering where all their good people went.

5. **Inclusion and voice is the force most often claimed and least often genuinely operational.** The research found that

organizations pointing to diverse hiring as evidence of inclusion were frequently maintaining structural exclusion below the surface — invisible to those it didn't affect, and exhausting to those it did. Staff from minority cultural backgrounds described calibrated self-presentation: carefully managing what they said, translating not just language but assumptions and expectations to navigate organizational life. That adaptation work was invisible to leadership but consumed the energy that should have gone into the work itself. Genuine inclusion requires multiple voice pathways, because no single channel works across all cultural frameworks — the public, formal, direct-challenge model that works for low-power-distance cultures actively excludes those for whom public disagreement violates relational order. When inclusion is structural rather than rhetorical, something measurable changes: problems surface earlier, innovation accelerates, and morale improves — not because work becomes easier, but because people experience themselves as contributors rather than managed resources.

Together, these forces form a system. Consistent leadership creates the safety within which honest communication becomes possible. Clear communication makes compelling vision legible rather than merely aspirational. Compelling vision gives growth culture a direction and a why. Growth culture creates the conditions in which genuine inclusion can take root. And genuine inclusion returns richer, more honest information to leadership — enabling more consistent, better-informed action. The cycle compounds in both directions. Tending all five is not an initiative. It is the daily discipline of building something meant to outlast you.

The Historical View

The tension between results and human dignity is not new. History offers powerful examples of leaders and movements that discovered—often through painful trial and error—that sustainable excellence requires both.

The Lowell Mill Experiment

In the 1820s, Francis Cabot Lowell founded textile mills in Massachusetts with a revolutionary premise: that industrial production need not destroy workers' lives. At the time, English mills were notorious for brutal conditions—children working fourteen-hour days, workers maimed by machinery, families broken by poverty wages. Lowell took a different approach. He recruited young women from New England farms, housing them in clean boardinghouses with strict but caring oversight. He paid wages that allowed savings. He created lending libraries and offered evening lectures. The "Lowell Mill Girls" became famous—literate workers who published their own literary magazine while producing textiles that competed globally.

For a season, the experiment worked. Production was high. Workers were healthy. The system demonstrated that results and dignity could coexist. But as competition intensified in the 1830s and 1840s, new management abandoned Lowell's principles. Wages dropped. Hours extended. Housing deteriorated. The system became extractive rather than developmental. The lesson endures: high-performance systems that honor humanity require constant intentionality. Market pressures naturally push toward extraction. Only deliberate commitment to human dignity preserves the balance.

Applying the Four Pillars:

- Clarity: Lowell's original system gave workers a clear understanding of what was expected, what they would receive in return, and why the arrangement existed. Workers knew the rules of the boardinghouses, the structure of their wages, and the purpose of the educational opportunities offered to them. That clarity created predictability—and predictability created trust. When new management took over, clarity eroded first. Expectations shifted without explanation. Workers who had understood the terms of their employment now found those terms quietly rewritten. The confusion this created was not incidental—it was the first sign that the system had begun to consume rather than develop.

- Consistency: The founding Lowell experiment held together because the values it proclaimed were actually practiced. Oversight of housing was strict but equitable. Wages were paid as promised. Educational opportunities were made genuinely available. Workers experienced an organization that did what it said. The unraveling of the 1830s and 1840s was, at its core, a consistency failure. New management retained the language of the original vision while abandoning its practice. Wages dropped, hours extended, and housing deteriorated—not because the mission statement changed, but because daily behavior drifted away from it. The rhetoric outlasted the commitment, and workers recognized the gap immediately.

- Contribution: Lowell's original design gave workers genuine agency over their own development. The lending libraries and evening lectures were not charity—they were an invitation to grow. Workers responded by publishing their own literary magazine, demonstrating what happens when people experience themselves as contributors rather than functions. When management shifted toward extraction, that sense of agency collapsed. Workers became interchangeable parts again. Their voice, their development, their initiative—all of it became irrelevant to a system focused solely on output. Contribution disappeared, and with it, the discretionary effort that had made the original system exceptional.

- Care: The boardinghouses, the savings-enabling wages, the attention to workers' physical and intellectual lives—these were expressions of care, however paternalistic they may appear through a modern lens. Lowell's founding vision held that workers were not costs to be minimized but human beings whose lives the enterprise had a responsibility to support. The departure from that care was not simply a business decision—it was a moral one. And workers understood it as such. The strikes and labor organizing that followed were not merely economic protests. They were responses to the experience of being seen, and then being unseen.

The Mondragon Cooperatives

In 1956, a Catholic priest named José María Arizmendiarrieta founded a worker-owned cooperative in the Basque region of Spain. Starting with five workers making paraffin heaters, Mondragon grew into one of the world's largest cooperative enterprises—employing over 80,000 people across manufacturing, retail, and finance. Mondragon's founding principle was radical: workers are not costs to be minimized but partners in a shared enterprise. Ownership is distributed. Wage ratios between highest and lowest paid are capped. Major decisions require democratic participation. When economic downturns hit, workers accept temporary pay cuts rather than laying off colleagues.

The results challenge conventional assumptions. Mondragon cooperatives have survived economic crises that destroyed traditional competitors. Worker satisfaction consistently outpaces industry averages. Innovation flourishes because workers who own their enterprise invest discretionary effort. Mondragon demonstrates that the four pillars—clarity about shared purpose, consistency in values, contribution through genuine voice, care expressed in mutual ownership—can sustain high performance across decades and economic cycles. The system works because it refuses the false choice between results and humanity.

Applying the Four Pillars:

- Clarity: Mondragon's founding clarity was structural, not merely rhetorical. The cooperative model itself communicated what the enterprise was for and whose interests it served. Workers did not need to wonder whether leadership's stated values aligned with actual practice—the ownership structure made alignment a requirement of the system, not a matter of individual goodwill. When economic downturns came, the clarity of shared purpose—we are all in this together, and the enterprise exists to sustain us all—gave workers a framework for understanding difficult decisions. Temporary pay cuts were not arbitrary impositions; they were expressions of a purpose workers genuinely shared.

- Consistency: Mondragon's capped wage ratios are perhaps the most visible expression of consistency in the cooperative model. In most organizations, statements about treating everyone fairly remain abstract. At Mondragon, the ratio between the highest and lowest paid is a structural constraint—consistency made concrete in policy. Democratic participation in major decisions creates a similar kind of built-in consistency: the process is the same regardless of the outcome, and that procedural reliability builds trust over time. Workers who have experienced this level of structural consistency develop a different relationship to the enterprise than workers who must simply trust that leadership's good intentions will hold under pressure.

- Contribution: Genuine contribution requires genuine voice, and Mondragon's democratic structure makes voice a feature of the system rather than a favor granted by leadership. Workers are not consulted—they participate in ownership and decision-making as a matter of right. This structural inclusion produces the discretionary effort that conventional enterprises struggle to coax through incentive programs: when people own the outcome, they invest differently than when they are merely rewarded for it. Innovation at Mondragon flourishes not because workers are more talented but because the system creates conditions in which their judgment, initiative, and creativity are genuinely wanted.

- Care: The decision to accept temporary pay cuts rather than lay off colleagues during economic downturns is perhaps the most powerful expression of organizational care in any of the historical examples in this chapter. It communicates something that no speech or recognition program can: we see you as a person, not a position. Your continued membership in this community matters more to us than protecting our own compensation. That is care expressed in structural terms, with real cost attached—and workers respond to it with the kind of loyalty and reciprocal investment that organizations built on extraction can never quite achieve.

Toyota's Production System

When Toyota developed its legendary production system in the 1950s, Western observers initially focused on technical innovations: just-in-time inventory, quality circles, continuous improvement. What they often missed was the human philosophy underneath. Taiichi Ohno, the system's architect, built on a simple premise: the workers closest to production understand problems best. Rather than treating assembly-line workers as interchangeable parts, Toyota invested in their development and gave them authority to stop production when they noticed defects. The famous "andon cord" allowed any worker to halt the entire line—a radical trust in human judgment.

This wasn't soft management. Toyota demanded excellence relentlessly. But the demand came paired with investment: extensive training, job security, genuine voice in improvement processes. Workers reciprocated with discretionary effort, problem-solving initiative, and loyalty that American manufacturers struggled to match. When American companies tried to copy Toyota's technical systems without adopting its human philosophy, they consistently failed. The lesson was clear: high performance isn't a set of techniques. It's a culture that honors human capacity while pursuing excellence.

Applying the Four Pillars:

- Clarity: Toyota's system gave every worker exceptional clarity—not just about their assigned tasks, but about why those tasks mattered and how they connected to the quality of the finished product. The andon cord was a clarity mechanism as much as a quality mechanism: it told every worker precisely what authority they held and exactly what to do when they identified a problem. That structural clarity communicated something beyond operational procedure. It communicated that problems were expected, that surfacing them was correct behavior, and that each worker's judgment was trusted. In most manufacturing environments, clarity flows downward—supervisors know, workers execute. Toyota's system made clarity distributed, and that distribution was inseparable from its performance.

- Consistency: Toyota's human philosophy was not a program that ran alongside the production system—it was embedded in the production system itself. Job security was not a promise that individual managers made when times were good; it was a structural expectation that shaped the entire employment relationship. Training was not an occasional event; it was continuous and expected at every level. The andon cord applied to everyone. Kaizen—the principle of continuous improvement—applied everywhere. Workers at Toyota experienced an organization where the standards and values were remarkably consistent across contexts, roles, and leadership changes, because those standards and values had been institutionalized rather than left to individual discretion.

- Contribution: The andon cord is perhaps the most vivid symbol of genuine contribution in any of the historical examples in this chapter. In manufacturing systems built on the assumption that workers execute while managers think, halting the entire line would be unthinkable—an act of disruption, even insubordination. At Toyota, it was the correct response to a quality problem, expected and respected. That single practice communicated the organization's actual belief about workers' capacity and value more clearly than any mission statement could. Workers who are trusted to stop the line to protect quality experience themselves as contributors to excellence, not executors of someone else's plan. That experience produces the discretionary effort, problem-solving initiative, and loyalty that Toyota's competitors could not replicate by copying the technical systems alone.

- Care: Toyota's investment in worker development—extensive training, genuine job security, inclusion in continuous improvement processes—expressed care in its most demanding and authentic form. It would have been easier and cheaper to treat assembly-line workers as interchangeable, to hire and lay off as production demands shifted, to reserve problem-solving authority for supervisors and engineers. Toyota's choice to invest instead was a statement about what workers are: people whose judgment matters, whose development is worth the cost, and whose stability is worth protecting. American manufacturers who copied Toyota's technical systems without this human philosophy were not simply missing a management technique. They were missing the conviction that made the technique worth using.

The Biblical View

Scripture consistently refuses to separate fruitfulness from faithfulness, results from righteousness, productivity from personhood. The biblical vision of work honors both excellence and human dignity.

Nehemiah: Building Walls While Building People

When Nehemiah arrived in Jerusalem to rebuild the city's destroyed walls, he faced a classic leadership dilemma. The task was urgent—enemies threatened, and the people's morale was broken. A results-focused leader might have driven the work relentlessly, sacrificing everything to speed. Nehemiah chose differently. Before organizing construction, he wept, fasted, and prayed for months (Nehemiah 1:4-11). He understood that sustainable results require spiritual foundation. When he finally arrived in Jerusalem, he didn't announce grand plans. He quietly surveyed the damage, understanding the situation before demanding action (2:11-16).

His organization of the work demonstrated all four pillars. Clarity: each family knew exactly which section of wall they were responsible for, and the work was recorded precisely (chapter 3). Consistency: Nehemiah applied the same standards to himself, refusing the governor's food allowance that previous leaders had taken (5:14-18). Contribution: workers were organized by family and neighborhood, building near their own homes, connecting personal stake to collective mission (3:10, 23, 28-30). Care: when Nehemiah discovered that wealthy Jews were exploiting poor laborers, he stopped construction to address the injustice, prioritizing human dignity over project timeline (5:1-13).

The wall was completed in fifty-two days—a remarkable achievement. But the greater achievement was how it was built: with people's dignity intact, relationships restored, and spiritual renewal kindled. Nehemiah demonstrates that godly leadership pursues results through human flourishing, not despite it.

Applying the Four Pillars:

- Clarity: Nehemiah's assignment of the wall sections in chapter 3 is a model of operational clarity. Every family, every group, every individual knew exactly which section they were responsible for—and the record of those assignments was precise enough to be preserved in Scripture. But Nehemiah's clarity went deeper than task assignment. Before organizing construction, he articulated the mission with theological and communal weight: "Come, let us rebuild the wall of Jerusalem, and we will no longer be in disgrace" (2:17). He connected the visible task to a larger purpose—the dignity of the people, the name of God, the possibility of a renewed community. Workers who knew both what they were building and why they were building it approached the work differently than a crew simply executing orders.

- Consistency: Perhaps no moment in Nehemiah's leadership demonstrates consistency more powerfully than his refusal of the governor's food allowance (5:14-18). Previous governors had placed heavy burdens on the people while enjoying the privileges of their position. Nehemiah, despite holding the same office, declined the same privilege—because he understood that consistency between stated values and personal behavior is the foundation on which trust is built. He could not call the community to sacrifice while exempting himself from it. His consistency was not merely personal virtue; it was a leadership strategy. When workers could see that the person asking them to work without rest was himself working without rest, and without special compensation, the credibility of his leadership was secured in a way that no speech could have achieved.

- Contribution: The assignment of families and neighbors to build near their own homes was an act of contribution design—connecting personal stake to collective mission in the most direct way possible. Workers building the section of wall nearest their own homes and families were not laboring for an abstract civic project; they were protecting their own people. That connection between personal investment and shared work is precisely what contribution looks like when it functions well. Nehemiah also demonstrated contribution in his willingness to stop everything and address the economic injustice that wealthy Jews were inflicting on poor laborers. By treating that complaint as worthy of interrupting construction—rather than a distraction from the real work—he communicated that workers' voices and experiences were part of the project, not peripheral to it.

- Care: The economic justice episode in chapter 5 is one of the most striking expressions of organizational care in Scripture. Nehemiah discovered that wealthy community members were charging interest to poor laborers who were already sacrificing to participate in the construction project—and he stopped work to address it. The wall mattered. The fifty-two-day deadline implies urgency. And Nehemiah stopped anyway. In doing so, he communicated something that no policy statement could: human dignity is not a value we pursue after the mission is secured. It is how we pursue the mission. The wall built on the exploitation of the poor would have been a contradiction of everything the reconstruction was supposed to restore.

Jesus and the Twelve: Development Over Extraction

Jesus had three years to launch a movement that would transform history. By worldly metrics, efficiency demanded maximizing output from His followers. Instead, Jesus invested extravagantly in twelve ordinary men—teaching, modeling, correcting, encouraging, and entrusting them with increasing responsibility.

His approach embodied the four pillars. Clarity: Jesus repeatedly explained His mission, using parables and direct teaching to ensure understanding (Mark 4:34). Consistency: His character remained constant whether facing crowds or solitude, success or opposition (Hebrews 13:8). Contribution: He sent the disciples out in pairs to practice ministry, then debriefed their experiences (Luke 10:1-20). Care: He noticed their exhaustion and insisted they rest (Mark 6:31). He washed their feet (John 13:1-17). He prayed for them by name (John 17).

Jesus could have accomplished more visible results in three years by working alone or driving His followers harder. Instead, He built capacity that multiplied after His departure. The disciples He developed transformed the ancient world. His investment in people, not extraction from them, produced lasting fruit. John 15 captures His philosophy: "I am the vine; you are the branches... apart from me you can do nothing" (John 15:5). Fruitfulness comes through abiding connection, not striving effort. High performance flows from relationship, not pressure.

Applying the Four Pillars:

- Clarity: Jesus' teaching ministry was characterized by a relentless commitment to ensuring genuine understanding, not mere information transfer. He did not speak in parables to obscure His message but to make it land in the soil of each listener's experience and culture. Mark's Gospel notes that He "did not say anything to them without using a parable. But when he was alone with his disciples, he explained everything" (Mark 4:34). That two-stage process—public teaching followed by private explanation—reflects a leader who understood that clarity requires more than transmission. It requires checking whether the message was received, answering questions, and translating abstract truth into lived application. When disciples misunderstood, Jesus corrected and re-explained. He did not move on and assume understanding had followed.

- Consistency: The theological truth of Hebrews 13:8—"Jesus Christ is the same yesterday and today and forever"—is also an organizational observation: His character remained constant across every context He navigated. He was the same with the crowds as with the disciples, the same at the Last Supper as at the feeding of the five thousand, the same under the pressure of opposition as in moments of apparent success. Disciples who follow an inconsistent leader spend energy reading the leader rather than doing the work. Disciples who follow a consistent leader can trust the relationship and invest their attention in the mission. Jesus' consistency was not rigidity—He responded differently to different people and situations with remarkable sensitivity. But His values, His care, His commitment to truth, and His identity never wavered. That consistency was the relational foundation on which genuine discipleship could be built.

- Contribution: The sending of the seventy-two in Luke 10 is a masterclass in contribution design. Jesus did not wait until

His followers were fully formed before entrusting them with real responsibility. He sent them out—in pairs, for mutual support and accountability—with clear authority and specific instructions, and then debriefed their experiences when they returned. That debrief was not a performance review; it was a learning conversation that treated their experiences as valuable input into shared understanding. The pairing ensured that contribution happened in community rather than isolation, and the debrief ensured that what was learned from the field came back into the team's collective knowledge. Over three years, Jesus progressively expanded His disciples' responsibility, moving from observation to participation to independent action—building contribution gradually rather than extracting performance immediately.

- Care: The moments of care in the Gospel accounts are numerous and specific, which itself is instructive: care that is genuine tends to be concrete and particular. Jesus noticed that the disciples were exhausted and created space for rest (Mark 6:31). He prayed for them by name and by specific need in John 17—not a generic prayer for "the team" but intercession that demonstrated knowledge of each person's situation. He washed their feet the night before His death, choosing a posture of service at the moment when He might most have claimed the right to be served. Care in Jesus' ministry was not a counterbalance to the demands of mission—it was inseparable from the mission itself. The disciples He sent to transform the world needed to experience transformation themselves first, and transformation requires being genuinely seen and genuinely loved.

The Proverbs 31 Woman: Excellence Through Wisdom

The Proverbs 31 portrait of an excellent wife is often misread as an impossible standard of productivity. Look closer, and you find a picture of high performance integrated with wisdom and care. She "works with eager hands" and "sets about her work vigorously" (verses 13, 17)—excellence matters. But notice the integration: she provides for her household's needs (verse 15), ensures her servants are cared for (verse 15), extends her hands to the poor (verse 20), and speaks with wisdom and faithful instruction (verse 26). Her productivity serves people, not just metrics.

The passage's conclusion reveals the heart: "Charm is deceptive, and beauty is fleeting; but a woman who fears the Lord is to be praised" (verse 30). Her excellence flows from reverence for God, not anxious striving. The fear of the Lord grounds her productivity in right relationship. This biblical vision challenges both extremes. Against those who sacrifice people for results, it insists on wisdom, care, and generosity. Against those who use "grace" to excuse mediocrity, it celebrates vigorous, excellent work. The integration is the point.

Applying the Four Pillars:

- Clarity: The Proverbs 31 portrait describes a woman who demonstrates remarkable clarity about what she is for—and that clarity is not primarily organizational but vocational and theological. She works with eagerness and vigor not because she is driven by anxiety or external pressure, but because she understands the purpose her work serves: the flourishing of her household, her servants, the poor, and her community. That clarity of purpose is what integrates her extraordinary range of activities into something coherent rather than exhausting. She is not trying to do everything; she is doing what she understands she is called to do. The fear of the Lord mentioned in verse 30 is ultimately the source of that clarity—her identity and purpose are grounded in relationship to God rather than in achievement or recognition, which frees her to work without the distortion that anxiety introduces.

- Consistency: The portrait in Proverbs 31 describes not a single exceptional day but a sustained pattern of life—a person whose character is consistent across seasons, contexts, and circumstances. She rises early and works late, not because she is performing for observers, but because her values shape her behavior whether anyone is watching or not. Her generosity to the poor (verse 20) and her wisdom in speech (verse 26) are not strategic moves designed to build reputation; they flow from character. The passage's commendation by her children and husband reflects the kind of recognition that follows sustained, consistent behavior over time—not impressive moments but a trustworthy pattern. That consistency is itself a form of leadership, even in a domestic context: those who depend on her can trust what they will receive because what they receive does not vary with her mood or circumstances.

- Contribution: The Proverbs 31 woman's contribution is notable for its reach. She contributes to her household's material needs, to her servants' wellbeing, to the poor in her community, to commercial activity, and to the wisdom of those who hear her speak. Her work does not merely produce outputs—it develops and serves people. That orientation—contribution that is human-centered rather than metric-centered—is precisely what the chapter argues genuine contribution looks like. Her productivity serves people, not just performance measures. The servants who benefit from her preparation, the poor who receive from her generosity, and the family who trusts her judgment all experience a leader whose contribution is directed outward. She is not building her own capacity at others' expense; she is building others' capacity and flourishing through hers.

- Care: Care is woven into the texture of the entire portrait. She ensures that her servants are not simply fed but fed well (verse 15). She extends her hands to the poor—not as a budget line item but as a personal act (verse 20). Her speech is characterized by wisdom and faithful instruction (verse 26)—care expressed in language that builds rather than diminishes. The theological grounding of the passage is important here: her care does not flow from obligation or social pressure but from the fear of the Lord, which means from right relationship with the God who made and loves the people she serves. Care rooted in theology rather than personality is more sustainable—it does not depend on whether she is appreciated, whether circumstances are favorable, or whether her efforts are recognized. It flows from conviction.

Nuances and Blind Spots

The rhetoric-reality gap. The most extractive systems often have the best language. Organizations that overwork and underinvest in people frequently use inspiring words about mission, excellence, and sacrifice — and the words sound right. The experience tells a different story. Watch what actually happens to people over time, not just what leadership says. When abundant talk about growth and development isn't matched by actual investment in training, realistic workloads, or career pathways, cynicism is the inevitable result.

Quiet quitting is a diagnosis, not a character flaw. Minimal effort, clock-watching, "not my job" responses — especially from people who previously showed initiative — are signals worth reading carefully. They usually mean someone has concluded they are being used rather than valued. Similarly, when your highest performers suddenly go quiet, withdraw, or show signs of burnout, pay attention: the people who care most leave first. They are the canaries.

Initiative punishment is slow and invisible. People stop speaking up not because they don't care, but because past attempts to help or improve were dismissed, criticized, or appropriated without credit. By the time voice has become risk, the pattern is already well-established — and leaders are often the last to know it exists.

Informal systems carry organizations — until they can't. Many organizations survive on peer training, relational knowledge transfer, and good people quietly compensating for inadequate systems. This works until those people leave, burn out, or reach capacity. Sustainable high performance requires institutionalizing what works, not hoping that dedicated individuals will keep absorbing the gaps indefinitely.

"High performance" isn't culturally neutral. Western frameworks tend to emphasize individual achievement, measurable outputs, and competitive drive. Other cultural frameworks prioritize group harmony, relationship quality, and collective success. Leaders who impose one definition of excellence — even unconsciously — will alienate team members whose equally valid frameworks simply look different. Cultural survival mode is a performance tax: when staff from minority cultures are constantly code-switching and carrying invisible translation labor, high performance for some is being subsidized by exhaustion from others.

Care without accountability isn't care — it's avoidance. Some leaders mistake niceness for genuine investment in people. They avoid difficult conversations, tolerate poor performance, and let problems fester in the name of grace. True care includes honest feedback, clear expectations, and accountability that actually helps people grow. Avoidance doesn't protect people — it abandons them to their weaknesses.

Consistency is tested in the exceptions. Anyone can uphold standards when it's easy. The real test is when making an exception would be convenient, when enforcing a standard is uncomfortable, when treating everyone fairly costs something. Watch how leaders handle the hard cases — those moments reveal whether fairness is a value or just a slogan.

Development requires tolerating inefficiency. Training people, giving feedback, allowing mistakes, and building capacity all take time that could otherwise be spent on immediate production. Organizations that won't accept this trade will never truly develop their people. They'll extract from existing capacity until it's exhausted — and then wonder why the revolving door keeps spinning.

The people who leave often understand the organization better than those who stay. Exit interviews, conducted honestly and without defensiveness, reveal patterns that current employees can't or won't articulate. Organizations that dismiss departing feedback as sour grapes lose some of their most valuable diagnostic information.

———◆○◆———

Try This Week

Choose ONE practice to implement consistently this week. Small actions, repeated faithfully, build momentum that grand initiatives rarely achieve.

Day 1-2: Clarify One Outcome

With your team, complete this sentence: "By the end of this month, we will _________________. This matters because _________________."

Example: "By the end of this month, we will complete training documentation for all new positions. This matters because it reduces anxiety for new hires and prevents knowledge loss when people transition."

Make it specific. Make it meaningful. Share it with at least three people.

Day 3-4: Ask About Barriers

In one conversation, ask a team member: "What makes it hard to do your best work right now?"

Listen for systemic issues—lack of resources, unclear expectations, cultural barriers, poor transition procedures. Don't let this become about whether someone is trying hard enough. Most people want to do well; barriers prevent them.

Follow up within 48 hours on something you heard. Even small follow-through demonstrates that voice leads to action.

Day 5: Take One Care Action

Choose one small action that communicates care—a personal check-in, solving a practical problem, offering schedule flexibility—and explicitly link it to your shared mission.

Say it out loud: "I'm doing this because ________________."

Example: "I'm arranging coverage so you can attend your family event because we believe families matter, and we can't ask you to serve others while neglecting your own."

This explicit connection prevents care from feeling arbitrary or conditional. It shows that care flows from values, not just personal preference.

Reflection Questions

Quick Check (1-2 minutes)

- Rate your organization 1-5 on each pillar: Clarity, Consistency, Contribution, Care

- Which pillar shows the biggest gap between what leadership believes and what staff experience?

Deeper Reflection (5-10 minutes)

- Where has your organization sacrificed human dignity for results? What was the long-term cost in turnover, trust, or capacity?

- How do newer or culturally marginalized staff experience "high performance" in your context? Don't assume—ask directly.

Experience often varies dramatically by role and tenure.

- If you could strengthen just one pillar in the next 90 days, which would create the most cascading positive effects?

- Are you operating with "lack of resources" as chronic excuse, or making strategic choices about what matters most? Real constraints exist, but progress comes from clarity about priorities.

Team Discussion (15-30 minutes)

- What would it look like to be known equally for excellent results AND deep care for people? Be specific about daily practices, not just values.

- Where might we be treating people as roles rather than image-bearers? How would we know?

Moving Forward

High performance for humans is not a destination—it's a direction. It is the daily choice to build systems that develop people rather than extract from them. To pursue results without abandoning dignity. To believe that honoring the image of God strengthens rather than weakens mission. Organizations don't arrive at high performance—they learn to walk toward it. Honesty about the journey matters: progress described as gradual, movement characterized as "starting to turn that way," assessments that acknowledge both strengths and gaps.

This is the reality of building human-centered performance: it's gradual, uneven, requiring constant attention and course-correction.

But direction matters more than pace. Organizations making genuine progress describe leadership with clear desires and goals, willingness to learn and adjust, and commitment to stay the course.

The alternative—productivity without humanity, or community without effectiveness—serves no one well. Neither honors God. Neither sustains mission over time. High performance for humans is both/and: results and relationships, excellence and dignity, challenge and care. It's the hard, holy work of building systems that let people flourish while pursuing a purpose larger than themselves. And it begins—as all good things do—with one clear, caring, consistent choice at a time.

PART TWO: BUILDING THE FOUNDATION

BUILDING THE FOUNDATION

Trust and Safety in Diverse Teams

Opening Scene

A staff member learns that a colleague was let go—without explanation. Another hears about a major curriculum change only after it's finalized. Rumors move faster than official emails.

The leader insists, "My door is always open." Staff reply quietly, "We never know what's coming next."

This pattern is achingly familiar in many organizations. When people don't know why decisions are made—or why people disappear—their imaginations fill the gap. And imagination, under uncertainty, almost always produces something worse than reality.

Over time, the result is predictable: fear replaces candor. People stop speaking up, not because they don't care, but because they don't feel safe enough to risk it. Trust isn't gone—but it's fragile, uneven, and shaped as much by memory as by the present.

Why Trust Is Harder in Multicultural Teams

Trust is complex in any organization. In multicultural teams, it is exponentially more fragile—not because people are unwilling to trust, but because they interpret the same actions through different cultural lenses. What feels fair and predictable to one person may feel cold or dismissive to another. What feels compassionate to one culture may feel arbitrary to another. Public correction, private feedback, flexibility, consistency—each carries different meanings depending on cultural expectations.

Good intentions are not enough. Trust in diverse teams is built—or eroded—through steady, observable patterns of behavior over time. When leaders fail to establish clear parameters for how decisions are made and how people are treated, organizations drift into what might be called a passive cold war: everyone knows something is wrong, everyone has an explanation for why, and no one feels safe enough to name it directly.

The Long Shadow of Organizational History

Trust is never built in a vacuum. It accumulates—or erodes—across leadership eras. In organizations that have experienced repeated leadership changes, shifting priorities, or periodic instability, trust doesn't reset automatically when new leaders arrive. The emotional residue remains. People who lived through previous uncertainty carry that memory forward, even when conditions improve.

This is why present experience and past experiences often tell different stories. Current staff may describe improvements—greater stability, clearer communication, less negativity—while those who left earlier remember unpredictability, anxiety, and silence. Both can be true. Trust doesn't move in straight lines. Like grief, it cycles—sometimes progressing, sometimes resurfacing—especially when old patterns are accidentally repeated.

Cultural Complexity and Competing Trust Frameworks

In multicultural organizations, multiple trust systems operate simultaneously. Some cultures build trust primarily through relationship—time spent together, mutual obligation, and demonstrated care. Trust develops slowly but deeply. Others build trust through competence and clarity—clear expectations, follow-through, and transparent processes. Trust can form quickly when systems work well. Still others emphasize authority and hierarchy, where trust comes from knowing who decides and seeing leaders behave consistently with their role. And some cultures prioritize consensus, where trust is built by being consulted, included, and brought along before decisions are finalized.

In real organizations, all of these frameworks coexist. Trouble arises when leaders default to only one—usually the one most familiar to them—and assume it should work for everyone. What one group experiences as efficiency, another experiences as disconnection. What one experiences as discretion, another experiences as secrecy. What one experiences as flexibility, another experiences as instability. Trust erodes not because leaders don't care, but because care is expressed in ways that don't translate.

The Three Dimensions of Trust

Trust is not a single quality. It emerges at the intersection of three dimensions. When all three move together, trust grows. When one lags behind, trust weakens—no matter how strong the others are.

1. Predictability—People Can Anticipate What Will Likely Happen

Predictability does not mean rigidity. It means people can reasonably answer the question: Based on past patterns, what will probably happen next?

In environments where leadership behavior shifts with mood, circumstance, or pressure, unpredictability produces chronic anxiety. People stop focusing on their work and start scanning for danger. When predictability improves, the change is palpable. Leaders who respond consistently, follow through, and remain visible create a sense of stability even amid change. People may not like every decision—but they understand the pattern. Where predictability tends to break down:

- Personnel decisions made without explanation

- Sudden changes without transition time

- Resource allocation that feels arbitrary

- Roles that come with responsibility but little support

What restores predictability is not certainty about outcomes, but clarity about process. When people understand how decisions are made and what generally stays stable, anxiety decreases—even when change continues.

2. Transparency—Decisions Are Explained at the Right Depth

Transparency is not oversharing, nor is it violating confidentiality. It is offering enough explanation that people can trust the logic and values behind decisions, even when details must remain private. Transparency often improves over time—but unevenly. Some people feel informed and included. Others feel decisions arrive fully formed, with little opportunity to understand or influence them. This gap creates a dangerous dynamic: those closest to leadership experience clarity, while those farther away experience opacity. Trust then distributes itself along lines of access rather than equity.

Cultural context complicates transparency further. In some cultures, direct public explanation protects trust. In others, it risks embarrassment or loss of face. Leaders must navigate this tension carefully—recognizing that silence meant as discretion may be interpreted as secrecy.

Transparency strengthens when leaders:

- Explain why before announcing what

- Clarify who was involved in decisions

- Name what is not changing alongside what is

- Close feedback loops by showing how input shaped outcomes

When people see that explanations are consistent and responsiveness is real, transparency stops feeling performative and starts feeling trustworthy.

3. Proximity—Leaders Are Close Enough to Hear Real Concerns

Proximity is not just physical availability. It is relational access and psychological presence. Leaders can have open-door policies and still feel distant if people don't believe walking through that door is safe. True proximity shows up when leaders listen well, know their people, and demonstrate that concerns raised actually matter. In diverse teams, proximity gaps often mirror structural divides:

- Faculty and staff

- Local and foreign employees

- Senior and junior roles

Left unaddressed, these gaps become trust fault lines. Proximity strengthens when leaders share the burdens they assign—when they don't ask others to do what they themselves would avoid. This kind of "in-the-trenches" leadership builds credibility across cultures far more effectively than slogans or policies ever could.

Trust and Psychological Safety

Trust and psychological safety are related but distinct. Trust is believing others won't intentionally harm you. Psychological safety is believing you can speak without punishment. An organization may have warm relationships and still lack safety. People may like their leaders and still choose silence if speaking up feels risky.

Psychological safety varies widely within the same organization. Some people speak freely. Others self-censor carefully. This difference is rarely about personality—it reflects perceived risk. When safety is low, people protect themselves by withdrawing effort, avoiding initiative, and waiting for instructions. Innovation slows. Engagement becomes conditional.

Trust Seen Through Three Layers

One of the most helpful lenses for understanding how trust actually works in multicultural organizations is the same three-layer framework introduced earlier in this book. Trust isn't a single experience happening on one plane. It operates simultaneously across the visible task layer, the relational climate layer, and the cultural undercurrent layer — and what looks like a trust problem on the surface is almost never exclusively a surface problem.

When a leader announces a personnel change without explanation, the visible task layer registers a simple fact: someone is gone. But the relational climate layer is registering something far more significant: *Am I safe here? Could this happen to me? Was there something I wasn't told?* And the cultural undercurrent layer is already running its own interpretive analysis: depending on a team member's background, the unexplained departure may signal leadership instability, disrespect for seniority, evidence of favoritism, or confirmation of a hierarchy they never fully trusted. Three people can receive the same announcement and arrive at three entirely different conclusions — none of them irrational, all of them shaped by the layer their trust framework most depends on. This is why trust erodes so unevenly in multicultural organizations. Leaders often address Layer One (what happened) while remaining unaware that Layers Two and Three are where the real damage is accumulating.

Layer One: Trust and the Visible Task

At the task layer, trust shows up as reliability. Did the policy actually change the way it was announced? Did the performance review criteria stay the same from cycle to cycle? Was the resources allocation actually equitable, or did some departments consistently receive preferential treatment regardless of what the org chart said?

When leaders are consistent at this layer, trust has something concrete to attach to. Geert Hofstede's decades of research across cultures pointed to something important here: uncertainty avoidance — the degree to which people find ambiguity threatening — varies widely across cultural backgrounds. For teams with high uncertainty avoidance, inconsistency at the task layer isn't merely inconvenient; it is experienced as a kind of danger. For them, predictable systems aren't bureaucracy — they are evidence that the organization can be trusted at all. Leaders who treat clarity about processes, policies, and roles as optional are, from the vantage point of high uncertainty-avoidance team members, not just disorganized — they are untrustworthy. But task-layer consistency alone is insufficient. Trust eroded at a deeper layer doesn't heal simply because the org chart looks tidy.

Layer Two: Trust and the Relational Climate

The relational climate layer is where trust lives most of the time for most people. This is the emotional weather system of the organization — the felt sense of whether you are seen, whether your concerns matter, whether leadership knows your name and not just your job title.

Amy Edmondson's research on psychological safety offers a crucial insight here: teams do not primarily make rational calculations about whether to speak up. They make *social* calculations. The question is not "Do I have relevant information?" but rather "If I share it, what happens to me?" Edmondson found that the single most important factor in whether people brought problems, questions, and creative ideas to the table was whether they believed they could do so without punishment or humiliation. Notably, her early research was largely conducted in Western, lower power-distance contexts — which matters, because the very definition of "safe" varies by cultural layer. For a team member from a high power-distance background, safety may mean having a private channel to express concern rather than a public invitation to challenge leadership in an open meeting. Safety is not one-size-fits-all. The relational climate must be safe in multiple modes to serve a multicultural team.

This is where proximity matters so much. A leader can have an open-door policy and still feel completely inaccessible if walking through that door carries social risk. Relational climate trust is built not through policies but through repeated interpersonal experiences: the leader who noticed you looked overwhelmed and asked about it privately, the feedback that was given respectfully rather than publicly, the check-in that happened not because it was on the calendar but because someone actually cared. Over time these experiences accumulate into a felt sense — a relational memory — that either says *this place is safe for me* or *this place requires careful navigation.*

When that relational memory is negative and layered over time, it doesn't reset automatically when a new leader arrives. The emotional residue of previous experiences shapes how current behavior is interpreted. A well-intentioned transparency initiative launched by new leadership can be received with deep skepticism by staff who have watched similar initiatives evaporate before. This is not cynicism without cause. It is rational self-protection.

Layer Three: Trust and the Cultural Undercurrent

The cultural undercurrent layer is where trust frameworks diverge most dramatically — and where leaders most commonly cause unintentional damage without ever knowing it. Erin Meyer's work on the Culture Map is useful here. She identifies trust as one of the primary axes along which cultures differ significantly: some build trust primarily through the relationship itself — shared meals, mutual disclosure, investing time before getting to business — while others build trust primarily through task performance, competence demonstrated, and promises kept. These are not personality preferences. They are deeply embedded cultural frameworks for what trust means and what it requires.

In a multicultural organization, multiple trust-building frameworks are running simultaneously. A Western task-oriented leader may feel they have built excellent trust by following through consistently, communicating clearly, and delivering results. Meanwhile, team members from relationship-oriented cultural backgrounds are experiencing something different: they don't feel known as people, there's no sense of shared life outside the immediate work, and a leader who gets straight to business without investing relational time feels cold, possibly calculating. Neither experience is a distortion of reality. They are simply reading the cultural undercurrent through different frameworks.

This is why trust distributes unevenly along cultural lines in diverse organizations. It isn't that some people are suspicious by nature. It's that the implicit trust-building practices of leadership match some cultural frameworks and miss others. The people whose frameworks match leadership's default approach feel included and secure. Those whose frameworks differ experience a persistent, low-grade sense that they don't quite belong — that the organization was built for someone else.

When Hofstede's dimension of power distance is also in play — as it almost always is in multicultural teams — the dynamic becomes even more complex. High power-distance team members may appear compliant and trusting on the surface while privately holding deep reservations they will never voice upward. In such contexts, the absence of complaint is not evidence of trust. It is evidence that speaking up feels too costly.

The Three Layers Working Together: What Trust-Building Actually Requires

Understanding the three-layer reality of trust has a direct implication for how leaders should think about trust-building practices. It is not enough to be consistent at the task layer if the relational climate is cold. It is not enough to invest in relationships if cultural frameworks are clashing invisibly at the undercurrent level. And it is not enough to develop cultural intelligence if the organization's systems are still arbitrary and unpredictable at the visible task level. All three require simultaneous, intentional attention.

This helps explain why trust in multicultural organizations can appear to be improving — leaders are doing better at the task layer, communication is clearer, processes are more consistent — while team members from particular cultural backgrounds are still reporting that something feels off. The problem may be that the relational climate layer hasn't caught up, or that cultural undercurrent assumptions are still causing misinterpretation. A single positive score on one layer does not compensate for deficits on the others.

It also helps explain the "passive cold war" dynamic described at the beginning of this chapter. In those organizations, surface-level functioning — the visible task layer — continues. People show up, do their jobs, participate in meetings. But beneath the surface, the relational climate has become one of careful, self-protective navigation. And at the cultural undercurrent layer, team members from non-dominant backgrounds have long since concluded that the organization's unspoken rules were never written with them in mind. Trust has not evaporated. It has simply retreated to whatever feels personally safe — which, in most of these environments, is the informal networks of people who share cultural frameworks, not the organization itself.

What the Three Layers Reveal About Rebuilding Trust

When trust has eroded, leaders often default to task-layer solutions: clearer policies, more regular updates, better-defined roles. These matter and should not be dismissed. But if the relational climate has been damaged, task-layer solutions feel beside the point to those most affected. What they need is evidence that leadership is willing to be close — relationally close, not just physically present. Proximity that costs something. Accountability that doesn't just apply downward.

Edgar Schein's work on organizational culture suggests that culture — and by extension, relational climate — is most visibly reinforced not through stated values but through what leaders actually pay attention to, what they measure, and how they respond to crises. The same is true of trust. What leaders pay attention to, and who they listen to, and whether they follow through on what they hear — these patterns, observed repeatedly at the relational and cultural layers, do more to build or destroy trust than any policy document.

For multicultural teams specifically, rebuilding trust requires one additional step that is often skipped: naming the layers explicitly. Most multicultural organizations do not have a shared vocabulary for the cultural undercurrents that shape interpretation. Leaders making entirely reasonable decisions based on their own cultural framework may genuinely not know that their choices are being read through a different cultural lens as evidence of exclusion. Creating space to talk about cultural frameworks — not defensively, not as a performance of diversity — but as a genuine practice of mutual learning, begins to make the invisible visible. And when the invisible becomes visible, the trust damage it has been quietly causing can finally be addressed.

Trust in multicultural organizations is not ultimately a problem of character or intention. It is a challenge of complexity — the complexity of human beings from different backgrounds interpreting the same environment through different layers of meaning. Leaders who understand this stop asking "Why don't they trust me?" and start asking "At which layer have I lost them, and how do I get back to them there?" That shift in question is the beginning of rebuilding trust that is equitable, durable, and genuinely shared.

The Cost of Low Trust

When trust erodes, the costs accumulate quietly but steadily. Turnover increases. Relationships never have time to deepen. Organizational memory leaks away. Voice diminishes. People stop offering ideas when effort feels unrewarded or unsafe. Anxiety rises. Uncertainty about roles, decisions, or security consumes emotional energy that could otherwise fuel creativity. Discretionary effort disappears. People give what is required—and no more. These are not moral failures. They are rational responses to an environment that feels unpredictable or unsafe.

Rebuilding Trust: What Actually Works

Trust can be rebuilt—but only through consistent, layered effort. Leadership change may create opportunity, but it does not create trust by itself. Trust grows when leaders repeatedly demonstrate:

1. Visibility and accessibility—showing up, responding, remaining present

2. Listening paired with action—not just hearing, but implementing when possible

3. Consistency over time—doing what was promised, again and again

4. Leading by example—sharing sacrifice, not just assigning it

5. Cultural intelligence in practice—ensuring trust is not distributed along cultural lines

These actions don't produce instant confidence. What they produce first is cautious hope. Over time, cautious hope becomes tentative trust. Eventually, if patterns hold, trust becomes assumed.

The Historical View

History offers powerful examples of trust being built—and broken—across cultural and organizational divides. These stories illuminate principles that remain relevant today.

The Rebuilding of Germany and Japan After World War II

After the devastation of World War II, the United States faced an unprecedented challenge: rebuilding trust with former enemies while transforming their societies. The Marshall Plan in Europe and the occupation of Japan under General Douglas MacArthur required navigating profound cultural differences and deep historical wounds. What made trust possible? In both cases, leaders demonstrated all three dimensions.

Predictability: American occupation forces established clear, consistent rules and followed them. Japanese citizens could anticipate how authorities would respond. The currency stabilized. Institutions functioned reliably. After years of wartime chaos, predictability itself became a form of care.

Transparency: MacArthur made decisions publicly and explained them through multiple channels. He used radio addresses, worked with Japanese media, and ensured that policies were communicated in culturally appropriate ways. People might disagree with decisions, but they understood the reasoning.

Proximity: Rather than governing from a distance, MacArthur made himself visible. He walked the streets of Tokyo. He met with Emperor Hirohito personally—a gesture that shocked many Americans but communicated profound respect to Japanese culture. His willingness to enter Japanese cultural space, rather than demanding Japanese conform to American norms, built trust across the cultural divide. The result was remarkable: within a decade, former enemies became allies. Trust emerged not despite cultural difference but through leaders who learned to build it across cultural frameworks.

The lesson: The postwar rebuilding succeeded not simply because resources were deployed or policies were implemented, but because leaders eventually learned to address all three layers. Task-layer decisions built institutional predictability. Relational-layer actions created the emotional conditions for cooperation. And cultural-layer adaptations made trust legible within frameworks that differed fundamentally from the occupiers' own.

The Truth and Reconciliation Commission in South Africa

When apartheid ended in South Africa, the nation faced a seemingly impossible challenge: building trust between communities that had experienced generations of systematic oppression, violence, and betrayal. The wounds were fresh. Justice seemed to demand punishment. Yet punishment risked perpetuating cycles of revenge. The Truth and Reconciliation Commission (TRC), led by Archbishop Desmond Tutu, chose a different path. Rather than trials that would establish winners and losers, the TRC created space for truth-telling, acknowledgment, and—where possible—reconciliation. The TRC embodied the three dimensions of trust in ways that crossed South Africa's deep cultural divides:

Predictability: The process had clear rules. Those who told the full truth about their actions could receive amnesty. Those who did not could face prosecution. The criteria were transparent and consistently applied—to perpetrators from all sides.

Transparency: Hearings were public. Testimonies were broadcast on radio and television. Victims told their stories. Perpetrators acknowledged their actions. The process was painful, but nothing was hidden. Transparency meant facing truth together, not papering over it.

Proximity: Tutu himself modeled what it meant to be present with suffering. He wept publicly during testimonies. He embraced both victims and perpetrators. He refused the distance that would have protected him emotionally but undermined his moral authority. His proximity to pain gave him credibility across communities. The TRC didn't achieve perfect reconciliation—South Africa continues to struggle with its legacy. But it demonstrated that trust can begin to rebuild even after profound betrayal, when leaders commit to predictability, transparency, and proximity across cultural lines.

The lesson: The TRC's work illustrates why trust-building after profound betrayal cannot operate at only one layer. Legal processes at Layer One provide structure but cannot restore relationship. Relational acts at Layer Two create the emotional conditions for change but need the structure of Layer One to be sustained and credible. And cultural wisdom at Layer Three — the ubuntu framework, the theological grounding, the broadcast hearings — is what makes the process legible and meaningful across communities who would otherwise interpret the same acts through entirely different lenses.

The Medici Bank and Cross-Cultural Commerce

In fifteenth-century Florence, the Medici family built the most successful banking network in Europe—one that operated across kingdoms, languages, religions, and cultures. Their success depended entirely on trust: merchants deposited money in one city expecting to withdraw it in another, based only on the Medici name. How did they build trust across such diversity? The Medici understood that trust required cultural translation. For Italian merchants, they emphasized family reputation and personal relationships—the relationship-based trust that dominated Mediterranean commerce. For Northern European traders, they emphasized precise record-keeping and contractual reliability—the task-based trust that Germanic cultures valued. For church officials, they demonstrated respect for hierarchy and proper deference to authority.

The Medici didn't choose one trust framework and impose it everywhere. They learned to build trust in culturally appropriate ways for each context while maintaining consistent integrity across all of them. Their ledgers were accurate everywhere. Their word was good everywhere. Their agents were reliable everywhere. When the Medici eventually fell, it wasn't because they lost the trust of one cultural group—it was because political overreach led them to betray the consistency that had made their name valuable. The lesson endures: trust across cultures requires both cultural flexibility and unwavering integrity.

The lesson: The Medici built a financial empire on the insight that trust is not a single currency that works the same way everywhere. It must be expressed in culturally appropriate forms at Layer Three, sustained by genuine relational investment at Layer Two, and grounded in rock-solid consistency at Layer One. Remove any layer and the structure weakens. Betray the foundational integrity and all the cultural fluency in the world cannot prevent collapse.

The Biblical View

Scripture offers profound wisdom about building trust, particularly across divisions that seem impossible to bridge. These stories reveal patterns that remain relevant for multicultural leadership today.

David's Mighty Men: Trust Forged Through Shared Hardship

Before David became king, he spent years as a fugitive, leading a ragged band of outcasts in the wilderness. The men who gathered around him were not Israel's elite—they were "all those who were in distress or in debt or discontented" (1 Samuel 22:2). Yet from this unlikely group emerged David's "mighty men"—warriors whose loyalty became legendary. How did David build such trust among such a diverse, troubled group? The account in 2 Samuel 23 provides clues.

Proximity: David shared their hardships. He lived in caves, went hungry, faced danger alongside them. When three of his men risked their lives to bring him water from the well at Bethlehem, David refused to drink it—he poured it out as an offering, honoring their sacrifice as too precious for personal consumption (2 Samuel 23:13-17). This wasn't a leader demanding service from a distance; this was a leader so close to his men that their risks became sacred to him.

Predictability: David's character was consistent whether in success or failure. When Saul—David's enemy—was vulnerable, David refused to harm him, even when his men urged him to (1 Samuel 24). This consistency proved that David's values didn't shift with circumstance. His men could trust that how he treated enemies predicted how he would treat them.

Transparency: David was honest about his struggles. The Psalms reveal a leader who expressed fear, doubt, and anguish openly. He didn't pretend invincibility. His transparency about weakness created space for others to be honest about their own struggles without losing standing. The result: men from different tribes, different backgrounds, different stories of failure became a unified force that conquered a kingdom. Trust built in the wilderness survived the transition to palace power—a transition that destroys most leadership teams.

The lesson: David's mighty men were not produced by effective management. They were produced by a leader who attended to all three layers simultaneously — delivering results at the task layer, investing in relational depth at the relational layer, and building a cultural framework that made honesty and loyalty possible across the diverse backgrounds of the men who followed him.

Barnabas: The Bridge-Builder Who Made Trust Possible

When the early church faced its most dangerous trust crisis, one man repeatedly stepped into the gap to build bridges no one else would risk. Barnabas—whose name literally means "Son of Encouragement"—demonstrated how trust is built across divides that seem impossible to cross. His story (Acts 9:26-27, 11:22-26, 15:36-39) reveals how the three trust dimensions work in practice.

When Saul converted to Christianity, no one believed it. This was the man who had dragged believers from their homes and consented to Stephen's murder. When Saul tried to join the disciples in Jerusalem, "they were all afraid of him, not believing that he really was a disciple" (9:26). Their fear was entirely rational—Saul could be a spy. Barnabas did what no one else would: "he took him and brought him to the apostles" (9:27). He vouched for Saul when Saul had no credibility. Later, when the gospel spread to Gentiles in Antioch, the Jerusalem church sent Barnabas to investigate. He arrived in a multicultural setting where Jewish and Gentile believers were building one church across enormous cultural differences. When controversy arose over John Mark's desertion during a missionary journey, Paul refused to give him another chance. Barnabas disagreed sharply enough that "they parted company" (15:39). While Paul wrote Mark off, "Barnabas took Mark and sailed for Cyprus" (15:39).

Proximity: Barnabas didn't investigate from a distance or send intermediaries. He personally spent time with Saul when everyone else avoided him. He stayed in Antioch long enough to understand what God was actually doing among Gentiles (11:23). He remained close to Mark after failure, investing in restoration when his ministry partner gave up. His proximity to risk, to cultural difference, and to failure didn't lead to rejection—it led to patient bridge-building.

Transparency: Barnabas told Saul's story to the apostles completely—the persecution and the transformation (9:27). He reported honestly to Jerusalem about the Gentile believers, not hiding cultural differences but also not catastrophizing them. He saw "evidence of the grace of God" and said so clearly (11:23). The disagreement with Paul was real and sharp—Scripture doesn't hide it. But Barnabas didn't let conflict prevent him from doing what he believed was right.

Predictability: Barnabas had a consistent pattern of believing the best about people and taking risks on them. He took a risk on Saul when no one else would. He built bridges to Gentile believers when others were suspicious. He invested in Mark when his ministry partner rejected him. His character was so consistent that when he vouched for someone, people trusted his judgment: "He was a good man, full of the Holy Spirit and faith" (11:24). The result: Saul became Paul the apostle. The multicultural church at Antioch became the launching point for mission to the Gentile world—"the disciples were called Christians first at Antioch" (11:26). And Mark, the deserter? Years later Paul wrote: "Get Mark and bring him with you, because he is helpful to me in my ministry" (2 Timothy 4:11). Trust built through proximity, transparency, and predictability produced fruit that outlasted the immediate cost.

The lesson: Barnabas's ministry demonstrates that the most important trust-building in an organization is often done not by those with formal authority but by those with relational credibility who are willing to be present at all three layers simultaneously — bridging task, relational, and cultural divides that formal structures cannot reach.

Jesus Restoring Peter: Trust After Betrayal

Peter's threefold denial of Jesus represents one of Scripture's most painful betrayals. At Jesus's moment of greatest need, Peter—who had sworn to die with him—claimed three times not to know him. The relationship seemed irreparably broken. After the resurrection, Jesus sought Peter out. The conversation recorded in John 21:15-19 demonstrates how trust is rebuilt after betrayal.

Proximity: Jesus didn't address Peter publicly, in front of all the disciples. He created intimate space around a breakfast fire—returning to the lakeside where their relationship had begun. The setting itself communicated that Jesus was willing to be close again, not holding Peter at arm's length.

Transparency: Jesus didn't pretend the betrayal hadn't happened. Three times Peter had denied him; three times Jesus asked, "Do you love me?" The questions were painful, but they named reality. Reconciliation required honesty about what had broken.

Predictability: Jesus's response to Peter's affirmation was consistent each time: "Feed my sheep." He didn't escalate punishment or add conditions. He demonstrated that his pattern was restoration, not retribution. Peter could trust that this Jesus—forgiving, commissioning, entrusting—was the same Jesus he would encounter going forward. The result: Peter, the denier, became Peter the rock—the leader of the early church who eventually gave his life for the faith he once fled. Trust rebuilt after betrayal can become stronger than trust that was never tested.

The lesson: Jesus's restoration of Peter illustrates that trust-rebuilding after betrayal must work at all three layers simultaneously. At Layer One, it requires the concrete reestablishment of role and responsibility — not vague forgiveness but specific recommissioning. At Layer Two, it requires the willingness to re-enter intimate relational space with the one who broke trust — proximity that costs something, that names what happened without pretending it didn't. And at Layer Three, it requires cultural wisdom about what accountability and restoration mean within the frameworks of those involved — neither ignoring the cultural weight of the failure nor accepting a cultural framework for punishment that forecloses the possibility of genuine restoration.

Nuances and Blind Spots

Leaders are usually the last to know. Job security anxiety, quiet resume updates, whisper networks more active than official channels — these are all signs that trust has already been eroding for some time before leadership notices. If you're genuinely surprised by resignations, it means people stopped telling you their real concerns long ago. The perception gap between "everything is fine" and what staff are actually experiencing is itself the problem, and it doesn't close on its own.

Trust has memory. New leaders inherit the trust — or distrust — created by their predecessors. Staff who experienced betrayal, broken promises, or unpredictability under previous leadership will respond to current leadership through that lens, even when current behavior is genuinely trustworthy. This isn't irrational; it's self-protective. Rebuilding inherited distrust requires patience, consistency, and explicit acknowledgment that the past was real — not just cheerful reassurance that things are different now.

Small betrayals accumulate. Trust rarely collapses from a single dramatic failure. More often it erodes through the quiet accumulation of small disappointments: the meeting where input was ignored, the promise that wasn't quite kept, the decision made without consultation. Each incident seems minor in isolation. Together they create a pattern — and once people have named that pattern internally, it takes far more than good intentions to undo it. Leaders who dismiss small concerns as unimportant are often missing the slow leak that eventually drains the tank.

Story fragmentation is a trust crisis. When different people describe the same event in completely different ways — "we heard three versions of why she left" — that's not merely a communication problem. It's evidence that official channels aren't trusted as sources of truth, and that people are filling informational voids with their own narratives. Whisper networks become dominant when transparent communication doesn't.

Privacy can feel like secrecy. Leaders often stay silent about sensitive matters out of genuine respect for confidentiality. But silence is never neutral — it's always interpreted. When explanations are absent, people construct their own, usually worse than reality. The question isn't whether to be transparent, but how to be appropriately transparent: enough to prevent harmful speculation, while still honoring legitimate constraints.

Trust distributes unevenly — and culturally. In most organizations, trust concentrates near leadership and thins at the margins. Those closest to power feel informed; those further away feel kept in the dark. This gap often maps onto cultural difference: those whose framework matches the dominant culture feel understood; others feel chronically misread. Over-politeness in diverse teams — everyone agreeing publicly, contradicting privately — isn't harmony. It's a warning sign, especially in high-context cultures where surface smoothness can mask deep fragmentation underneath. Effective leaders regularly audit who actually has access to trust, and who doesn't.

Cultural trust frameworks compete. Relationship-oriented team members who receive purely task-focused communication feel uncared for. Task-oriented team members who must wade through extensive relational investment before getting to the point feel their time is wasted. Neither reaction is wrong — but both erode trust when leaders fail to recognize and bridge the frameworks at play.

Psychological safety isn't the same as trust. You can trust someone's competence and character while still feeling unable to disagree with them safely. Psychological safety requires explicit, active cultivation — it doesn't follow automatically from good relationships or good intentions. Leaders must create visible conditions where challenge, dissent, and honest questions are genuinely welcomed, not merely tolerated in theory.

Trust is rebuilt in public, not just private. Individual conversations matter, but restoring trust across an organization requires visible patterns that everyone can observe. When a leader admits a mistake openly, keeps a difficult promise where others can see, or demonstrates consistency under pressure — those moments build collective trust in ways that private reassurances simply cannot replicate.

Try This Week

Choose ONE practice to implement consistently this week. Trust builds through repeated small actions, not grand gestures.

Monday: Over-communicate one upcoming decision

Pick one decision you're about to announce. Before you do, prepare answers to these questions: What is changing? Why this decision? Who was involved in deciding? What stays the same? What happens next? How can people give input? Who should they ask with questions?

Share all of this when you communicate the decision, not just the conclusion. Count how many questions you get. If you get fewer than usual, your explanation worked.

Tuesday-Wednesday: Check in with people who hear news last

Identify two staff members who are typically last to know about changes. This might be because of their role, their schedule, their cultural communication style, or simple proximity to leadership.

Schedule 15-minute informal check-ins. Don't make it about work tasks. Ask: "What are you wondering about lately?" "What's one thing you wish more people understood about your role?" "Is there anything you've heard through the grapevine that I should clarify?"

Just listen. Take notes. Thank them for their honesty. Follow up on something specific within a week.

Thursday: Address a cultural trust gap

If your team includes people from both relationship-oriented and task-oriented cultures, do one thing that honors both:

- Send a clear email with decision details (task), then have coffee with key people to explain it personally (relationship)

- Hold a structured meeting with agenda (task), then stay after for informal conversation (relationship)

The goal is demonstrating that both approaches matter to you.

Friday: Practice transparency through admission

In a team meeting or email, acknowledge one past miscommunication or mistake. Use this structure:

"I need to acknowledge something. When [describe what happened], I [describe what you did or didn't do]. I've realized this had the impact of [name the impact on others]. Going forward, here's what I'm doing differently: [specific new behavior]."

This kind of admission doesn't weaken authority—it builds the kind of trust that makes authority meaningful.

Reflection Questions

Quick Check (1-2 minutes)

- Rate your organization 1-10 on each trust dimension: Predictability, Transparency, Proximity. Which needs most attention?

- When was the last time someone on your team shared a genuine concern or admitted a mistake to you?

Deeper Reflection (5-10 minutes)

- What recent decisions have raised anxiety or confusion among your team? How were they communicated? If you could replay that communication, what would you do differently?

- In what ways might your leadership be predictable to you but not to others? What would a skeptical team member say about your consistency?

- Who currently feels farthest from you relationally? What might that mean for their trust in the organization? What would it take to close that proximity gap?

- Which cultural trust frameworks (relationship-based, task-based, authority-respecting, consensus-seeking) are most natural for you? Which are hardest? How might that create trust gaps with certain team members?

Team Discussion (15-30 minutes)

- As a leadership team, discuss: "If we asked our team members anonymously what most damages trust in our organization, what would they say?" Write down guesses without defending or explaining. Then find a way to actually ask—anonymous survey, trusted third party, exit interview data. Compare your guesses to reality. What surprises you?

Moving Forward

Trust provides the foundation—but trust alone isn't sufficient. Organizations also need pathways for people to actually use their voice, share concerns, and influence decisions. Without structured ways for input to flow, even high-trust environments can inadvertently silence important perspectives.

You cannot promise perfect trust forever. But you can commit to being trustworthy for a while—long enough that people stop waiting for the other shoe to drop. The biblical model for this is covenant faithfulness. God doesn't ask His people to trust Him because He's explained everything perfectly—He asks them to trust Him because He's proven faithful again and again. He shows up. He keeps promises. He stays present through difficulty.

Leaders who want to build trust in diverse teams do the same: show up consistently, keep the promises you make, stay present when things are hard. Do this not just for a month or a season, but long enough that people stop scanning for danger and start focusing on mission. That's when trust moves from fragile hope to lived reality. And that's when multicultural teams can finally shift their energy from self-protection to shared purpose.

Voice, Feedback, and Fairness

Opening Scene

The meeting agenda listed "Staff Input on New Initiative" as the final item. The executive director smiled warmly: "We really want to hear your thoughts before we finalize this."

Silence stretched across the room. Finally, Tom from finance spoke: "I think it sounds great. Really innovative." Others nodded. The director glanced around hopefully. "Anyone else? Questions? Concerns?" More nodding. Someone mentioned a minor logistical detail. The director thanked everyone for their input and closed the meeting.

In the hallway five minutes later, a completely different conversation erupted. "This is going to be a disaster." "Did you see how fast they want to implement it?" "There's no way this works with our current staffing." "Why do they even ask for input when they've clearly already decided?"

Maria from programs caught Ana, one of the quieter team members, at the elevator. "Why didn't you say anything in there? You work most directly with this." Ana looked uncomfortable. "What's the point? They already have their plan. And you know how it goes—if you speak up, you're labeled as 'not a team player.'" Maria pressed: "But if we don't speak up, nothing changes." Ana shook her head. "When I raised concerns about the last initiative, nothing changed anyway. They just got defensive. I learned my lesson."

Leadership left the meeting pleased with the smooth consensus. Staff left the meeting confirmed in their belief that voice doesn't actually matter. The initiative would launch with foreseeable problems that could have been prevented if the real feedback had been accessible.

Why Silence Doesn't Mean Agreement

The opening scene illustrates one of the most consequential mistakes leaders make in multicultural organizations: interpreting silence as consent. In reality, silence can signal many things—disagreement, uncertainty, cultural respect for hierarchy, exhaustion from previous failed attempts to contribute, fear of consequences, or lack of trust that input matters.

Research on organizational voice reveals that silence is rarely about personality or lack of opinions. It's about the organizational context. When people consistently choose silence over voice, it signals that the organizational environment has made speaking up feel futile, risky, or culturally inappropriate. Researchers identify three types of silence: **acquiescent silence** (resignation that speaking won't help), **quiescent silence** (fear of negative consequences), and **prosocial silence** (withholding information to benefit others or the organization). In multicultural contexts, a fourth type operates: culturally-shaped silence, where cultural frameworks about hierarchy, harmony, and appropriate communication determine when and how voice is expressed.

The cost of silence is substantial. Employees withhold information about errors, inefficiencies, concerns, and improvement opportunities. Organizations lose access to critical knowledge held by people closest to actual work. Problems that could have been prevented become crises. Good ideas remain unspoken. Innovation stagnates. Leaders must understand: voice is not primarily a personality trait (some people are naturally outspoken while others are quiet). Voice is primarily a response to organizational systems and cultural context. The same person who appears passive in one organizational setting can be highly vocal in another where the conditions support it.

What Research Tells Us About Voice and Fairness

Van Dyne, Ang, and Botero identified three distinct forms of organizational silence that help explain why quiet rooms aren't what they appear to be. Acquiescent silence is resignation — the belief that speaking up won't change anything anyway. Quiescent silence is fear — the calculation that the cost of speaking outweighs the benefit. Prosocial silence is protective — withholding information to shield a colleague, a team, or the organization from harm. All three can look identical from across the table.

All three can be mistaken for agreement. Edmondson's research on psychological safety established something equally important: the willingness to speak is not a personality trait. It is a response to the perceived safety of the environment. When people stay silent, the relevant question is not "why won't they talk?" It is "what has this organization taught them happens when they do?" These two bodies of work point in the same direction. Silence is organizational feedback, not personal passivity. And it compounds over time — the longer honest input goes unrewarded, the safer silence becomes.

But there is a fourth form of silence these frameworks don't fully name. In multicultural contexts shaped by high power distance and relational norms — particularly in collective cultural settings — there is silence that is neither resignation, nor fear, nor protection. It is relational silence: the natural, appropriate withholding of voice when the relationship required to carry it hasn't been built yet. People don't share honest feedback with strangers. They share it within relationships.

And in many cultural frameworks, what counts as a "real enough" relationship to carry difficult truth is far more substantive than a title on an org chart or an open-door policy on a website. This matters because most organizational voice systems are built to address the first three types of silence. They rarely address the fourth. You can add anonymous surveys and open forums and feedback forms — and still find that the people you most need to hear from remain quiet, not because they're afraid, but because the relationship isn't there yet.

Voice is Not a System, It is a Relationship

What field research in multicultural organizational settings consistently reveals is this: leadership is relationship. The concept of guanxi — rooted in Confucian thought and studied extensively by researchers including Li and colleagues, Kuo and colleagues, and Ameyaw and colleagues — describes the relational ecosystem within which meaningful exchange actually happens. It is not simply a network of connections. It is a living web of cultivated trust, reciprocal investment, and mutual dignity that determines what can flow between people and what cannot.

Guanxi holds within it four interdependent dynamics. Understanding them changes how voice and fairness actually work in practice. Ganqing is the affection and sincere care that develops between people over time — not performed warmth, but the accumulated evidence of genuine investment in another person's wellbeing. In every multicultural context where trust is low, what changes things is rarely a new policy. It is a relationship — the slow accumulation of evidence that the person across from you actually sees you and cares.

Voice is a form of vulnerability. People don't make themselves vulnerable to institutions. They make themselves vulnerable to people — and only when the accumulated evidence suggests it's reasonably safe to do so. When leaders treat voice as a structural problem to be solved with better systems, they skip the relational work that makes any system usable. Renqing is reciprocal relational investment — the sense that genuine care creates a bond of mutual accountability. It is not transactional. You don't give in order to receive. But when leaders consistently demonstrate genuine investment in their people — in their growth, their dignity, their lives beyond the job — something shifts. People give back. Not because they have to. Because the relationship has earned their engagement.

This is directly connected to what Kim and Beehr, and Wang and colleagues, describe as affective organizational commitment — the emotional attachment that develops when employees genuinely feel supported and seen. When that commitment is present, people offer more. Including honest feedback. Including the kind of voice that costs something to give. Mianzi is the concept of face — personal prestige, social credit, and dignity that a person carries and that can be honored or diminished by others. In collective cultural contexts, mianzi is not pride. It is social currency. To give someone face is to honor their standing. To cause someone to lose face — even without intending to, even through a well-meaning but careless dismissal in a meeting — is to damage something with real relational consequences.

The interactional fairness literature, developed by Bies and Moag, asks whether people are treated with dignity during organizational processes. Mianzi adds specificity that the Western framework often misses. It is not enough to be respectful in the abstract. The specific ways dignity is demonstrated vary across cultural frameworks — and leaders who default to their own cultural norms for what respect looks like will routinely cause interactional injustice without recognizing it. In multicultural contexts, dignity is not a universal gesture. It is a culturally specific practice that must be learned — and leaders who skip that learning will cause harm they never intended and never see.

Xinren is trust — not in a system, but in a specific person, built through consistent honesty, reliability, and the alignment of words with actions. It is accumulated slowly and damaged quickly. And it is the foundation beneath everything else. Edmondson established that psychological safety is the precondition for voice. Xinren is the relational content of that safety. It is not a feeling people have about organizations. It is a conviction they develop about specific leaders — through lived experience, over time, that can't be manufactured by a policy announcement or a team-building retreat.

A Relational Framework for Voice and Fairness

The established research on organizational justice — the distributive, procedural, and interactional framework developed by Greenberg and by Bies and Moag — is a genuinely useful map. Distributive justice asks whether outcomes are fair. Procedural justice asks whether processes are transparent and consistent. Interactional justice asks whether people are treated with dignity along the way. Cross-cultural research, including the work of Leung, demonstrates that different cultures weight these dimensions differently. In more individualistic contexts, people tend to weight distributive outcomes most heavily. In more collectivist contexts, the procedural and interactional dimensions often carry more weight — how decisions are made and how people are treated in the making of them matters as much or more than what the decision actually was.

What this framework adds is a layer beneath all three: the relational foundation that determines whether any of them are actually experienced as fair. Distributive justice lands differently when there is xinren. When people trust that a leader is honest, they extend more benefit of the doubt to outcomes that don't favor them. The same decision, made by a leader people trust and a leader they don't, will be experienced as fair or unfair along relational lines more than logical ones.

Procedural justice requires mianzi to function. It is not enough that a process is technically consistent. If the process causes people to lose dignity along the way — if they are corrected publicly, talked over, or invited to speak and then dismissed — the technical fairness of the procedure is invisible behind the relational injury. Protecting mianzi through the process is what makes procedural fairness felt rather than merely documented. Interactional justice becomes transformative when it is carried by ganqing. When a leader treats someone with care during a difficult conversation and that care is experienced as an extension of a genuine, ongoing relationship — rather than a performance of managerial competence — it lands differently. It is received as real.

And renqing — the reciprocal investment that builds over time — is what makes people willing to engage in the participatory processes that all three justice dimensions ultimately depend on. When employees have experienced genuine investment from their leader, they invest back. They show up to shape decisions, not just receive them. They offer honest feedback, not just managed responses. This framework does not replace the established taxonomy. It roots it in the relational soil from which it actually grows.

Why Fairness Determines Whether Voice Mattes

Voice only matters if it connects to fairness. People may tolerate imperfect decisions if they believe the process was just. They rarely tolerate decisions that feel arbitrary, opaque, or biased. Fairness operates on three levels — and in multicultural teams, how each level is experienced is inseparable from the relational conditions beneath it.

1. **Distributive Fairness**: *Are resources and recognition allocated fairly?* Fairness isn't only about pay. It includes access to support, recognition, development opportunities, and relational investment. Perceived favoritism — between roles, departments, or cultural groups — undermines trust quickly, even when leaders believe they are being practical or efficient. And when xinren is absent, people tend to assume the worst about why the outcomes are distributed the way they are.

2. **Procedural Fairness**: *Are decisions made transparently and*

consistently? This is where many organizations struggle. When people don't understand how decisions are made — or why — they fill the gaps with speculation. Unclear personnel decisions, shifting expectations, and inconsistent support generate fear. Procedural fairness requires consistency, clear criteria, and genuine opportunity for input before decisions are finalized. But in multicultural contexts, it also requires protecting mianzi throughout the process — ensuring that the way people are treated while decisions are being made doesn't undercut the fairness of the outcome. Even small daily ambiguities can erode trust over time.

3. **Interactional Fairness:** *Are people treated with dignity and respect?* Respectful treatment — listening, explaining decisions, acknowledging effort — goes a long way. Many organizations do this well in principle. But gaps emerge along invisible lines: role differences, cultural groupings, informal power networks. When leaders speak the language of equality but protect the dignity of some people more than others in practice, the mismatch is visible to everyone it affects — and it damages the relational trust that makes voice possible.

Culture Shapes How Voice and Fairness Are Experienced

Silence, directness, disagreement, and feedback all mean different things across cultures. In some contexts, silence signals respect. Indirectness signals care. Public challenge signals disrespect. In others, silence signals agreement or apathy. Directness signals honesty. Challenge signals engagement. Problems arise when one framework is treated as universal — when Western assumptions about what "speaking up" should look like become the invisible standard against which everyone else is measured and found lacking. The solution is not choosing one style. It is designing for many: multiple pathways for voice, clear norms, adequate time, and the relational investment that makes each pathway genuinely accessible.

The Three Pathways for Voice

Effective multicultural organizations create multiple pathways for voice because no single channel works for everyone. The goal isn't choosing one best method but orchestrating several complementary approaches. Understanding voice as a relational phenomenon changes how each pathway should be understood. These are not simply logistical options. They are different relational environments, each of which honors different cultural frameworks for what it means to speak with trust and dignity.

1. Public Voice: Meetings, group discussions, open forums

Public voice — speaking up in front of peers and leaders — is often treated as the default standard of engagement. In some cultural contexts, it is the most legitimate way to participate. In others, it is deeply uncomfortable — and not because people have nothing to say. For people shaped by cultures that value harmony, hierarchy, and the protection of mianzi, public disagreement can feel disrespectful or risky. This is not passivity. It is relational intelligence operating according to a different set of norms. Silence in these contexts doesn't mean agreement. It means restraint.

Meanwhile, leaders from more direct cultures may assume that if no one objects, everyone is on board. Neither assumption is malicious. Both are incomplete. Public voice also requires relational foundation to function well. A meeting room with an announced open-door policy but no accumulated xinren will produce the same managed silence as the opening scene of this chapter — people performing agreement while the real conversation happens somewhere else.

Public voice works best when the organizational culture explicitly values direct, open exchange; when power dynamics are relatively flat;

when enough relational trust has been built through real investment; and when time allows for genuine dialogue rather than structured announcement. Public voice improves when leaders create structured opportunities rather than open-ended invitations, ask specific questions instead of "any thoughts?", and make it unmistakably clear that disagreement will not be remembered against the person who offered it. Even then, public voice alone is insufficient. When speaking up remains optional — and primarily exercised by the confident — it becomes uneven and exclusionary.

2. Private Voice: One-on-ones, written feedback, anonymous input, trusted intermediaries

Private voice is not a lesser alternative to public voice. In many cultural frameworks, it is the primary and most legitimate channel for genuine expression. This matters because leaders who treat private feedback as informal — as something less serious than what gets said in a meeting — have fundamentally misread both the feedback and the culture. In contexts shaped by mianzi and high power distance, honest critique and serious concerns are almost never offered in group settings by choice. They are shared in settings where the relational dynamics allow for directness without the social cost of public disagreement.

In collective cultural environments, the deeper and more difficult the concern, the more likely it is to arrive privately — if it arrives at all. The willingness to bring a concern privately to a leader is itself a relational act, an expression of trust that the leader will receive it well. Leaders who respond to private voice with defensiveness, dismissal, or — worst of all — by raising it publicly without permission, will not hear private voice again.

Private voice also carries special importance for people from marginalized backgrounds across every cultural context. The same feedback carries different risk depending on who is giving it. A senior person questioning a decision faces minimal consequences. A junior employee from a minority background raising the same concern risks being labeled difficult or disloyal. Private channels reduce that asymmetry —

not by pretending the power differential doesn't exist, but by offering a pathway that doesn't require someone to expose themselves to it.

Private voice becomes stronger when anonymous options genuinely exist, when trusted intermediaries can surface themes without attribution, and when leaders visibly act on what they hear through private channels — demonstrating that private input carries the same weight as public input.
Seeing even partial change validates the channel. And it begins building the xinren that eventually makes more direct voice feel possible.

3. Participatory Design: Involving people before decisions are finalized

The most powerful form of voice happens before decisions are made. Participatory design invites people into the shaping process rather than asking for approval afterward. When done well, it builds ownership, surfaces practical insight, and develops leadership capacity throughout the organization. It positions people as co-creators rather than commentators — and that distinction has deep relational significance.

In the relational logic of guanxi, contributing to something that matters creates investment. The person who helped shape the direction has a stake in it that the person who was simply informed about it does not. Participatory design generates renqing — the reciprocal bond that forms when genuine investment is offered and received. When leaders create real opportunities for team members to influence direction before it is set, they are extending a form of relational trust that carries weight across cultural frameworks.

What people across multicultural settings describe as the most meaningful leadership moments are rarely the times they were kept well-informed. They are the times their actual contribution shaped something real — when they could trace a thread from what they said to what became of it. That experience is what transforms voice from a transaction into a relationship. When done poorly, participatory design feels performative. And people can tell immediately.

The difference between "help us think this through" and "we've already decided — any comments?" is not subtle. When participation is performative, it doesn't merely fail to build trust. It actively destroys it. It teaches people that their investment in the relationship was not reciprocated — and that lesson is harder to undo than never having asked at all. Participatory design also requires cultural adaptation. Western-style brainstorming — where individuals call out ideas quickly, in a group, with the reward going to the boldest — doesn't translate well across cultural frameworks. In many contexts, people need time to consult within their own relational networks before sharing perspectives more broadly. The format of participation must match the cultural logic of the people being invited to participate — not the preferences of the person designing the process.

And it requires relational responsiveness: closing the loop, explaining what was heard, what will be done with it, and why. This is not communication hygiene. It is a relational act. It says: your investment in this mattered, I took it seriously, and our relationship is real enough that you deserve to know what became of what you offered. When participatory design is genuine, consistent, and culturally adapted, people stop asking "is it safe to speak?" and begin thinking "my input matters." That is the compound effect this chapter is ultimately after.

The key insight: voice isn't just about creating channels. It's about creating channels that are carried by relationships. One pathway is never enough. And no pathway works without the relational investment that makes it trustworthy.

The Historical View

History offers compelling examples of how voice systems shape organizational health — and what happens when they fail or succeed across cultural divides.

The Iroquois Confederacy: Voice Across Nations

Long before European contact, the Iroquois (Haudenosaunee) Confederacy created one of history's most sophisticated systems for voice across cultural difference. Five distinct nations — Mohawk, Oneida, Onondaga, Cayuga, and Seneca — each with their own traditions and interests, united under the Great Law of Peace while preserving their individual identities.

The Confederacy's genius was relational before it was structural. Major decisions required genuine consensus, not majority rule — which meant the larger nations had to build enough xinren with the smaller ones that minority perspectives were treated as worth the time. The Onondaga served as "firekeepers," a role that was less about authority and more about ganqing — the patient, ongoing investment in ensuring every nation felt genuinely heard before anything was decided. You can't hold that role without having built the relational trust to carry it.

Critically, women held significant voice through the Clan Mothers, who selected and could remove chiefs. This wasn't tokenism — it was structural protection for a constituency that could otherwise have been absorbed into silence. The system recognized that different groups needed different pathways to influence, and it built those pathways in rather than expecting people to find their own way in. When decisions couldn't reach consensus, the matter was tabled rather than forced through. Relational silence — the silence of an unresolved relationship — was treated as a signal worth heeding, not a problem to be overridden by efficiency.

The lesson for modern organizations: sustainable unity across cultural difference requires all three voice pathways, structural protections for minority perspectives, and a relational investment patient enough to wait for genuine consensus rather than performing it.

The British East India Company's Fatal Silence

The British East India Company offers a cautionary tale about what happens when voice systems serve only the dominant culture — and when the relational foundation for honest exchange is never built. Indian soldiers (sepoys) had legitimate grievances: religious insensitivity, broken promises, systematic disrespect. But the Company's structure made raising concerns nearly impossible. British officers had no ganqing with the soldiers they commanded — no genuine investment in their wellbeing, their dignity, their concerns. Without that relational foundation, the channels that did exist were unusable. Indirect expressions of concern, the natural voice of high power distance cultures protecting mianzi, went unnoticed or were dismissed as insubordination rather than heard as the signal they were.

This is the cost of having only public voice — a single pathway designed for a single cultural framework — and no relational trust beneath it. The sepoys weren't without opinions. They were without a relationship through which those opinions could safely travel. The result was the Sepoy Mutiny of 1857. Investigators later found that warning signs had been everywhere. The information existed. The voice pathways to carry it did not.

The lesson: organizations that build voice systems without building the relationships beneath them aren't just unfair — they're fragile. Relational silence accumulates until it has nowhere left to go.

The Apollo 13 Mission: Voice Under Pressure

When an oxygen tank exploded aboard Apollo 13 in April 1970, what saved the crew wasn't a policy. It was a culture that had been built, relationship by relationship, before the crisis arrived. Flight Director Gene Kranz had established something closer to xinren than procedure — a genuine, demonstrated trust that speaking up would be received rather than punished, regardless of rank. Junior engineers could challenge senior assumptions because the relational history of the team had made that safe. That kind of trust isn't created in a crisis. It is revealed by one.

Multiple pathways existed because Kranz understood that no single channel reaches every voice. Engineers could escalate through supervisors, go directly to flight directors, work through colleagues, or flag data anomalies that triggered automatic review. What mattered was that honest information reached the people who needed it — not that it arrived through the approved route.

When unconventional solutions emerged, Kranz didn't defend existing plans. He asked questions. That receptivity — that modeled openness — is what renqing looks like under pressure: the leader's genuine investment in the team's contribution, returned through the team's willingness to give everything they had.

The lesson: crisis reveals whether voice systems actually work. The relational investment required to build them must happen long before anyone needs them.

The Biblical View

Scripture provides rich examples of voice, feedback, and fairness — including how God Himself creates space for human voice and how leaders should respond when people speak up.

Moses and the Daughters of Zelophehad: Voice That Changes Law

Numbers 27:1-11 records a story of voice that changed Israelite inheritance law. Zelophehad had died without sons. Under existing law, his daughters would receive nothing. The five daughters — Mahlah, Noah, Hoglah, Milcah, and Tirzah — came forward and stood before Moses, the priest Eleazar, the leaders, and the whole assembly. In a patriarchal culture with steep power distance, this was not a small act. They chose public voice because no private channel existed that could carry a challenge this significant. Their argument was direct and grounded in the very principles the law already claimed to uphold: why should their father's name disappear simply because he had no son?

What matters as much as their courage is Moses's response. He didn't defend existing policy. He didn't explain why the rules were the rules. He brought their case before God and genuinely sought an answer — an act of procedural fairness that honored both their mianzi and the legitimacy of their claim. The law was changed. Not just for these five women but for all future cases. This is what relational responsiveness looks like from a leader with authority: the concern is received, elevated, and answered — and the answer closes the loop in a way that honors the dignity of everyone who brought it.

Nathan Confronting David: Speaking Truth to Power

2 Samuel 12 shows what it costs to deliver honest feedback to someone with the power to destroy the messenger — and what cultural intelligence in voice actually looks like. Nathan didn't burst in with accusations. He used a story — a rich man who stole a poor man's beloved lamb — and let David arrive at his own verdict before revealing that David was the man. This was not evasion. It was precision. Nathan understood that direct public accusation of a king would trigger defensiveness, not reflection. He chose a pathway — indirect, private in its framing, relational in its approach — that gave the feedback the best possible chance of being genuinely received.

This is the same logic that makes private voice essential in high power distance contexts. The form of delivery is not weakness. It is intelligence about how truth can actually travel. David's response is the model for what leaders must do when voice reaches them: "I have sinned against the Lord." No excuses. No defensiveness. No attacking the messenger. Voice that costs something to give deserves a response that costs something to offer.

The Early Church Widows: When Voice Requires Structural Change

Acts 6:1-7 describes the early church's first organizational crisis — and one of Scripture's clearest examples of what it looks like when leaders respond to a voice complaint with genuine structural change rather than managed reassurance. The Hellenistic Jewish widows were being overlooked in the daily distribution of food. This was a distributive justice failure, a procedural failure, and an interactional failure all at once — and it fell along a cultural fault line. The system had been built by and for one group, and the other group was falling through its gaps.

Notice what the apostles didn't do. They didn't dismiss the complaint. They didn't defend their intentions. They didn't ask the Hellenistic community to adapt to how things were done. They acknowledged the problem plainly and created a participatory design solution: choose seven leaders from among yourselves — your community, your voice — and we will give them the authority to ensure this works.

All seven chosen leaders have Greek names. That was not coincidental. It was the apostles recognizing that ensuring fair treatment for the Hellenistic widows required Hellenistic leaders who understood their context, protected their mianzi, and carried the relational trust — the xinren — of their own community. The result was growth, not fracture. When voice led to structural change that addressed cultural inequity, the community that could have split instead deepened.

The lesson: voice systems fail when they're designed only for the dominant culture. They succeed when leaders invest in the relationships and structures that allow every group to be genuinely heard — and when complaints become the occasion for building something more just rather than defending what already exists.

Nuances and Blind Spots

Asking for input isn't the same as creating voice. "Any questions?" at the end of a presentation often signals the opposite of openness — it signals that the presentation is over and agreement is expected. Genuine voice requires multiple channels, adequate time, explicit invitation of dissent, and — critically — demonstrated responsiveness to what gets shared. When feedback is solicited and then disappears without acknowledgment or explanation, it doesn't just fail to help. It actively teaches people that their voice is performative, that leadership wants to *appear* open without actually being influenced. That lesson is harder to undo than never having asked at all.

The loudest voices aren't the most important ones. The people who speak most confidently in public settings are often simply those whose cultural background, personality, or organizational position makes public speaking comfortable. The most valuable perspectives may belong to people who will never voluntarily speak in a group meeting but will share profound insights through a private conversation or a written channel — if those pathways exist and are genuinely valued. Predictable speakers dominating every meeting isn't a sign of healthy participation; it's a sign that only one communication style feels safe.

Voice pathways have cultural signatures. Every feedback mechanism carries embedded assumptions. Anonymous surveys assume literacy and comfort with written expression. Open forums assume low power distance and direct communication norms. One-on-one meetings assume individuals can speak for themselves without consulting their group. When certain cultural or linguistic groups consistently use only one pathway — always private, never public — the instinct is to see that as a quirk. The better question is: *Who does each pathway actually work for, and who does it quietly exclude?*

Power shapes what can be said. The same feedback carries entirely different risk depending on who's giving it. A senior leader questioning a decision faces minimal consequences. A junior employee from a minority background raising the same concern risks being labeled difficult, ungrateful, or not a team player. Fair voice systems don't just offer channels — they account for these power differentials and actively work to reduce the cost of speaking honestly for those with the least protection.

Selective listening is a trust killer. When leaders consistently act on suggestions from certain people — often those culturally similar to themselves — while identical suggestions from others go unacknowledged, the pattern is visible to everyone except, usually, the leader. It reveals whose voice actually carries weight in the room, regardless of what the official culture says about inclusion.

The best feedback often arrives packaged poorly. Input from frustrated, marginalized, or culturally different team members frequently comes in forms that are easy to dismiss — too emotional, too indirect, too blunt, poorly timed, or tangled up with complaints about other issues. Leaders who only hear feedback delivered "professionally" — by their own cultural standards of what professional sounds like — are filtering out precisely the information they most need. Mature voice systems are built to receive imperfect delivery without discarding the substance inside it.

Fairness isn't sameness. Equal access to voice doesn't mean identical channels for everyone. It means ensuring that people from all cultural backgrounds have *equally effective* pathways to influence — which often requires different mechanisms for different people. This can feel unfair to those who don't understand why multiple pathways exist. That discomfort is worth addressing directly rather than dissolving the pathways to make everyone feel equally served by a single system that actually works well for only some.

Post-meeting hallways are diagnostic. When the real conversations — the honest assessments, the actual concerns, the genuine disagreements — consistently happen after official channels close, that gap is the data. It means the formal setting isn't safe enough for truth. The distance between what people say in the meeting and what they say walking to their cars is a reliable measure of how well voice is actually functioning in your organization.

Try This Week

Choose ONE practice to implement this week:

Practice 1: Add One New Voice Pathway

Identify which pathway your organization currently lacks or under uses. If you only have public forums, add private channels (anonymous feedback form, written input option, one-on-one office hours). If you only have feedback systems, create a participatory design opportunity (working group to shape an upcoming initiative). Announce the new pathway and use it genuinely—don't just create it and ignore input.

Practice 2: Receive Without Defense

Next time someone shares a concern or critique, practice receiving it without defending, explaining, or solving. Try this script: "Thank you for telling me. Help me understand more—can you give me an example?" Then listen, ask clarifying questions, summarize what you heard, and say "Let me think about this and get back to you by [specific date]." Then actually follow up.

Practice 3: Close One Open Loop

Identify one piece of feedback, suggestion, or concern that was raised but never resolved. This week, close the loop: explain what you did with the input, why you did or didn't implement it, what you learned. Even if the answer is "we couldn't implement this because X," closure matters. It signals that voice was heard even if the answer wasn't yes.

Practice 4: Diversify One Invitation

Look at who you typically invite to give input or join planning processes. This week, intentionally invite someone from a different cultural background, department, or position level than your usual go-to people. Frame it specifically: "I want your perspective because..." Make clear their input will genuinely shape the outcome, not just validate predetermined plans.

Reflection Questions

Quick Check (1-2 minutes)

- Which of the three voice pathways (Public, Private, Participatory Design) is strongest in your organization? Which is weakest or missing entirely?

- When was the last time you changed a decision based on employee input? Can your team name a specific example?

Deeper Reflection (5-10 minutes)

- Think about your most recent significant decision. Who had opportunity to influence it before it was finalized? Who was only informed afterward? What pattern do you notice?

- Which voices are easiest for you to hear and receive? Which voices require more effort? What makes the difference—and what might that reveal about your cultural assumptions?

- If you asked your team anonymously, "Does your input actually influence decisions here?"—what percentage would say yes? What evidence supports your estimate?

- When have you received feedback that was poorly packaged but contained important truth? How did you respond? What might you have missed?

Team Discussion (15-30 minutes)

- As a leadership team, map out one recent initiative from conception to implementation. At what points did you create opportunity for voice? Whose voices were included? Whose were not? If you could redesign the process, what would you change to create more genuine participatory design rather than post-decision feedback?

Moving Forward

Creating pathways for voice is essential—but voice alone isn't sufficient if leaders lack the cultural intelligence to understand what they're hearing. The same words mean different things across cultural frameworks. Silence signals different messages. Feedback comes packaged in culturally-shaped communication styles that require interpretation.

The daughters of Zelophehad spoke up—and Moses had the wisdom to recognize their voice as legitimate rather than dismissing it as inappropriate challenge to established norms. Nathan delivered difficult feedback indirectly—and David had the humility to receive it rather than defending himself. The early church heard a complaint about cultural inequity—and created a system that ensured ongoing fairness across difference.

These examples share a common thread: voice systems work when leaders genuinely want to hear, create multiple pathways for expression, and respond to what they learn. They fail when leaders want the appearance of openness without the vulnerability of actually being influenced.

Fair voice isn't about creating identical channels for everyone. It's about ensuring that people from all backgrounds have equally effective access to influence. This requires cultural intelligence—the ability to recognize how different cultural frameworks shape communication, to create pathways that work across those differences, and to interpret input accurately once it arrives.

Shared Vision and Leadership

Opening Scene

The executive director's office light was still on at 9 PM. Again. Through the glass wall, staff could see her hunched over her laptop, reviewing budgets that should have been handled three levels down, editing emails that department heads had already drafted, double-checking decisions that team leads were qualified to make.

In the conference room, three department heads were waiting—still—for her approval on a proposal they'd submitted two weeks ago. "She's just so busy," Susan rationalized. "She'll get to it." But David shook his head: "It's not just being busy. She doesn't actually trust us to make decisions. Everything has to go through her."

The pattern had become painfully clear: promising initiatives stalled waiting for executive approval. Team members stopped taking initiative because it was faster to wait for direction than to have their decisions questioned and revised. Junior staff learned to ask permission for everything rather than risk getting it wrong. The executive director worked 70-hour weeks while her team worked 40—not because they were lazy, but because the system couldn't function without her constant involvement.

When she finally left for a two-week sabbatical, everything ground to a halt within three days. "We couldn't make decisions without her," Susan explained. "We didn't know what she'd want." The executive director returned exhausted rather than refreshed, realizing what her team hadn't said: the organization had become completely dependent on her presence. She'd created a system that couldn't function without her—and it was killing her and stunting everyone else's growth.

The Cost of Centralized Leadership

The opening scene illustrates what researchers James MacGregor Burns and, more recently, Joseph Rost's critique call 'heroic leadership' -- the assumption that organizational success depends primarily on a single leader's vision, decisions, and constant involvement. This model dominates Western leadership thinking but creates predictable problems across every organizational context it inhabits.

- **Leader Burnout**: When everything flows through one person, that person becomes overwhelmed. Heroic leadership is unsustainable.

- **Follower Initiative Dies**: Team members stop developing judgment, taking risks, or offering ideas. Centralized leadership systematically diminishes the capability of everyone not at the center.

- **Organizational Learning Stagnates**: When only the leader's perspective shapes decisions, the organization loses access to crucial knowledge held by people closest to actual work.

- **Succession Becomes Crisis**: When leadership is centralized, no one else develops the capability to lead. Departure or incapacity of the central figure creates organizational crisis.

- **Innovation Declines**: New ideas require risk-taking and experimentation. When all decisions require approval from the top, innovation slows to whatever the top leader can personally evaluate and endorse.

In multicultural contexts, centralized leadership carries additional costs. Team members from high power distance cultures may defer to authority without offering input even when they have crucial insights. Team members from low power distance cultures may become frustrated and leave. The bottleneck problem intensifies because cultural frameworks for decision-making vary — but all must conform to the leader's single approach.

What Research Tells Us About Shared Leadership

Shared leadership — distributing influence and responsibility across multiple people rather than concentrating it in a single leader — consistently outperforms traditional hierarchical models in complex, knowledge-intensive work. Research by Lorinkova and Bartol, Gu and colleagues, and Evans and colleagues demonstrates that teams with shared leadership show higher performance, particularly on tasks requiring diverse expertise and ongoing adaptation. However, shared leadership isn't leaderless. It requires clear boundaries about who can decide what, explicit processes for coordination, high trust, and strong communication. Without these elements, shared leadership devolves into confusion rather than empowerment.

Empowering leadership research — developed extensively by Tang and colleagues, O'Donoghue and van der Werff, and Wang and colleagues — identifies four key behaviors that enable healthy distributed leadership:

- **Authority Delegation**: Leaders explicitly grant decision-making authority at appropriate levels rather than hoarding it.

- **Accountability Clarification**: People know both what they're empowered to decide and what they're accountable for delivering.

- **Self-Directed Decision Making**: Teams have latitude to determine how they'll accomplish objectives, not just execute prescribed methods.

- **Information Sharing**: People have access to the information needed to make good decisions, not just instructions to follow.

Cross-cultural research reveals that empowerment looks different across cultural frameworks. In individualistic cultures, empowerment often means individual authority and autonomy. In collectivist cultures, it might mean team-based decision-making with shared accountability. In high power distance cultures, empowerment requires explicit permission from authority; in low power distance cultures, people assume more autonomy naturally. Effective multicultural leaders recognize these differences and create empowerment structures that work across cultural frameworks rather than imposing a single model.

The Relational Readiness Conditions

The five levels of decision authority described later in this chapter are a genuinely useful structural map. But they rest on an assumption that multicultural leaders must examine carefully: that empowerment, once announced, can be received. It cannot — not always, and not across all cultural frameworks. Empowerment is not a policy transfer. It is a relational act. And in contexts shaped by high power distance, collective values, and relationship-based trust, the relational conditions that determine whether empowerment is receivable must be established before any structural announcement of authority will function.

This framework draws on the guanxi relational ecosystem — rooted in Confucian thought and documented extensively by Li and colleagues, Kuo and colleagues, and Ameyaw and colleagues — to name four relational preconditions that determine whether each level of decision authority can actually be exercised by the person to whom it is offered.

Ganqing: The Precondition for Empowerment Without Abandonment

Ganqing is the affection and sincere care that develops between people over time — not performed warmth, but accumulated evidence of genuine investment in another person's wellbeing. Without ganqing, a leader who transfers authority has not offered a gift. They have created exposure.

When authority is transferred without relational investment, the person receiving it faces a predictable set of questions they cannot answer from a job description: Does this leader actually believe I can do this? If I make a mistake, will they protect me or publicize my failure? Is this empowerment — or is this offloading?

Ganqing does not answer these questions through policy. It answers them through history. A leader who has invested in someone's growth, noticed their struggles, remembered their circumstances, and followed through on small commitments has built a relational account from which authority transfer can be drawn.

Diagnostic question: Before transferring authority to someone, ask honestly — have I invested in this person the way I would want a leader to invest in me? If the answer is no, the empowerment announcement may succeed on paper and fail in practice.

Renqing: The Precondition for Reciprocal Engagement

Renqing is the reciprocal relational investment that builds between people over time — the bond that develops when genuine care creates mutual accountability. It is not transactional. Leaders don't build renqing by doing favors in exchange for loyalty. They build it by consistently demonstrating genuine investment, which over time generates genuine investment in return.

Renqing is what makes shared leadership feel like shared ownership rather than additional burden. When a team member who has experienced consistent investment from their leader is offered more responsibility, renqing generates the intrinsic motivation to carry it well — not because they have to, but because the relationship has earned their engagement. This is directly connected to what Kim and Beehr, and Wang and colleagues, describe as affective organizational commitment: the emotional attachment that develops when employees genuinely feel supported, and that generates discretionary effort that no policy can manufacture.

When renqing is absent, empowerment tends to be received as an expectation rather than a trust. People comply minimally, perform adequately, and invest no further than required — not because temperament disengages them, but because the relational conditions for genuine engagement were never established.

Diagnostic question: Does this person experience their relationship with me as reciprocal? Have I given as consistently as I have asked?

Mianzi: The Precondition for Empowerment Without Threat

Mianzi is the concept of face — personal prestige, social credit, and dignity that a person carries and that can be honored or diminished by others (Guan and Ploner; Li; Zhuo and Yuan). In collective cultural contexts, mianzi is not pride. It is social currency that enables participation. And it is the dimension of empowerment that most multicultural leaders from low power distance, direct-communication backgrounds miss.

When someone exercises authority and makes a mistake, what happens to their dignity is not incidental to their willingness to exercise authority again. It is the primary determining factor. In contexts where mianzi matters, public correction of a mistake made in good faith under delegated authority is not experienced as feedback. It is experienced as relational damage that makes the exercise of future authority feel genuinely threatening.

Leaders who want team members to operate at higher levels of decision authority must create explicit mianzi-protection around the exercise of that authority: mistakes addressed privately, errors normalized as part of growth, corrections framed in ways that preserve the dignity of the person who tried. This is not softness. It is the architecture of sustainable empowerment in high-mianzi-sensitivity contexts. The inverse is equally important. When leaders publicly honor someone's exercise of authority — recognizing the decision, noting the outcome, celebrating the initiative — they are adding to that person's mianzi in ways that make future initiative feel safer, not just more motivated.

Diagnostic question: Have I created conditions where this person can make a mistake under delegated authority without losing standing — with me, with their peers, with the organization?

Xinren: The Precondition for Trust in the Boundaries

Xinren is trust — not in a system, but in a specific person, built through the consistent alignment of words with actions over time (Kuo and colleagues; Migge and colleagues; Chen and Bedford). It is accumulated slowly and damaged quickly.

The five levels of decision authority function as a map. But xinren is what determines whether people trust the map. A leader who has told team members they are empowered to decide, and then overridden those decisions; who has said mistakes are learning opportunities, and then punished them; who has announced open-door access and then been consistently unavailable — has undermined xinren. And without xinren, no structural announcement of empowerment will be believed.

Edmondson's research on psychological safety established that the willingness to speak and act is a response to perceived environmental safety, not a personality trait. Xinren is the relational content of that safety — the specific, accumulated evidence about this leader, in this relationship, over this period of time, that tells a person whether the empowerment offer is real.

Diagnostic question: Have my actions consistently matched my words around authority, mistake-tolerance, and access? Does this person have reason, from lived experience, to trust that what I say about empowerment is true?

Applying the Relational Readiness Conditions

These four relational conditions are not sequential. They develop together, through the same sustained investment. A leader who is building ganqing is also building renqing and xinren. A leader who protects mianzi is also building xinren. The framework is a diagnostic, not a checklist.

The practical implication is this: before asking why empowerment isn't working structurally, ask whether it is receivable relationally. The five levels of decision authority describe what to offer. The relational readiness conditions describe the soil in which that offer can take root.

A note on cultural variation: In low power distance, task-based trust cultures, the relational threshold for receivable empowerment is lower. Clear criteria, defined boundaries, and demonstrated competence may be sufficient. In high power distance, relationship-based trust cultures, the relational conditions described above are not supplementary — they are foundational. Effective multicultural leaders calibrate accordingly, without assuming their own threshold is universal.

Relational Empowerment Bias

One of the most persistent and least examined failure modes in multicultural shared leadership is what this framework names relational empowerment bias: the pattern by which authority flows more readily to those whose relational style most closely resembles the leader's own — not because they are more capable, but because the leader has more naturally built the relational preconditions of empowerment with them.

This is rarely conscious. Leaders don't decide to empower some cultural groups and not others. They build ganqing more naturally with people who demonstrate care the way they recognize it. They extend xinren more readily to people whose reliability signals match their own cultural patterns for what trustworthiness looks like. Renqing accumulates more easily between people who reciprocate in culturally familiar ways. Mianzi is protected more instinctively for people whose dignity signals the leader has learned to read.

The result is empowerment that tracks relational familiarity rather than competence — and in multicultural contexts, relational familiarity tends to follow cultural lines. People from backgrounds that share the leader's communication style, decision-making norms, and relationship-building patterns accumulate relational capital faster. They move up the authority levels more quickly, receive more public recognition, get more developmental investment, and are trusted with higher-stakes decisions — not because they are better at the work, but because the relational ecosystem between them and the leader developed more naturally.

The research on selective delegation names this pattern at the organizational level: the insider/outsider dynamic that forms when empowerment becomes selective, and the way dissent that cannot find a relational channel becomes toxic rather than constructive. What the research adds is the mechanism: selective delegation in multicultural contexts is not primarily a failure of intention. It is a failure of relational range — leaders investing relationally only within the bandwidth of their own cultural framework.

Diagnosing Relational Empowerment Bias

Because relational empowerment bias operates below the level of conscious decision-making, diagnosing it requires tracking patterns rather than intentions. The following questions are diagnostic, not accusatory:

- Who in this organization operates at Level 4 or Level 5 authority? What do they have in common beyond competence?

- Who receives public recognition for initiative? Who receives it privately, or not at all?

- With whom have I invested relationally — one-on-ones, developmental conversations, personal investment — and does that group reflect the cultural diversity of the organization?

- Who are the people in this organization with whom I have the least relational history? What cultural patterns do they share?

- When empowerment has been extended and then retracted, what was the pattern? Did corrections tend to fall on certain cultural groups more than others?

The purpose of these questions is not guilt. It is accuracy. Leaders who cannot see their relational empowerment bias cannot correct it — and the cost falls not on the leader but on the team members whose capability never receives the relational infrastructure it requires to develop.

Expanding Relational Range

The corrective for relational empowerment bias is deliberate relational investment beyond the leader's natural bandwidth. This means learning to recognize trustworthiness signals in cultural forms other than the ones that feel instinctive — learning what reliability looks like for someone from a relationship-based trust culture versus a task-based one, what care looks like in high-context communication versus direct communication, what reciprocity looks like in collective versus individual frameworks.

This is what cultural intelligence, in the formulation of Asfar and colleagues and Egwuonwu and colleagues, actually requires: not just knowledge about other cultures, but the metacognitive and motivational investment to build genuine relationship across cultural difference. Leaders who develop this range don't just become fairer in how they distribute formal empowerment. They become genuinely more capable, because the relational channels through which the organization's most important information travels — voice, feedback, constructive challenge — open to them.

Voice as Empowered Deviance

Positive deviance — constructive behavior that departs from organizational norms in ways that advance the mission — has been studied extensively by Mula and Pierro, Sharma, Edosomwan and colleagues, and Déprez and colleagues. It encompasses whistle-blowing, creative problem-solving, principled organizational dissent, and proactive behaviors that go beyond job description for the mission's sake. The research literature distinguishes it clearly from destructive deviance, which violates norms in ways that harm the organization.

In multicultural contexts shaped by high power distance and collective values, there is a specific and particularly demanding form of positive deviance that this framework names: voice as empowered deviance — the act of speaking up with concerns, critique, or challenge in cultural environments where that act violates social norms. This is not a metaphor. In organizations operating within collective, harmony-oriented cultural frameworks, the person who raises a concern in a meeting, who challenges a leader's assumption, who names a problem that others are managing around — that person is not exercising a default right of organizational participation. They are breaking a social norm. They are accepting personal relational risk in service of organizational health. They are doing something that their cultural context has taught them carries cost.

This means that voice, in these contexts, is not simply a feedback mechanism. It is the most demanding form of empowerment a leader can ask for. And it requires the most complete relational foundation to function.

The Relational Requirements of Voice as Deviance

Voice as empowered deviance requires all four relational readiness conditions — and requires them more completely than lower-stakes forms of empowerment. Consider the calculus: A person considering whether to raise a concern publicly must believe — from lived relational experience, not from policy — that the leader has genuine investment in their wellbeing (ganqing), that the relationship can survive the friction of honest challenge (renqing), that their dignity will be protected if the concern is received badly or turns out to be wrong (mianzi), and that the leader's stated openness to feedback is actually true (xinren).

Without all four, the rational choice is silence. Not acquiescent silence, not quiescent silence, not prosocial silence — but relational silence: the appropriate withholding of voice when the relationship required to carry it has not been built. The person is not passive. They are reading the relational environment accurately. This is why organizations can install every structural voice mechanism available — anonymous surveys, open forums, regular one-on-ones, suggestion boxes — and still find that team members from collective, high-power-distance backgrounds do not use them for substantive input. The channels exist. The relational foundation that makes them safe to use does not.

Cultivating Voice as Positive Deviance

Leaders who want to cultivate voice as positive deviance in multicultural contexts must understand that the work happens before the speaking up — in the relational investment that makes speaking up survivable. Several practices follow from this:

- Frame voice explicitly as valued contribution rather than as organizational right. In collective cultures, the individual assertion of a right is not a natural frame. But contributing to the group's health through honest input — when that frame has been set by a leader who is trusted — is culturally coherent.

- Model the relational risk yourself. Leaders who share their own uncertainties, mistakes, and concerns openly demonstrate that relational risk is survivable at the top of the power gradient. If the most powerful person in the room can be wrong and remain standing, others receive permission to be wrong too.

- Protect voice publicly when it arrives. When someone offers critique or concern — especially in a group setting, where mianzi is at stake — the leader's immediate, visible response determines whether anyone in the room will do it again. A response that defends, explains, or minimizes the concern teaches everyone watching that voice carries cost. A response that receives, thanks, and elevates the concern teaches them the opposite.

- Distinguish voice from disruption. Not all challenging behavior is positive deviance. Leaders must be able to name the difference — between the person who raises a concern to advance the mission and the person who raises objections to advance themselves — and respond differently to each. The distinction is relational: does this voice serve the collective, or does it serve only the speaker?

When voice is successfully cultivated as positive deviance in a multi-cultural organization, something significant shifts. The silence that once marked meetings gives way to something more substantive. Not louder meetings — more honest ones. Not more voices, necessarily, but deeper ones. And the leader gains access to the information the organization most needs: the honest assessment of people closest to the actual work.

The AMOR Framework

The ability-motivation-opportunity (AMO) framework, developed in the organizational psychology literature and connected to HPWS research by Malik and Lenka and Ma and colleagues, offers a useful diagnostic for empowerment. It asks: does this person have the ability to exercise authority well? Are they motivated to do so? Do they have the opportunity — the structural access and the formal permission?

This framework has been foundational in understanding what makes empowerment work or fail. But in multicultural contexts, particularly those shaped by high power distance and relationship-based trust, the AMO framework is incomplete. It identifies three necessary conditions for effective empowerment — and misses the fourth, which determines whether the first three are accessible.

The expanded framework is AMOR: Ability, Motivation, Opportunity, and Relationship. The fourth dimension — Relationship — is the foundation that determines whether ability is expressed, whether motivation is sustained, and whether opportunity is genuinely available. Without it, all three of the original conditions can be present and empowerment still fails.

A — Ability

The question: Does this person have the skills and knowledge to exercise authority well?

Fails when: Preparation is insufficient, expectations are unclear, or no developmental investment has been made.

Relational link: Ganqing. Investment in growth is relational before it is instructional. A leader who has genuinely invested in someone builds the relational confidence that makes new capability feel safe to attempt.

M — Motivation

The question: Does this person genuinely want to exercise authority and engage with the mission?

Fails when: There is no sense of ownership, empowerment feels like additional burden, or the person has quietly disengaged.

Relational link: Renqing. Reciprocal relational investment generates the intrinsic motivation that policy cannot manufacture. Motivation gaps in otherwise capable people are frequently relational deficits wearing a performance label.

O — Opportunity

The question: Does this person have formal permission, structural access, and real space to decide?

Fails when: Decisions are overridden after being delegated, authority is not actually granted, or boundaries are so undefined that the person cannot exercise authority without risking correction.

Relational link: Mianzi. Opportunity must include protection of dignity when mistakes occur. A formal authority transfer that carries significant face-risk will not be exercised in high-mianzi-sensitivity contexts, regardless of the structural permission granted.

R — Relationship

The question: Does this person have sufficient relational history with this leader to trust that the empowerment offer is genuine?

Fails when: Authority is announced but not believed, empowerment is offered but not exercised, or relational silence holds despite structural invitation.

Relational link: Xinren. Accumulated evidence that this leader's words and actions align is the foundation beneath all three other dimensions. Without it, A, M, and O are structurally present and functionally inaccessible.

Applying AMOR in Practice

The AMOR framework changes the diagnostic sequence for empowerment failures. Before asking what structural adjustment is needed, it asks:

- Ability gap? Address through preparation, training, and developmental investment — but frame that investment relationally (ganqing), not just instructionally.

- Motivation gap? Investigate the relational history. Is there reciprocal investment (renqing)? Does this person experience their relationship with leadership as genuine? Motivation gaps in otherwise capable people are often relational deficits wearing a performance label.

- Opportunity gap? Clarify boundaries and formalize authority — but also examine whether the opportunity includes mianzi-protection for mistakes. A formal authority transfer that carries significant face-risk will not be exercised in high-mianzi-sensitivity contexts.

- Relationship gap? This is the foundational question, and it must come first. Without xinren — without the leader's demonstrated alignment of words and actions around empowerment — ability, motivation, and opportunity are structurally present and functionally inaccessible.

The practical value of naming Relationship as a fourth dimension is that it makes relational investment a leadership accountability, not a cultural amenity. In high-performing multicultural organizations, building the relational soil for empowerment is not optional or supplementary. It is leadership work — as essential as any structural design.

The Relational Leadership Pipeline

In multicultural organizations shaped by collective values and high power distance, one of the most consistent and least theorized findings is this: leadership development moves most effectively through relational networks, not institutional programs. The peer-driven development model — where team members rely on one another for training, vision clarity, and professional growth, building leadership capacity throughout the organization without formal program design — is not a workaround for inadequate institutional investment. It is the primary culturally intelligent leadership development model in collective-value contexts. Institutional programs are the supplement. The relational network is the engine.

This matters because most organizational leadership development thinking assumes the opposite. It assumes that programs, training sessions, formal mentorship structures, and developmental curricula are primary — and that informal peer learning is what happens when the formal structures are absent or insufficient. In individual-value, low-power-distance contexts, that assumption is often correct. But in collective, relationship-oriented contexts, it inverts the effective order.

Why the Relational Pipeline Works in Collective Cultures

Several dynamics explain why leadership development travels through relational networks more effectively than institutional channels in high-power-distance, collective-value contexts.

First, it is relationally lower-risk. Asking peer colleagues for help, learning through proximity, developing capability through collaborative problem-solving — none of these require the individual initiative or public display that institutional programs often demand. The learning happens within established relational channels, protected by existing xinren and mianzi dynamics, rather than requiring people to step into exposed, unfamiliar developmental territory.

Second, it generates renqing. When one team member invests in another's development — shares knowledge, models a skill, coaches through a problem — the relational bond between them deepens. The organization accumulates not just developing individuals but a web of relational mutual accountability that makes collective performance more resilient. Each developmental exchange adds to the organizational relational capital.

Third, it is contextually intelligent in ways institutional programs cannot be. The peer colleague who has navigated the same organizational culture, faced similar power distance dynamics, and built trust with the same leaders understands the specific relational landscape of this organization. Their development investment carries contextual wisdom that external programs cannot replicate.

The Leader's Role in the Relational Pipeline

If leadership development travels through relational networks, the leader's primary developmental role is not program design. It is relational environment creation. Specifically, the leader must:

- Build enough organizational xinren that team members trust peer development is valued and won't be perceived as the organization's failure to invest formally.

- Create relational safety (mianzi-protection) around the expression of not knowing — so that asking for help from a peer doesn't carry the same face-risk as asking a leader.

- Recognize and celebrate peer development publicly, adding to the mianzi of both the one who invested and the one who received, making the relational exchange organizationally honored rather than merely tolerated.

- Design enough structural space — time, permission, natural collaboration opportunities — that relational development can actually happen. The relational pipeline requires slack to flow.

What the leader does not need to do is design the curriculum. The content and sequence of peer development is more accurately calibrated by the people doing the work than by any formal program. The leader's job is to create the conditions — relational, structural, and cultural — in which the network develops leadership organically.

From Grassroots Development to Organizational Pipeline

Over time, the relational leadership pipeline produces something institutional programs rarely achieve: a leadership bench that reflects the cultural diversity of the organization. Because development travels through peer relationships rather than formal programs, it reaches people across cultural backgrounds, communication styles, and power distance orientations — provided the relational environment is healthy enough that those networks cross cultural lines.

This is the point at which relational empowerment bias intersects with the relational leadership pipeline. If the relational networks through which development travels are themselves culturally homogeneous — if peer learning happens primarily within cultural groups rather than across them — the pipeline reproduces the relational empowerment bias at scale. Leaders from one cultural background develop other leaders from similar backgrounds. The cultural diversity of the organization's formal membership does not translate into the cultural diversity of its leadership capacity.

The corrective is the same as for relational empowerment bias: deliberate relational investment across cultural lines, by leaders who have developed enough relational range to build genuine ganqing and xinren beyond their own cultural bandwidth. This is not a program. It is a practice — sustained, intentional, and relational all the way down.

The Historical View

History offers compelling examples of shared leadership enabling extraordinary achievement -- and centralized leadership creating spectacular failure. But read through the lens of the relational frameworks developed in this chapter, these stories reveal something that standard organizational histories often miss: the structural arrangements that get celebrated were almost never the primary cause of the outcomes. The relationships built before authority was distributed were.

Nelson's Band of Brothers: Relational Readiness Before Distributed Authority

Admiral Horatio Nelson's approach to the Battle of Trafalgar (1805) is often cited as a masterclass in distributed decision-making. Twenty-seven British ships defeating thirty-three French and Spanish vessels, with each captain making independent tactical decisions in the fog and chaos of battle -- captains who could adapt, act, and lead because Nelson had explicitly empowered them to do so. What the standard account underemphasizes is what Nelson spent years doing before he ever gave those captains authority to act independently.

Nelson did not simply announce distributed authority and trust the structure to hold. He invested, repeatedly and specifically, in the relational conditions that would make distributed authority receivable. His captains called themselves his 'band of brothers' -- a phrase that does not describe a reporting structure. It describes ganqing: the accumulated affection and trust that develops when a leader genuinely invests in the people he is about to empower. Nelson gathered his captains before battle not to issue orders but to share intent, build shared understanding, and ensure that every man in that room knew that his judgment was trusted and his questions were welcome. That is not a briefing. That is relational investment at scale.

The mianzi dimension of what Nelson built is easy to miss. In the Royal Navy of 1805, public failure by a captain could end a career. Nelson had to create conditions where a captain could make an independent decision -- including a wrong one -- without catastrophic face-loss. He did this by framing the entire enterprise relationally: 'I have no great secrets. I communicate my thoughts to all.' When captains knew that their leader shared everything he knew with them, they could exercise authority without the anxiety that they were acting on incomplete information and would be punished for gaps they could not have known.

Consider what happened when Nelson was killed during the battle. The fight continued. His captains did not freeze, panic, or wait for orders that would never come. They exercised the authority he had spent years making them ready to exercise. The structural empowerment -- the explicit permission to decide independently -- held because the relational foundation beneath it held.

This is the AMOR framework made visible in history. Nelson's captains had ability -- he had developed it over years of shared service. They had motivation -- the renqing built through genuine relationship meant they were fighting for the mission and for each other, not just for orders. They had opportunity -- the explicit authority to make decisions in their domain. And they had relationship -- xinren built through consistent, demonstrated trust that what Nelson said about their authority was actually true.

Remove any one of those four dimensions and Trafalgar looks different. Captains with ability and opportunity but no relational trust would have sought confirmation before acting, and the battle would have been decided before they could reach each other. Captains with trust and motivation but no prepared capability -- no developed judgment -- would have acted boldly and incorrectly. Nelson understood this, even if he did not name it in these terms. He built all four conditions simultaneously, over years, before the crisis that would test them.

The lesson: Distributing authority without first building relational readiness is not empowerment -- it is exposure. The structural permission to act is only as stable as the relational foundation beneath it. Nelson spent years building that foundation before he ever needed to test it.

Napoleon's Marshals: Relational Empowerment Bias at the Highest Level

Napoleon Bonaparte is history's most instructive lesson in what happens when a leader of extraordinary individual capability cannot bring himself to build what his organization needs most: distributed relational investment. Napoleon's marshals were not incapable men. Ney, Davout, Massena -- these were soldiers of genuine brilliance. But Napoleon kept information closely held. He shared strategy only partially. He expected subordinates to execute his plans rather than exercise judgment. And critically, he built deep personal renqing with almost no one. The relationship between Napoleon and his marshals was not a relational ecosystem -- it was a hub-and-spoke system with Napoleon at the center of every spoke, managing each relationship individually, ensuring that the depth of connection required for genuine independent leadership never developed.

What Napoleon created was a form of relational empowerment bias operating at the command level. His marshals were trusted to execute in domains where Napoleon had personally invested in them -- where their competence matched Napoleon's own framework for what competence looked like. But they were never trusted to lead independently, never developed as people whose judgment could be trusted without his oversight, never given the xinren that would have made them capable of the kind of adaptive authority Nelson's captains demonstrated at Trafalgar.

The consequences emerged wherever Napoleon could not be present personally. In Spain, his marshals could not coordinate because none of them had been developed to lead within a shared framework -- they had only been developed to follow within Napoleon's framework. In Russia, subordinate commanders lacked the judgment to adapt when circumstances diverged from the plan, because adapting required exactly the independent relational authority Napoleon had systematically withheld. He recognized the problem himself: 'I have made my marshals forget how to fight.' What he meant, in the language of this framework, was: I never built the relational conditions that would have made their independent authority receivable.

There is a deeper pattern here worth naming. Napoleon's inability to develop his marshals as independent leaders was not simply a management oversight. It reflected something about what his relationship with them actually was. A leader who hoards information cannot build xinren -- because xinren requires consistent alignment of words and actions, and the consistent action of withholding says clearly what the words of confidence cannot undo. A leader who never shares strategic intent cannot build ganqing -- because ganqing requires genuine investment in the other person's capacity to understand and contribute, not just their capacity to execute.

Napoleon's empire collapsed not because his enemies were stronger but because its leadership capacity ended where Napoleon's personal presence ended. The organization had ability. It had, in some measure, opportunity. What it never had was the relational dimension -- the foundation that would have allowed ability and opportunity to function in the leader's absence.

The lesson: Individual brilliance that does not invest in relational empowerment creates organizations that can only function at the top. When the center holds, they are extraordinary. When the center is absent, they dissolve. The leader who believes their own capability makes distributed leadership less necessary has misunderstood what organizations are for.

The Roman Centurion System: The Relational Leadership Pipeline at Scale

The Roman army's centurion system is often analyzed as an organizational design achievement -- the distributed leadership structure that allowed a single empire to project military force across three continents for five centuries. That analysis is correct as far as it goes. What it misses is that the centurion system was not primarily a structural achievement. It was a relational pipeline.

Rome did not appoint centurions and give them authority. Rome built centurions -- through extended periods of shared service, demonstrated competence in progressively more demanding roles, and the accumulated relational investment of the legions they served in. A soldier who rose to become a centurion had not simply been assessed and promoted. He had been developed through relationships -- with the men he fought beside, with the officers who observed his judgment under pressure, with the institutional culture of a legion that had its own xinren, its own renqing, its own accumulated relational history.

This is the relational leadership pipeline in its most fully realized historical form. Leadership development did not travel primarily through instruction or formal training. It traveled through relationship -- the peer learning of soldiers who taught each other what the manuals could not capture, the mentorship-through-proximity of observing senior officers in real situations, the trust-building of shared hardship that no assessment process can manufacture. The centurion who eventually commanded eighty soldiers had built, over years, the relational infrastructure that made his authority believable to the men he led.

The mianzi dimension of this is visible in how Rome handled mistakes. Centurions were held to high standards and faced serious consequences for genuine failures. But the system was designed to distinguish between mistakes made in the course of courageous action and failures of character or judgment -- a distinction that requires exactly the kind of relational knowledge that only develops over time. A centurion's reputation was protected when he acted decisively and imperfectly, in a way that made it safe for other centurions to act decisively rather than cautiously preserving their standing.

What the centurion system demonstrates is that the relational leadership pipeline is not a modern innovation or a culturally specific practice. It is the structural truth of how human organizations actually build leadership capacity. When Rome's enemies had more men or better individual warriors, they still lost -- because Rome had distributed relational authority at every level of the organization, and its enemies had concentrated authority at the top. When a Roman general was killed, the legion adapted. When a Carthaginian general was killed, the army often collapsed. The difference was not tactical genius. It was the depth and distribution of the relational infrastructure.

The lesson: Leadership pipelines that travel through relationships produce the organizational resilience that formal programs alone cannot generate. Rome's military dominance was not primarily an achievement of structure or training. It was an achievement of relational investment, repeated and distributed across hundreds of thousands of soldiers over hundreds of years.

The Biblical View

Scripture does not offer idealized portraits of shared leadership. It offers honest ones -- including the failures, the costs, the relational conditions that made empowerment work and the relational absences that made it fail. Read through the frameworks developed in this chapter, the biblical stories of distributed authority reveal something more demanding and more hopeful than a simple argument for organizational decentralization.

The Twelve Spies: When Distributed Authority Meets Relational Unpreparedness

The story of the twelve spies (Numbers 13-14) is often read as a story about courage and faith. It is also, read carefully, a story about what happens when authority is distributed to people who have not been made relationally ready to exercise it well. Moses did exactly what shared leadership frameworks recommend: he did not go himself, he sent representatives, he distributed the authority to assess to people closest to the actual situation. All twelve were qualified by position. All twelve gathered the same information. All twelve came back with accurate facts. And then ten of them used their authority to dismantle the mission.

What the ten lacked was not information. It was formation. They had the A, M, and O of the AMOR framework -- ability to scout, motivation to serve, opportunity to report. What they did not have was the relational readiness to carry the weight of their authority. Specifically, they lacked the xinren between themselves and the God who had promised them the land -- the accumulated evidence of consistent words and actions that would have allowed them to interpret the giants of Canaan through the lens of what they already knew to be true. Without that relational trust as foundation, their accurate observations produced catastrophic conclusions.

Caleb and Joshua had the same facts and arrived at opposite conclusions. The difference was not courage in the abstract. It was a specific form of relational trust -- the xinren of people who had accumulated enough lived experience of God's consistency to believe that what He said about their authority was actually true. 'If the LORD is pleased with us, he will lead us into that land' is not optimism. It is a relational assessment: based on what we have seen of this relationship, the offer of authority it contains is genuine.

This is what relational unpreparedness looks like when authority is distributed too early, or to people who have not been formed through the relational investments that make authority receivable. The ten were not bad men. They were men whose relational foundation could not carry the weight of the decision they had been empowered to shape. They had been given Level 5 authority -- full ownership of the assessment that would determine the nation's direction -- without the relational formation that Level 5 authority requires.

Moses's response to this failure is itself instructive. He did not immediately redistribute the authority to someone better prepared. He waited. Forty years in the wilderness was not punishment alone -- it was formation. By the time Joshua led the conquest, he had been developed through four decades of proximity to Moses, of shared hardship, of observing how a leader navigated between God and people. The relational leadership pipeline had done its work. Joshua entered the land with the same authority the twelve spies had been offered -- and with the relational formation to exercise it.

The lesson: You can distribute authority before you have built the relational readiness that makes authority exercisable well. The twelve spies had positions and permission. What they lacked was the accumulated relational trust -- the xinren -- that would have allowed those positions to produce faithful rather than fearful conclusions. Empowerment without relational formation does not produce empowered people. It produces people who use their influence to spread what they are afraid of.

Deborah and Barak: Empowering Across the Relational Distance Between Leaders

The story of Deborah and Barak (Judges 4-5) is one of Scripture's most nuanced accounts of what happens when a leader of greater capability tries to empower a leader of lesser confidence -- and what both the success and the limitation of that empowerment reveal about the relational conditions empowerment requires.

Deborah held the most complete version of authority available in Israel: prophet, judge, arbiter of national disputes. When she summoned Barak and gave him his commission -- lead ten thousand men, engage Sisera, the LORD will give him into your hands -- she was offering an act of full organizational empowerment. She had the authority to give this mission, and she gave it clearly. The mission, the army, the boundary of responsibility, the promised outcome: all of it was Barak's.

Barak's response -- 'If you go with me, I will go; but if you don't go with me, I won't go' -- has often been read as weakness or lack of faith. Read through the relational readiness framework, it is something more specific: it is the honest declaration of a person who knows that the relational foundation for the authority being offered is not yet sufficient to carry it alone. Barak was not saying he lacked military competence. He was saying, in effect: I do not yet have enough xinren with this commission to trust it without the ongoing presence of the one who gave it. The promise of God's presence in battle is a relational claim -- it asks Barak to trust not just a directive but a relationship. And Barak's honest answer was that he needed the visible, embodied relational presence of Deborah to hold that trust steady under the pressure of actual combat.

What Deborah did next is the model response to this kind of honest relational disclosure. She did not shame Barak. She did not withdraw the commission. She agreed to go -- and she named clearly, without cruelty, what the relational cost of his condition would be: the glory of the final victory would belong to someone else. This is the mianzi-aware response to relational unreadiness: the authority remains available, the support is provided, and the consequence is named in a way that honors the person's dignity while being transparent about the reality.

Notice also what Deborah did not do. She did not command the battle herself. She accompanied Barak, remained present, provided the spiritual authority and the decisive moment of release -- 'Go! This is the day the LORD has given Sisera into your hands' -- and then let

Barak lead the actual military execution. This is the relational leadership model in its most sophisticated form: not abandonment, not control, but the kind of alongside-presence that makes someone else's authority stable enough to exercise. Deborah built the relational conditions for Barak's empowerment in real time, during the event itself, because she understood that the relational foundation he needed had not been built before it was required.

There is also a relational empowerment bias dimension to this story worth noting. In a culture with steep power distance and strong patriarchal norms, Deborah held ultimate authority -- and Barak, a military commander of higher cultural status in some respects, still needed her presence to function. The cultural expectation would have been that military authority flows to men and spiritual authority defers to military judgment. Deborah inverted this without apology and without forcing Barak to choose between his cultural framework and his mission. She made his empowerment possible within his actual relational capacity, not within the idealized version of it.

The lesson: Empowerment is not a single act. It is a sustained relational practice. Deborah's gift to Barak was not simply a commission. It was ongoing relational presence that made the commission stable enough to act on. Leaders who empower people and then withdraw entirely have not empowered them -- they have exposed them. The goal is to build the relational foundation that makes the leader's ongoing presence unnecessary. Deborah did this over the course of the battle itself.

The Disciples After Pentecost: The Relational Pipeline That Changed the World

The transformation of the disciples between the Gospels and the book of Acts is one of history's most dramatic examples of what distributed relational empowerment actually produces -- and why the leader's most important work is often the relational investment that precedes the formal transfer of authority.

Jesus spent three years with twelve people. By any efficiency measure, this was an extraordinary allocation of time and relational investment to a very small group. He taught them, but the teaching was embedded in relationship -- meals, travel, shared hardship, private conversations, public moments of correction and affirmation. He built ganqing with them through genuine, unobligated investment in their growth and wellbeing. He built renqing through a pattern of consistent giving that eventually generated the kind of commitment that would cost them everything to honor. He built xinren by demonstrating, repeatedly, that what He said about His authority and their future authority was actually true -- not through announcements but through evidence.

The disciples' inability to function independently during Jesus's earthly ministry is often read as a failure. Read through the AMOR framework, it is something different: it is the accurate reflection of a group in which ability, motivation, and opportunity were developing, but in which the relational foundation -- the xinren specifically -- had not yet been completed. They could not fully trust their own authority because they had not yet seen it exercised and sustained independent of Jesus's physical presence. The resurrection appearances, the forty days of continued relational investment after the resurrection, and the promise of the Spirit were the final phase of the relational preparation. Jesus did not distribute authority and then leave. He built the relational conditions for distributed authority to be receivable -- and then left.

Pentecost is the moment the relational leadership pipeline became visible as a pipeline. The Spirit distributed to all of them -- not just the apostles -- activated relational authority that had been built through three years of proximity and investment. Peter's boldness was not new personality. It was xinren completing its work: accumulated evidence, now fully present, that the authority he had been offered was genuine and would hold. The disciples did not become different people at Pentecost. They became people who finally trusted what they had always been told was true about themselves.

The Acts 6 distribution of leadership to the seven Greek-named deacons is the relational pipeline becoming organizational structure. When the Hellenistic widows were being overlooked, the apostles did not simply create a new administrative role. They specifically empowered leaders from within the affected community -- leaders who already had xinren with that community, who understood its mianzi dynamics, who carried the relational authority of their own people. This was not diversity for representation's sake. It was the recognition that distributed leadership only functions when the people carrying authority have the relational infrastructure within their communities to make that authority believable and effective.

The persecution of Acts 8 reveals what the relational pipeline had built. When the church was scattered, it did not collapse. Every believer became a minister, because the relational foundation for leadership had been distributed across the entire community rather than concentrated in the apostles. The organization that dispersed under pressure was more resilient precisely because its leadership had been built relationally rather than positionally. When the positions were forced to scatter, the relationships -- and the authority embedded in them -- went with the people.

This is the deepest argument for the relational leadership pipeline. Positional authority is what you hold while you're in place. Relational authority is what you carry wherever you go. Jesus built the kind of authority that could not be confiscated, because it had been built into relationships rather than into roles. The empire that tried to destroy the early church by destroying its leaders discovered that it had misunderstood what made those leaders effective. Their authority was not in their positions. It was in their relationships.

The lesson: The goal of leadership development is not producing people who can follow well. It is producing people who can lead independently -- people whose relational authority has been built deeply enough that it holds when the original leader is absent, when the structure changes, or when the organization is forced to scatter. Jesus worked himself out of positional necessity not to diminish his influence but to multiply it. Every leader who genuinely develops others is doing the same thing.

Nuances and Blind Spots

Permission paralysis is a leadership creation. When people consistently wait for approval before acting on matters they're fully qualified to handle, the problem usually isn't their initiative — it's that initiative has been punished. When people who take independent action within their role get questioned, corrected, or second-guessed, they learn quickly to wait for direction rather than risk being wrong. The leader who then complains about a lack of ownership helped build the very passivity they're frustrated by.

Responsibility without authority is a setup for failure. Holding people accountable for outcomes while withholding the decision-making power needed to achieve them doesn't create high performance — it creates frustration, learned helplessness, and eventually departure. This pattern is worth examining carefully, because it often coexists with the language of empowerment while functioning as its opposite.

Centralization is often disguised as quality control. Leaders who struggle to share authority frequently frame their bottlenecking as concern for excellence: "I just want to make sure it's done right." Unchecked, this prevents others from developing and creates dependency rather than capability. True quality concern includes investing in others' capacity to produce quality — not remaining the sole guarantor of it. The leader who believes "only I can do this" may be protecting standards, or may be protecting their own sense of indispensability. It's worth knowing which.

Empowerment requires preparation, not just permission. You can't simply hand authority to people who haven't been developed to exercise it. Shared leadership without capability development creates confusion, not empowerment. Different cultural contexts compound this: in high power distance cultures, people may not exercise authority unless it's explicitly granted by someone they recognize as legitimate. In low power distance cultures, people may assume authority that was never offered. Effective empowerment structures are explicit enough for the former and bounded enough for the latter.

Selective empowerment is visible to everyone. When certain people — often those culturally or relationally closest to leadership — are trusted with authority while others of equal competence aren't, the pattern registers across the organization even when it's never named. Empowerment distributed along cultural or relational lines rather than demonstrated capability quietly communicates who is truly trusted and who is merely tolerated.

The leader's identity may be the real bottleneck. For many leaders, centralized authority isn't just a management style — it's identity. "I'm the one who decides" becomes, underneath, "I'm the one who matters." Sharing leadership can trigger genuine anxiety about relevance and value. Leaders who haven't developed an identity grounded in *developing others* rather than being indispensable will find structural empowerment initiatives quietly undermined by their own behavior.

Shared leadership requires more communication, not less. When authority is centralized, coordination happens inside one person's head. When it's distributed, coordination requires deliberate infrastructure — shared vision, clear boundaries, regular check-ins, transparent information flow. Organizations that distribute authority without building that infrastructure don't get empowerment. They get confusion with extra steps.

Mistakes must be allowed — and distinguished. Distributed leadership means people will make decisions you wouldn't have made, some of which will be wrong. If every mistake triggers recentralization, shared leadership can never take root. The critical discipline is distinguishing between mistakes that require learning and support versus mistakes that require removal of authority. Treating all errors the same way — either with punishment or with unlimited tolerance — both undermine the system.

Empowerment isn't abandonment. Some leaders overcorrect from control to neglect and call it delegation. Genuine empowerment includes ongoing access to guidance, resources, and support. The goal is autonomous decision-making with available backing — not isolated decision-making without help. People left alone to sink or swim don't feel trusted. They feel set up.

Try This Week

Choose ONE practice to develop shared leadership:

Practice 1: Clarify One Decision Zone (20 minutes)

Pick one recurring decision that currently requires your approval. Write down: (1) Who should make this decision? (2) What information do they need? (3) What boundaries exist? (4) What happens if it goes wrong? Share this clarity with the decision-maker. Let them actually make the decision without interference unless boundaries are violated.

Practice 2: Publicly Recognize Initiative (5 minutes in next team meeting)

Identify one time someone took initiative and made a good decision without asking permission. Thank them publicly: "I appreciated how you [specific action]. That's exactly the kind of ownership we need more of." This signals that initiative is valued, not punished.

Practice 3: Ask "If You Owned This..." (10 minutes in next one-on-one)

Instead of telling someone what to do, ask: "If you owned this decision, what would you do?" Listen to their answer. If it's reasonable, respond: "That sounds good—go ahead." If concerns exist, ask questions rather than giving answers. Develop their judgment; don't bypass it.

Practice 4: Competence-Building Conversation (15 minutes)
Identify someone ready for more authority. Have an explicit conversation: "I want you to start making decisions about X. Here's what you have authority to decide. Here's what still needs approval. I'm available for questions, but I trust you to handle this." Then actually let them handle it—resist the urge to intervene.

Reflection Questions

Quick Check (1-2 minutes)

- What percentage of decisions in your organization require your personal approval? What would healthy delegation reduce this to?

- When was the last time someone on your team made a significant decision without checking with you first? How did you respond?

Deeper Reflection (5-10 minutes)

- What decisions are you holding that others could handle with proper preparation? What makes you reluctant to let go?

- If you were unavailable for two weeks, what would break? Why? What does this reveal about your leadership structure?

- Who on your team is ready for more authority but hasn't been given it? What's preventing you from empowering them?

- How does your cultural background shape your assumptions about authority, delegation, and hierarchy? How might team members from different backgrounds experience your leadership style?

Team Discussion (15-30 minutes)

- As a leadership team, map out major decision categories (budget, hiring, programs, operations, communication). For each: Who currently makes these decisions? Who should make them? What preparation would enable better distribution? Create a 90-day plan to redistribute at least three decisions appropriately.

Moving Forward

Distributed leadership enables organizations to function at scale and develop people's capacity. But shared authority without shared vision creates chaos rather than coordination. People need to know not just what they're authorized to decide, but why those decisions matter and how they connect to larger purpose.

The executive director in our opening scene didn't just need to delegate more—she needed to develop her team's capability, clarify decision boundaries, and build the trust that makes genuine empowerment possible. Shared leadership isn't a single decision to "let go." It's an ongoing practice of developing others, clarifying authority, extending trust, and resisting the pull toward centralization that feels safer but creates fragility.

Nelson's captains could lead independently at Trafalgar because Nelson had invested years building their judgment and establishing shared understanding. Moses could distribute leadership because God had already identified capable people and provided the Spirit to empower them. Jesus could send seventy-two followers because He had taught, modeled, and prepared them for independent ministry.

The question isn't whether you should share leadership—the biblical and practical case is overwhelming. The question is how you develop the people, structures, and trust that make shared leadership work across cultural differences in your specific context.

<hr>

PART THREE: LEADING FOR THE LONG HAUL

<hr>

LEADING FOR THE LONG HAUL

Vision That Transcends Backgrounds

Opening Scene

The conference room buzzed with energy as the leadership team unveiled their new vision statement, projected in bold letters across the screen: "Empowering communities through innovative, sustainable partnerships."

They'd spent three months crafting it—wordsmithing every phrase, debating whether "transforming" was better than "empowering," ensuring it sounded both aspirational and achievable. The executive director beamed: "This captures who we are and where we're going. Let's get this on our website, in our materials, on the wall in reception."

Six months later, she sat in her office troubled by what she was hearing. In separate conversations, she'd asked team members: "What's our organization's vision?" The answers were all over the map.

Grant from finance: "We're about innovative solutions—disrupting old models, trying new approaches, being on the cutting edge." He emphasized speed and experimentation.

Lin from programs: "We build sustainable partnerships—long-term relationships based on mutual respect and trust." She emphasized patience and harmony.

Amara from outreach: "We empower communities—helping people take collective action, building grassroots movements." She emphasized solidarity and shared power.

David from development: "We develop individual leaders—giving people tools to succeed and create their own opportunities." He emphasized personal capacity and achievement.

They'd all heard the same vision statement. They'd all memorized the same words. But Lin's Taiwanese background emphasized relationships and collective harmony. David's American framework prioritized individual empowerment. Amara's Kenyan experience valued community solidarity. Grant's German training emphasized systematic innovation.

The vision wasn't uniting people around shared purpose—it was functioning as a mirror, reflecting each person's cultural assumptions back to them while everyone believed they were aligned. The words were universal enough to mean anything, which meant they effectively meant nothing.

Why Vision Matters in Multicultural Organizations

Vision serves multiple critical functions in organizations. A clear, compelling vision drives organizational cohesion, facilitates goal alignment across teams, and functions as a core leadership competency that distinguishes effective from ineffective leaders. In multicultural contexts, vision becomes even more crucial—and more complex. Without clear parameters, organizations risk what researchers call "mission drift"—gradual departure from core purpose as different cultural groups interpret ambiguous vision through their own frameworks.

The challenge is real: language that seems clear in one cultural framework can be genuinely ambiguous in another. "Empowerment" means individual authority and autonomy in individualistic cultures but collective action and shared power in collectivist ones. "Innovation" suggests rapid change and disruption in low uncertainty avoidance cultures but calculated, systematic improvement in high uncertainty avoidance cultures. "Partnership" implies formal equality in low power distance cultures but may suggest hierarchical relationships with mutual obligation in high power distance cultures.

Vision that transcends backgrounds doesn't ignore cultural difference or demand cultural uniformity. Instead, it articulates purpose rooted in universal values while allowing flexible execution that honors diverse cultural frameworks.

Vision Doesn't Work Alone: The Five Forces Connection

One of the most important findings from research with multicultural organizations is this: vision only functions as a unifying force when the other organizational forces support it. A compelling vision statement, however well-crafted, cannot do its work in isolation. Research identifies five reinforcing forces that together create organizational health in multicultural contexts: Consistency, Communication, Vision, Growth Culture, and Inclusion. These aren't independent qualities—they are interdependent. Vision is one pillar, but the others must be load-bearing too. Consider what happens when vision operates without the other forces:

- **Vision without consistency becomes cynicism**. When leaders articulate inspiring purpose but make decisions that contradict it, staff learn quickly that the vision is decorative. Over time, even a genuinely good vision loses credibility because the behavior that surrounds it tells a different story.

- **Vision without communication becomes noise**. When purpose is announced but not continuously interpreted—especially during organizational change—it goes silent at exactly the moments people most need to hear it. Staff fill the vacuum with speculation and anxiety.

- **Vision without inclusion becomes a monoculture**. When vision language is crafted by a homogeneous leadership team and presented to a diverse staff, it encodes the cultural assumptions of those who wrote it. It may resonate deeply for some and feel entirely foreign to others—not because those people lack commitment, but because the vision was never genuinely theirs.

- **Vision without a growth culture becomes pressure without support**. When purpose is clear but people don't feel safe to experiment, fail, or push back, vision becomes a standard used to judge rather than a story used to invite.

The practical implication: if your vision isn't landing, the problem may not be the vision itself. It may be that the surrounding forces—consistency in decision-making, openness in communication, genuine inclusion in the process—aren't strong enough to carry it. When leaders articulate vision consistently, connect it to day-to-day decisions, and demonstrate alignment in their own behavior, staff report greater cohesion and a sense of pulling together even amid limited resources. That cohesion isn't produced by vision alone. It's produced by vision operating inside a system where all five forces are functioning.

The Vision-Change Gap: When Organizations Need Vision Most, It Goes Silent

There is a specific and recurring failure pattern that multicultural organizations need to name clearly: the Vision-Change Gap. This is what happens when vision communication lags behind structural change. Leadership transitions, accreditation shifts, curriculum reforms, budget restructuring, rapid growth, key staff departures—these are exactly the moments when people most urgently need a clear answer to the question: "Do we still know where we're going?" And these are precisely the moments when leaders, consumed by managing the change itself, stop talking about vision.

The consequences are predictable. In the absence of vision language, staff from different cultural backgrounds revert to their own cultural defaults to make sense of what's happening. Some interpret the silence as instability. Others interpret it as evidence that the organizational direction has changed. Still others simply disengage, waiting to see what the new normal will be before reinvesting.

Research from multicultural settings makes this pattern visible. When leadership change brings new consistency and clearer communication, the difference is described as "night and day." But the legacy of the vision gap lingers: staff who lived through the silence period remain cautious longer, require more behavioral evidence before they re-engage, and carry a learned wariness that a new vision announcement, however sincere, cannot immediately dissolve.

Closing the Vision-Change Gap requires a counterintuitive discipline: in seasons of transition and uncertainty, increase—don't decrease—the frequency with which you name what remains constant. Leaders who say "Here's what is changing, and here's what is not" give people the anchors they need to stay oriented. Vision doesn't need to be fully resolved to be communicated. Saying "We're working through what this means for our direction, and here's our best current understanding" is far more stabilizing than silence.

The principle: Vision communication should be most frequent during transition, not most sparse. Organizations that go silent about purpose when facing change don't protect themselves from confusion—they guarantee it.

Two Different Failures: Vision Drift and Vision Fragmentation

Not all vision failures are the same, and treating them as if they were leads to ineffective responses. Research and organizational experience reveal two distinct failure modes that require different interventions.

Vision Drift

Drift happens when the whole organization quietly moves away from its stated purpose together. No one announces the change. No dramatic conflict occurs. But over time, under the pressure of immediate demands, resource constraints, and convenience, the organization gradually does something other than what it said it existed to do. Drift is often invisible from the inside because everyone drifts together—there's no friction to signal the departure. Drift requires anchoring interventions: regular story-keeping that surfaces examples of vision lived out, resource allocation audits that ask whether spending patterns actually reflect stated priorities, and rituals that return people to the founding purpose.

Vision Fragmentation

Fragmentation is what happened in the opening scene of this chapter. The organization doesn't drift—it fractures. People stay committed and energetic, but they're committed to different interpretations of the same stated vision. Fragmentation is often invisible precisely because it looks like alignment: everyone affirms the vision statement, everyone can recite the words, but the meanings have diverged along cultural and experiential lines.

Fragmentation requires a clarifying process—not a better communication strategy, but a participatory conversation that surfaces how differently the same words are being heard. This isn't a communication problem; it's a diagnostic problem. The right question isn't "How do we explain our vision better?" but "What do we learn when we ask people to tell us what our vision means to them?" The practical distinction matters because the interventions are opposite. Drift calls for repetition and reinforcement of what the vision says. Fragmentation calls for conversation about what the vision means—and often, honest revision of language that seemed universal but wasn't.

Two Different Failures: Vision Drift and Vision Fragmentation

Not all vision failures are the same, and treating them as if they were leads to ineffective responses. Research and organizational experience reveal two distinct failure modes that require different interventions.

VISION DRIFT

Drift happens when the whole organization quietly moves away from its stated purpose together. No one announces the change. No dramatic conflict occurs. But over time, under the pressure of immediate demands, resource constraints, and convenience, the organization gradually does something other than what it said it existed to do. Drift is often invisible from the inside because everyone drifts together—there's no friction to signal the departure.

What it looks like: Everyone moves away from purpose together; no friction signals the problem.

Root cause: Insufficient anchoring; immediate pressures override long-term purpose.

Intervention needed: Story-keeping, resource audits, regular return to founding purpose.

Drift requires anchoring interventions: regular story-keeping that surfaces examples of vision lived out, resource allocation audits that ask whether spending patterns actually reflect stated priorities, and rituals that return people to the founding purpose.

VISION FRAGMENTATION

Fragmentation is what happened in the opening scene of this chapter. The organization doesn't drift—it fractures. People stay committed and energetic, but they're committed to different interpretations of the same stated vision. Fragmentation is often invisible precisely because it looks like alignment: everyone affirms the vision statement, everyone can recite the words, but the meanings have diverged along cultural and experiential lines.

What it looks like: Everyone affirms vision but pursues different interpretations; appears aligned.

Root cause: Culturally ambiguous language; vision crafted without diverse input.

Intervention needed: Participatory diagnosis; ask what vision means, not just whether people know it.

Fragmentation requires a clarifying process—not a better communication strategy, but a participatory conversation that surfaces how differently the same words are being heard. This isn't a communication problem; it's a diagnostic problem. The right question isn't "How do we explain our vision better?" but "What do we learn when we ask people to tell us what our vision means to them?"

THE PRACTICAL DISTINCTION

The practical distinction matters because the interventions are opposite. Drift calls for repetition and reinforcement of what the vision says. Fragmentation calls for conversation about what the vision means—and often, honest revision of language that seemed universal but wasn't. If your organization is drifting, repeat and re-anchor the vision more consistently. If your organization is fragmenting, stop repeating and start listening—find out what the vision actually means to people across cultural backgrounds before saying another word about it. Misdiagnosing one for the other makes things worse. Leaders who respond to fragmentation with louder, more frequent repetition of the vision statement are not solving the problem—they are deepening it.

Vision Equity: Whose Cultural Framework Is Centered?

Earlier chapters introduced the concept of structural fairness—the recognition that voice and dignity aren't just matters of individual interaction but of how organizational systems are designed. The same framework applies to vision. When vision language consistently resonates with one cultural group and feels foreign to another, the problem isn't communication skill. It's a structural equity issue: the vision was built on one group's cultural assumptions and presented to everyone as universal.

This is almost always unintentional. Leaders who share cultural backgrounds don't experience their assumptions as cultural—they experience them as obvious. "Excellence," "community," "empowerment," "accountability"—these feel like plain language to people who share a cultural framework in which those words have settled meanings. But in multicultural contexts, those words carry entirely different weights and connotations depending on the cultural soil they land in.

The structural equity question is: Who was in the room when the vision was shaped? Not who was invited to the announcement, but who genuinely influenced the language, the priorities, the framing. If the answer is primarily one cultural group—even a well-intentioned one—the vision will reflect their cultural assumptions, regardless of how universal the language sounds to them.

Research consistently shows that when vision is crafted by homogeneous groups and presented to diverse staff, those staff can often identify the cultural fingerprints in it—even when leadership cannot. The staff member who says "I'm not sure this vision really fits how we think about community in my culture" is offering a diagnostic gift, not a complaint. The leader who hears this as resistance rather than insight loses an opportunity to build something genuinely transcendent.

The practical standard: Vision is equitable when staff from every cultural background in your organization can articulate it in their own language and genuinely locate themselves inside it—not because they've learned to parrot the official version, but because it was built with their voices included.

The Vision Equity Audit

Before finalizing or relaunching any vision statement, apply these diagnostic questions:

- Who was in the room (or conversation) when this vision was shaped? Did that group represent the cultural diversity of the full organization?

- What cultural assumptions are embedded in the key words? (Test: ask staff from different backgrounds what each major term means to them.)

- Which cultural groups find this vision immediately resonant? Which groups require more explanation before it connects?

- If you asked staff from your least-represented cultural group to rewrite the vision in their own language, what would change?

- Does the vision require cultural translation for some people to own it—while requiring no translation for others? If so, why?

Calling: The Integrative Force Vision Statements Can't Manufacture

Research into what actually holds multicultural organizations together across cultural friction, resource constraints, and leadership transitions reveals something that vision statements alone cannot produce: shared sense of calling. Calling is more than purpose. Vision describes where the organization is going. Calling describes why people are there at all—the sense that this work is not just a job but a vocation, a contribution to something larger than any single cultural framework or organizational structure. In contexts where people come from genuinely different cultures, shared calling can bridge differences that shared language cannot, because calling operates at the level of meaning rather than information.

In study after study of multicultural organizations that successfully navigate cultural difference, participants describe not primarily the clarity of the vision statement but the sense that their work matters in ways that transcend the immediate context. Teachers who stay through leadership transitions and resource constraints are often those who articulate a clear sense of calling—a conviction that their presence serves something larger than any particular organizational form.

This has a specific implication for how vision is constructed and communicated. Vision that is only organizational—about what this institution will accomplish—can resonate or fail to resonate based on cultural distance from the organization's framework. But vision that connects organizational purpose to something the person experiences as calling—to their convictions about human dignity, their commitments to future generations, their sense of participation in something spiritually meaningful—creates a bond that organizational documents cannot manufacture.

The biblical material in this chapter—Abraham's calling to bless all nations, Isaiah's vision of a light for the Gentiles, Philip's encounter with the Ethiopian—is not incidentally spiritual illustration. It is the structural form of transcendent vision: purpose that connects to something larger than any single organization, culture, or era. Leaders who can help people see their work inside that larger frame are doing something qualitatively different from leaders who simply clarify objectives.

The practical question: Does your vision connect only to organizational outcomes, or does it also connect to the deeper reasons people gave up other options to be part of this work? Vision that speaks to calling rather than just purpose has staying power that organizational clarity alone cannot achieve.

What Makes Vision Transcend Cultural Backgrounds

Based on research and observation of organizations successfully navigating this challenge, several elements consistently appear:

1. Rooted in Universal Values, Not Cultural Preferences

Vision must connect to values that resonate across cultures—dignity, justice, compassion, excellence, stewardship—rather than values that feel culturally specific. "Maximizing shareholder value" is a culturally Western concept. "Creating flourishing for all stakeholders" translates better across cultures. "Individual freedom" is culturally loaded. "Human dignity" resonates more universally. This doesn't mean eliminating all cultural specificity—organizations exist in specific contexts. But the core vision should connect to something broader than any single cultural framework.

2. Clear Purpose with Flexible Execution

Transcendent vision articulates WHAT we're ultimately trying to accomplish and WHY it matters, while allowing HOW to vary across cultural contexts. "We exist to ensure every child can read by third grade" is clear purpose. The methods for achieving it can honor different cultural approaches to education, family involvement, and community engagement. Contrast this with vision that prescribes method: "We deliver phonics-based reading instruction through standardized curriculum." This dictates approach, making it culturally rigid rather than transcendent.

3. Continuously Connected to Daily Decisions

Vision transcends when it's not just words on a wall but a lived framework that shapes actual decisions. This requires leaders regularly asking: "How does this choice connect to our vision?" and ensuring the connection is clear across cultural frameworks. When vision only appears in annual reports and donor communications, it's decorative rather than functional. When it shapes budget decisions, hiring criteria, program design, and conflict resolution, it becomes real.

4. Owned by Many, Not Just Leadership

Vision transcends when people throughout the organization can articulate it in their own words and explain how their work connects to it. This requires more than top-down communication—it requires participatory processes where diverse voices help shape and interpret vision. In the opening scene, the vision was crafted by leadership and announced to staff. A more effective approach: gather diverse team members to discuss "What are we ultimately trying to accomplish? Why does it matter?" Let vision emerge from that conversation rather than imposing it.

5. Creates Identity and Direction Simultaneously

Transcendent vision answers both "Who are we?" and "Where are we going?" It provides identity (the kind of organization we are) and direction (the impact we're pursuing). Organizations with only identity become self-focused. Organizations with only direction lose coherence. Both are needed. "We are people who believe every human being deserves dignity and opportunity" (identity), "pursuing a world where systemic barriers don't determine life outcomes" (direction). This works across cultures because dignity and opportunity are universal values, while specific barriers and interventions can vary by context.

The Costs of Vision Failure

Research identifies several consequences when vision fails to unite diverse organizations:

- **Mission Drift and Fragmentation**: Different parts of the organization pursue different interpretations of purpose, creating fragmentation rather than cohesion. This is particularly damaging in multicultural contexts where cultural frameworks naturally pull in different directions.

- **Stagnation and Low Productivity**: When people don't understand how their work connects to larger purpose, discretionary effort declines. They do what's required but rarely go beyond minimum expectations.

- **Leadership Barriers**: Leaders struggle to make decisions and resolve conflicts without clear vision to reference. Every choice becomes negotiated from scratch rather than evaluated against shared purpose.

- **Loss of Collective Engagement**: Team members operate as individuals pursuing personal goals rather than as a community pursuing shared purpose. This is especially problematic in collectivist cultures where collective identity matters deeply.

- **Reduced Collective Efficacy**: Collective efficacy—a group's shared belief in their capability to accomplish goals—depends on clear, compelling vision. Ambiguous vision undermines collective efficacy, reducing both motivation and actual performance.

The Historical View

History offers compelling examples of vision that united diverse peoples—and vision failures that fragmented them. Read through the lens of the failure modes and framework concepts above, these historical cases become richer diagnostic tools.

The Council of Nicaea and Constantine's Vision of Christian Unity (325 AD)

When Constantine convened the Council of Nicaea in 325 AD, he brought together bishops from across the known world—Greeks, Egyptians, Syrians, North Africans, Persians, Romans, and others—speaking different languages, shaped by different philosophies, and holding sharp theological disagreements. These were not colleagues who liked each other. Many bore physical scars from persecution under prior emperors. Some had theological positions they considered worth dying for.

What Constantine faced was not merely a theological dispute—it was an advanced case of vision fragmentation. Every bishop was committed to the faith. All of them could recite the same scriptures. But the meanings they carried in those shared texts had diverged along cultural, philosophical, and regional lines. The words were the same; the vision had fractured.

Constantine articulated a unifying vision not rooted in doctrinal uniformity (he himself was not yet baptized) but in a purpose every bishop shared: a unified church that could speak with one voice on essential beliefs. His opening address framed internal division as a greater threat to the church than external persecution had ever been—a striking claim that reframed the stakes from "who is right" to "what we lose if we can't agree." Notice the structure: he named the Vision-Change Gap explicitly. The church was in a moment of structural transition. He insisted that vision communication increase, not decrease, at precisely that moment.

The Council produced the Nicene Creed—a statement of core shared belief broad enough to unite participants from radically different theological and cultural traditions, while leaving room for diverse expressions in worship, governance, and practice. It didn't resolve every dispute; it established shared identity around irreducible essentials. This was a direct response to fragmentation, not drift. The intervention was clarifying process—naming what the vision actually meant—not simply repeating it louder.

Constantine's genius was distinguishing between the core (what all Christians must hold in common) and the periphery (where diversity was permissible). The vision wasn't "become theologically identical"—it was "agree on what is essential so the church can move forward together." Bishops who disagreed on much found they could unite around what mattered most. This is vision equity in practice: not forcing everyone into one cultural-theological framework, but finding the ground broad enough for genuine, diverse ownership.

The Council also shows the danger of conflating organizational power with transcendent vision. When Constantine used imperial pressure to force consensus, he produced outward unity without inward alignment—a problem that haunted the church for centuries afterward. Transcendent vision cannot be coerced. It must be genuinely owned. Forced agreement is the opposite of vision equity; it is vision uniformity imposed by power, which creates compliance without calling.

The lesson for modern leaders: The most durable vision documents—those that unite diverse people across generations—distinguish clearly between essentials and non-essentials. When organizations try to unify around everything, they fragment. When they identify what is truly irreducible and give freedom on everything else, diverse people can genuinely align. And when fragmentation has already occurred, the answer is not louder repetition of the vision statement—it is participatory conversation about what the vision actually means.

The Founding Vision of the United States

The American founding offers both inspiration and cautionary lessons about transcendent vision—and a vivid case study in both drift and fragmentation operating simultaneously. The Declaration of Independence articulated vision in universal terms: "We hold these truths to be self-evident, that all men are created equal, that they are endowed by their Creator with certain unalienable Rights." This vision was powerful precisely because it appealed to universal values—equality, dignity, rights inherent in humanity itself. It could inspire people from vastly different backgrounds because it grounded identity in shared humanity rather than particular cultural traditions.

But the founding vision suffered from a structural equity failure from the beginning. The language felt universal to those who wrote it—landed, white, property-owning men—because it resonated with their cultural framework. "All men" didn't include enslaved Africans, Native Americans, or women in practice. The universal language masked particular exclusions. This is a precise example of vision crafted by a homogeneous group and presented as universal: those inside the cultural framework heard clear purpose; those outside it heard words that explicitly contradicted their lived experience.

The result was not drift—the founders didn't gradually move away from their intentions. The result was fragmentation on a civilizational scale. Different groups held genuinely different understandings of what the founding vision meant and who it included. That fragmentation required a civil war to partially address, and remains unresolved in significant ways.

Yet the American story also shows how transcendent vision can expand over time. The same language that initially excluded—"all men are created equal"—became the basis for movements that demanded inclusion. Frederick Douglass, the women's suffrage movement, and civil rights leaders all appealed to the founding vision while challenging its limited application. They were, in effect, demanding vision equity: insisting that the language be applied to those it had excluded. Transcendent vision, well-articulated, can call organizations to become more than they currently are—but only if its exclusions are named and addressed, not papered over.

The lesson for organizations: Universal language isn't enough. Transcendent vision must be genuinely inclusive in practice, not just in rhetoric. And when stated vision contradicts lived reality for some groups, it becomes a source of cynicism rather than unity—a vision-values gap that erodes trust faster than no vision at all.

The Red Cross and Universal Humanitarian Vision

When Henry Dunant witnessed the Battle of Solferino in 1859, he saw thousands of wounded soldiers from multiple nations left to die without care. His response was to articulate a vision that transcended the national and cultural divisions that had caused the war: care for all wounded soldiers, regardless of which side they fought on.

The Red Cross is a compelling case study precisely because it avoided the fragmentation and drift failures that plague many organizations. Dunant's vision had structural clarity on the five dimensions identified in this chapter. It was rooted in universal values (compassion for suffering, dignity of human life) rather than cultural preferences. It was clear about purpose (relieve suffering impartially) while flexible about execution (how aid is delivered varies by context). It was connected to calling—volunteers didn't join because of organizational affiliation but because of a personal conviction about human dignity. And it was designed for equity—the Red Cross symbol itself was later adapted (Red Crescent, Red Crystal) to honor different cultural and religious sensibilities rather than requiring everyone to work under one culturally specific symbol.

That last point is often overlooked: the Red Cross's willingness to adapt its own symbol rather than insist on uniformity is an act of vision equity in practice. The vision (relieve suffering impartially) remained constant; the cultural expression of membership in that vision was made accessible to people for whom a cross carried different or exclusionary meaning.

The Red Cross also demonstrates something important about the Vision-Change Gap. Organizations built around calling rather than only organizational structure are more resilient during transitions, because when the organizational structure changes, the calling remains. Volunteers who joined because of a personal conviction about human dignity don't lose their anchor when leadership turns over or administrative structures shift. The calling carries what organizational vision alone cannot.

The lesson: Vision that transcends isn't culturally neutral—it's rooted in values broad enough to resonate across cultures while specific enough to guide action. And organizations that build their identity around calling rather than only around institutional purpose are more capable of surviving the structural changes that will inevitably come.

The Biblical View

Scripture demonstrates both the challenge of unity across difference and the power of transcendent vision to create it. Read carefully, the biblical material also illuminates the specific failure modes—fragmentation, drift, vision equity failures—and shows what genuine transcendence looks like in contrast.

Abraham's Vision: A Nation That Blesses All Nations

When God called Abram out of Ur, He gave him a vision that was both radically specific and universally expansive: "I will make you into a great nation, and I will bless you; I will make your name great, and you will be a blessing... and all peoples on earth will be blessed through you" (Genesis 12:2–3).

What is often missed is how this vision addressed what would become the central cultural temptation of Israel: to treat their particular calling as the whole story. The blessing promised was not for Abraham's cultural group—it flowed through that group to all peoples. The vision was, from the beginning, structurally designed to resist cultural insularity. God named the universal scope explicitly, so that no future generation could mistake particular identity for the whole purpose.

This is the vision equity principle in its deepest form. Abraham's calling didn't erase his cultural particularity—he remained a man of his time and place, and his descendants remained a distinct people. But the vision gave his particularity a universal purpose. His cultural identity was honored; it was also relativized. The vision was bigger than the culture that carried it.

Notice also the structure of the promise: the WHAT was specific (descendants, land, blessing), but the HOW remained mysterious for decades. Sarah was barren. They were nomads. The path to fulfillment was completely opaque. Abraham sustained his commitment to the vision through extended periods of not knowing how it would be accomplished—which is to say, through extended periods of what felt like a Vision-Change Gap. The clarity of the calling carried him when the organizational path forward was invisible.

The vision was continuously reinforced across generations. When Isaac nearly lost his life on Mount Moriah, God renewed the promise: "Through your offspring all nations on earth will be blessed" (Genesis 22:18). When Jacob received the covenant, the same universal scope appeared: "All peoples on earth will be blessed through you and your offspring" (Genesis 28:14). This is not accidental repetition—it is the anchoring discipline that prevents vision drift across generations. Every time the story could have narrowed into a merely tribal one, the universal purpose was restated.

The lesson for modern leaders: Transcendent vision connects to needs and values broader than any single cultural group. It must be large enough that no one cultural expression can exhaust it, and specific enough that people know what they're committing to. And it must be repeated at every major transition point, precisely because transitions are when organizations are most vulnerable to narrowing their vision into something smaller than it was meant to be.

Isaiah's Vision: A Light for the Gentiles

The prophet Isaiah received a vision for Israel's calling that repeatedly broke beyond ethnic boundaries—and that spoke directly to the problem of cultural insularity as a form of vision failure. The clearest statement comes in Isaiah 49:6: "It is too small a thing for you to be my servant to restore the tribes of Jacob and bring back those of Israel I have kept. I will also make you a light for the Gentiles, that my salvation may reach to the ends of the earth."

"Too small a thing." God's word to a people who had developed a sophisticated religious culture, an elaborate vision for their own restoration, a complete theological framework for understanding their identity—is that their vision had fragmented into something culturally enclosed. They had drifted from the universal scope of Abraham's calling into a vision defined almost entirely by their own cultural-religious boundaries.

Isaiah's intervention is a vision equity correction at the prophetic level. Israel's particular identity was not erased—they remained God's servant, a specific people with a specific calling. But that particular calling had universal purpose: "a light for the Gentiles." The vision had to expand to include those it had implicitly excluded. The same correction that Frederick Douglass would later demand of the American founding—insist that universal language be applied to those it had excluded—was what God demanded of Israel through Isaiah.

What makes Isaiah's vision structurally transcendent is that it held both the particular and the universal without collapsing either. Israel didn't stop being Israel. The Gentiles didn't become Israel. The vision was large enough to honor both particular identity and universal purpose. That is the goal for multicultural organizations: a vision in which people don't have to abandon their cultural identity to participate, but also can't reduce the whole vision to their cultural expression.

Notice too that this vision involved explicit cost: the Servant would be "despised and rejected" (53:3), bearing "the sin of many" (53:12). Transcendent vision often demands sacrifice from those who carry it—a reality that purely aspirational vision statements conceal. When people sense that the vision costs nothing, they rightly suspect it means nothing. Vision that has genuine stakes, that requires something real from those who hold it, carries a credibility that comfortable mission statements cannot manufacture.

The lesson for modern leaders: Vision that truly transcends names the universal purpose explicitly—and honestly. It tells particular groups clearly that their calling is bigger than themselves, without erasing what makes them who they are. And it does not hide the cost of carrying it.

Philip and the Ethiopian: Vision Breaking Cultural Barriers

Acts 8:26–40 tells the story of Philip, a Greek-speaking Jewish Christian, meeting an Ethiopian court official on a desert road. This encounter demonstrates what happens when vision is genuinely transcendent—when calling, clarity, cultural intelligence, and inclusion work together in real time.

The Ethiopian was an outsider on multiple levels: ethnically African (not Jewish), religiously a God-fearer (likely a eunuch, unable to fully join Israel per Deuteronomy 23:1), geographically from the ends of the known world, and socially a court official serving a foreign queen. From a cultural equity standpoint, he had no access to the existing organizational vision. The existing religious structure had, in effect, designed a vision that excluded him.

Philip's response to the Spirit's direction—"Go to that chariot and stay near it"—demonstrates the first requirement for vision equity: following divine direction even when it leads across cultural comfort zones, before you know where it's going. Philip didn't strategize about how to make the gospel culturally relevant to Ethiopians. He just went.

What he found was a man already reading Isaiah 53—the Suffering Servant passage, the same material that articulated Israel's calling to be a light for the Gentiles. The transcendent vision embedded in Scripture had already created a bridge that Philip didn't have to build. The Ethiopian asked: "Tell me, please, who is the prophet talking about?" The vision had reached him before the messenger arrived.

Notice what Philip did not do: he did not tell the Ethiopian to become more Jewish before receiving the gospel. He did not require cultural conversion as a condition of full inclusion. He began with the text the Ethiopian was already reading and moved from there into the good news about Jesus. This is vision equity in practice: the same core purpose, accessed through the cultural and intellectual framework of the person receiving it—not watered down, not compromised, but genuinely translated.

When they came to water, the Ethiopian asked: "What can stand in the way of my being baptized?" The answer was: nothing. Full inclusion, immediately, without requiring the Ethiopian to stop being Ethiopian. After baptism, he "went on his way rejoicing"—not to Jerusalem, but back to Ethiopia, carrying the vision into his own cultural context. That is what transcendent vision enables: people become full participants in a shared purpose without surrendering the cultural particularity that makes their contribution distinctive.

The lesson for modern leaders: The goal of transcendent vision is not that everyone becomes culturally identical to the organization's founders. It is that everyone can genuinely locate themselves inside the shared purpose—fully included, fully themselves, fully part of the mission. Philip's encounter shows that when vision is genuinely transcendent, cultural barriers become bridges rather than walls. The Ethiopian didn't stop being Ethiopian when he became Christian. That's what you're building toward.

Nuances and Blind Spots

Poster-only vision is worse than no vision. When a beautifully crafted statement lives on walls and websites but never appears in actual decision-making, it doesn't just fail to inspire—it actively breeds cynicism. People learn quickly whether vision is functional or decorative by watching what gets referenced when real choices get made under pressure.

Words that seem universal often aren't. Terms like "empowerment," "excellence," "innovation," and "community" feel universal to the people who coined them, usually because those people share similar cultural frameworks. Across cultures, the same words can land as hollow, threatening, foreign, or simply meaningless. Transcendent vision requires testing language across cultural groups, not just wordsmithing within leadership.

Vision crafted by homogeneous groups reflects their assumptions. When leadership teams lack cultural diversity, their vision naturally encodes their shared—and often unconscious—cultural frameworks, then presents the result as universal. Genuinely transcendent vision requires diverse voices in the crafting process, not just diverse faces in the audience when the finished product is unveiled.

Clarity about "what" matters more than poetry about "why." Many vision statements are eloquent about aspirational values but vague about actual objectives. Vision that can't be connected to daily work by frontline staff isn't transcendent—it's abstract. Concrete purpose that people can see themselves inside is more powerful than beautiful language they can only admire from a distance.

Vision must be translated, not just communicated. Announcing a vision statement isn't the same as creating alignment. Different cultural groups need to hear vision expressed through frameworks that connect to their own—not different messages, but the same core purpose articulated through multiple cultural entry points. When vision doesn't resonate across groups, the reflex of "they just need to understand it better" is almost always the wrong diagnosis.

Alignment requires ongoing work, not a one-time unveiling. Vision alignment isn't established at a launch event—it's built through continuous reinforcement: connecting daily decisions to stated purpose, telling stories that show what vision looks like in practice, checking understanding across cultural groups, and adjusting articulation when it isn't landing.

Vision without resource allocation is just aspiration. People learn what an organization actually values not by reading its wall plaques but by watching what gets funded, rewarded, and protected. If the vision emphasizes relationships but the budget prioritizes efficiency, the real vision is efficiency.

The loudest objections may not be the most important ones. Some cultural frameworks express disagreement vocally; others express it through silence, gradual withdrawal, or quiet non-compliance. Leaders who only respond to audible pushback may remain entirely unaware that vision isn't resonating with their quieter cultural groups—mistaking silence for consensus long past the point where engagement has already been lost.

⸺◆O◆⸺

Try This Week

Choose ONE practice to strengthen transcendent vision:

Practice 1: Share One Vision Story

Instead of repeating vision words, tell a specific story: "Last month when we faced [situation], we chose [action] because [connection to vision]." Make the connection between daily decisions and larger purpose visible. Ask: "Can you think of other times when we lived out this vision?" Collect stories that illustrate vision in practice.

Practice 2: Test Vision Understanding Across Cultures

Ask 3–5 team members from different cultural backgrounds individually: "What is our organization's vision? What does it mean to you? How does your work connect to it?" Don't correct or explain—just listen. Notice where understanding varies. Pay particular attention to whether different cultural groups give systematically different answers—that's a vision equity signal, not just a communication gap.

Practice 3: Name What Isn't Changing

If your organization is currently in any kind of transition—leadership change, structural shift, new initiative, budget pressure—write down three things that are NOT changing, rooted in your vision and values. Share them explicitly with your team this week. Practice closing the Vision-Change Gap proactively rather than waiting for anxiety to surface.

Practice 4: Connect One Decision to Vision

Before announcing any significant choice this week, write down: "We're choosing [option] because it [connection to vision]. This reflects our commitment to [core value]." Share both the decision AND the vision connection. Model making the link explicit rather than assuming everyone sees it.

Practice 5: Audit One System for Vision Alignment

Pick one organizational system (hiring criteria, evaluation rubrics, budget priorities, meeting agendas). Ask: "Does this system reinforce or undermine our stated vision?" Identify one concrete change that would better align system with vision. Implement it.

Reflection Questions

Quick Check (1–2 minutes)

- Can you recite your organization's vision from memory? More importantly, can your team—and does their version match yours?

- Think about the last three major decisions made. Were they explicitly connected to vision? Could you explain how?

- Is your organization currently in a transition of any kind? If so, when did you last explicitly communicate what is NOT changing?

Deeper Reflection

- If you asked team members from different cultural backgrounds what your organization's vision means, would their answers be similar or wildly different? What does that reveal?

- Does your vision statement resonate equally across all cultural groups in your organization? If not, what cultural assumptions might be embedded in how it's articulated—and whose assumptions are they?

- Looking at the past month: Where did you see vision come alive in actual practice? Where did daily pressures override vision commitments?

- What stories does your organization tell about itself? Do those stories illustrate vision in action, or do they focus on something elseentirely?

- Is what your organization funds and rewards actually aligned with what your vision says it values? Where is the gap?

Team Discussion

- As a leadership team, examine your vision statement word byword. For each key term, ask: "What does this word mean in different cultural frameworks? Could it be interpreted in conflicting ways?" Then ask: "What are we REALLY trying to say here? What's the core idea beneath the words?"

- Then ask the harder question: "Who was in the room when we wrote this? Whose cultural assumptions are embedded in it? Who needs to beat the table for a genuine revision?"

Experiment with articulating vision in multiple ways that communicate the same core purpose but might resonate differently across cultural frameworks. The goal isn't to have five different visions—it's to have one vision that can be genuinely translated into multiple cultural languages without losing its core.

⸻◆⸻

Moving Forward

Vision provides direction—the destination toward which a diverse organization moves together. But the research is clear: vision alone doesn't produce the cohesion it promises. It must operate inside a system where consistency, communication, growth culture, and inclusion are all functioning. When one force fails, the others cannot fully compensate.

The executive director in our opening scene discovered that her carefully crafted vision meant different things to different people. The words were universal enough to mean anything—which meant they effectively meant nothing. Moving forward requires more than better wordsmithing. It requires genuinely diverse voices in shaping vision, concrete clarity about what success looks like, continuous connection between vision and daily decisions, translation of vision across cultural frameworks, and particular vigilance during transitions—when the Vision-Change Gap most threatens to undo the work of alignment.

It also requires distinguishing between drift and fragmentation, because the interventions are different. Drift calls for anchoring; fragmentation calls for honest conversation. Both call for humility—the willingness to ask not just "Do people know our vision?" but "Do people own it? And if not, whose cultural assumptions did we build into it that made ownership harder for some than others?"

Abraham understood this: his vision of blessing for all nations united people across generations because it connected to universal human needs while allowing diverse expressions—and because it was continuously re-anchored at every major transition point. Isaiah understood this: his vision explicitly told Israel their calling was bigger than themselves, and named the cost of carrying it. Philip understood this: he included the Ethiopian fully without demanding cultural conversion, and the transcendent vision did its work before Philip even arrived.

For many Christian leaders, faith profoundly shapes their values and vision. But leading from conviction in multicultural contexts requires wisdom: How do you honor the role of calling without reducing it to institutional loyalty? How do you create organizations where the vision is large enough that no one cultural expression can exhaust it—where diverse people are fully included not despite their differences but because of them?

That's the kind of transcendent vision that endures. Not because it found the perfect words, but because it was built by many, tested across cultures, anchored in calling deeper than any organizational structure, and repeated most faithfully in exactly the moments when it was most needed.

Faith, Values, and Workplace Spirituality

Opening Scene

The weekly staff prayer meeting had become increasingly uncomfortable. For the first few years, everyone participated naturally—sharing requests, praying together, weaving faith into work conversations. But as the organization grew more diverse, the dynamics shifted.

Kelly, who came from a Pentecostal background, prayed with passion and length. Michael, from a more reserved Lutheran tradition, shifted uncomfortably at the emotional intensity. Wei, a Buddhist who joined because she believed in the mission, stopped coming entirely. When her supervisor asked why, she said carefully: "I support the organization's Christian foundation. But I feel like I don't belong in those meetings."

Leadership faced a dilemma. Some staff members said: "This is a Christian organization. Prayer is who we are—we shouldn't apologize for it." Others worried: "Are we making people feel excluded? Are we using spiritual language to avoid difficult conversations?"

The tension crystallized in a budget meeting. When discussing staff pay inequities, the executive director said: "I've been praying about this, and I sense God wants us to trust Him with provision rather than focus on comparing salaries." One team member—a committed Christian herself—spoke up: "I appreciate your faith. But 'pray and trust God' can't be the answer to systemic injustice in our pay structure. Faith should drive us toward justice, not become an excuse for avoiding it."

The executive director felt defensive: "Are you saying I'm being unjust?" The team member clarified: "I'm saying that spiritual language doesn't make difficult decisions easier—it should make them more urgent. If we really believe everyone bears God's image, how can we tolerate pay inequities based on arbitrary factors?"

The meeting ended awkwardly. Everyone believed faith mattered. But they were discovering that faith doesn't eliminate complexity—it requires navigating the tension between conviction and coercion, between spiritual richness and respect for different consciences, between values that inspire and values that manipulate.

A Theological Foundation for Workplace Spirituality

Before exploring practice, we need theological grounding for why faith matters in organizational leadership:

1. **Stewardship, Not Ownership**: Christian leaders hold authority as stewards, accountable to God for how they use power, manage resources, and treat people. This fundamentally reframes leadership from "my organization" to "God's organization entrusted to me." Stewardship creates both permission for bold action and constraint against exploitation.

2. **Imago Dei**—Every Person as Image-Bearer: Genesis 1:27 declares: "God created mankind in his own image." This isn't about similarity to God—it's about bearing God's representation on earth. Every human being, regardless of cultural back-

ground, religious belief, or performance level, carries divine dignity. This prohibits treating people as means to ends, resources to extract, or obstacles to manage.

3. **Calling, Not Just Career**: Ephesians 2:10: "We are God's handiwork, created in Christ Jesus to do good works, which God prepared in advance for us to do." Work isn't just about earning income or achieving success—it's about participating in God's purposes. This elevates all legitimate work, not just "ministry," as spiritually significant.

4. **Servant Leadership, Not Self-Advancement**: Jesus's model is explicit: "Whoever wants to become great among you must be your servant, and whoever wants to be first must be slave of all. For even the Son of Man did not come to be served, but to serve, and to give his life as a ransom for many" (Mark 10:43-45). This inverts typical power dynamics—authority exists to serve, not to be served.

5. **Justice as Divine Requirement**: Micah 6:8 provides the clearest summary of what God requires: "He has shown you, O mortal, what is good. And what does the LORD require of you? To act justly and to love mercy and to walk humbly with your God." This isn't optional for faith-informed leaders—justice, mercy, and humility are non-negotiable expressions of authentic faith in organizational practice.

These theological commitments should shape how Christian leaders operate—but the question is HOW to embody them in multicultural contexts where not everyone shares these convictions.

The Challenge of Faith-Informed Leadership

For Christian leaders, faith isn't compartmentalized—it shapes every-thing. How you view people (imago Dei), work (stewardship), justice (biblical imperative), suffering (redemptive purpose), and hope (eternal perspective) all flow from theological convictions. But leading from faith in multicultural contexts introduces genuine tensions. Research on workplace spirituality demonstrates that authentic integration of spiri-tuality with work correlates with increased organizational commitment, job satisfaction, and employee engagement. However, these benefits only appear when spirituality is authentic rather than coercive, inclusive rather than exclusionary.

The opening scene illustrates three common challenges:

1. **Spiritual Pressure Masquerading as Conviction**: When "I've prayed about this" becomes code for "this discussion is closed," spiritual language shuts down rather than enriches dialogue. Faith becomes a trump card that ends conversation instead of a foundation that deepens it.

2. **Cultural Differences in Spiritual Expression**: Wei's discom-fort at prayer meetings wasn't about rejecting Christianity—it was about feeling like one particular expression of Christianity was the only acceptable form. Kelly's passionate prayer was au-thentic to her tradition. Michael's quieter approach was equally authentic. Neither was more spiritual—they were culturally different.

3. **Spiritual Language Avoiding Difficult Realities**: The team member's challenge wasn't rejecting prayer or faith—it was rejecting the use of spiritual language to avoid addressing con-crete injustice. "Trust God" is appropriate when facing circum-stances beyond our control. It's spiritual bypass when applied to problems we have power and responsibility to fix.

Research on responsible leadership in multicultural faith-based organizations emphasizes that value alignment—the consistency between stated values and lived practices—is critical. When spiritual language doesn't match organizational behavior, the resulting authenticity gap erodes trust faster than having no spiritual language at all.

What Research Reveals: Finding Common Moral Ground Across Traditions

One of the most practically useful findings from qualitative research in multicultural Christian organizations is that shared values don't require shared theology. In multicultural environments where staff come from Christian, Confucian, Buddhist, and secular backgrounds, the organizations that functioned best weren't those that required everyone to adopt identical theological convictions—they were those that discovered a shared moral vocabulary across different traditions.

The overlap is more substantial than many leaders realize. Christian commitments to diligence, loyalty, community care, love of learning, and respect for those who came before find a strong resonance in Confucian values around the same themes—not as coincidence, but as a convergence of wisdom traditions developed across centuries of human experience. Likewise, the Buddhist emphasis on compassion, present-mindedness, and the dignity of all sentient beings intersects meaningfully with Christian convictions about imago Dei and servant leadership. These traditions use different language and different theological frameworks, but they often arrive at strikingly similar ethical commitments in the workplace.

This matters enormously for faith-informed leaders. The temptation in Christian organizations is to frame all values conversations in explicitly Christian language—which creates an implicit test that non-Christian or differently-Christian staff cannot fully pass. The wiser practice is what might be called moral vocabulary mapping: looking for where your tradition's deepest commitments overlap with the language and frameworks that colleagues from other backgrounds bring.

The leader who says "we treat every person with dignity because they bear God's image" is making a genuinely Christian claim. The leader who adds "and I know that resonates in different ways for each of you based on your own convictions—but it lands us in the same place" is practicing moral vocabulary mapping. The destination—human dignity, fairness, care for the vulnerable—is shared even when the route that leads there differs.

When Spiritual Language Gets Weaponized: The Institutional Stress Pattern

Research across multicultural Christian organizations surfaces a pattern that leaders rarely intend but frequently create: spiritual bypass tends to appear not randomly, but predictably—at the precise moment when leaders feel most exposed and most in need of a rationale for inaction.

When organizations are under genuine stress—resource scarcity, declining enrollment or revenue, leadership instability, high staff turnover—the pressure on leaders intensifies. Budgets that should be addressed get deferred. Systemic problems that require structural change feel overwhelming. Honest conversations about organizational survival feel too frightening to have. In these moments, spiritual language becomes especially tempting as a cover: "God will provide." "We just need to trust more." "This is a season of refining."

None of these statements is theologically false. God does provide. Trust does matter. Difficulty can refine. The problem is not the theology—it's the timing and function. When these phrases appear in response to problems that the leader actually has the power and responsibility to address, they cease to be expressions of faith and become expressions of avoidance. Staff—especially those without institutional power—learn to recognize the difference between a leader who prays while also acting and a leader who prays instead of acting.

One research finding is particularly striking: in organizations that had navigated significant change and instability, the spiritual language most associated with trust erosion wasn't hostile or manipulative in intent. Leaders who genuinely believed what they were saying deployed it. Their problem wasn't insincerity—it was a failure to distinguish between circumstances genuinely beyond their control (where trust and prayer are entirely appropriate responses) and circumstances within their control that required decision, action, and accountability.

The diagnostic question is simple: Do I have the power to change this? If yes, spiritual language that substitutes for action is spiritual bypass. If no—if the circumstance genuinely lies outside your agency—then faith-filled trust is the appropriate and honest response.

Crucibles of change—seasons of organizational hardship, instability, and stress—can either refine leaders or calcify them. The difference often lies precisely here: whether the hard season drives them toward honest assessment and courageous action, or toward the comfort of spiritual language that protects them from having to act. The leaders who emerge from difficult seasons more trusted are those who said both "we are praying" and "here is what we are doing"—and who demonstrated that their faith made the hard decisions more urgent, not less.

The Compounding Effect: Spiritual Language and Cultural Hierarchy

Research in multicultural organizations with high-power-distance cultural dynamics—settings where deference to authority is deeply embedded as a cultural norm—reveals a compounding effect that leaders in Western Christian contexts frequently miss entirely. In many Asian, Latin American, African, and Middle Eastern cultural contexts, challenging a leader's decision publicly is not merely uncomfortable—it violates a deep social script about appropriate respect and relational harmony. Staff from these backgrounds often communicate concern indirectly, through trusted intermediaries, or in private rather than public challenge. Their silence in group settings doesn't indicate agreement; it indicates cultural respect for hierarchy.

When spiritual language is added on top of this existing cultural dynamic, the silencing effect compounds dramatically. Consider what happens when a leader in a high-power-distance context says "I've prayed about this, and I believe God is directing us to proceed." The staff member who was already culturally constrained from challenging the leader now faces a double bind: to disagree is simultaneously to commit a cultural transgression (challenging the authority figure) and a spiritual one (questioning God's direction). The cost of speaking up has just doubled—and the incentive to stay silent has never been higher.

This is not a hypothetical risk. Qualitative research in multicultural Christian organizations consistently finds that staff from high-power-distance backgrounds are most likely to report feeling unable to raise concerns, most likely to internalize spiritual pressure as both cultural and theological constraint, and most likely to exit the organization quietly rather than advocate for change. Leadership often interprets their departure as personal rather than systemic—which means the pattern repeats.

Leaders who genuinely want honest input from multicultural teams must understand that creating the conditions for honest voice requires actively dismantling the compounding effect. This means separating institutional decisions from theological claims (saying "I believe this is the right direction" rather than "God told me to do this"), creating private and indirect feedback pathways that honor high-power-distance cultural frameworks (not just relying on open-meeting input), and explicitly inviting disagreement in ways that make cultural safety as clear as spiritual openness.

The Authenticity Gap as Spiritual Injury

Research consistently demonstrates that gaps between stated values and actual practices erode trust in any organization. But in faith-based organizations, the authenticity gap produces a harm that goes deeper than ordinary trust damage—it inflicts what can only be called spiritual injury. In secular organizations, when stated values don't match lived practices, staff feel deceived and disillusioned. In Christian organizations, when stated spiritual values don't match lived organizational experience, staff feel spiritually deceived—and the damage extends to their relationship with the values themselves. When an organization proclaims that it values servant leadership, imago Dei, and Micah 6:8 justice, but practices favoritism, opaque decision-making, and uneven support, staff don't just experience poor management. They experience a form of spiritual betrayal that calls into question whether the values themselves are real or merely useful language.

The pain isn't just that leadership didn't live up to their stated values—it's that leadership used the language of those values to justify or obscure unjust practices. When "we're a grace-filled community" becomes a cover for avoiding accountability, and when "God's provision" becomes language for inadequate compensation, staff don't just distrust the leader—they can begin to distrust the language of faith itself.

This is why the team member in the opening scene was responding to something more than a management failure. Her pushback wasn't primarily a critique of the executive director's budgetary reasoning—it was a defense of faith itself against being co-opted to justify injustice. When she said "faith should make this more urgent, not provide language for avoiding it," she was articulating what research confirms: the authenticity gap in faith-based organizations isn't merely an organizational problem. It's a theological one.

The practical implication is serious. The larger the gap between spiritual language and organizational practice, the more toxic the environment becomes—not just for morale, but for people's relationship with faith in the workplace. Faith-informed leaders carry a specific responsibility that their secular counterparts do not: to steward the credibility of the values they invoke. Using those values instrumentally—to motivate or silence rather than to genuinely shape practice—corrupts the organizational culture in ways that are harder to repair than ordinary trust damage.

The Devotional Life of the Organization: Asset or Liability?

One of the more counterintuitive findings from research in multicultural Christian organizations is this: shared daily spiritual practices—morning devotions, communal prayer, values-based reflection embedded in the workday—function as a powerful retention and resilience mechanism that secular organizations simply cannot replicate through compensation alone.

In organizations facing resource constraints, high turnover, and competitive pressure, staff who participate authentically in shared spiritual practices report staying committed for reasons that go beyond salary or career advancement. The sense of participating in something with eternal significance, of working alongside people who share a common calling, and of having institutional anchors that provide meaning during difficult seasons creates a form of organizational loyalty that organizational behavior research calls "normative commitment"—staying not because of what you get but because of what you believe.

This is genuine organizational strength. It explains why faith-based organizations can often retain gifted staff at below-market compensation, why staff persist through seasons of institutional difficulty that would trigger mass exodus in purely transactional environments, and why the culture of many Christian organizations carries a quality of care and mutual investment that peers in secular settings sometimes find remarkable.

But the research reveals the limit with equal clarity: the same practices that anchor and retain some staff can actively alienate others—depending entirely on how they are conducted, who designs them, whose cultural expression of faith is privileged, and whether participation feels genuinely voluntary or subtly coerced.

Wei's departure from the prayer meeting illustrates this precisely. Her absence wasn't a rejection of the organization's Christian mission—she believed in the mission enough to work there. It was a response to a practice that had become culturally exclusive without anyone intending it to be. The meeting had drifted from being an expression of shared commitment into being an expression of one tradition's particular form—and that form communicated, implicitly but powerfully, that some people belonged more fully than others.

Research in this area suggests three conditions that determine whether shared spiritual practices function as organizational assets or liabilities:

1. **Voluntary participation without social penalty**. Staff who feel they must attend to demonstrate loyalty—or who feel their absence will be noted and judged—are not participating freely. Coerced spiritual participation produces performance rather than authenticity, and performance is corrosive to the culture that these practices are meant to create.

2. **Cultural diversity in practice design**. Organizations that rely on a single cultural expression of faith for all communal spiritual practices inadvertently signal that one tradition is more legitimately "Christian" than others. Rotating leadership, honoring different styles of prayer and reflection, and explicitly welcoming diverse expressions communicates that the Spirit moves across cultures—not just through the dominant one.

3. **Integration with concrete practice, not substitution for it**. Devotional life is strengthening when it drives people toward the hard work that faith demands: justice, honesty, generosity, accountability. It becomes a liability when it substitutes

for that work—when the prayer meeting replaces the difficult conversation, or when "God is in control" replaces the leader's responsibility to act.

When Faith Functions Well—And When It Doesn't

Faith in organizational leadership can create tremendous strength—or significant harm. The difference lies in how it's embodied.

<u>When Faith Functions Well</u>

- **Motivation Through Difficulty**: Faith provides resources for perseverance when circumstances are hard. The conviction that God is present in suffering, that setbacks aren't final, that faithfulness matters more than immediate success—these beliefs sustain leaders and teams through difficulty without denying the pain.

- **Framework for Navigating Conflict**: Biblical principles about reconciliation, truth-telling, forgiveness, and justice provide guidance for addressing conflict constructively. Faith doesn't eliminate disagreement but can shape how disagreement is handled.

- **Source of Resilience**: Research on religious coping demonstrates that positive religious coping correlates with better psychological adjustment and health outcomes. Leaders who draw on faith for strength without imposing it on others model healthy resilience.

- **Common Ground Across Cultural Difference**: In multicultural Christian organizations, shared faith often creates stronger bonds than national or ethnic identity. And as research in cross-cultural settings reveals, the moral vocabulary of faith—dignity, justice, care, diligence—finds resonance even in traditions that approach the same commitments from different theological starting points.

<u>When Faith Functions Poorly</u>

- **Spiritual Pressure to Silence Dissent**: "Have you prayed about this?" or "Where's your faith?" used to shut down legitimate concerns. Questioning decisions gets reframed as questioning God. Disagreement becomes spiritual rebellion. In high-power-distance cultural contexts, this silencing effect is especially severe—as the compounding dynamic discussed earlier makes clear.

- **Theological Gatekeeping**: Subtle (or explicit) messages that only those from certain theological traditions, with certain doctrinal positions, or expressing faith in certain ways fully belong. This fractures rather than unites.

- **Performance Spirituality**: Creating pressure to demonstrate piety through language, participation in spiritual activities, or visible devotion. People learn to perform spirituality for acceptance rather than integrating it authentically. The devotional practices that should anchor organizational culture instead become tests of belonging.

- **Covering for Dysfunction**: Using spiritual language to avoid addressing concrete problems. "God will provide" substituting for responsible budgeting. This pattern tends to intensify under institutional stress—the very moments when honest leadership is most needed.

The cost of spiritual dysfunction is severe: authenticity gap (people can't be honest), trust erosion (spiritual language becomes manipulative), moral injury (faith gets associated with harm), innovation suppression (can't question what's framed as God's will), and talent exodus (gifted people leave rather than navigate toxic spirituality).

The Historical View

History offers compelling examples of faith shaping workplace practice—both for good and for ill.

The Quaker Business Revolution

In eighteenth and nineteenth century England, Quakers (Society of Friends) transformed business ethics through faith-informed practice. Though a small minority—never more than one percent of the population—Quakers founded and led businesses like Barclays Bank, Lloyds Bank, Cadbury, and Rowntree—companies that pioneered ethical business practices.

Several Quaker theological convictions shaped their revolutionary approach. Their belief in integrity as spiritual discipline led to fixed prices at a time when haggling was standard, quality products without deception, and honest advertising. Their conviction that "that of God" existed in every person—not just in fellow Quakers, not just in Christians, but in every human being—gave them an instinctive expectation that moral wisdom and human dignity would be found across different backgrounds and traditions. This is moral vocabulary mapping in historical practice: the Quakers employed skilled workers who didn't share their faith, extended the benefits of their theological convictions to those who held different beliefs, and found that the values resonated across the difference.

George Cadbury explicitly rejected the idea that business existed primarily to enrich owners—he believed it existed to serve workers, customers, and communities. Quaker meetings practiced corporate discernment where business decisions were examined by the faith community, creating accountability that prevented the misuse of spiritual language. Business owners couldn't invoke God's direction to justify practices their faith community would scrutinize—a structural constraint on spiritual bypass that most modern Christian organizations lack.

The lesson: Faith-informed values work in multicultural contexts when they're lived authentically, create genuine benefit for all stakeholders, welcome people who don't share the faith but appreciate its practical expression, and are held accountable by communities rather than claimed unilaterally by leaders.

The Guinness Brewery

In 1759, Arthur Guinness signed a 9,000-year lease on a brewery at St. James's Gate in Dublin. What emerged was not just a successful business but a model of faith-informed care for workers that would influence industrial practices across Europe.

The Guinness family's Christian conviction about human dignity translated into concrete daily practices decades before they became industry standard: free healthcare for workers and their families, quality housing at below-market rates, schools for workers' children, libraries, skill development programs, above-market wages, and pension plans. By 1890, Guinness workers received benefits that wouldn't become standard in British industry for another sixty years.

What made Guinness remarkable connects directly to the research finding about devotional practices as organizational assets. The family's faith convictions weren't expressed primarily through mandatory chapel attendance or spiritual performance—they were expressed through the structural and material conditions of workers' lives. The theological conviction (imago Dei—every worker bears God's image) produced tangible workplace practices that benefited workers who didn't share the family's Christian beliefs. This is the distinction that matters: faith-informed convictions landing in justice and dignity for everyone, rather than faith-informed language requiring performance from those who don't share the faith.

The lesson: When faith drives leaders toward justice and human dignity rather than justifying exploitation, it creates environments where people flourish—regardless of whether they share the underlying theological convictions. The authenticity is verified not by spiritual language but by structural reality.

Toyohiko Kagawa: Faith That Moved into the Slums

In 1909, a young Japanese seminary student named Toyohiko Kagawa made a decision that shocked his peers. He moved into the Shinkawa slum of Kobe—then one of Japan's most desperate neighborhoods—taking a six-foot-square shack as his home. He stayed for fourteen years. The choice wasn't symbolic. It was theological: he had read the Sermon on the Mount and concluded that faith without incarnational presence wasn't faith at all.

What Kagawa built from that shack offers a direct response to the compounding silence problem identified in research. His authority came not from his theological position or organizational role, but from his willingness to share the conditions of those he led. In a high-power-distance cultural context—Japan in the early twentieth century—Kagawa's downward movement was itself a dismantling of the hierarchy that silences. He organized Japan's first modern labor unions and founded agricultural and consumer cooperatives that gave workers structural voice, not just the invitation to speak in a meeting designed by those with power.

His cross-cultural witness is particularly instructive. Kagawa's Japanese Christian convictions produced outcomes that resonated across cultural boundaries precisely because authentic faith expressed through concrete justice proves universally legible. Western missionaries came to observe. Labor movements in other countries studied his cooperative models. He didn't adapt his message to Western sensibilities or require others to adopt his cultural expression of Christianity—he embodied the moral vocabulary of justice, dignity, and solidarity in ways that translated across difference.

The contrast with coercive faith is instructive. Kagawa's authority came from his willingness to share the conditions of those he led, not from his position above them. Faith that moves toward people, rather than requiring people to perform for it, creates something different—communities where dignity isn't just preached but structurally protected.

The Biblical View

Scripture consistently presents faith as shaping practice, not just private belief. Several examples illuminate healthy integration—and the research findings above give us new eyes to see what these examples are actually demonstrating.

Lydia: Moral Vocabulary Across Difference

Acts 16 introduces Lydia, "a dealer in purple cloth from the city of Thyatira, who was a worshiper of God." Several details matter—including one that speaks directly to the moral vocabulary question.

Lydia was already "a worshiper of God" before encountering the full gospel. She had arrived at genuine faith convictions through a path that didn't follow the expected route—a Gentile woman, a businesswoman in a male-dominated trade, drawn to the synagogue in Philippi as a God-fearer without being fully Jewish. Her integrity and business practice were faith-shaped before her theology was complete. When Paul spoke, she recognized the fuller expression of what she had already been reaching toward.

What Lydia demonstrates is precisely what research confirms: shared moral ground can precede shared theology. Her business success was built on convictions that hadn't yet found their full theological home.

When they did, she responded immediately—not because faith was new to her, but because the fuller vocabulary finally matched what she had already been living. Her home became the meeting place for the Philippian church: a space where faith had already been expressed concretely, through integrity, competence, and generosity, long before the formal community gathered.

For multicultural leaders, Lydia is a model of what to look for in people from different backgrounds: not whether their theological vocabulary is complete, but whether their lives already evidence the moral commitments that their tradition—whatever it is—calls forth. The moral vocabulary mapping the leader does isn't creating alignment where none exists; it's recognizing alignment that was already there.

The Jerusalem Church's Economic Practice: Authenticity Without Coercion

Acts 2 and 4 describe the early church's radical economic sharing: "All the believers were together and had everything in common. They sold property and possessions to give to anyone who had need" (Acts 2:44-45). "There were no needy persons among them" (Acts 4:34).

This wasn't coerced—it was the organic expression of shared faith and mutual love. When Ananias and Sapphira tried to deceive the community about their giving (Acts 5), Peter's rebuke makes clear the giving was voluntary: "Didn't it belong to you before it was sold? And after it was sold, wasn't the money at your disposal?" (Acts 5:4). The sin wasn't keeping some money—it was lying about it.

Notice what the Ananias and Sapphira story reveals about the authenticity gap as spiritual injury. Their deception wasn't merely financial fraud—it was the use of spiritual performance (the appearance of radical generosity) to claim spiritual status they hadn't earned. Peter names it as lying "not just to human beings but to God" (Acts 5:4). The early church understood that using the language and appearance of faith to claim belonging you aren't living is a qualitatively different kind of harm than ordinary deception. It corrupts the community's spiritual currency.

Leaders who use spiritual language to perform values they aren't embodying are doing something structurally similar—with consequences that research confirms are proportionally severe. The authenticity gap in faith-based organizations is costly precisely because, as in the Jerusalem church, the spiritual stakes are higher when faith is invoked. When faith is authentic, generosity flows naturally. When it's coerced or performed, resentment—and, as research confirms, eventually moral injury—builds.

Proverbs and Daniel: Faith That Works Across Cultural Power Distance

Proverbs repeatedly connects faith to work practices: "The LORD detests dishonest scales, but accurate weights find favor with him" (11:1). These aren't uniquely Israelite values in their practical expression—neighboring cultures had similar commercial ethics—but for believers they are grounded in theological conviction about God's character and requirements. They represent exactly the kind of moral vocabulary overlap that research identifies: different traditions, same commitment to fairness in practice.

Daniel offers the most direct biblical engagement with the high-power-distance compounding problem. Daniel served in Babylon—an empire with maximum power distance between the king and everyone else. His faithfulness required navigating a context where challenging authority could cost him his life, where spiritual language was constantly weaponized by those in power, and where the pressure to perform loyalty was extreme.

What Daniel demonstrates is a path through the double bind: he maintained deep personal conviction without requiring others to adopt his theological framework, found ways to serve with excellence in a pluralistic environment, expressed his conscientious objections through structured dialogue rather than direct confrontation (Daniel 1's negotiated dietary arrangement rather than public refusal), and built the kind of credibility over time that gave him standing to speak difficult truths to power when it mattered most. His authority didn't come from claiming divine direction for every decision—it came from demonstrated integrity that made his convictions legible even to those who didn't share them.

For leaders navigating multicultural environments with high-power-distance dynamics, Daniel's example is clarifying: faithfulness doesn't require constantly invoking theological authority. Sometimes it requires the kind of patient, consistent integrity that earns standing to speak—without creating the double bind that spiritual claims layer onto cultural hierarchy.

Nuances and Blind Spots

Spiritual language can close conversations rather than open them. "God told me" or "I've been praying about this" can signal genuine discernment—or it can signal that the decision is already made and dissent will be read as opposing God. The same phrase creates entirely different experiences depending on the listener's history, cultural background, and position in the organization. In high-power-distance contexts, this isn't merely uncomfortable—it creates the double bind that research identifies as the primary driver of exit among staff from those backgrounds.

Authenticity matters more than intensity. Quiet, consistent embodiment of values builds more trust than passionate spiritual rhetoric. The leader who reliably treats people with dignity does more for faith's credibility than the one who speaks eloquently about it while the gap between stated values and actual practices quietly widens. When compassion, integrity, and justice are the stated values but exploitation, deception, and inequity are the lived experience, the spiritual language doesn't soften that contradiction—it deepens the injury.

Theological gatekeeping creates hierarchy where there should be community. Subtle messages that only certain expressions of faith are acceptable—the right vocabulary, the right emotional register, the right tradition—create a tiered spirituality where some people are quietly marked as "more spiritual" than others. The research finding about shared devotional practices applies here: the same practices that create belonging for some create exclusion for others, depending entirely on whose cultural expression defines the default.

Cultural expressions of faith vary dramatically—and legitimately. What feels reverent in one tradition feels cold in another. What feels Spirit-filled in one tradition feels chaotic in another. Organizations with cultural diversity also contain diversity in how faith is practiced, expressed, and integrated into work. Leaders who privilege one cultural form of spiritual expression as the standard aren't protecting orthodoxy—they're enforcing cultural conformity under a theological label.

Faith doesn't replace competence, and grace doesn't replace accountability. "We're a ministry, not a business" can quietly become cover for poor systems, inadequate training, and tolerated incompetence. Biblical stewardship demands doing things well. Similarly, organizations that use "grace" to avoid difficult conversations have confused kindness with avoidance. Grace-filled organizations can still have honest feedback, clear expectations, and real consequences for harmful behavior.

Spiritual bypass is a genuine danger—and it is most predictable under pressure. When institutions face genuine stress, the temptation to substitute spiritual language for courageous action intensifies precisely when courageous action is most needed. The diagnostic question: do I have the power to change this? If yes, "just trust God" is bypass. If no, trusting God is genuinely appropriate. The honest leader knows the difference and refuses to use the language of faith to cover what is actually a failure of leadership will.

Vulnerability builds more trust than projected certainty. Leaders who admit doubt, struggle, and uncertainty create space for others to be honest about their own. Leaders who perform constant spiritual confidence create pressure for everyone around them to fake a certainty they don't feel. Faith that has room for lament, questions, and wrestling is more honest—and ultimately more trustworthy—than faith that only displays triumph.

The quiet servants are often the truest measure. People who faithfully embody values through humble, unremarkable service frequently go unrecognized while those who perform spirituality visibly get rewarded. When an organization's recognition patterns consistently elevate spiritual rhetoric over authentic practice, it has inverted what it claims to value—and the people paying closest attention will notice.

Try This Week

Choose ONE practice to embody healthy faith-informed leadership:

Practice 1: Acknowledge One Hard Reality Without Spiritual Clichés

Find one difficult situation and name it honestly without immediately spiritualizing it. Instead of "God will work this out" or "We just need to trust more," try: "This is genuinely hard. I don't have easy answers. But I believe we can find a way forward together." Honesty builds more trust than spiritual platitudes.

Practice 2: Do a Moral Vocabulary Check

In your next discussion of a core value or decision, try naming it in your own tradition's language, then asking: "Does this connect with how you think about it from your background?" Notice where moral common ground already exists. Build from the overlap rather than requiring theological alignment as the price of full belonging.

Practice 3: Bypass Audit

Ask yourself honestly: Where am I using spiritual language in response to problems I actually have the power to change? List three organizational problems you've referenced faith about in the last month. For each one, ask: Is this genuinely outside my control—or am I avoiding the difficult decision I need to make? Choose one and act.

Practice 4: Highlight Quiet Service

Identify someone who embodies organizational values through humble, consistent service without drawing attention to themselves. Thank them publicly and specifically: "The way you [specific action] reflects our commitment to [value]. This is what living our values looks like." Make visible the service that spiritual performance often obscures.

Practice 5: Invite Non-Spiritual Feedback

Ask someone you trust: "I want to lead with integrity. Where do you see gaps between our stated values and actual practices? I won't get defensive—I genuinely want to know." Listen completely before responding. Thank them. Follow up with action within a week.

Reflection Questions

Quick Check (1-2 minutes)

- If you asked team members anonymously whether they feel free to disagree with leadership, what percentage would say yes?

- When was the last time you admitted uncertainty or mistake without softening it with spiritual language?

Deeper Reflection (5-10 minutes)

- Where might you be using faith language to avoid addressing concrete problems you have power to fix? What would change if you took responsibility instead of spiritualizing?

- Think about your organization's communal spiritual practices.

Who feels anchored by them? Who might feel excluded or pressured by them? What would you need to change for both groups to experience them as genuine rather than performative?

- If someone from a different faith tradition or no faith observed your organization for a month, what would they say you actually value based on behavior, not stated beliefs?

- Who on your team might be experiencing the double bind—feeling both cultural and spiritual pressure not to raise concerns? What signals—subtle or obvious—create that pressure?

Team Discussion (15-30 minutes)

- As a leadership team, discuss: "What are our three most important values?" Then ask: "What behaviors or decisions from the past month demonstrate those values? What behaviors or decisions contradict them?" Be honest about gaps. Then ask the harder question: "Where have we used spiritual language in ways that may have functioned to close conversations rather than open them? What would we do differently?" Pick one gap and create a concrete plan to close it in the next 90 days.

Moving Forward

Faith-informed values create organizational culture at its best—inspiring purpose, shaping character, calling people to something larger than themselves. The Quakers demonstrated that authentic faith produces practices that benefit everyone, including those who don't share the faith, and that moral wisdom finds resonance across traditions when leaders take the time to look for it. The Guinness family showed that conviction about human dignity translates into tangible improvements in workers' lives—regardless of whether those workers share the family's theology. Kagawa showed that faith that moves toward people rather than requiring performance from them builds communities where dignity is structurally protected, not just proclaimed. Lydia modeled business competence integrated with faith-shaped generosity, and demonstrated that moral alignment can precede theological alignment. The early church demonstrated economic sharing that was generous without being coercive—and showed, through the Ananias and Sapphira story, that the authenticity gap in faith-based communities carries specifically spiritual stakes.

But the opening scene reminds us that faith doesn't eliminate complexity—it requires navigating it. The prayer meeting that excluded Wei. The budget discussion where spiritual language avoided hard questions. The different cultural expressions of faith that created friction rather than unity. The silent staff member from a high-power-distance background who found herself facing a double bind every time institutional decisions were framed as divine direction. These aren't failures of faith; they're failures to embody faith with wisdom across difference.

What research in multicultural Christian organizations consistently confirms is this: the organizations that navigate these tensions well are not those with the most spiritual language—they are those with the smallest gap between spiritual language and organizational practice. They are those whose leaders distinguish between circumstances that genuinely require trust and circumstances that require action. They are those whose communal spiritual practices are voluntary, culturally inclusive, and integrated with concrete justice rather than substituting for it. They are those whose leaders actively dismantle the double bind rather than inadvertently constructing it.

The executive director's challenge wasn't whether to lead from faith—it was how to lead from faith in ways that honored conviction without coercion, created space for diverse expressions, and drove toward justice rather than away from it. Her team member was right: if we really believe everyone bears God's image, and if we take Micah 6:8 seriously about acting justly and loving mercy, then faith should make addressing inequity more urgent, not provide language for avoiding it.

Values get tested most severely not in ideal circumstances but in crisis. When resources run short, when budgets get cut, when pressures mount—that's when authentic values prove themselves or reveal themselves as mere rhetoric. And it's precisely in those moments that the temptation to reach for spiritual language as a substitute for courageous action is strongest.

The leaders who build organizations where faith genuinely flourishes are those who resist that temptation—who let their convictions drive them toward the hard work that faithfulness actually demands, who cultivate the shared moral vocabulary that creates belonging across difference, and who hold themselves accountable not just to the language of faith but to its fruits.

Practices to Offset Scarcity Mindset

Opening Scene

The email from the board chair landed in the executive director's inbox at 4:47 PM on Friday: "Budget projections show 18% shortfall for next fiscal year. Need plan for cuts by Monday board meeting."

Sarah sat staring at the screen, her stomach knotting. Eighteen percent. That wasn't trimming around the edges—that was eliminating entire positions, cutting programs, or both. She pulled up the org chart, mentally calculating: two staff positions would get them to 15%. Cutting the newest program would add another 5%. But the newest program served the community with the greatest need. And the two newest staff members were the only ones from minority backgrounds.

Over the weekend, she drafted three scenarios. Each felt like choosing who to harm. Option A: Cut junior staff (least expensive, most culturally diverse). Option B: Cut newest program (serves most vulnerable population). Option C: Ask remaining staff to take 15% pay cuts (keeps everyone but creates hardship for those already stretched financially).

Monday morning, she presented the options to the leadership team.

The operations director immediately favored Option A: "Last hired, first fired—that's standard. It's not about diversity, it's about seniority and budget math." The programs director pushed back: "We just spent two years recruiting diverse staff. Cutting them first sends a clear message about who we value." The finance director added: "Option C sounds fair but it's not—15% pay cut is manageable for those making $80K. It's devastating for those making $35,000."

The conversation revealed what scarcity does: it turns colleagues into competitors, forces impossible choices, and tempts leaders to make decisions based on what's easiest rather than what's right. Sarah felt pressure to decide quickly, pressure to appear decisive and in control. But rushing this decision to relieve her own discomfort could damage the organization for years.

"I know the board wants an answer today," she finally said. "But I'm not ready to give one. These decisions will shape our culture for the next decade. We need to make them well, not just quickly."

The room fell silent. Some faces showed relief. Others showed anxiety about the uncertainty. But something shifted: they weren't just reacting to scarcity—they were choosing how to navigate it. And crucially, Sarah hadn't yet asked the question that would prove most important: not just "what do we cut?" but "who bears the weight of what we decide—and is that just?"

The Reality and Psychology of Scarcity

Every organization eventually faces scarcity—declining revenue, budget cuts, resource constraints, unexpected financial pressures. How leaders navigate scarcity reveals their true values more than any vision statement or stated commitment. Research on scarcity mindset demonstrates that resource constraints don't just limit what we can do—they fundamentally alter how we think. Scarcity creates cognitive load, narrows focus to immediate concerns, reduces capacity for long-term thinking, and increases the likelihood of making decisions we later regret.

The scarcity trap operates this way: when resources are tight, we focus intensely on the immediate shortage. This narrow focus causes us to neglect other important considerations—relationships, values, long-term consequences. We make decisions that address the immediate problem but create larger problems downstream. Then those new problems demand immediate attention, perpetuating the cycle.

In multicultural organizations, scarcity creates additional and compounding challenges. Budget cuts often impact those with least power most severely: junior staff, who are frequently more culturally diverse, get laid off while senior staff, who are frequently less so, remain. Programs serving marginalized communities get cut while core programs—often serving majority populations—continue. When organizations respond to scarcity by cutting staff, freezing development, or reducing benefits, trust declines. People feel expendable. Cultural minorities, already navigating additional barriers in the workplace, become particularly cautious about investing in organizational success when they see others treated as disposable.

Scarcity also pressures organizations toward decisions with immediate financial benefit but long-term cultural cost. Eliminating professional development saves money now but hampers capability building. Cutting diversity initiatives shows quick savings but abandons hard-won progress. And when resources are limited, teams can shift from collaboration to competition—departments protecting their budgets, individuals hoarding information, everyone looking out for themselves. This competitive scarcity mindset is particularly damaging in multicultural contexts where trust already requires extra intentionality.

Research on resource dependence shows that how organizations manage scarcity determines long-term sustainability more than how they manage abundance. Organizations that respond to scarcity with panic, short-term thinking, and value compromise often don't survive. Those that navigate scarcity with wisdom, maintain values, and think long-term emerge stronger.

The Grief Arc of Organizational Scarcity

Change never unfolds in a straight line. Organizational researchers have long noted the parallel between how individuals process loss and how organizations process crisis: there is shock, then denial, then anger or blame, then bargaining, then a period of low energy and depression, and finally—if leadership holds—a horizon of hope and reorientation. Most organizations don't move through these stages cleanly. They cycle. They get stuck. They rush forward before grief has been acknowledged, then collapse back into the earlier stages.

Leaders and staff navigating sustained scarcity, high turnover, and leadership transition often describe their situation in strikingly similar terms: frenetic hope, the sense of simultaneously responding to residual consequences of earlier crises while planning a reorganization for the future. This is the bargaining stage made visible. The bargaining stage is distinctive: it is characterized by a kind of frenetic hope, a belief that the right combination of policy changes, restructuring, or effort can forestall further loss. It is a stage where leaders are tempted to overpromise and where followers are tempted to perform stability they don't actually feel.

What makes the bargaining stage particularly risky in multicultural organizations is that different cultural backgrounds shape how people interpret these organizational signals. Staff from contexts where institutions have historically failed them may read bargaining-stage optimism as a precursor to abandonment. Those whose cultural frameworks emphasize collective endurance may quietly absorb distress without naming it. And those who rely on spiritual resources—prayer, faith community, a sense of divine providence—may appear untroubled to a leader watching for visible signs of anxiety, while carrying significant internal weight.

Leadership at each stage of the grief arc looks different. In the shock and denial phases, the leader's primary task is honest naming: this is real, this is serious, here is what we know. In the anger and blame phases, the task is to receive that anger without deflecting it and to resist the temptation to manage rather than hear it. In the bargaining phase—where most organizations spend the longest time—the task is to differentiate between realistic hope and false optimism, to make commitments that can actually be kept, and to protect people from the exhaustion of performing recovery before it has arrived. In the depression phase, the task is presence: showing up, maintaining care, refusing to let institutional memory evaporate while waiting for conditions to improve.

And when hope genuinely begins to return, the leader's task is to name it publicly and specifically, to celebrate what has been rebuilt, and to resist the powerful temptation to pretend the difficult period never happened. Organizations that skip the honest reckoning rarely develop the resilience to navigate the next crisis well.

How People Actually Respond to Scarcity and Change

One of the most practically significant patterns that emerges in multicultural organizations under stress is that people do not respond uniformly. Three distinct groups emerge—not defined primarily by role or seniority, but by how individuals orient themselves toward difficulty. Understanding these groups is not about placing people in fixed categories. It's about recognizing that different people need meaningfully different things from leadership during hard seasons, and that a one-size-fits-all response to organizational crisis will serve some people reasonably well and others not at all.

The first group are the active fighters. These individuals stay engaged under pressure. They push through, maintain their energy, and often seek out additional ways to contribute when the organization is struggling. They are assets in a crisis—but they are also the most likely to burn out if leadership doesn't manage their workload realistically. Active fighters can carry an organization through a difficult season, but they cannot carry it indefinitely, and their visible engagement can mask how depleted they actually are. What they need from leaders is clear direction, permission to innovate and adapt, and honest workload calibration. They need to be told: "Your effort is visible and valued, and we are paying attention to sustainability."

The second group are the accepters and compromisers. These individuals comply, adjust, and go with the flow. They are not disengaged; they are adaptive. They do what is asked without loud resistance, often because they have learned—from previous organizational experiences or from cultural backgrounds that emphasize deference to authority—that visible opposition carries risk. The danger with this group is that leaders can mistake their compliance for genuine alignment. Accepters and compromisers often have significant concerns that they never voice, not because they don't have them, but because no structure has been created where voicing them feels safe. What they need from leaders is regular, private check-ins, specific affirmation that their contributions are seen, and genuine invitation to participate in shaping solutions. They need evidence that voice is actually welcomed, not just formally available.

The third group are the faith-reliers. These individuals draw their primary stability from spiritual resources—prayer, religious community, a sense that a larger divine purpose is at work even in difficult circumstances. In organizations with a faith-based mission, this group may be a significant proportion of the staff. What's important for leaders to understand is that faith-reliance as a coping mechanism is not the same as passivity or avoidance. Individuals in this group often demonstrate remarkable endurance through extended difficulty. But they can be poorly served by leaders who either dismiss their spiritual orientation as irrelevant to organizational life or who co-opt it—using faith language to minimize the legitimacy of their concerns or to discourage them from advocating for change. What this group needs from leaders is genuine patience, acknowledgment of the spiritual dimension of their experience, and care not to instrumentalize their faith as a management tool.

People move between these groups over time. Someone who enters a crisis as an active fighter may migrate toward faith-reliance when their reserves are depleted. An accepter who feels genuinely heard and involved may begin to engage more actively. The leader's task is not to sort people once and manage them accordingly, but to remain curious about which orientation is active in each person at a given moment—and to adjust their leadership accordingly.

Scarcity, Diversity, and the Inequality Beneath the Numbers

One of the most persistent and damaging patterns in organizational scarcity is what might be called the equality illusion—the tendency to design responses that are equal in form but deeply unequal in impact. A 10% pay cut is an inconvenience for someone earning $120,000. For someone earning $38,000, it is a financial crisis. A "last hired, first fired" policy sounds like principled neutrality; in organizations that have spent years building diversity, it systematically concentrates the cost of financial difficulty on those whose hiring was most recently achieved—who are disproportionately from underrepresented backgrounds.

This pattern is not usually the result of malicious intent. It is the result of applying technically neutral rules to a context that is not neutral—where historical patterns of who has held power, who has been hired longest, and who carries the most financial margin are themselves shaped by decades of inequity. The scarcity moment doesn't create these inequalities. It reveals and amplifies them.

Staff in multicultural organizations consistently name perceptions of unequal work distribution and unequal influence over decisions as among the most significant threats to organizational trust. When scarcity decisions were made that seemed to protect those with the most power while falling hardest on those with the least, the damage to cross-cultural trust was severe and lasting. People remembered—not with bitterness, but with clarity—how they were treated when it mattered most.

This is why Sarah's instinct to slow down was right, but it needed to be paired with a specific analytical move: before finalizing any scarcity response, leaders must ask who bears the cost of this decision and whether that distribution is just. Not just what percentage of the budget does it address, but what percentage of their livelihood does it take from each person affected. Not just what programs are technically optional, but whose communities are served by those programs—and whether cutting them is a resource decision or a statement about whose needs matter.

This kind of analysis is not comfortable. It requires leaders to sit with the discomfort of naming inequity explicitly, of acknowledging that some options that appear neutral are not, and of sometimes choosing the more complicated path because it is the more just one. But organizations that navigate this honestly—that make the equity analysis visible rather than hiding it behind efficiency language—emerge with their multicultural trust largely intact. Those that don't will find that trust is among the hardest things to rebuild.

Across multicultural organizations, a recurring cluster of growth barriers tends to surface precisely during moments of financial and organizational stress. Perceived inequality in work distribution and autonomy, alongside inconsistent leadership behavior during change, are both activated and amplified precisely when organizations are under financial stress. Scarcity does not create these barriers; it is the pressure that makes visible what was already fragile beneath the surface.

The Handover Problem: When Knowledge Walks Out the Door

Turnover compounds scarcity in a specific and often underestimated way. When people leave organizations—whether through budget cuts, burnout, or simply finding better opportunities—they take with them not just their skills but the accumulated relational and contextual knowledge that makes organizations function. Who trusts whom. Why a particular policy was written the way it was. Which community partner needs a personal call rather than an email. What the student who seems disengaged is actually dealing with at home. This knowledge is not in any manual. It exists in the minds of people who built it through years of showing up.

This pattern appears with painful consistency across organizations under pressure. New hires receive minimal handover and are left to self-teach content, processes, and relationships. The burden this created was not equally distributed: remaining staff carried emotional fatigue from repeatedly orienting new colleagues, while new hires carried the anxiety of performing competence in contexts they hadn't had time to understand. And those the organization exists to serve experience the disruption as inconsistency, confusion, and the unsettling sense that the institution is perpetually starting over.

High turnover also creates a specific cultural dynamic: people stop investing in relationships because they know the people they're investing in may not be there next year. This relational shallowness is not character failure; it is rational adaptation to repeated loss. But it becomes self-reinforcing: shallow relationships make the organization a less compelling place to stay, which increases turnover, which reinforces shallowness. The leader who breaks this cycle does so not by demanding deeper investment but by demonstrating through institutional memory practices that the organization itself will hold what individuals cannot.

This is the purpose of what we might call a Knowledge Bridge Protocol—a structured approach to preserving and transferring what departing staff carry. The idea is straightforward: before someone leaves, create a deliberate process to capture what they know in a form that doesn't depend on their continued presence. This includes documented processes, yes—but more importantly, it includes relationship maps (who are the key contacts and what do they need to feel respected), contextual notes (what would someone new need to know that isn't in any policy document), and cultural navigation guidance (what are the unwritten expectations, sensitivities, and communication norms that shape how work actually happens here).

In resource-constrained organizations, the pressure is always to skip this step. People are busy. Departures often happen quickly. The person leaving may not feel obligated to invest time in transition when the organization has just reduced their role. But the cost of skipping it is paid in the months that follow, by everyone who remains. A minimal handover practice—even a few hours of structured conversation and documentation—returns its investment many times over. And critically, how an organization handles departures is itself a visible signal to everyone who stays. It communicates whether the institution treats its people as interchangeable units or as bearers of irreplaceable knowledge and relationship.

A Framework for Navigating Scarcity Wisely

Across organizations that navigate scarcity well, several principles consistently appear. These are not steps to be executed in sequence. They are orientations that together create the conditions for wise navigation of difficulty.

Slow Down When Pressure Says Speed Up

Scarcity creates urgency: we must decide now. But rushed decisions under stress are precisely when we're most likely to violate values, miss important considerations, and create unintended consequences. Wise scarcity navigation includes deliberate pause: this is important enough to do well, not just quickly. Gather input from those most affected. Consider multiple options. Test decisions against stated values. Sleep on major choices. The board may want an answer Monday. But a hasty decision Monday that damages culture for years is worse than a delayed decision that preserves organizational integrity.

Make Values Visible, Not Just Viable

Scarcity tests whether stated values are real or rhetorical. Organizations claiming "people first" but cutting staff casually reveal what they actually value. Organizations claiming commitment to diversity but eliminating diverse staff first show their real priorities. Navigating scarcity well requires explicit connection between decisions and values: we value justice, so we are examining whether cuts burden those with least power disproportionately. We value development, so even in scarcity we are maintaining minimal investment in staff growth. Values don't eliminate difficult choices. They shape how choices get made and what factors weigh most heavily.

Distribute Burden Thoughtfully, Not Just Proportionally

Different scarcity responses distribute burden differently. Layoffs concentrate burden on those who lose jobs while others remain unaffected. Pay cuts distribute burden across everyone but impact those with lower salaries more severely. Benefit reductions affect those most dependent on benefits, who are often lower-paid staff. Program cuts impact service recipients who have no voice in the decision. Wise leaders examine: who bears the cost of our scarcity response? Is that distribution just? Are we asking those with least margin to carry the heaviest burden? Sometimes the answer is yes, because there are no good options. But at minimum, leaders should name this reality rather than pretending decisions are neutral.

Communicate Honestly, Not Optimistically

Scarcity tempts leaders toward false optimism. People see through it. It damages trust. Honest communication acknowledges reality: this is genuinely difficult, I don't have easy answers, we are navigating real constraints. This creates space for authentic problem-solving rather than performing positivity no one believes. False optimism is its own form of information hoarding. Leaders who perform positivity don't protect their teams from anxiety—they just add the burden of pretending to believe something they don't. In multicultural contexts, communication style matters additionally. Some cultural backgrounds value direct, explicit information. Others prefer more indirect, relationship-preserving communication. Leaders need multiple communication pathways to ensure diverse staff actually understand the situation.

Preserve Future Capacity, Not Just Current Operations

Organizations in scarcity often cut anything not immediately essential: training, development, strategic planning, relationship building, innovation. These cuts provide quick savings but eliminate capacity for future growth. When professional development is cut during scarcity, skill gaps tend to persist long after financial conditions improve—a cost that rarely shows up on the spreadsheet that drove the cut. Wise scarcity navigation maintains some forward-looking investment even when painful. This signals hope and investment in the future, not just survival in the present. Even a reduced commitment to development communicates that this is a temporary hardship, not a permanent abandonment of organizational values.

Invite Participation, Not Just Announcement

Top-down scarcity decisions create resentment even when necessary. Participatory approaches—how might we navigate this together?—create ownership and often surface creative solutions leaders wouldn't have considered. This doesn't mean consensus decision-making on everything. But it means genuine invitation for input before decisions are finalized, particularly from those most affected. In multicultural organizations, participation must be genuinely structured—not a meeting where the dominant voices are already dominant. Seeking input from accepters and compromisers, from faith-reliers, from staff who have less positional power requires intentional design, not just open doors.

From Scarcity to Abundance: The Transition Leaders Miss

Most leadership attention in organizations goes to navigating the crisis itself. Far less attention is given to the transition out of it—and this neglect is costly. Organizations that emerge from genuine scarcity without intentionally naming and marking the transition often find that the scarcity mindset persists long after financial conditions have stabilized. Staff who learned to protect themselves, to not invest in relationships that might dissolve, to not advocate for needs that seemed unlikely to be met—they don't automatically unlearn those adaptations when a budget improves. The crisis ends, but the posture remains.

Leaders must actively and publicly mark the transition. This means naming what was hard and acknowledging it honestly—not pretending it didn't happen, but also not staying there. It means visibly reinvesting in what was cut: if professional development was eliminated, announcing and funding its return. If diverse staff were lost, recommitting visibly and with specific plans to rebuilding that diversity. If community relationships were damaged by program cuts, returning to those communities and acknowledging the disruption.

It also means being patient with the lag between changed conditions and changed behavior. An organization that survived two years of scarcity may need another year before its people genuinely believe that abundance has returned. Staff who have experienced leadership instability are cautious about trusting new signals of stability—not because they are cynical but because they have learned through experience that stability is fragile. The appropriate leadership response is not frustration at this caution but sustained demonstration, over time, that the new conditions are real.

The three-group framework matters here too. Active fighters may be among the first to re-engage with energy and optimism. Accepters and compromisers may need explicit invitation and evidence before they will advocate for their own needs again. Faith-reliers may express gratitude and hope while still carrying unprocessed weight from the difficult period. Leaders who pay attention to these different paces of recovery—rather than assuming that a budget turnaround equals an immediate team turnaround—are far more likely to help the whole organization genuinely move forward.

The Historical View

History offers compelling examples of leadership functioning under scarcity conditions and either how they came out for the better or the worse for it..

Valley Forge: Leadership in Extreme Scarcity

The winter of 1777–1778 at Valley Forge represents one of history's most studied examples of leadership through extreme scarcity. George Washington's Continental Army faced conditions that would break most organizations: inadequate food, insufficient clothing, no pay, desertion rates climbing, disease spreading, and the very real possibility of total collapse. The scarcity was brutal and visible. Soldiers lacked basic winter clothing—many were barefoot in freezing conditions. The army had no money to purchase supplies and limited credit to acquire them.

Washington faced what the grief arc framework names as its most dangerous moment: an organization in the shock and depression phases simultaneously, with no guarantee of hope ahead. His response illustrates the principles of wise scarcity leadership with striking clarity.

He practiced shared sacrifice: Washington lived in similarly austere conditions as his troops. He refused to retreat to comfortable quarters while his men suffered. This wasn't symbolic—it was substantive shared burden that preserved his moral authority to ask sacrifice from others. He communicated honestly: Washington wrote repeatedly to Congress describing conditions accurately and urgently. He didn't minimize the crisis. He maintained discipline with flexibility: punishments for desertion were real but not unnecessarily harsh given the circumstances. He recognized that harsh response to soldiers desperate from hunger would have been unjust.

Most instructively for our framework: even in crisis, Washington invested in future capacity. He brought in Baron von Steuben to train troops in military tactics—not immediately essential for survival, but critical for long-term effectiveness. This is the preserve future capacity principle made concrete under conditions of genuine deprivation. The investment during scarcity created capability that proved decisive later. And Washington distributed leadership: he relied heavily on his officers not because he was weak but because the complexity required distributed decision-making. He could not micromanage in such crisis. He needed competent leaders at every level—precisely the kind of shared leadership structure that allows organizations to navigate difficulty without centralizing all burden on one person.

The result: the army didn't just survive Valley Forge—it emerged more disciplined, better trained, and more unified than when it entered. The shared suffering created bonds that held through the rest of the war. Washington's leadership through scarcity proved more formative than any abundance phase. Notably, the three-group response pattern was visible even here: some soldiers were active fighters who stayed engaged and pushed through; others were accepters who complied and endured; still others drew their strength from something larger than themselves—faith in the cause, in Providence, in the meaning of what they were fighting for. Washington's genius was that his leadership held space for all three.

The Irish Famine Response: When Ideology Overrides Compassion

The Great Irish Famine (1845–1852) offers a contrasting example of how leadership failure in scarcity creates catastrophe. When potato blight destroyed Ireland's primary food source, the dominant British government response was shaped by ideology rather than reality. The Whig government believed that market forces should resolve the crisis without government interference. They maintained food exports from Ireland even as millions starved. They created work programs that required exhausting labor from people too malnourished to work. They blamed Irish dependency rather than addressing the crisis.

Viewed through the grief arc lens, the British government was stuck in the denial and bargaining phases—insisting that their economic framework was correct even as evidence of mass death mounted around them. They performed a kind of institutional bargaining: if we adjust the work programs slightly, if we import some corn, perhaps the market will correct itself. The distance—physical, cultural, social—between decision-makers in London and the dying in Connaught enabled decisions that up-close contact would have made unconscionable.

The equity analysis that Sarah's leadership team eventually had to face was never honestly performed by the British government. They treated proportional policy as just policy—the market applies equally to everyone—while the actual impact was catastrophically unequal. The burden fell entirely on the most vulnerable, while those with resources survived and even benefited. And critically, the response failed the three-group test: the active fighters among the Irish population were actively suppressed; the accepters and compromisers were ground down by impossible conditions; and the faith-reliers—whose endurance of suffering became a formative element of Irish Catholic identity—were offered no meaningful partnership from institutional authority.

The famine killed over a million people and drove millions more to emigrate. The failure wasn't lack of resources—Britain was the world's wealthiest nation. It was failure of leadership: ideology overriding compassion, distance enabling cruelty, blame replacing responsibility. The handover of institutional knowledge that might have helped—local knowledge held by Irish community leaders, clergy, landholders—was systematically disregarded.

Lincoln Electric: Shared Burden as Organizational Culture

During the Great Depression of the 1930s, most American manufacturers laid off workers en masse. The Lincoln Electric Company in Cleveland, Ohio, took a different approach that would define its culture for the next century. Facing severe economic contraction, Lincoln Electric's leadership guaranteed continued employment for all workers rather than layoffs. This required painful sacrifices from everyone.

Rather than concentrating hardship on those laid off, Lincoln Electric reduced everyone's hours and pay proportionally. Senior leaders took the largest percentage cuts. The company shifted to a four-day work week, then three days when conditions worsened. Everyone hurt, but everyone survived. This was the thoughtful burden distribution principle at institutional scale: the question was not just what percentage of salary to cut, but what level of sacrifice was genuinely shared rather than concentrated on the most vulnerable.

Workers participated in finding efficiencies and cost savings—a direct application of the invite participation principle. The advisory board, composed of elected employee representatives, worked with management to identify waste and streamline processes. Solutions came from those doing the work, not imposed from above. Management shared financial data openly. People understood why sacrifices were necessary and could see that leaders were being honest about the situation. This maintained trust even during difficulty.

Lincoln Electric also preserved future capacity: even during crisis, it continued its profit-sharing and bonus system (though bonuses were smaller) and kept training programs running. The message was clear: this is temporary hardship, not permanent abandonment. The knowledge preservation was also deliberate—workers who stayed through the Depression carried institutional memory that became the foundation of Lincoln Electric's post-Depression competitive advantage.

Looking at Lincoln Electric through the three-group lens: the organization's response was structured specifically to prevent the collapse of the active fighters, to give genuine voice and dignity to the accepters and compromisers, and to honor the faith-reliance that characterized many of its long-tenured workers without requiring that it replace structural action. The results were extraordinary: Lincoln Electric not only survived the Depression but emerged with employee loyalty so strong that the guaranteed employment policy became permanent.

The Biblical View

Scripture consistently presents stories of men and women moving through times of scarcity and confusion. Several examples illuminate healthy responses—and the research findings above give us new eyes to see what these examples are actually demonstrating.

The Widow's Offering: Faithful Generosity in Scarcity

In Mark 12:41–44, Jesus observed people giving offerings at the temple. Wealthy people gave large amounts. Then a poor widow came and put in two very small copper coins, worth only a few cents. Jesus called his disciples and said: "Truly I tell you, this poor widow has put more into the treasury than all the others. They all gave out of their wealth; but she, out of her poverty, put in everything—all she had to live on."

What's instructive here is not only the widow's generosity but what her presence reveals about how we evaluate sacrifice. The wealthy givers gave proportionally less of their actual resources. The widow gave proportionally everything. This is the equity analysis that organizational leaders must perform: the same dollar amount is not the same sacrifice from different people. The same percentage cut is not the same burden across different salary levels.

For leaders navigating scarcity, this teaches something additional: generosity and trust don't wait for abundance. The widow's scarcity didn't eliminate her faithfulness—it revealed its authenticity. Values tested in scarcity prove themselves real or reveal themselves as fair-weather commitments. And the community that honors the widow's offering rather than dismissing it as negligible is one that has learned to read contribution in terms of cost rather than quantity. That reorientation—from what did you give to what did it cost you?—is precisely the one leaders must make when designing scarcity responses in multicultural organizations.

Hezekiah's Crisis Leadership During Siege

When the Assyrian army surrounded Jerusalem (2 Kings 18–19, 2 Chronicles 32), King Hezekiah faced existential scarcity. The most powerful military in the world was besieging the city. Resources were limited. Options were few. Terror was spreading. Hezekiah's response maps directly onto the framework of wise scarcity navigation.

He did not perform optimism. When Assyrian officials tried to demoralize the people with propaganda—essentially communicating that resistance was futile and surrender was rational—Hezekiah addressed it directly. He didn't pretend the threat wasn't real. He acknowledged the danger while pointing to reasons for genuine hope, and he communicated clearly to his people: "Be strong and courageous. Do not be afraid or discouraged because of the king of Assyria and the vast army with him, for there is a greater power with us than with him" (2 Chronicles 32:7). This is not false optimism. It is honest acknowledgment of the threat paired with a clear account of why hope is nevertheless warranted.

Hezekiah also practiced shared burden, standing with his people rather than above them, and invested in future capacity rather than surrendering to the present crisis. He secured the water supply by building a tunnel—a significant infrastructure investment during siege, not immediately essential for the next few days but critical for sustained resistance. He did not treat the crisis as a reason to stop thinking strategically about the future. And he prayed without passivity: he spread the threatening letter before God (2 Kings 19:14–19), modeling a spirituality that acknowledges the full weight of difficulty rather than minimizing it.

Hezekiah's leadership also suggests something important for the three-group framework. He communicated in ways that could reach all three orientations: practical military preparation for the active fighters, clear institutional communication for the accepters, and explicit spiritual grounding for the faith-reliers. He did not assume that one message would serve everyone. Jerusalem survived the siege—and the lesson for organizational leaders is that crisis leadership requires holding multiple registers simultaneously: practical, communicative, and spiritual.

Ezra's Organizational Reforms: Change Without Destroying Community

When Ezra led returning exiles back to Jerusalem (Ezra 7–10), he found organizational chaos: mixed practices threatening community identity, corruption among leaders, systems that had broken down during the exile. He needed massive organizational reform during resource scarcity and cultural upheaval. His approach demonstrates the grief arc in action, navigated with wisdom.

Ezra began with public grief and honest naming. When he learned of the problems, he tore his clothes and sat appalled (Ezra 9:3). He did not minimize the crisis or pretend everything was fine. He modeled honest response to organizational failure—moving through shock into genuine acknowledgment rather than rushing to solutions before grief had been named. This gave the community permission to do the same: they wept together, acknowledged the problems together, and developed solutions together (Ezra 10:1–5). The difficult decisions had community ownership because people participated in making them.

The reforms happened systematically over time (Ezra 10:16–17), not through panic decisions. People were given time to respond. The process balanced urgency with dignity—which is precisely what the equity analysis principle calls for: not pretending that time doesn't matter, but also not sacrificing people's dignity on the altar of institutional efficiency. And Ezra built future capacity even while addressing current crisis: he established systems for ongoing instruction in the Law (Ezra 7:10, 25), investing in the knowledge infrastructure that would sustain the community long after the immediate reforms were complete. This is the Knowledge Bridge made institutional—not just preserving what individuals knew, but building structures that would hold community wisdom across successive transitions.

What Ezra demonstrates is the integration of all six principles into a coherent leadership posture: slowing down despite pressure, making values visible through public accountability, distributing burden through community participation, communicating honestly beginning with his own grief, preserving future capacity through structural investment, and inviting participation so thoroughly that the community's solutions became the community's own.

Nuances and Blind Spots

Scarcity reveals values—it doesn't create them. Organizations don't become different during hard times; they become more visibly what they already were. If people are treated as expendable during cuts, that wasn't a crisis decision—it was always the underlying reality, and scarcity just removed the packaging. The "we're family" rhetoric that evaporates the moment layoffs begin doesn't represent a change in values. It represents their exposure.

Panic decisions trade future capacity for present relief. Scarcity creates urgency that can override wisdom—eliminating training, cutting development, reducing the very investments that make recovery possible. Leaders who can slow down enough to ask what are the long-term consequences of this choice—even under genuine pressure—make better decisions than those who reach for the fastest option.

Temporary measures have a way of becoming permanent. Pay cuts, benefit reductions, increased workloads, and eliminated positions introduced as crisis responses frequently outlast the crisis. Leaders must be intentional about defining end points and actually following through on restoring what was cut when conditions improve. The failure to do so is remembered—and shapes whether people trust leadership's word the next time.

The people who leave during scarcity aren't always the ones you'd choose to lose. Voluntary departures during hard times often include your most capable people—those with options. Those who remain may be a mix of genuinely loyal team members and those who simply lack alternatives. Scarcity can inadvertently sort your workforce in ways you wouldn't choose deliberately.

Cultural backgrounds shape how scarcity is experienced and processed. Some frameworks emphasize individual resilience and self-reliance in hard times. Others expect collective support and shared burden. Some expect leaders to make unilateral decisions during crisis; others expect participatory processes even then. The pattern is clear: value compromise rationalization—"we can't afford to care about diversity or development right now"—compounds this by treating values as luxuries that apply only in abundance rather than as the architecture that holds things together precisely when everything is hard.

Scarcity can become identity long after the crisis passes. Some organizations get so habituated to "we can't afford that" that it becomes a reflexive response to any new idea, even when resources have recovered. The trauma of scarcity creates ongoing caution that prevents growth. Leaders must intentionally work to shift the organizational mindset when conditions genuinely change. Announcing that scarcity is over is not enough: leaders must visibly reinvest in what was cut, publicly name the transition, and give people time to believe that abundance is real before they will act from it.

How you handle scarcity shapes who will trust you in abundance. People remember how they were treated during hard times with unusual clarity. Organizations that navigated scarcity with integrity—protecting the vulnerable, communicating honestly, distributing burden fairly—earn a loyalty that prosperity alone can never purchase. Those that revealed their true priorities during difficulty will find that trust, once lost that way, is among the hardest things to rebuild.

Try This Week

Choose one of the following. Do it this week, not someday.

Practice 1: Run the Equity Impact Assessment on One Decision

Identify one current or recent scarcity-driven decision. Work through all five questions. Write down the answers. If you don't like what the analysis reveals, that's important information—sit with it before deciding whether to change the decision or change your values.

Practice 2: Name the Grief Stage

Using the Grief Arc Stage Assessment, identify where your organization currently is. Then identify one specific leadership action that stage calls for—and do it this week. Tell at least one colleague what you're doing and why.

Practice 3: Identify Your Three-Group Reality

Name one person in each of the three response groups on your team. Schedule a brief, private conversation with someone in the group you most tend to neglect. Ask: "How are you really doing? What would help you most right now?" Then act on what you hear.

Practice 4: Start a Knowledge Bridge

Identify one role in your organization that has high turnover or significant institutional knowledge concentrated in one person. Have a conversation with that person about what would need to be documented if they were leaving next month. Start the document. Don't wait for someone to announce departure.

Practice 5: Honest Communication Draft

For one ongoing challenge or change, draft a communication using the Change Communication Grid. Before sending it, review: does it name what we know and don't know honestly? Does it specify when the next update will come? Does it provide a real channel for questions? If not, revise before sending.

Scarcity, turnover, and change will continue. The question is not whether you will face them. It is whether you will face them in ways that reveal and strengthen your values, or in ways that expose and deepen their absence. These tools are companions for the former.

Reflection Questions

Quick Check (1–2 minutes)

- When facing resource constraints, do you typically make decisions quickly to relieve anxiety, or slowly to make them well?

- In your last significant scarcity decision, who bore the primary burden? Was that distribution just?

Deeper Reflection (5–10 minutes)

- What does your organization actually value based on how scarcity decisions get made—not just what you say you value?

- Where might you be using scarcity as an excuse to avoid difficult conversations you should have regardless of budget?

- Which of the three groups—active fighters, accepters/compromisers, or faith-reliers—are you most naturally attentive to? Who might you be missing?

- What stage of the grief arc is your organization currently in? What does that stage ask of you as a leader right now?

- If you had to navigate scarcity in a way that strengthened rather than damaged organizational culture, what would you do differently than you have done before?

Team Discussion (15–30 minutes)

- As a leadership team, map your last significant scarcity season: What decisions did you make? How? Who participated? Who bore the burden? What were the long-term consequences—intended and unintended?

- For each of the three response groups, identify one or two people in your current team. What does each person need from you right now that they may not be getting?

- What is one thing your organization has said is "temporary" that has quietly become permanent? What would it take to make good on the original promise?

Moving Forward

Scarcity forces difficult decisions about resources, priorities, and sometimes people. Sarah's Friday email demanded a response by Monday—but she was right to slow down. And she was right that the decision wasn't just about budget math. It was about who would bear the cost, whether that distribution was just, and what kind of organization they would be when the difficulty had passed.

Washington at Valley Forge demonstrated that scarcity leadership requires shared sacrifice, honest communication, preserved values, and investment in future capacity even when the present is desperate. The Irish Famine response showed what happens when ideology overrides compassion and distance enables cruelty. Lincoln Electric proved that organizations can navigate severe economic crisis without abandoning the people who make them work, and that the way they navigate it shapes who will trust them for generations.

The biblical witness is consistent: faith doesn't deny scarcity but navigates it through honest acknowledgment, generous response, community burden-sharing, and trust in God's provision. Hezekiah didn't perform optimism—he acknowledged the threat and named the hope. Ezra didn't rush to solutions—he let grief be present before action was taken. The widow at the temple gave from poverty, not surplus, teaching that authentic generosity doesn't wait for abundance.

The organizations that navigate scarcity well are not those that avoid difficult decisions. They are those that make difficult decisions with integrity—that perform the equity analysis, that hold the three-group framework in mind, that build knowledge bridges before people leave, that mark the transition back to abundance when it comes, and that remain honest about all of it throughout.

Scarcity, turnover, and change will continue. That is the reality of organizational life. The question is not whether you will face them but whether you will face them in ways that reveal and strengthen your values or in ways that expose and deepen their absence.

Managing Turnover and Transitions

Opening Scene

The Slack message appeared without warning on a Tuesday morning: "Hi team, I want you to hear from me first. After much prayer and consideration, I've accepted a position elsewhere. My last day will be two weeks from Friday. I'm grateful for my time here and wish you all the best."

Maria stared at her screen. James was leaving. He had been program director for four years — institutional memory, key relationships, critical knowledge about systems that had never been written down anywhere. And he was giving two weeks' notice for a role that would take months to fill and longer to master.

Within an hour, the whisper network was running at full speed. "I heard he'd been looking for months." "Did you know he was unhappy?" "Who's going to run the fall program — that's entirely in his head." Some staff felt betrayed: How could he just leave us like this? Others felt something more complicated — a kind of quiet envy. Maybe I should start looking too. Leadership felt blindsided: Why didn't he tell us he was struggling?

By Thursday, three more resignation letters arrived. Whatever had prompted James to leave was apparently affecting others too. The executive director sat in her office, overwhelmed: How did we get here? How do we stop the bleeding? How do we manage all this transition without everything falling apart?

What she didn't realize: the turnover wasn't the problem. It was the symptom. And how she responded now would determine whether remaining staff stayed or quietly accelerated their own exit timelines.

Two weeks later, James's last day arrived. There was no goodbye gathering, no formal transition process, no exit interview. He simply didn't show up Monday morning. His knowledge left with him. His relationships evaporated. The remaining team members felt abandoned and uneasy: If we become inconvenient, we'll just disappear too.

Six months later, the program James had led was limping along under someone promoted before she was ready. Morale was low. Two more people had left quietly. And the organization was still trying to understand what had happened and how to prevent it from happening again.

Understanding Turnover in Multicultural Organizations

Employee turnover is expensive, disruptive, and — in most organizations — poorly managed. Replacing an employee typically costs somewhere between half and double their annual salary once you account for recruitment, onboarding, lost productivity, and knowledge that walks out the door with them.

But the costs go deeper than finances. Turnover damages organizational memory, disrupts relationships, demoralizes survivors, and creates a low-grade anxiety that cascades through teams. In multicultural organizations, these costs multiply in particular ways. Diverse teams take longer to form and gel. Trust builds more slowly across cultural difference. And cultural knowledge — knowing how to navigate the organization across different frameworks, reading unwritten rules, bridging communication styles — is perhaps the hardest kind of knowledge to transfer. When a culturally fluent person leaves, they often take invisible bridges with them.

There are different kinds of turnover worth distinguishing, because each requires a different leadership response.

Voluntary departure — someone choosing to leave — is different from **involuntary separation**. Losing a low performer who was dragging the team down is categorically different from losing a high performer who held things together. And turnover driven by organizational factors — inadequate pay, poor management, lack of development, feeling unseen — is different from turnover driven by genuinely external factors like relocation or family need. The first kind can be addressed. The second kind usually cannot. The mistake many leaders make is treating all turnover as if it belongs to the second category, when substantial portions of it belong to the first.

In multicultural organizations, one additional category matters enormously: **culturally-driven turnover**. This describes departures that are specifically rooted in cultural dynamics — feeling perpetually excluded from informal networks, carrying the invisible tax of constantly translating between cultural frameworks, lacking role models or sponsors who share your background, or simply exhausting yourself navigating microaggressions that no one else seems to notice. This kind of turnover is particularly costly because it tends to cluster: cultural minority staff leave disproportionately, undermining diversity efforts even when leadership is genuinely committed to them. If your exit interviews show that departures are concentrated among particular groups — by cultural background, role type, or years of service — you don't have a general turnover problem. You have a targeted one, and it requires targeted investigation.

The opening scene reveals a cluster of common failures: no early warning system to catch dissatisfaction before it becomes departure, exit without dignity or knowledge transfer, survivors left feeling insecure, and leadership caught entirely reactive. None of these failures are inevitable. They are the predictable result of operating without sustainable rhythms and systems.

How People Navigate Change: Three Patterns Worth Knowing

When organizations go through significant disruption — financial pressure, leadership change, staff departures, restructuring — people don't respond uniformly. Understanding the typical response patterns can help leaders lead more effectively through the turbulence rather than offering generic reassurance that lands differently for different people.

Research on organizational crisis and change consistently surfaces three broad groups among staff navigating upheaval.

1. **Active fighters:** Engaged, energetic, pushing through — sometimes impatiently

   - *They Need:* Clear direction, real problems to solve, honest acknowledgment of difficulty without catastrophizing

2. **Accepters / adapters:** Compliant, adjusting, going with the flow — sometimes too quietly

   - *They Need:* Regular check-ins, genuine appreciation, real voice in decisions that affect them

3. **Faith-reliers:** Finding strength in spiritual grounding, meaning-making, endurance

   - *They Need:* Assurance that core values and purpose remain intact; patience; spiritual community

The first group stays actively engaged throughout the difficulty. They show up, push through, maintain energy and initiative even when the ground feels unstable. They tend to need clear direction and real problems to sink their energy into. Without those, their energy can curdle into frustration or leave the organization looking for somewhere it can be usefully spent.

The second group accepts and adapts. They comply, adjust to new realities, and generally go with the flow of organizational change. They're not disengaged — they're cautious. Regular check-ins, genuine appreciation, and real voice in the process matter disproportionately to this group. When they feel ignored, they don't usually push back. They quietly disengage or begin to consider leaving.

The third group finds its primary strength in spiritual or values-based grounding. They endure difficulty through faith, meaning-making, and a conviction that something larger than the immediate situation is at work. This group doesn't need to feel that everything will be fine — they need to feel that the organization's core purpose and values are still intact even when circumstances are turbulent. Dismissing or inadvertently mocking this orientation creates alienation at precisely the moment when this group's stabilizing influence on others could be most valuable.

The practical implication is that a single communication style or support approach will not reach all three groups equally. Good leaders learn to read which people are in which mode — and to recognize that people shift between modes as circumstances evolve. Someone who was actively fighting through the first month of a crisis may be quietly depleted by month four. The person who appeared to accept and adapt may be carrying unexpressed concerns that will surface eventually, one way or another.

The Seasonal Arc of Transition

When a freeze hits overnight, we call it a weather event. But what follows — the thaw, the muddy ground, the slow reawakening of root systems — that is a season. Organizations confuse these constantly. The announcement of a departure or a structural change is a weather event. What people carry inside them afterward is a season, and seasons cannot be rushed. Every significant organizational change launches an internal journey in the people who experience it. Managing the announcement is not the same as leading people through that journey. Most organizations are reasonably good at the former and almost entirely unprepared for the latter.

Stage One: Winter — The Season of Loss

When something ends — a colleague departs, a role dissolves, a team restructures — people enter Winter. Winter is not failure. It is not weakness. It is the natural and necessary response to real loss. We know from the study of grief that loss moves through us in layers: shock first, then denial, then the slow ache of reality setting in. Organizations that announce a change on Monday and expect full productivity by Wednesday are ignoring the fact that human beings are not systems to be rebooted. They are ecosystems, and ecosystems need time to process what has died before they can receive new growth.

In multicultural organizations, Winter carries particular weight. In collectivist cultures, the loss of a colleague is not merely the loss of a task-partner — it is the loss of a relational anchor, a known quantity in an uncertain world. The colleague who helped you navigate unspoken organizational rules, who instinctively understood what you meant even when your English was imperfect, who provided a kind of cultural companionship — their departure is a different order of loss than purely individual frameworks tend to account for. Grief in these communities runs deeper and wider than Western productivity frameworks tend to accommodate. When leaders rush past Winter, they don't avoid the grief — they just delay its expression into less visible and less manageable forms.

What leaders must do in Winter: Give permission. Name the loss out loud. Do not project false spring. The leader who says "I know this is hard, and it's okay that it's hard" does more for team recovery than the one who insists on optimism before the ground has thawed.

Stage Two: Early Spring — The Season of Disorientation

Winter doesn't end with a date on the calendar. It ends when the ecosystem is ready. And in that liminal stretch — when winter's grip has loosened but spring has not yet arrived — everything feels uncertain. The ground is soft and unreliable. The landscape looks different but hasn't fully transformed.

This is also where a different kind of pressure emerges. When patterns feel destabilized, some team members will attempt to recreate old routines as a coping mechanism. Others will freeze. Still others will announce prematurely that everything is fine and the organization should move forward immediately. None of these responses mean the person is weak or difficult — they are recognizable human responses to ambiguity. But if leaders mistake any of them for genuine resolution, they'll find themselves managing a second crisis beneath the surface of an apparent calm.

In multicultural contexts, high uncertainty-avoidance cultures find this season particularly destabilizing. The absence of clear structure can feel like organizational failure rather than natural transition. People from these backgrounds may interpret ambiguous communication as leaders hiding something or preparing for worse news. This isn't paranoia — it's a reasonable inference from cultural experience with instability. Leaders who name uncertainty honestly and explicitly — who say "I don't yet know, and here is what I'm doing to find out, and here is when I'll update you" — are far more effective with these teams than leaders who offer generic reassurance.

What leaders must do in Early Spring: Normalize the disorientation.

Communicate what is stable even when much is not. Resist the pressure to manufacture certainty that doesn't exist. Stay present with discomfort rather than trying to resolve it prematurely.

Stage Three: Full Spring — The Season of Emergence

Spring doesn't arrive because we demanded it. It arrives because Winter was endured and Early Spring was navigated. New growth emerges from ground that has been cleared by loss. New patterns solidify. The team finds its rhythm again — different from before, but alive.

New beginnings in organizations follow the same logic. They cannot be announced into existence. They must be earned through the preceding seasons. A team that was given space to grieve in Winter, and was steadied through Early Spring, will arrive at Full Spring with something that forced transitions never produce: genuine renewed commitment, rooted in shared experience rather than mandate.

What leaders must do in Full Spring: Celebrate. Name what's new. Acknowledge the journey the team has made together. Don't treat the new normal as if the preceding seasons never happened — that history is the source of the new season's depth.

A Note on Multicultural Timing

Different people enter and leave each season at different times. In nature, a south-facing slope thaws faster than a north-facing one. Neither is broken. Both will reach summer. Leaders of diverse teams must resist the impulse to synchronize everyone to a single emotional timeline. Some will need longer Winters. Some will reach Early Spring faster but linger there longer. Patience with varied timelines is not permissiveness — it is ecological wisdom. The gardener who pulls seedlings upward to make them grow faster kills them. The one who tends the conditions and trusts the process is the one who gets a harvest.

The Scarcity Trap — And How to Navigate It

James's departure didn't happen in a vacuum. In most multicultural organizations experiencing significant turnover, resource scarcity is part of the backdrop — limited budgets, lean staffing, stretched facilities, volatile enrollment or client numbers. Scarcity and turnover are not independent problems. They feed each other.

Scarcity creates cognitive pressure that narrows thinking. When resources are tight, leaders focus intensely on immediate shortages, which causes them to neglect longer-term considerations — relationships, values, development investments that build future capacity. Decisions made under this kind of pressure can address the immediate problem while creating larger problems downstream. Then those new problems demand immediate attention, and the cycle perpetuates itself.

In multicultural organizations specifically, scarcity creates several compounding dynamics. Budget cuts tend to impact those with least organizational power most severely. Junior staff — frequently those who bring cultural and demographic diversity — get reduced or eliminated while senior staff hold on. Programs serving communities that are already marginalized get cut while core programs continue. This pattern may not be intentional, but its effect is to undo diversity progress even when organizations are genuinely committed to equity.

Scarcity also erodes trust in ways that are culturally specific. When organizations respond to financial pressure by cutting staff, freezing development, or reducing benefits, the message received by those who already navigate additional barriers is: you are more expendable than you thought. Cultural minority staff who have invested in building relationships and demonstrating value can absorb this message in ways that their majority colleagues don't. The trust damage is real, and it accumulates.

Perhaps most corrosively, sustained scarcity pushes organizations toward competitive rather than collaborative dynamics. Departments protect their budgets. Individuals hoard information because sharing it costs them something and they're not sure they can afford to be generous. Teams that were once interdependent become islands. This is particularly damaging in multicultural contexts where trust is the foundational currency and always requires more intentional investment than it does in culturally homogeneous settings.

How organizations navigate scarcity reveals character more than how they navigate abundance. Several principles consistently appear in organizations that manage financial difficulty without losing their cultural health.

The first is slowing down when pressure says speed up. Scarcity creates urgency: we must decide now. But rushed decisions under stress are precisely when organizations are most likely to violate values, miss important perspectives, and create unintended consequences. Wise scarcity leadership includes a deliberate pause: this is important enough to do well, not just quickly. Gathering input from those most affected. Considering options rather than defaulting to the most obvious one.

The second is naming reality clearly. Organizations that navigate difficulty well don't hide problems. They communicate with honest specificity: here is what is true right now, here is what we are doing about it, here is what will not change. Clarity like this reduces speculation. The rumor network in any organization is remarkably active precisely when official communication is vague or delayed. People don't imagine the worst because they are pessimists — they imagine the worst because uncertainty is neurologically aversive and their minds fill the gap with something plausible.

The third is protecting what actually sustains people. During scarcity, the temptation is to cut everything that seems optional. But professional development, team-building time, margin for reflection — these look optional in a crisis but are precisely what prevent total collapse. They're not luxuries. They're the conditions that make sustained performance possible. Organizations that eliminate them in the name of efficiency frequently find that they've saved money in the short term and spent it back in turnover costs and burnout.

The Power of Small Practices

The opening scene reveals what happens when organizations lack systematic practices for managing transitions. James's departure became crisis because no ongoing rhythms existed for knowledge transfer, relationship maintenance, or early warning about dissatisfaction. The crisis didn't begin when James sent that Slack message — it began months earlier, when the signals of his disengagement went unnoticed because no structure existed to catch them.

Research on habits and organizational change consistently shows that sustainable transformation comes through small, consistent practices rather than dramatic initiatives. Tiny changes compound over time into significant results — and their absence creates gradual decline that only becomes visible in crisis. In multicultural organizations, this principle has particular force. Trust across cultural difference builds slowly through repeated positive interactions, not through occasional grand gestures. Cultural intelligence develops through regular practice, not periodic training. Inclusive environments emerge from daily micro-behaviors — who is greeted first in the morning, who gets interrupted in meetings, whose ideas get credited — not from diversity statements. The question isn't whether your organization will face turnover, scarcity, and change. It will. The question is whether daily rhythms have built enough resilience to navigate these challenges, or whether their absence has created fragility that makes every disruption a potential crisis.

Consider what a few consistent practices might have changed in the opening scene. A weekly five-minute check-in rhythm that gave leaders early signal about James's growing dissatisfaction. A quarterly knowledge-mapping practice that had already documented critical systems before they became urgent. A departure ritual that honored James's four years of contribution and made the transition visible and meaningful rather than abrupt and demoralizing. None of these are dramatic. All of them compound over time. None of them exist in organizations operating purely in reactive mode.

The Historical View

One of the greatest ways to plan for succession and to weather the uncertainties of the sea of transition is to look to the historical records of others who have managed to go through both, either successfully or as lessons to learn from but avoid repeating.

Johns Hopkins Hospital's Residency System

In 1889, Johns Hopkins Hospital fundamentally changed how medical knowledge was transmitted by creating the first formal residency program in America. Before this, young doctors learned by watching senior physicians with no systematic approach — knowledge transferred haphazardly, and what any attending physician knew largely left with them when they moved on. What Hopkins created was a structure that made knowledge transfer not incidental but central.

The key design decision was graduated responsibility. Residents progressed through structured levels — intern, junior resident, senior resident, chief resident — with each level bringing increased autonomy and accountability. No one was thrown into full responsibility they weren't prepared for. This created natural mentorship by design: you always had someone slightly more experienced guiding you and someone slightly less experienced depending on you.

Clinical knowledge got documented rather than kept in people's heads. Procedures were written down, studied, standardized. Attending physicians conducted daily rounds with residents, teaching while treating. When a senior physician rotated off service, their knowledge remained in documented form and in the people they had been shaping.

Perhaps most importantly, transitions were overlapping rather than abrupt. When one resident completed training, another had already been working alongside them for months. The departure wasn't a knowledge cliff — it was a gradual handoff with built-in redundancy. And departures were honored: graduation ceremonies marked the transition from training to independent practice, honoring the journey, celebrating achievement, and providing genuine closure.

What's instructive is that Hopkins didn't prevent turnover — residents were designed to leave after completing training. The entire system was built around constant departure. But the systematic practices meant those departures strengthened rather than weakened the institution. Each generation learned from the previous, then taught the next. Knowledge accumulated rather than evaporating with each person who moved on.

The lesson for multicultural organizations navigating high turnover: organizations can thrive through constant change if they systematize knowledge transfer before they need it urgently, create graduated responsibility that develops people over time, document critical knowledge, ensure overlap during transitions, make teaching core work rather than optional extra, and honor departures with genuine dignity. What Hopkins built wasn't a system for preventing loss. It was a system for making loss generative.

Southwest Airlines and the Transmission of Culture

Southwest Airlines has maintained a distinctive organizational culture for over fifty years despite multiple complete turnovers of their entire workforce. Most airlines struggle to maintain culture through a single generation of employees. How Southwest has sustained it is a study in what intentional culture transmission actually looks like.

The starting point is deliberate hiring. Southwest doesn't just assess skills — they hire for alignment with their values of humor, servant's heart, and what they call warrior spirit. Interview processes are specifically designed to surface whether candidates embody these characteristics rather than simply whether they can do the job. The implicit assumption is that skills can be developed but fundamental orientation is harder to change — and that cultural fit matters enough to be a hiring criterion rather than an afterthought.

New employees then go through intensive orientation that is less about learning procedures and more about being enculturated into Southwest's history, values, and distinctive way of seeing their work. Stories of company founders and cultural heroes get told and retold in ways that make abstract values concrete and memorable. This isn't accidental — it's systematic transmission of what the organization believes about itself.

Culture-keeping responsibility is distributed rather than centralized. Employee-led culture committees at every location organize events, recognize exemplars, and actively maintain the Southwest way. This matters enormously because culture that depends on leadership attention alone doesn't survive leadership transitions. When anyone can become a culture keeper, the culture becomes more resilient than any individual.

Leadership almost always comes from within. External hires into senior leadership positions are rare. This ensures that the people with the most organizational influence have been shaped by the culture they're now responsible for protecting — rather than bringing in different assumptions and values that gradually erode what took decades to build.

For multicultural organizations, Southwest's approach carries an important caveat as well as an important lesson. The lesson is that culture survives turnover through deliberate practices: hire for alignment, invest heavily in early enculturation, distribute culture-keeping responsibility, celebrate culture exemplars publicly, protect informal relationship time. The caveat is that the culture being sustained must itself be examined. If the culture being transmitted is one that certain people must constantly adapt to while others find effortless, then these same practices that create belonging for some may systematically exclude others. Culture transmission and cultural equity are related questions, not separate ones.

Pixar's Braintrust and the Compounding of Creative Wisdom

Pixar Animation Studios produces consistently excellent films despite constant project turnover — teams form for a film, then disband when it's complete. This should make sustained quality nearly impossible. The mechanism that makes it possible is called the Braintrust: a systematic practice for preserving and transmitting creative wisdom across project teams and across time.

The Braintrust brings every film in development before a group of senior creative leaders on a regular review schedule. This creates predictable feedback rhythm rather than sporadic crisis intervention. The culture of these sessions is deliberately direct — Braintrust members name what isn't working clearly and honestly, without the social softening that can make feedback useless. The permission to be honest, even uncomfortably so, is treated as a feature rather than a bug.

One structural decision makes the whole system work: the Braintrust has no authority to mandate changes. They identify problems but cannot dictate solutions. This preserves the director's creative ownership while providing expert perspective — preventing the group from becoming a committee that dilutes individual vision into a safer but blander consensus.

Because the Braintrust reviews all films, learning from one project becomes available to all others. A problem solved on one film becomes a resource for the next director facing something similar. Knowledge compounds across projects rather than staying siloed within teams.

Pixar also explicitly documents principles learned through experience. When patterns emerge across multiple projects — what makes characters feel real, what makes audiences disengage, what structural moves tend to save failing stories — those patterns get named and written down. Wisdom that might otherwise stay tacit and individual becomes institutional and transferable.

The lesson for multicultural organizations: creative and organizational excellence don't depend on preventing turnover or keeping the same people together indefinitely. They depend on systematic practices that capture learning, transmit it across people and time, and sustain a culture of honest feedback that makes improvement possible. When people leave, their wisdom can remain in documented principles and in the people they've shaped — if the systems exist to make that possible.

The Biblical View

Scripture is ripe with stories of turnover and transitions, successions going well and those that were never planned. It bodes well for leaders to read these stories.

Moses and Joshua: Succession as Ongoing Stewardship

Moses didn't leave succession to chance. Decades before his death, he appointed Joshua as military leader. He included Joshua on the mountain during revelatory moments. He sent him as one of the twelve spies into Canaan. He kept him close through long years of wilderness wandering. When God told Moses his time was ending, Moses didn't panic — he asked God immediately to appoint a successor so that the community would not be "like sheep without a shepherd." God designated Joshua. Moses laid hands on him before the entire assembly. Authority began transferring while Moses was still present to provide continuity.

But Moses didn't stop with the ceremonial. In Deuteronomy 31, he committed God's instructions to writing and handed Joshua a documented body of knowledge to lead from. He stood beside him publicly before the entire assembly to speak words of commissioning, naming explicitly what Joshua was taking on and what resources he had to do it. He charged Joshua repeatedly with the kind of direct personal encouragement that acknowledges real difficulty without pretending it away: be strong and courageous, do not be afraid, for God will be with you wherever you go.

The handoff worked. Joshua stepped into authority with the confidence of the people not because he demanded it but because they had watched the transition unfold deliberately, publicly, and over time. The community had been given the chance to transfer their trust, not simply ordered to.

What this reveals is the pattern that Moses embodied: effective succession requires three elements working together — long-term investment in developing a successor, deliberate knowledge transfer before departure, and public commissioning that signals to the whole community that the new leader carries genuine authority. Moses had no succession crisis because he treated succession as ongoing stewardship rather than a last-minute scramble.

Organizations that wait until someone announces their departure to think about who comes next create the crisis that James's executive director found herself managing. The knowledge in people's heads — relationships, institutional memory, unwritten rules, hard-won wisdom — doesn't transfer automatically. It transfers through time, intentional overlap, and documentation. Moses began Joshua's preparation before either of them knew exactly when the transition would come. That's the pattern worth imitating.

Samuel's Succession to Saul: Dignity at Every Stage

When Israel demanded a king, God instructed Samuel to manage a transition from one form of governance to another — a genuinely disruptive organizational change with enormous stakes. What's remarkable is how Samuel structured the process. He first met Saul privately, anointed him, and gave him specific signs to confirm his calling. Saul had time to process this enormous change before any public announcement. There was no surprise press release, no Slack message at 7 a.m. that the organization was going in a different direction. There was private preparation.

Then Samuel gathered Israel publicly and revealed God's choice through a process the people could witness. The transition had both private preparation and public legitimation — the new leader wasn't simply installed over people's heads; they watched the process and participated in it. Samuel didn't simply announce Saul's kingship — he explained the rights and duties of kingship, wrote them down, and deposited them formally. The new role was documented, not just described verbally in a meeting that half the people would misremember. This is ancient wisdom about knowledge transfer: if it matters, write it down.

Samuel didn't then disappear. He remained engaged during Saul's early leadership, available for guidance, willing to confront when confrontation was necessary. When his active leadership ended, he gathered Israel and publicly reviewed his own tenure — naming his record, inviting testimony, giving account of his stewardship. Then he moved to an advisory rather than active role, remaining available without crowding his successor.

The entire arc demonstrates something essential about transitions done well: dignity at every stage. Dignity for the departing leader, whose record gets acknowledged rather than erased. Dignity for the incoming leader, who receives public support rather than being thrown into the water alone. Dignity for the community, who are given space to make meaning of the change rather than simply being informed of it.

The Rhythm of Sabbath: Rest as Organizational Wisdom

God built rhythm into creation itself. By the seventh day, creation was complete and God rested — not from exhaustion, but establishing rest as part of the pattern of good creation. The Sabbath commandment extended this rhythm to human life: six days of work, one day of rest, repeated weekly across generations.

The Sabbath principle teaches that sustainable faithfulness requires rhythm. Work without rest leads to burnout. Intensity without recovery leads to breakdown. This isn't a concession to human weakness — it's recognition of how human beings are actually made. Organizations that ignore rhythm, celebrating overwork and treating rest as laziness, eventually pay the price in turnover, burnout, and diminished creativity. The machine can run continuously; humans cannot.

Sabbath also teaches trust: stopping work one day in seven requires believing that God provides, that the world doesn't depend entirely on our effort, that productivity isn't the ultimate value. For organizations, this means building rhythms of restoration into work life — not as concessions to weakness but as recognition of human design. The organizations that navigate scarcity and turnover and change with the most resilience are almost always the ones that have maintained rhythms of rest, reflection, and renewal even when pressure made them feel like luxuries. The rhythms that feel most optional are often most essential.

Nuances and Blind Spots

Systems beat intentions every time. Leaders often believe that genuine care for people will naturally produce dignified departures, smooth knowledge transfer, and supported transitions. But intentions without systems produce inconsistent results. The organization that means to handle departures well but has no actual departure ritual will do it beautifully when the right person remembers and has energy, and skip it entirely otherwise. Consistency requires structure, not just goodwill.

Daily practices compound in ways that dramatic gestures don't. A five-minute weekly check-in sustained for a year builds deeper early-warning capacity than an annual retreat. Brief monthly knowledge-sharing maintained across years creates organizational memory that survives any individual departure. The power is in repetition, not intensity — and this is exactly why rhythm collapse is so devastating. When sustainable practices depend on one person's energy rather than organizational systems, that person's departure takes the practices with them.

Crisis reveals rhythm absence at the worst possible time. Organizations discover they lack sustainable practices precisely when crisis hits — which is the worst moment to build them. Ghost employees, knowledge loss, replacement rush, survivor insecurity — these aren't caused by the departure itself. They're caused by the absence of systems that should have been in place before the departure happened. Build rhythms before you need them urgently.

Transitions are normal — treating them as failures makes them worse. Organizations that respond to every departure with barely concealed panic create ambient anxiety that accelerates future turnover. People watching how leadership handles someone else's exit are already calculating what their own exit would look like. The goal isn't preventing all turnover — it's building rhythms that make transitions manageable rather than catastrophic, and that honor what people contributed rather than pretending they simply vanished.

Exit interviews done badly are a missed diagnostic opportunity. Conducting exit interviews that never inform retention strategy or surface systemic problems isn't demonstrating care for departing staff — it's performing care. The same applies to rushing back to normal without processing loss, or managing collective discomfort by talking negatively about the person who left. Both prevent the organization from learning what the departure was actually telling it.

Rhythms must match culture — imported ones create friction. Western organizational rhythms often assume individual autonomy and linear time. Collectivist cultures may need rhythms that emphasize group cohesion. Cultures with different relationships to time may need different pacing. Imposing rhythms without cultural adaptation doesn't create sustainability — it creates one more thing that certain people must constantly translate while others find it effortless. The rhythm that helps some staff feel grounded may make others feel constrained. This is worth naming and designing for.

Heroic leadership undermines rhythm by design. Leaders who personally intervene to solve every problem feel indispensable — and are, because they've prevented sustainable systems from developing. The organization becomes dependent on the hero's energy rather than building capacity that survives any individual. Genuine rhythm requires leaders to step back enough for systems to actually function, which means tolerating some imperfection in the short term to build something that lasts.

Rest is productive, not its opposite. Organizations that celebrate overwork and treat recovery as laziness eventually pay the price in burnout, turnover, and diminished creativity. Sustainable rhythms include rest, reflection, and renewal as non-negotiable features — not rewards for high performance, not luxuries to be earned, but the biological and organizational reality that makes continued high performance possible at all.

❖

Try This Week

Choose one practice from below — just one, done consistently, is more valuable than five done sporadically.

Practice 1: Honor One Ending

When someone leaves — or has recently left — gather the team briefly. Ask: What did [person] contribute that we'll miss? What did we learn from working with them? Let people share. Don't rush it. Acknowledge loss before moving to next steps. This gives permission to grieve and honors the person's contribution without requiring that you have everything figured out yet.

Practice 2: Create a Knowledge Transfer Map

Don't wait for departures. Identify three critical roles in your organization. For each, document: What knowledge would leave if this person left tomorrow? What relationships are they maintaining that others don't know about? What would someone need to know to step into this role? Start building succession documentation now, before urgency makes it feel impossible.

Practice 3: Establish One Sustainable Rhythm

Identify one healthy practice your organization does inconsistently. It might be regular check-ins, knowledge sharing, celebrating contributions, or reflecting on lessons learned. Create a system to make it consistent: put it on the calendar, assign responsibility, create accountability. Start the rhythm even imperfectly — small and consistent beats large and occasional.

Practice 4: Support Survivors

After any departure, check in individually with remaining team members: How are you doing with this transition? What do you need? What concerns you most right now? Don't assume everyone's fine because no one has said otherwise. Transition creates anxiety even when departure was expected and positive. The question itself communicates something important.

Reflection Questions

Quick Check (1–2 minutes)

- Think about the last person who left your organization. Did they leave with dignity and honored contribution, or did they simply disappear?

- What daily or weekly rhythms does your organization maintain consistently, regardless of who's present or what crises have emerged?

Deeper Reflection (5–10 minutes)

- If your highest performer gave notice tomorrow, do you have systems for knowledge transfer — or would their expertise leave with them?

- What does your turnover rate tell you about organizational health? Are certain roles or demographic groups leaving disproportionately? What might that reveal about your rhythms and practices?

- When was the last time you personally experienced significant transition? How long did it take you to feel grounded again? Are you extending your team similar patience?

- Where is your organization dependent on individual heroics rather than sustainable systems? What would need to change for that to be different?

Team Discussion (15–30 minutes)

- As a leadership team, review the last five departures. For each: Why did they leave? How was the departure handled? What knowledge left with them? How long did the transition actually take? What would you do differently? Then identify one systemic rhythm to implement that would make future transitions more manageable — not because departure is bad, but because people who contributed deserve to be honored and what they carried deserves to survive them.

◄O►

Moving Forward

The opening scene revealed an organization without sustainable rhythms. James's departure became crisis because no systems existed for early warning, knowledge transfer, or dignified transition. The three additional resignations that arrived within days suggested a deeper pattern — problems that consistent daily practices might have caught and addressed before they became departures.

Johns Hopkins revolutionized medical training through graduated responsibility, systematic knowledge transfer, and overlapping transitions. Southwest Airlines maintains cultural identity through five decades of complete workforce turnover via deliberate hiring, intensive enculturation, and distributed culture-keeping. Pixar sustains creative excellence through constant team flux via regular review rhythms, candid feedback culture, and documented principles.

None of these examples depended on extraordinary leaders or dramatic interventions. They depended on ordinary practices, repeated consistently, compounded across time. The power was in rhythm, not intensity. Scripture confirms this pattern. Sabbath rhythm built into creation itself. Moses preparing Joshua for decades before the transition came. Samuel managing a governance change with private preparation, public commissioning, documented expectations, gradual authority transfer, and ceremonial farewell. Elijah developing Elisha through extended apprenticeship rather than abrupt handoff. The pattern is consistent across very different contexts: prepare before you need to, document what matters, honor transitions publicly, invest in the relational depth that makes all of it possible.

Sustainable organizations don't just manage crises well — they build rhythms that prevent crises from becoming catastrophic and create resilience for challenges that can't be prevented. These rhythms aren't glamorous. They don't make headlines. But they're precisely where organizational health is built or eroded, one small practice at a time. The question isn't whether scarcity, turnover, and change will come. They will. The question is whether you've built the rhythms to navigate them — or whether the next departure will catch you the same way James's did.

PART FOUR: SUSTAINABLE TRANSFORMATION

SUSTAINABLE TRANSFORMATION

Personal Development

Opening Scene

The leadership conference had been transformative. Brenda filled three notebooks with insights about multicultural leadership, trust-building, cultural intelligence, and organizational change. She flew home energized, ready to revolutionize her organization.

Monday morning, she arrived early to review her notes and create an implementation plan. By 9 AM, three urgent emails demanded attention. By 10 AM, she was in an unscheduled crisis meeting about a program deadline. By noon, she'd fielded two personnel issues and rescheduled her afternoon to handle a donor concern. By 5 PM, she realized she hadn't looked at her conference notes once.

Tuesday, she blocked two hours on her calendar specifically for "Conference Implementation." But a board member called, the blocked time disappeared, and she spent the afternoon on a funding proposal. Wednesday was consumed by budget meetings. Thursday by site visits. Friday by catching up on everything that had piled up during the week.

Three weeks later, she found her conference notebooks in her bag, unopened since the flight home. All that inspiration, all those insights, all that investment — consumed by the relentless pressure of immediate needs that crowded out important-but-not-urgent changes. The gap between what she wanted to do and what she actually did felt insurmountable.

She wasn't lazy. She wasn't uncommitted. She was simply overwhelmed by the relentless pressure of immediate needs that crowded out important-but-not-urgent changes. And she was learning what research on organizational change confirms: big dramatic initiatives fail far more often than they succeed. Real transformation happens through small, consistent practices repeated over time — micro-practices that become habits that shape culture.

But how do you create those practices when you can barely find time to breathe?

What makes Brenda's story worth examining carefully is that it isn't really about her. It's about a pattern that shows up in organizations everywhere, across cultures and contexts. The conference inspiration is real. The commitment to change is genuine. The urgency that consumes it is also real. And the gap that results — between what leaders know matters and what they actually do — quietly undermines organizational health one deferred intention at a time. Research in multicultural settings consistently finds that this gap is one of the primary drivers of what might be called leadership inconsistency: leaders whose values and behaviors are out of sync not because of bad faith but because the environment is systematically optimized for the urgent rather than the important.

The Science of Habit Formation

Approximately 43% of daily behaviors are habitual — performed automatically without conscious deliberation. This matters profoundly for organizational leadership: if nearly half of what we do is habitual, changing behavior requires changing habits, not just increasing willpower or motivation. The basic structure of habits involves a cue (trigger), routine (behavior), and reward (payoff). Habits form when this loop repeats enough times that the routine becomes automatic in response to the cue.

For organizational change, this means:

- **Willpower Isn't Enough**: Brenda's conference inspiration lasted as long as her willpower held out — about three days. Sustainable change requires building new habits, not just trying harder. Willpower is a finite resource that depletes under cognitive load, time pressure, and emotional stress — precisely the conditions that define most organizational leadership. Habits, by contrast, run on autopilot. The goal is to build practices so deeply into the rhythm of organizational life that they no longer require willpower to sustain.

- **Environment Shapes Behavior**: The strongest determinant of whether habits form is environmental cues, not individual motivation. If Brenda's environment constantly cues crisis response — every surface pinging with urgency, every hour fragmented by incoming demands — that is what becomes habitual regardless of her intentions. Organizations that want different behaviors must design environments that actively cue those behaviors. This is why purely aspirational approaches to development rarely work. The environment teaches people what is actually expected, and it teaches through structure, not speeches.

- **Small Beats Big**: Research on what has been called "tiny habits" shows that starting with behaviors so small they're almost trivial creates sustainable change better than dramatic overhauls. "Read one conference note daily" works better than "implement comprehensive cultural change initiative." The friction of beginning matters more than the scale of the goal. A practice small enough to do on a hard day will compound into something transformative over months. A practice sized for ideal conditions will be abandoned the first week things get difficult.

- **Identity Precedes Behavior**: Lasting behavior change comes from identity shifts: "I am the kind of leader who…" rather than "I want to do…" When practices align with who a person understands themselves to be, they are far more likely to persist through difficulty and distraction. This is one reason that development programs which treat growth as external performance rarely hold. When people come to own their development as part of their identity as a leader — not a task on a list but a reflection of who they are — the internal cue to practice becomes far stronger than any external accountability system.

In Multicultural Organizations, Habit Formation Faces Additional Challenges

- **Cultural Variation in Habits**: What feels natural and automatic varies across cultures. Time orientation, communication patterns, decision-making styles, and approaches to feedback are all culturally shaped habits — invisible to those who hold them precisely because they're automatic. When organizations try to shift habits, they are asking people to reroute patterns that have been reinforced across a lifetime of cultural experience. A habit that feels effortless for someone from one cultural background may feel deeply unnatural, even disrespectful, to someone from another. Effective development in multicultural settings begins by taking cultural habit seriously, not as resistance to overcome but as context to work with.

- **Collective Habits Matter**: Organizational culture is essentially collective habits — shared patterns of behavior that persist across personnel changes. This is why cultures are so resistant to individual intervention: one leader's new behavior presses against the gravitational pull of the group's existing norms. Changing organizational habits requires changing not just individual behaviors but the shared expectations, cues, and rewards that the group maintains together. Research in multicultural organizations shows that the most durable cultural changes happen when practices become communal — when enough people are doing them that the group norm begins to shift, and the behavior is no longer swimming against the current.

- **Power Dynamics Affect Habit Formation**: Leaders' habits shape organizational culture disproportionately. If the executive director habitually responds to every email within five minutes, that creates expectation and pressure for everyone else to do the same — whether or not it was intended as a norm. In high power distance contexts, where the authority of leaders is especially significant, this effect is amplified. Leaders' micro-behaviors are watched and mimicked in ways they often don't realize. This is both a warning and an opportunity: the same mechanism that allows leaders to accidentally install unhealthy habits can be used deliberately to model the habits a culture needs.

The Power of Micro-Practices

Micro-practices are deliberately designed small behaviors — so small they take less than two minutes — that cumulatively create cultural change when practiced consistently. They are not a workaround for serious organizational development. They are the mechanism of it. The research on how cultures actually shift consistently points to the same conclusion: incremental, embedded, repeated behavior changes the norms of a group far more reliably than periodic dramatic interventions. Why micro-practices work:

- **Low Resistance**: A two-minute practice doesn't trigger the resistance that a two-hour initiative does. "Before each meeting, I'll ask 'What cultural dynamics might I be missing?'" is achievable under pressure. "I'll completely overhaul how we run meetings" isn't. The threshold of resistance matters enormously for whether a practice survives contact with organizational reality. Research on multicultural organizations found that development initiatives requiring significant time investment were the first things abandoned when operational demands spiked — which, in most organizations, is most of the time. Practices small enough to sustain under pressure are the ones that actually shape culture.

- High Repetition: Because they're small, micro-practices can be repeated frequently. Frequency matters more than intensity for habit formation. A daily two-minute practice creates more neural reinforcement in a month than a monthly two-hour training. In multicultural organizations where trust and cultural intelligence must be cultivated continuously, daily micro-practices create far more cumulative impact than quarterly programs, however well-designed. The brain learns through repetition; culture shifts through the accumulation of shared, repeated behaviors.

- **Visible Modeling**: When leaders practice micro-behaviors consistently and visibly, others notice and begin adopting them. The practice spreads organically rather than requiring mandated implementation. This is especially significant in organizations with high power distance, where leadership behavior carries enormous normative weight. A leader who consistently pauses after presenting information — who visibly waits for others to speak before filling the silence — is not just building a personal habit. They are gradually establishing a new group norm about whose voice matters and when it's welcome.

- **Cumulative Impact**: Individual micro-practices seem trivial. But three to five practices repeated daily for six months create substantial cultural shift. The change accumulates rather than arriving dramatically. This is perhaps the hardest thing for leaders oriented toward visible results to accept: the practices that most reliably reshape organizational culture are often invisible in the short term. Their impact becomes legible only when looking back over months or years.

- **Sustainable Under Pressure**: When crisis hits — and in multicultural organizations navigating scarcity, turnover, and change, crisis is a near-constant condition — two-hour development initiatives get abandoned. Two-minute practices can continue. They don't require special time or conditions. They can be done on the hardest days. And it is precisely on the hardest days that culture is most decisively formed: how leaders behave under pressure tells their organizations far more about what is actually valued than how they behave when things are going well.

For Building Trust:

- Start each 1-on-1 with "How are you actually doing?" and listen completely before moving to agenda. Not "How is the project going?" — but the person. This practice, done consistently, signals that the relationship has priority over the transaction, which is foundational to trust especially across cultural contexts where relational investment is a prerequisite for working trust.

- End each week by emailing one team member thanking them

for something specific. Not "great job" — something observed and named. Specificity signals genuine attention. Generic appreciation reads as performance; specific acknowledgment reads as witness.

For Voice and Participation:

- In meetings, after presenting information, pause ten seconds before moving forward. Count silently. Ten seconds feels uncomfortably long — that discomfort is data about how little space has previously existed for response. The pause signals genuine invitation. In cultures where speaking without invitation is inappropriate, or where processing time before speaking is normal, this small practice can meaningfully shift whose voice enters the conversation.

- When someone shares an idea, respond first with "Tell me more" before evaluating. This single practice disrupts the reflexive evaluative response that shuts down contribution, especially from people who are already cautious about whether their input is welcome.

For Cultural Intelligence:

- Before major decisions, ask explicitly: "What cultural considerations might I be missing?" The act of asking the question publicly normalizes cultural attention as part of leadership judgment, not a specialty topic reserved for training days.

- Notice when you are uncomfortable in cross-cultural interaction and ask yourself: "What cultural assumption of mine might be operating here?" Discomfort is often a signal that a default assumption is being challenged. The habit of pausing to examine that assumption rather than reacting from it is one of the most powerful cultural intelligence practices available.

For Distributed Leadership:

- Once daily, ask someone "If you owned this decision, what would you do?" instead of telling them what to do. This practice develops judgment in others, signals that their thinking matters, and gradually shifts the organization toward empowered rather than dependent followership — one of the most consistent findings in the research on high-performance multicultural teams.

- Weekly, identify one decision you made that someone else could have made, and commit to delegating similar decisions going forward. Leaders often hold decisions they've outgrown out of habit rather than necessity. This practice builds the habit of actively releasing authority rather than passively retaining it.

For Managing Transition:

- When someone leaves, schedule fifteen minutes with the team to ask "What will we miss about how they worked?" before rushing to replacement planning. Naming what is lost honors the person and surfaces the institutional knowledge, relational skills, or cultural wisdom that needs to be carried forward intentionally rather than assumed to persist.

- For new hires, schedule brief check-ins at three days, three weeks, and three months. The consistency signals that the person matters — not as a role to be filled but as someone whose experience of joining is worth attending to. In multicultural settings, where the experience of being welcomed varies dramatically by cultural background, this simple practice can meaningfully reduce the anxiety and social risk of early tenure.

Pick one to three practices maximum. Do them consistently for 90 days before adding more. Let them become automatic before expanding. The research on habit formation is unambiguous on this point: attempting to build multiple habits simultaneously dramatically reduces the likelihood that any of them will stick. The goal is not a comprehensive practice portfolio. It is one practice so deeply embedded that it no longer requires intention — just execution.

Development as Organizational Priority

Too many organizations invest heavily in results while assuming people will "just develop" through experience. They provide technical training but neglect leadership development. They hire for today's competencies without building tomorrow's capabilities. They focus on doing more with existing people rather than helping people become more through deliberate growth. This approach fails for several reasons that compound over time.

Capability gaps widen. When organizations don't develop people, skill gaps that could have been addressed gradually become crises when key people leave or when new challenges demand capabilities that were never cultivated. What looked like adequate functioning was actually managed by a small number of highly capable individuals. When they go, the gap becomes visible — and large.

Talent leaves. High-potential people who don't see development pathways find organizations that offer them. Research consistently shows that "no growth opportunities" appears among the top reasons people leave organizations — often in the same exit interviews where leaders express surprise at the departure. The cost of turnover — in recruiting, onboarding, lost institutional knowledge, and team disruption — almost invariably exceeds the cost of the development that might have retained the person. Organizations that treat development as an expense they can't afford are paying for it anyway, just in the far more costly currency of departure.

Innovation stagnates. Organizations that don't develop new capabilities can't adapt to changing environments. The skills that worked five years ago are not necessarily adequate for the challenges of today, and today's competencies won't be sufficient for what comes next. Without deliberate capability development, organizations become progressively less able to navigate the complexity their contexts require — not because people stop caring, but because they were never given the tools to respond to what changed.

Cultural knowledge fails to transfer. In multicultural organizations, cultural intelligence must be deliberately developed — it doesn't emerge automatically through exposure or proximity. Research on faith-based multicultural organizations found that cultural intelligence and cross-cultural communication skill varied widely across staff and was rarely addressed through formal development. Organizations that assume cultural competency will develop naturally through experience reliably discover that it doesn't — and they discover it at the worst possible moments, when cross-cultural misunderstanding has already produced damage that patient, consistent development could have prevented.

Effective development requires several things working together. It requires individualized pathways, because different people start from different places and learn differently. One-size-fits-all development programs waste resources and frustrate participants — particularly in multicultural contexts where learning styles, relationships to authority, and orientations toward feedback vary significantly across cultural backgrounds. It requires practice, not just knowledge — development happens through application, not information transfer. It requires honest feedback loops, because people cannot improve what they cannot clearly see. And it requires a long-term perspective, because meaningful development takes months and years. Organizations that treat development as a program they run annually are missing the far more important question: how is development woven into the ordinary fabric of organizational life?

The Historical View

History is full of stories and examples of individuals who exemplified personal and organizational development, as well as more than a few where this lack of development brings ruin.

The Benedictine Rule and Daily Rhythm

Benedict of Nursia, writing around 530 CE, created a Rule for monastic life that has sustained communities for nearly 1,500 years. What makes the Benedictine Rule remarkable isn't its theological brilliance or organizational complexity — it's its profound, practical understanding of how daily rhythms shape character and community over time.

Benedict was a careful observer of human nature, and his Rule reflects a clear-eyed realism about what people are actually capable of sustaining. He did not write a heroic document. He famously described it as "a little rule for beginners" — and that modesty was deliberate and wise. Rules that demand extraordinary effort fail when extraordinary effort isn't available, which is most of the time. Rules that require only faithful daily attention can be kept even in exhaustion, distraction, and the ordinary difficulty of human life.

The structure of the Rule built development into the rhythm of each day rather than reserving it for special occasions. Times for prayer, work, study, meals, and rest — each given its place, each treated as formative. The movement between activities wasn't merely practical scheduling. It was a theology of transformation: that character forms not through infrequent intense experiences but through repeated small acts embedded in daily life. The monk who prays eight brief times each day will be formed differently, over a decade, than the monk who attends one elaborate annual ceremony. Frequency beats intensity for lasting formation. This is what the research on habit formation says in the language of neuroscience; it is what Benedict built into organizational life fifteen hundred years earlier.

Several aspects of the Rule are directly instructive for organizational leaders today.

- **Balance of Activities**: Benedict balanced contemplation and action, individual and communal time, work and rest. No single activity dominated. This balance was not a concession to human limitation — it was a design principle. Sustained excellence requires sustainability. Leaders and organizations that optimize entirely for output at the expense of rest, reflection, and relationship produce high performance for a season and burnout over time. The Rule's insistence on balance was a long-game strategy.

- **Modest Expectations**: The achievability of the Rule is part of its genius. Practices small enough to maintain even under difficulty create consistent formation. Practices sized for ideal conditions create cycles of aspiration, failure, guilt, and renewed aspiration — exactly the pattern Brenda experienced with her conference notebooks. The leaders and organizations that actually develop people over time are, almost without exception, those who chose modest, consistent practices over ambitious, intermittent ones.

- **Rhythm Over Intensity**: Prayer eight times daily rather than once in elaborate ceremony. The cumulative effect of consistent, brief practice mattered more than the intensity of any single instance. Organizations habitually invert this logic, investing in periodic high-intensity development events while neglecting the daily rhythms that would do most of the actual formation work. The conference Brenda attended was probably genuinely valuable — but without daily practices to receive and reinforce what she learned, it had nowhere to land.

- **Communal Accountability**: Practices were shared by the community, creating mutual accountability and shared culture. Individual willpower wasn't the load-bearing structure — the community rhythm was. When any single monk's motivation flagged, the community schedule carried them. This is a critical insight for organizational development: the most resilient practices are those embedded in shared structures, not dependent on individual initiative. Development that requires any one person's sustained enthusiasm to maintain is fragile. Development built into communal rhythms is not.

- **Gradual Formation**: New members entered through stages — postulant, novice, finally professed monk. Each stage had appropriate expectations matched to the person's place in the journey. Formation was unhurried by design. This patience was not passivity; it was the mechanism of deep transformation. Rushed development produces compliance. Patient, graduated development produces changed character. The organizations that develop people most profoundly are those willing to play a longer game than the quarterly calendar encourages.

- **Long-Term Sustainability**: The proof is in the longevity. Benedictine communities have sustained these practices for fifteen centuries across enormous cultural and historical upheaval. The daily rhythm proved more durable than any individual's enthusiasm because it wasn't dependent on individual enthusiasm. It was a system, sustained by community, resistant to the inevitable variation in any person's motivation over time.

What is directly applicable is this: transformation through daily rhythm isn't a modern innovation — it is ancient wisdom. Communities that want to sustain distinctive culture across time don't rely on dramatic events or heroic individuals. They create rhythms of practice small enough to maintain, consistent enough to form character, and communal enough to create shared identity. Every high-performing multicultural organization has something that functions like this, even when they don't call it that.

The Apprenticeship Model of Medieval Guilds

Medieval craft guilds developed sophisticated systems for growing people over time. A young person entered as an apprentice, typically around age twelve to fourteen, and spent seven to ten years learning a craft before becoming a journeyman, then eventually a master. This system wasn't arbitrary — it was calibrated to the actual time required for genuine mastery, and it embodied a set of developmental principles worth examining carefully.

- **Learning Through Doing**: Apprentices learned by working alongside masters, not by studying theory. Knowledge transferred through practice, observation, and graduated responsibility. The master's expertise didn't move through explanation primarily — it moved through the sustained, attentive relationship of someone who knew doing something well alongside someone learning it. Organizations that assume classroom instruction or structured training will develop capability are missing what the guilds understood intuitively: most of what matters about doing something well cannot be told. It must be shown, practiced, corrected, and shown again.

- **Graduated Challenge**: Apprentices began with simple tasks and took on progressively more complex work as capability developed. The challenge level was matched to the developmental stage — always slightly ahead of current comfort but not recklessly beyond it. This calibration is one of the most demanding aspects of effective development, and one of the most commonly neglected. It requires actually knowing where someone is in their development well enough to design appropriate challenge. Leaders who give everyone the same challenge level are either over-stretching the newer staff or under-developing the more experienced ones — usually both simultaneously.

- **Extended Timeline**: The guild system took mastery seriously enough to give it the time it required. Seven to ten years is not a training program — it is a formation process. The patience embedded in that timeline communicated something important: genuine capability is worth waiting for. The dominant organizational logic today pushes in exactly the opposite direction. We promote people on shorter timelines, move roles faster, and expect managers newly into their roles to perform at levels that the guild system would have recognized as requiring years more formation. The cost of that acceleration is the capability we don't develop.

- **Quality Standards**: Journeymen had to produce a "masterpiece" demonstrating competence before becoming masters. Standards were clear, externally assessed, and publicly visible. This combination — clear expectations, external evaluation, community acknowledgment — created a developmental environment where progress was legible and standards were real rather than negotiated downward to protect feelings. Organizations that lack clear developmental standards don't protect people from failure. They deprive them of the feedback necessary to improve.

- **Community of Practice**: Learning happened within community — masters, journeymen, and apprentices working together. Knowledge passed through relationships, not just formal instruction. The community itself was a developmental resource: different levels of expertise in visible proximity, each learning from what was above and solidifying their own understanding by teaching what was below. Organizations that develop people in isolated training cohorts miss the richness of what learning communities make possible.

- **Identity Formation**: The guild system didn't just teach skills — it formed identity. Apprentices became craftsmen. The transformation was about who they were, not only what they could do. This is the deepest kind of development, and the rarest. It requires an organizational culture that takes seriously the formation of people — that sees the organization's relationship to staff not just as a performance contract but as a relationship with people who are in the process of becoming something.

The Failure of "Sink or Swim" Development

In contrast, many organizations practice what might be called "sink or swim" development: place people in challenging situations with minimal support and see who figures it out. This approach seems efficient — no formal development investment required, and those who succeed demonstrate they can handle pressure. But it produces predictable failures:

- **High failure rates**: Many capable people drown not because they lack potential but because they lack support. Organizations lose talent they could have developed — and rarely count the cost accurately because the losses are attributed to the individuals rather than to the system.

- **Survivor bias**: Those who succeed through sink-or-swim often conclude that's simply how capable people develop, perpetuating the pattern. They don't see the talent that was lost, only the talent that persisted. This creates a self-reinforcing cycle: the system keeps producing leaders who think the system is fine, because it worked for them.

- **Cultural homogeneity**: Sink-or-swim tends to favor those whose background, cultural framework, and existing networks match the dominant culture of the organization. Those from different backgrounds face not just role challenge but cultural translation challenge simultaneously — a significantly heavier load with significantly less support. The "survivors" therefore tend to be culturally similar, and leadership progressively narrows toward the existing center. Diversity suffers — not through malice but through a development system that was never designed with diverse starting points in mind.

- **Limited innovation**: People developed through survival mode learn what works right now. They develop the capabilities required to navigate the current environment, not necessarily the broader or more adaptive capabilities that come from more deliberate formation. Organizations built on sink-or-swim development find themselves with staff highly adapted to the present moment and inadequately prepared for what changes.

Organizations that rely on sink-or-swim development mistake survival for excellence. They settle for the capability that emerges by accident rather than building the capability they actually need.

The Biblical View

Scripture consistently portrays development as intentional investment over time, not accidental growth through experience. Three passages in particular illuminate how God designs growth — and what that design suggests for organizational leaders.

The Feeding of the Five Thousand: Participation in Provision

When Jesus faced a hungry crowd of five thousand men plus women and children (John 6:1-14), He could have simply created food miraculously and distributed it. The miracle was entirely within His capacity. He didn't need anyone's participation to accomplish the provision. And yet He turned to Philip and asked a question: "Where shall we buy bread for these people to eat?" The text is explicit that He asked this to test Philip — not because Jesus lacked information, but because Philip needed the experience of being in the question.

Philip's response was honest and accurate. He calculated the cost against the crowd: more than half a year's wages, and that wouldn't even cover a small bite for each person. The math was right. The conclusion — impossibility — was where the disciples were at that moment in their development. Andrew added his own version of the same conclusion: "There is a boy here who has five barley loaves and two fish, but what are they for so many?" It isn't quite despair. It is something more familiar — the exhausted realism of people who can see the gap clearly and haven't yet experienced the kind of provision that changes what they believe is possible.

Then Jesus did something that was as much about formation as provision. He told the disciples to have the people sit down. He took the bread, gave thanks, and distributed it — through their hands. Not around them. Through them. They were the ones passing out bread that kept coming. They held in their hands more than there should have been. They filled twelve baskets with what was left over after five thousand ate. The miracle passed through their bodies, not just their eyes.

This is how Jesus developed the disciples throughout his ministry. Not through lecture, not through explanation, but through participation in situations beyond their capacity — situations where the gap between what they could do and what was needed made space for experiencing both their inadequacy and God's sufficiency at the same time. Development came through doing the thing with support, not through being told about the thing from a distance.

For organizations, the implication is direct. Development often happens not through removing challenges from people's paths, but through supporting people as they face challenges that stretch them beyond current capability. The growth comes in the gap between what they can do alone and what becomes possible through participation in something larger. Leaders who shield developing people from difficulty in the name of care are withholding exactly what the disciples received: the chance to hold the bread in their own hands. The protection feels kind. The deprivation is real.

Elisha and the Widow's Oil: Gradual Increase Through Daily Action

When a widow came to Elisha in desperate poverty (2 Kings 4:1-7), she was facing creditors ready to take her sons as payment for her debt. The urgency was extreme. The resources were minimal: one small jar of oil. What Elisha gave her in response to her crisis was not immediate relief. He gave her a process.

"Go around and ask all your neighbors for empty jars. Don't ask for just a few. Then: go inside, close the door behind you and your sons, and pour oil into all the jars — and as each is filled, set it to one side." The widow obeyed. She gathered jars — how many depended on her own initiative and her own faith about what might be possible. Then she poured. The oil flowed. Jar after jar was filled and set aside. The process went on until she ran out of containers, and only then did the oil stop. When she reported to Elisha, the instruction was practical: go, sell the oil, pay your debts, and live on what remains.

There are several things worth sitting with in this story. The provision was gradual — not a single dramatic moment but a repeated small action, jar by jar. It required her participation at every step: gathering, pouring, setting aside. The total provision was bounded by her preparation; she could not have received more oil than she had containers to hold. The multiplication matched her readiness and her willingness to act faithfully in small ways over time.

The instruction not to ask for just a few jars is particularly striking. Elisha was telling her not to limit what she went looking for. Her expectation about what was possible would literally determine the ceiling on the outcome. Leaders and organizations that approach development with limited imagination — assuming people can only grow so much, or that their role is to manage current capacity rather than cultivate future capability — are asking for only a few jars. They will receive exactly as much as their expectation prepared room for.

For organizations, this pattern is instructive at multiple levels. Growth rarely arrives as sudden transformation. More often it comes jar by jar — through repeated small actions, each one requiring a measure of faithful effort, each one building on the last. The developing person is not a passive recipient of growth but an active participant whose engagement shapes what becomes possible. Development systems designed for gradual, consistent, supported practice understand something that dramatic intervention approaches miss: the work of formation is slow, and its slowness is a feature, not a failure.

The Parable of the Talents: Faithful Stewardship and Development Over Time

Jesus told a parable about a master entrusting servants with different amounts of money — five talents to one, two to another, one to a third — "each according to his ability" (Matthew 25:14-30). Then he went on a journey.

The first two servants put their talents to work immediately and doubled them. When the master returned, both offered the same account: here is what you gave me, here is what it became. The commendation was identical for both, regardless of the size of their original gift: "Well done, good and faithful servant! You have been faithful with a few things; I will put you in charge of many things." The standard was not the amount produced but the faithfulness of the stewardship. Five talents producing five more and two talents producing two more both receive the same response. Proportional faithfulness is what the master recognizes.

The third servant's account is revealing. He didn't claim to have lost the talent. He didn't claim bad conditions. He explained: "I was afraid." Fear — not incompetence, not laziness, not malice — was what caused him to bury what he'd been given. He was protecting what he had against the risk of losing it, and in doing so forfeited both the growth and the trust that faithful engagement would have built. The master's response was sharp: even minimal effort — depositing with the bankers, the lowest-risk option available — would have demonstrated faithfulness. The condemnation was not about the size of the return. It was about paralysis in the face of responsibility.

For development, the parable is a diagnosis. When staff operate in environments where failure is met with judgment rather than learning, they bury their talents. They do what is safe. They avoid the stretch that might produce imperfect results. They stop bringing their full capability to work and begin managing exposure instead — appearing productive without taking the risks that growth requires. The result is organizations full of buried potential: people carrying capability they will not risk in an environment that does not feel safe for honest effort and honest failure.

The parable also reframes the goal of development. The master's standard was not that everyone produce the same outcome. It was that everyone be faithfully engaged with what they've been given, growing from their own starting point. Organizations that design development systems oriented toward uniform outcomes will inevitably frustrate some people while leaving others unchallenged. Systems that ask "how is this person growing from where they are?" — and that create environments safe enough for people to actually try — are closer to what the parable commends.

Fear-based cultures that punish risk-taking produce buried talents. Trust-based cultures that celebrate faithful effort produce multiplication. The creation of that trust-based environment is not a soft aspiration. The parable frames it as fundamental stewardship — not of money, but of the people and their potential that leaders have been entrusted to develop.

Nuances and Blind Spots

Development happens in the ordinary, not the extraordinary. Most growth occurs through daily work, regular feedback, and consistent challenge — not through special programs, conference highs, or dramatic interventions. The inspiration that fades within weeks after an event wasn't false; it just had nowhere to land because no sustainable daily practices were built to receive it. Organizations that invest heavily in formal development programs while neglecting the developmental quality of ordinary work miss the majority of their growth opportunity. If the experience of everyday work doesn't develop people — if meetings aren't environments for learning, if feedback isn't a regular part of relationships, if stretch isn't built into how roles are designed — no supplemental program will compensate for that deficit.

Imperfect consistency beats perfect inconsistency. The pattern of abandoned initiatives — starting strong, adding complexity, then watching things collapse under their own weight — creates something more damaging than the original problem: cynicism about whether any future development effort is real. "We'll have weekly two-hour development sessions" won't happen consistently, and everyone knows it before it starts. Small practices sustained over time compound into genuine transformation. All-or-nothing thinking is among the most reliable predictors of organizational stagnation — the enemy of actual growth.

Hero dependency is a development failure disguised as commitment. When development requires one leader's constant energy to maintain — stopping entirely when they're absent, traveling, or burned out — it was never really organizational development. It was personal energy temporarily wearing the costume of a system. Sustainable development must be built into organizational rhythms that function independently of any single person's presence or enthusiasm. The measure of a development culture is not what happens when the most committed leader is fully present. It is what happens when that person is gone for three weeks.

Development requires challenge and support in calibrated combination. Research on human development is consistent here: challenge without support produces stress and failure; support without challenge produces comfort and stagnation. The combination — genuinely stretching challenge held within genuinely adequate support — creates the conditions for growth. What makes this demanding is that the right calibration differs for every person and changes as they develop. Leaders must actually know the people they are developing well enough to read where each person's growing edge is and what kind of support will help them stay in the difficulty rather than retreat from it. Uniform expectations applied to diverse people waste resources on those who need less while quietly overwhelming those who need more.

The leader's development sets the ceiling for everyone else's. Organizations rarely grow beyond the leader's current capacity — not because leaders prevent growth intentionally, but because every developmental ceiling a leader hits becomes a cultural norm. If the executive director doesn't know how to give honest developmental feedback, the organization won't have a culture of honest developmental feedback regardless of what values are stated. Leaders who wear overload as an identity marker — who treat margin as weakness and busyness as a badge of commitment — model exactly the posture that prevents sustainable development at every level below them. Exempting oneself from the development one asks of others doesn't go unnoticed. It quietly teaches that development is for the people who need fixing, not for those who are already leading.

Feedback is not optional. Development without honest, specific, timely feedback is like practicing archery without ever seeing where the arrows land. People cannot improve what they cannot clearly see. Organizations that avoid difficult feedback conversations — in the name of kindness, relationship preservation, or cultural harmony — are not protecting their people. They are preventing the growth they claim to want. There is often a subtle avoidance at work: leaders who track numbers carefully and measure outputs obsessively are sometimes doing so as a substitute for the harder, more personal work of telling someone the truth about their growth. Measurement is not development. Feedback is.

Development is investment, not expense. Organizations that cut development during difficult times treat it as optional overhead. But development builds the capability that creates future success — cutting it saves money today while systematically undermining tomorrow. The same logic applies to cultural intelligence: cross-cultural capability doesn't emerge automatically through exposure or proximity. It requires intentional investment — frameworks, practice, feedback, and honest reflection. Organizations that assume it will "just happen" reliably discover it doesn't, and they discover it at precisely the moments when it matters most.

Adding without subtracting guarantees collapse. Piling new development activities onto already overloaded people isn't generosity — it's a reliable recipe for initiative exhaustion. Genuine development requires replacing ineffective patterns with better ones, not simply accumulating more. Before launching any new development practice, the honest question is: what are we willing to stop doing to make room for this? The question isn't only what should we add, but what should we stop doing to create space for what actually works.

Try This Week

Choose ONE micro-practice to start — just one.

Practice 1: The Daily Question

Before leaving work, ask yourself one question: "Did I invest in someone's development today?" Not "Was I perfect?" but "Did I practice?" Write one sentence answer. Do this daily for 90 days. Track streaks. This builds awareness and accountability through minimal time investment.

Practice 2: Meeting Pause Practice

After presenting information in meetings, count to 10 silently before moving forward. This creates space for response from people who need processing time or whose cultural framework makes immediate speaking uncomfortable. Ten seconds feels long — that's the point. It signals you genuinely want input, not just performing consultation.

Practice 3: Weekly Development Email

Every Friday before leaving, send one email to one team member with specific developmental feedback: "I noticed [specific behavior]. The impact was [result]. To grow further, consider [suggestion]." Rotate through team. Balance affirmation with challenge. This builds developmental rhythm consistently over time.

Practice 4: Start With "How Are You?"

In every 1-on-1, start with "How are you actually doing?" and wait for a real answer before moving to agenda. If they say "fine," follow up: "What's been hard this week?" or "What are you learning?" Consistently starting with the person before productivity builds the relational foundation for developmental conversations.

Reflection Questions

Quick Check (1–2 minutes)

- What percentage of your leadership time goes to developing others versus doing the work yourself?

- Think about the last person you developed effectively. What made that development work?

Deeper Reflection (5–10 minutes)

- If someone shadowed you for a week, what would they conclude you actually value about development based on what you consistently do, not what you say?

- What small developmental practice, if you did it daily for a year, would fundamentally change your team's capability?

- Who on your team has the most developmental potential that you're currently not investing in? What would it take to start?

- How does your own ongoing development affect your capacity to develop others? Where are you growing? Where have you stagnated?

Team Discussion (15–30 minutes)

As a leadership team, each person shares: (1) One way you've been developed that made lasting difference, (2) What made it effective, (3) How you're passing that kind of development to others. Then together, identify one team-level developmental practice you could adopt — something small enough to do consistently that would grow the team's collective capability. Commit to 90-day trial.

Moving Forward

Brenda's conference notebooks, unopened three weeks after her return, represent a common failure pattern: dramatic inspiration without sustainable practice. The insights she gained were real. Her commitment was genuine. But without micro-practices that fit into daily rhythm, transformation remained aspiration rather than reality.

The Benedictine Rule has sustained communities for fifteen centuries through daily rhythm, modest expectations, and communal accountability. Medieval guilds developed master craftsmen through graduated challenge, extended timelines, and learning communities. Jesus involved the disciples in feeding five thousand, developing them through participation in impossible situations — holding in their own hands bread that kept coming. The widow's oil multiplied through repeated small actions, jar by jar, provision bounded by preparation and faithful daily participation. The parable of the talents teaches that faithful stewardship of what we're given, in the environment of trust rather than fear, leads to multiplication — while fear produces only the careful preservation of what was already there.

These examples share common elements: patience with process, consistency over intensity, relationship as the context for growth, graduated challenge matched to capability, and long-term perspective that allows deep formation rather than superficial change. None of them relied on drama. All of them relied on faithfulness.

Growing people isn't an optional extra for organizations with resources to spare. It's a fundamental requirement for organizations that want to thrive over time. The capability to navigate multicultural complexity, build trust across difference, distribute leadership effectively, and sustain mission through challenge — none of this emerges automatically. All of it must be deliberately developed. The question isn't whether to invest in development — organizations that don't develop people inevitably decline. The question is whether development will happen through intentional investment or be left to chance. The organizations that thrive are those that choose intention. And that choice begins, most reliably, with one small practice done faithfully today.

Growing People, Not Just Results

Opening Scene

The annual review conversation wasn't going well. Vivi had been a solid performer for three years—reliable, competent, delivering what was expected. But when her supervisor asked, "Where do you see yourself in five years?" Vivi went quiet.

Finally: "Honestly? I don't know. I thought maybe I'd be leading a team by now. But we've never talked about development or leadership preparation. We've only talked about getting my current work done better and faster."

Her supervisor felt defensive: "We've sent you to training. You went to that project management conference last year."

Vivi nodded. "That was helpful for technical skills. But it didn't prepare me to lead people, navigate conflict, or make strategic decisions. I know how to execute better. I don't know how to lead."

The supervisor realized the gap: The organization invested in training for current roles but nothing for future ones. They developed technical competence but not leadership capacity. They measured results but not growth. People either figured out leadership on their own or they didn't advance—and often they left for organizations that took development seriously.

Across the organization, the pattern repeated. New managers struggled because they'd never received leadership development—just technical training and a promotion. Seasoned staff hit plateaus because no one invested in their continued growth. Talented people left after two or three years saying, "I'm not learning anymore."

The organization was producing results but not developing people. And increasingly, that meant they couldn't sustain results because capability wasn't deepening. They were extracting value from people rather than investing in growth—and eventually, people stopped offering their best because they stopped believing the organization cared about their development.

The executive director reviewing retention data saw the pattern: exit interviews consistently mentioned "no growth opportunities" as the primary reason for departure. Yet the organization's budget included substantial training line items. They were spending money on development but not actually developing people. Something fundamental was missing.

Why Development Matters

Evidence and experience point toward a truth many leaders resist: the most fruitful leaders see their work as forming people, not just producing outputs. Intentional development of competencies—self-awareness, emotional resilience, communication, ethical judgment—matters as much as technical skill.

When organizations invest in growing people, performance improves as competence deepens. Retention increases because people feel valued. Leadership pipelines develop naturally. Culture strengthens through shared learning. Mission advances through multiplied capacity.

When organizations neglect development, talent stagnates. High performers plateau. Good people leave for places that will invest in them. Succession becomes a crisis when key people depart. Culture turns transactional rather than developmental. Mission suffers as organizational capacity fails to keep pace with organizational ambition.

The data on this is consistent and sobering. In cross-cultural settings especially, staff from minority cultural backgrounds are often the first to notice when development is distributed unevenly—and the first to leave when they conclude the pattern is deliberate. What leaders experience as a vague retention problem is often, at its root, a development equity problem: certain people receiving formative investment while others receive only task assignments.

One pattern surfaces repeatedly in multicultural organizations: some staff experience rich learning and genuine leadership pathways, becoming administrators and program leaders over time, while others find themselves repeatedly assigned new responsibilities without adequate training, support, or debriefing. The first group thrives. The second group burns out or leaves. And organizations often mistake the exits for attitude problems rather than recognizing them as diagnostic signals about how development is—or isn't—flowing.

The Deeper Truth: Development as Calling

Here's the deeper truth: growing people isn't just strategic—it's theological. Humans were created with capacity for deep intellectual, relational, and spiritual growth. Leadership, rightly understood, is helping people fulfill that God-given purpose. It's nurturing strengths, providing meaningful challenges, creating opportunities for contribution, and walking with people through seasons of refinement.

When you invest in someone's development, you're not just improving organizational performance. You're participating in what God is doing to form people into who they were created to be. Training, feedback, and accountability become means of grace. Job design becomes an expression of respect for people's God-given capacities. Leadership development becomes preparation for lifelong service, not just career advancement.

This reframing changes everything. The question isn't whether you have budget for development. The question is whether you care enough to make the time—and whether you see your role as extracting performance from people or growing people while pursuing performance. That choice shapes everything that follows.

How People Actually Develop: The 70-20-10 Framework

Research on how leaders develop reveals that formal training, while important, accounts for only about 10% of developmental learning. The 70-20-10 framework shows:

• 70% from experience (challenge assignments, new responsibilities, stretch opportunities, learning by doing)

• 20% from relationships (coaching, mentoring, feedback, observation of role models, peer learning)

• 10% from formal training (courses, workshops, conferences, structured programs)

Most organizations invert this. They spend the majority of their development budget on formal training—the 10%—while neglecting the 70% of developmental experiences and the 20% of relationships that actually create growth.

Vivi's organization sent her to a project management conference—the 10%—but never gave her stretch assignments that developed leadership capability, provided coaching or mentoring for leadership growth, created opportunities to observe and learn from experienced leaders, or offered feedback on her leadership behaviors rather than only on task completion. The training helped her execute better. It didn't develop her as a leader.

What changes when leaders understand this framework is not just what they spend money on—it's how they think about their daily role. Every stretch assignment is a developmental act. Every feedback conversation is developmental investment. Every time a senior leader brings a developing staff member into a strategic conversation and debriefs it afterward, that's the 20% at work. The most powerful development tools cost nothing except intentionality.

Why This Matters Especially in Multicultural Organizations

Development needs vary across cultural frameworks in ways leaders often don't anticipate. Individualistic cultures may emphasize independent stretch assignments where a person proves themselves through solo initiative. Collectivist cultures may prioritize mentoring relationships and peer learning, where growth happens in community rather than through individual achievement. High power-distance cultures may expect formal developmental investment from authority figures as a sign of genuine regard. Low power-distance cultures may assume people take initiative for their own development and may interpret a leader's direct offer of mentoring as condescending.

Effective development in multicultural settings requires all three elements of the 70-20-10 framework delivered through multiple pathways that honor diversity not just in identity but in how people learn and grow.

There's a subtler dynamic as well. In multicultural organizations, the staff who most need developmental investment are often the least likely to ask for it. Cultural humility can look like low ambition to leaders unfamiliar with the difference. Deference to authority can mask genuine readiness. And because developmental conversations require a baseline of trust and psychological safety, staff who don't yet fully trust that leadership cares about them will rarely volunteer their aspirations in a formal review setting.

This means the developmental conversation—"What do you want to learn? What would stretch you?"—has to be built on a foundation of genuine relationship, not just asked as a performance review checkbox. Staff need to believe their honest answer won't be held against them and that something real will come of it.

Assessing and Building Developmental Readiness

Not everyone is ready for every development opportunity. Developmental readiness depends on three factors: capability (do they have the foundational skills needed for next-level challenges?), motivation (do they actually want to grow in this direction?), and opportunity (does the organization have the roles and projects that would develop them?).

Mismatches at any point create problems. High capability with low motivation means pushing development someone doesn't want, which creates resentment rather than growth. High motivation with low capability means promoting before someone is ready and setting them up for visible failure. High capability and motivation with no opportunity is perhaps the most damaging of all—it produces the exit interviews that say "I'm not learning anymore" and sends talented people to organizations that will invest in them.

Cultural frameworks shape all three dimensions of readiness in ways leaders often miss. Capability varies because different cultures emphasize different competencies. Someone highly capable in a relationship-oriented culture may need development in task-oriented environments and vice versa—but that doesn't mean they lack capability overall. It means they need developmental experiences that expand their range, not leaders who confuse cultural style with competence ceiling.

Motivation is culturally shaped in ways that can be genuinely invisible to leaders from majority cultures. In some cultural frameworks, openly expressing leadership aspiration is expected and admired. In others, it is seen as presumptuous or inappropriate unless an authority figure extends an invitation first. Leaders who mistake cultural restraint about ambition for actual lack of ambition will systematically overlook some of their most capable people.

Opportunity often reflects cultural bias even when it isn't intended to. Developmental assignments tend to flow most naturally to people who communicate and relate in ways that feel comfortable and familiar to the leaders distributing those assignments. This isn't usually deliberate—it's the path of least resistance. But the aggregate effect is that people culturally similar to leadership get developed, while those who aren't continue to be assigned tasks rather than formed for leadership.

Creating Developmental Opportunities

Effective organizations deliberately create growth pathways rather than waiting for them to appear organically. The range of tools available is broader than most leaders realize. Stretch assignments give someone a project slightly beyond their current capability, requiring new skills—real work with real responsibility and appropriate support. Acting roles give someone temporary leadership during a transition or absence, letting them discover capacities they didn't know they had. Cross-functional exposure to different parts of the organization builds systemic understanding that task-focused roles never provide.

External representation—asking someone to present to stakeholders, speak at a conference, or represent the organization publicly—does something subtle and powerful: it signals trust, expands networks, and often crystallizes confidence in ways internal opportunities can't replicate. Problem-solving teams that tackle strategic or complex challenges develop judgment. Mentoring others develops the mentor as much as the mentee. Leading a specific initiative with defined outcomes and adequate support is one of the most powerful developmental tools available.

The key in each case is the same: match the developmental experience to the person's actual readiness, provide genuine support during the stretch rather than abandoning them once the assignment is made, debrief the learning explicitly afterward rather than moving on, and distribute opportunities equitably across cultural backgrounds and role types. Development doesn't happen automatically through experience—it happens through experience plus reflection plus support. Remove any of the three and the investment is incomplete.

What Patterns Reveal About Development in Practice

Across multicultural organizations, a consistent pattern emerges when leaders ask honestly about how development actually flows. Formal training systems often exist and function reasonably well. But the informal systems—who gets brought into strategic conversations, who gets introduced to key relationships, who gets offered a stretch assignment when one opens up—reveal a different picture. Those informal systems tend to reproduce whatever cultural patterns already exist at the leadership level, not because anyone planned it that way, but because trust and familiarity are the currency of informal development, and both tend to flow most easily between people who share cultural frameworks.

What changes this isn't a policy—it's intentionality at the individual decision level. When leaders begin asking explicitly, "Who is ready for more responsibility that I haven't yet offered more responsibility to, and why?" the answers often surface patterns no one had previously named. Naming the pattern is the first step toward changing it.

There's also a category of staff who build the organization's developmental capacity from the inside without formal recognition or resources—colleagues who train each other, senior teachers who mentor newer ones, staff who create informal peer learning networks. In understaffed, under-resourced organizations especially, this relational infrastructure often carries the organization for seasons when formal systems are inadequate. Wise leaders identify these informal developers, acknowledge what they're contributing, and find ways to formalize and support it rather than extracting it invisibly.

The organizations that sustain high performance over time are consistently the ones that treat development as ongoing infrastructure rather than occasional initiative. When development budgets get cut in hard seasons, those cuts signal something deeper than financial constraint—they signal whether the organization actually believes that its people are its primary long-term asset. Staff notice. And they respond accordingly.

The Historical View

History offers compelling examples of how sustained investment over time creates extraordinary capability—and how its absence creates mediocrity.

Carnegie's Executive Development System

Andrew Carnegie built not just a steel empire but a legendary leadership pipeline—one of the most deliberate executive development systems in American industrial history. Where competitors focused on machinery, Carnegie focused on people, believing that the systematic development of human talent was his greatest competitive advantage.

Carnegie's approach centered on identifying potential early. He actively sought young workers who showed character and capability, then gave them graduated responsibilities over years—not weeks. His famous principle, "Put all your eggs in one basket, and watch that basket," applied as much to people as to capital. He concentrated his developmental investment in those with the most promise, watching them closely and advancing them deliberately.

The results were remarkable. Carnegie developed Charles Schwab from a stake driver to president of Carnegie Steel. He cultivated Henry Frick, Henry Phipps, and dozens of others who became transformational leaders in their own right. His organization produced more great executives than any competitor—not because of superior training programs but because of a cultural commitment to developing people through real responsibility, close observation, and patient promotion.

What distinguished Carnegie's system was its multi-generational thinking. He wasn't developing people for their current roles—he was preparing them for roles that didn't yet exist. He built internal capacity across decades, trusting that sustained investment in people would compound into organizational strength that no competitor could quickly replicate.

There's a challenge embedded in Carnegie's story that contemporary leaders need to sit with: his system worked, but it also reflected the biases of his era. His developmental investment flowed almost exclusively to men who looked and moved in ways that felt familiar to him. The lesson isn't to replicate Carnegie's system—it's to take his core insight about sustained, deliberate developmental investment and apply it without the cultural blind spots that limited who benefited from it. Development that changes organizations happens over years and decades, not quarters. And it only produces the full return on investment when it reaches across, not just down, cultural lines.

Tuskegee and the Long Work of Building People

In 1881, Booker T. Washington arrived in Tuskegee, Alabama to lead a new school with a promised state allocation, no campus, no buildings, and no equipment. What he found was an abandoned church and a shanty. What he built over the next three decades became one of the most instructive examples in American history of what happens when an institution commits—without reservation—to developing people rather than merely producing outputs.

Washington's foundational conviction was that genuine development couldn't be rushed or faked. Students at Tuskegee didn't just study in buildings—they built them. They learned brickmaking by making bricks, farming by farming, carpentry by constructing the campus they would inhabit. This wasn't poverty making do—it was a deliberate philosophy that learning divorced from practice produced incomplete people. Washington wanted graduates who could not only think but build, not only aspire but execute. He was developing whole persons, not credentialing students.

Development was the core work, not a byproduct. Washington never treated student formation as secondary to institutional outcomes. The institution existed to develop people; whatever else it accomplished flowed from that. This priority structured every decision about curriculum, campus life, and leadership practice. When opportunities for faster growth or larger enrollments appeared, Washington turned them down if they would compromise the depth of development he was committed to. Growth that outpaced the institution's capacity to form people well was, in his framework, not growth at all.

In 1896, Washington recruited George Washington Carver—already being courted by better-resourced institutions—because Carver shared the developmental philosophy. Carver would spend 47 years at Tuskegee, consistently choosing the long work of mentoring students and serving poor farmers over personal advancement. He turned down offers from Thomas Edison and Henry Ford. When asked why, he pointed to the students he was developing and the farmers whose lives his agricultural research was transforming. He had taken the long view.

Carver refused to patent the vast majority of his discoveries—over 300 products derived from peanuts, sweet potatoes, and other crops—so that the people who most needed them, small farmers with no resources, could access them freely. He was developing an ecosystem of human flourishing, not extracting personal benefit from his expertise. That posture—placing the development of others above personal advancement—is rare in any era. It's the posture Tuskegee's endurance depended on.

Tuskegee remains a functioning university today, nearly 145 years after Washington arrived at that abandoned church. That endurance came directly from its commitment to developing people deeply rather than producing outputs efficiently. Washington and Carver both operated with time horizons longer than their own careers. They were building something they knew they wouldn't see completed—and they invested their best work into it anyway.

The contrast with extractive development is precise: institutions that treat people as means to organizational ends produce short-term results and long-term fragility. Institutions that treat development of people as the primary work find that results follow—and that what they build lasts beyond any individual's tenure. For leaders navigating resource-constrained, multicultural environments where the pressure to produce outcomes is relentless, Tuskegee's example is not inspiration about the past—it is instruction about what's possible when development conviction is genuine and sustained.

The Moravian Missions: Sustained Commitment Across Centuries

The Moravian church, beginning in the eighteenth century, sent missionaries to some of the world's most difficult mission fields—Caribbean slave communities, Arctic Greenland, Native American territories. What distinguished Moravian missions was sustained commitment across generations.

Moravian missionaries often spent their entire lives in a single location. When they died, others took their place. The mission continued regardless of individual outcomes. This long-term perspective produced results that short-term presence never could. Moravians were willing to invest years building relationships before seeing any visible fruit. They learned languages, understood cultures, and earned trust through sustained presence. When missionaries died or departed, others continued their work. Knowledge transferred. Relationships maintained. The mission's identity transcended individual missionaries.

There's a development principle embedded in this pattern that translates directly to organizational life: the most powerful investment leaders make in people is often not a single transformative intervention but the cumulative weight of sustained, consistent presence over years. The leader who checks in monthly for three years, who notices growth and names it, who provides progressively more challenging opportunities as readiness develops—that leader shapes people in ways that the leader who runs an intensive development program and then disappears never does.

Compound impact is real. Decades of faithful presence created impact that short-term efforts never could. Communities transformed gradually through sustained relationship, not through dramatic interventions. For leaders who are tempted to measure developmental ROI on quarterly timelines, the Moravian example is a needed corrective: some of the most important seeds take years to germinate and cannot be forced.

The Biblical View

Scripture consistently portrays leadership as a developmental calling—growing people, not just accomplishing tasks.

Anna the Prophetess: 84 Years of Faithful Service

Luke 2:36–38 introduces Anna, a widow who had devoted herself to the temple—worshiping night and day with fasting and prayer—for 84 years. She is one of Scripture's most striking portraits of long obedience. Anna did not see immediate results from her faithful service. There were no dramatic miracles attributed to her prayers during those decades, no crowds gathering to hear her teach, no political power accrued from her presence. She simply showed up—day after day, decade after decade—serving faithfully in the place God had given her.

What sustained 84 years of faithful presence when visible results were absent? Anna's story suggests it was purpose larger than outcomes. She wasn't serving to achieve a measurable goal; she was serving because faithfulness itself mattered. The work was the calling, not merely the means to a visible end.

Then, in the fullness of time, her patient faithfulness positioned her for something generations of Israel had longed to witness. When Mary and Joseph brought the infant Jesus to the temple, Anna was there—present because she had always been present—and she recognized the Messiah. Her 84 years of showing up made her available for the moment that mattered most.

For leaders investing in people's development, Anna's story is both challenge and encouragement. The challenge: Are you willing to invest faithfully for years without seeing immediate results? The encouragement: sustained faithfulness positions you—and those you develop—for moments of profound impact that impatient approaches never reach. Development that compounds over years becomes impossible to replicate through intensive short-term investment. You cannot buy in a quarter what only time and faithful presence can produce.

David Preparing Solomon: Succession as Development

Near the end of his life, David received word that he would not build the temple he'd dreamed of constructing for God. His son Solomon would complete that work. David's response is one of Scripture's most instructive portraits of leadership succession.

Rather than becoming passive or bitter, David spent years preparing Solomon for the work he would inherit. First Chronicles 28–29 details his preparations: David gathered gold, silver, bronze, iron, wood, and precious stones—everything Solomon would need. He organized the priestly divisions. He drew up architectural plans. He secured the political relationships that would make the temple possible. He prepared for work he would never see completed.

Then David publicly commissioned Solomon before all Israel's leaders—not a quiet handoff but a formal, communal investment in the next generation's authority. He shared the plans God had given him. He charged Solomon with both the work and the character it required: "Be strong and courageous, and do the work. Do not be afraid or discouraged, for the Lord God, my God, is with you." In his final charge to Solomon in 1 Kings 2, David passed on not just resources but wisdom accumulated across a lifetime of leading—lessons learned through victories and failures, through faithfulness and sin, through the full arc of a life lived before God. This was mentorship at its deepest: not technique transfer but wisdom transmission.

What makes David's succession planning remarkable is its scope. He didn't just prepare Solomon for the next stage; he gathered resources, organized systems, and created conditions for work that would unfold across generations. His investment extended beyond his own tenure into a future he would never see.

This is what genuine succession planning looks like—not emergency preparation for unexpected departures, but sustained developmental investment in people who will carry the work forward after you are gone. Knowledge hoarding, protecting expertise as job security, is the precise inversion of David's example. David transferred everything he knew, gathered everything the next generation would need, and made Solomon's success possible through deliberate generosity with what he had learned. Organizations build that kind of culture one succession decision at a time.

Jeremiah's Field: Investing in a Future You Cannot See

The city was under siege. The army of Babylon surrounded Jerusalem. Jeremiah was in prison for prophesying disaster. And into this moment came an instruction from God that must have seemed like a cruel joke: buy a field. Not just any field—a field in Anathoth, which would shortly be occupied enemy territory. Jeremiah's cousin Hanamel came to him in the courtyard of the guard, just as God had said he would, offering the property for sale. "Buy my field," he said. And Jeremiah did. He weighed out seventeen shekels of silver. He signed the deed. He had it witnessed. He sealed one copy and left another open for reference. Then he handed the documents to Baruch with careful instructions for their preservation: "Take these deeds... and put them in a clay jar so they will last a long time. For this is what the Lord Almighty, the God of Israel, says: Houses, fields and vineyards will again be bought in this land" (Jeremiah 32:14–15).

Then Jeremiah prayed—honestly, wrestling with what he had just done: "You have said to me, Lord my God, 'Buy the field with silver and have the transaction witnessed.' Yet the city will be given into the hands of the Babylonians." He had obeyed. He didn't fully understand. And he said so.

What makes this instructive for developing people: Jeremiah's field purchase is one of Scripture's most concrete pictures of investment in a future the investor will not personally see or benefit from. He wasn't planting seeds and waiting for his own harvest. He was documenting, preserving, and bearing witness to a promise whose fulfillment would come to people not yet born. The care he took—signing deeds, sealing documents, explicit instructions for preservation—shows that faith in a long future doesn't make present faithfulness careless. It makes it more deliberate.

Leaders who develop people are always buying fields under siege. The staff member you invest in this year may not reach their potential for a decade. The culture you are slowly building may not be visible until after you are gone. The person everyone else has written off may become, years from now, someone indispensable—but only if someone was willing to pay the price of investment when the returns were invisible.

Jeremiah's act of faith was not passive waiting. It was costly, documented, witnessed, and carefully preserved. That is what genuine investment in people looks like: not optimistic hope that things will work out, but deliberate, costly action in full awareness of present difficulty, grounded in confidence that God's purposes outlast any individual's career or any organization's current crisis. What this reveals: growing people requires leaders who can hold two realities simultaneously—honest acknowledgment of present difficulty and confident investment in a future they may not live to see. The fields you buy today, when they make no immediate sense, are often the ones that matter most.

Nuances and Blind Spots

Most developmental investment is invisible—and therefore undercounted. The experiences and relationships that actually develop people don't show up in training budgets or program enrollments. Organizations can appear to invest heavily in development through workshops and formal programs while neglecting the 70% that happens through stretch assignments, daily challenge, and meaningful feedback. Initiative churn—constantly launching new programs and abandoning them before they can bear fruit—is expensive precisely because it consumes budget while bypassing what actually works.

Development without equity reproduces what already exists. Without deliberate attention, developmental opportunities flow naturally to people who look, communicate, and relate like current leadership. Homogeneous development isn't usually intentional—it's the path of least resistance. Diversifying leadership requires actively identifying and investing in people from underrepresented backgrounds, not simply hoping they'll surface on their own. The same applies to promotion decisions: sink-or-swim approaches and the Peter Principle—promoting people until they reach their level of incompetence—disproportionately harm those who already have less access to informal mentorship and organizational insiders who might catch them before they fail.

**Succession planning is development—not emergency prepara-

tion. Organizations that treat succession planning as a contingency exercise miss what it actually is: the ongoing, sustained development of multiple people capable of stepping into expanded roles. You don't identify successors; you create them, over years, through consistent investment. Knowledge hoarding—senior people protecting expertise as job security—is the direct opposite of this, and it guarantees that leadership capacity stays concentrated rather than distributed.

Patience is countercultural, and that makes it hard. Modern organizational culture celebrates speed and rapid results. Patient investment over years feels wrong—surely we should be seeing outcomes by now? But lasting transformation requires a timeline that feels uncomfortably slow by contemporary standards. Some fruit takes decades. The person you develop today may not show the full results of that investment for twenty years. Long-term thinking requires the willingness to act on faith that investment matters even when results aren't yet visible—and the discipline not to abandon the effort when it is.

Faithful presence outperforms dramatic intervention. Organizations that maintain consistent developmental investment through difficulty and abundance alike outperform those that intensify development in good times and cut it when things get hard. Consistency compounds; inconsistency erodes. This applies to individual leaders as much as to organizations: leaders who stop growing create organizations that stop growing. Continued investment in your own development isn't self-indulgence—it's the prerequisite for everything else in this chapter.

Development as reward creates a ceiling for the whole organization. When only high performers receive developmental investment, those who most need growth have no pathway to it—and the cycle entrenches itself. Underdeveloped managers promoted from strong individual contributors without leadership training compound the problem: they weren't given what they needed, and now they're the ones responsible for giving it to others. Real development culture treats growth as a universal condition of belonging, not a prize for those who've already arrived.

Exit for growth is an organizational diagnosis. When talented people consistently leave because the only path to development is an external move, that pattern is data. It means the organization is funding other organizations' futures while neglecting its own. The question worth sitting with isn't just why they left—it's what would have had to be true for them to have stayed and grown.

Try This Week

Choose ONE practice to start developing people systematically:

Practice 1: Schedule Development Conversations

Separate from performance reviews, ask each person: What are you learning? What do you want to learn? What opportunity would stretch you positively? What support do you need? Document the answers. Within two weeks, provide one concrete developmental opportunity or resource based on the conversation. Track quarterly.

Practice 2: Create One Stretch Assignment

Identify someone ready for next-level development. Design one stretch assignment: slightly beyond their current capability, real responsibility with real impact, appropriate support provided, defined timeline, explicit debrief afterward. This is the 70%—experience—that actually develops people. Make it real work, not a fake exercise.

Practice 3: Implement Developmental Feedback

When you observe someone handling a situation well—or struggling—provide immediate specific feedback: "When you [behavior], the result was [outcome]. Here's what I noticed [observation]. Next time you might try [suggestion]." Make it developmental (helping them learn) not just evaluative (judging performance).

Practice 4: Audit Development Equity

List developmental opportunities provided in the past year—stretch assignments, conference attendance, coaching, special projects. Who received them? Note gender, ethnicity, tenure, and role level. Are opportunities distributed equitably? If not, what systemic pattern exists? Commit to intentionally diversifying next quarter's developmental investments.

Reflection Questions

Quick Check (1–2 minutes)

- If you asked your team "Does this organization invest in your development?" what percentage would say yes?

- What's the longest sustained developmental investment you've made in another person? What made it possible?

Deeper Reflection (5–10 minutes)

- Who on your team has significant potential but hasn't received meaningful developmental investment? Why not? What would change if you committed to their development for the next three years?

- What does your organization's budget reveal about actual—not stated—commitment to developing people? Where is the gap between rhetoric and resource allocation?

- If you looked at who gets developmental opportunities, what patterns would you see? Are opportunities distributed equitably across cultural backgrounds, genders, and tenure levels?

- What would "long obedience in the same direction" look like for your leadership? What would you need to sustain for a decade to see real transformation?

Team Discussion (15–30 minutes)

- As a leadership team, each person identifies one person they could invest in developmentally over the next year—not just this quarter. Describe what the person's developmental edge is, what opportunities you could provide over twelve months, what support they will need, and how you will maintain investment when other pressures arise. Create mutual accountability for sustained investment.

Moving Forward

Vivi's frustration—"We've never talked about development or leadership preparation"—represents a common organizational failure. The organization sent her to training, checked the development box, and wondered why she wasn't growing into leadership. They invested in the 10% while neglecting the 70% and 20% that actually create growth.

Carnegie's systematic development of leaders across decades, Tuskegee's multi-generational vision of forming whole people, the Moravian missionaries' sustained cross-cultural presence—all demonstrate that meaningful development unfolds over timespans longer than most modern leaders plan for.

Anna's 84 years of faithful temple service reminds us that sustained presence—without visible results for decades—can position us for the moments that matter most. David's preparation of Solomon shows that the greatest leaders invest their final years preparing the next generation for work they'll never see completed. Jeremiah's deliberate purchase of a field under siege—all point to the same conviction: investment in people is never wasted, even when the returns are invisible, delayed, or delivered to someone else.

The question isn't whether you can transform your organization this quarter. The question is whether you can sustain faithful investment for a decade. Whether you can plant seeds whose harvest you may never see. Whether you can run the race marked out for you with perseverance, fixing your eyes on Jesus, the pioneer and perfecter of faith.

That's the long obedience. That's how people grow and organizations transform. One faithful step at a time, sustained across years, compounding into transformation that dramatic initiatives never achieve.

Building Learning Organizations

Opening Scene

The same mistake happened again. Not in the same department—this time in a different location, with different people, six months later. But essentially identical: a program launched without adequate community input, initial enthusiasm, growing resistance, eventual failure, and a painful shutdown after wasting resources and damaging relationships.

When the executive director saw the pattern, she was frustrated: "We already learned this lesson. Why are we making the same mistake again?" But as she dug deeper, she discovered the answer.

The previous failure had been in the East Coast office. Lessons learned were discussed extensively—in that office. A detailed after-action review was conducted—and filed in that office's records. The program director who led the analysis left three months later. Her successor never saw the report. When the West Coast office proposed a similar program, no one connected it to the previous failure because the people involved didn't know it had happened.

The organization had individual learning—people in the East Coast office had learned something real. But it had no organizational learning—the organization as a whole didn't get smarter. Knowledge stayed trapped in individual heads or specific locations. When people left, their learning left with them. Mistakes that should have been prevented got repeated. Successful innovations that should have spread stayed isolated.

During a leadership retreat, someone asked: "How many times have we reorganized our programs in the past five years?" After counting, the answer was four. "And how many of those reorganizations achieved their intended outcomes?" Silence. "Do we know why the previous ones failed?" More silence. "So we're launching a fifth reorganization without analyzing why the first four didn't work?"

The painful realization: they were an organization of smart, dedicated people who kept making the same organizational mistakes. They had lots of individual intelligence but almost no collective intelligence. They weren't building organizational memory or systematic learning. They were hoping that good intentions and hard work would compensate for lack of systematic knowledge management. It wasn't working.

What Makes Organizations Learn—or Not

A learning organization is one where people continually expand their capacity to create results they genuinely want—where new and expansive patterns of thinking are nurtured, where collective aspiration is set free, and where people are continually learning how to learn together. Organizations that embody this consistently outperform their peers in innovation, adaptation, and long-term sustainability. But creating them requires deliberate systems, not just good intentions.

The challenge most organizations run into is that they confuse individual learning with organizational learning. The distinction matters more than it first appears.

Individual Learning: A person gains knowledge, develops capability, and changes their behavior. This is valuable—and insufficient.

Organizational Learning: The organization as a whole develops collective knowledge, capabilities, and behavioral patterns that persist even when individual people leave. This is rare—and essential.

Organizations where only individuals learn face predictable problems. Knowledge loss is the first: when people leave, their expertise leaves with them, and critical knowledge exists only in individual heads rather than accessible systems. Then comes the reinventing-the-wheel problem, where different parts of the organization solve the same problems independently, wasting resources duplicating effort. Repeated mistakes follow—errors made in one location or time period get made again elsewhere because there's no system for capturing and sharing lessons. Good ideas stay trapped in individuals or teams rather than spreading systematically across the organization. And because learning happens individually and sporadically rather than collectively, the organization responds slowly to change.

In multicultural organizations, these challenges intensify in specific ways. Knowledge may be culturally encoded—making intuitive sense in one framework while remaining opaque in another. Communication barriers prevent knowledge from flowing across cultural and linguistic groups. Different cultural traditions value different types of knowledge as legitimate. And power dynamics mean that knowledge from cultural minorities often gets discounted even when it's the most valuable information available.

Teams that have navigated this well tend to share a common insight: the most dangerous knowledge in an organization is the knowledge that lives only in certain people's heads. Not because those people are untrustworthy, but because they will eventually leave, get promoted, burn out, or retire—and when they do, the organization loses what they knew unless deliberate systems have transferred it somewhere it can persist.

Building the Cathedral: What Organizational Learning Actually Requires

Consider what it took to build a medieval cathedral. Not the finished building—the soaring nave, the rose window catching afternoon light—but the generations of work that produced it. A cathedral of any scale might take a century or more to complete. The archbishop who laid the cornerstone would never see the spire. The master mason who designed the vaulting might train three generations of apprentices before the ceiling was raised. The glaziers, the stonecutters, the carpenters, the theologians who shaped the iconography, the community members who hauled stone and funded campaigns—none of them could build it alone, and none of them could stop the others from needing to.

This is not merely a metaphor for patience or vision, though it is that too. It is a picture of what genuine organizational learning requires—and why most organizations never achieve it.

Every Worker Carried Knowledge the Others Didn't Have

The stonecutter knew how granite behaved under weight and how limestone fractured in frost. The glazier understood light and color and lead in ways the mason never would. The theologian knew what the building was supposed to mean—which scenes to cut into the tympanum, which figures to place where the eye would fall first. The master builder had to understand enough of each trade to coordinate them, without pretending to master any of them fully.

This is the first condition of organizational learning: recognizing that the knowledge needed to build something enduring is distributed. It does not live in any one person, any one role, or any one cultural tradition.

Leaders who treat their own framework as complete—who design systems without asking what those systems look like from the front lines, who communicate without asking whether their words actually translate, who solve problems without sitting with the people closest to them—produce organizations that move in circles, repeating the same failures with different names.

Organizational learning begins with the intellectual humility to acknowledge that you cannot see the whole building from any single vantage point. The person quarrying the stone at the base knows something about load and foundation that the person setting the pinnacle will never observe. Both pieces of knowledge are necessary. Neither is optional.

The Apprentice Who Never Asked Questions Left the Trade

Cathedral construction was built on apprenticeship—not merely the transfer of technique but the cultivation of judgment. An apprentice did not simply learn to cut stone by watching stone get cut. He learned by cutting, failing, correcting, trying again, and gradually developing the internal compass that allowed him to assess a new problem he had never encountered before.

Organizations that treat learning as the delivery of content miss this. Training that tells people what to do produces compliance. Training that builds judgment produces adaptability. The people who grew into broader roles in the organizations studied for this book tended to share a common characteristic: they had been given space to try, to fail visibly without punishment, and to reflect on both. They didn't just carry out directives—they developed the capacity to handle situations the directives hadn't anticipated.

But apprenticeship only worked when it was genuinely reciprocal. The master who was too proud to learn from the apprentice's fresh eyes missed the adaptations the craft needed. In multicultural organizations, this dynamic becomes pointed. Senior leaders, often from the dominant cultural tradition, carry positional authority and organizational history. Junior staff, often from different cultural backgrounds, carry contextual intelligence—they know how the community outside the walls actually experiences the organization, how the language the organization uses actually lands in practice, where the gap between stated values and lived reality is widest. Organizations that allow information to flow in only one direction—downward from authority—are apprenticeship structures where only half the learning happens.

The Cathedral Had a Vision That Outlasted Any Individual

No single generation built a cathedral. What allowed the work to continue across decades and leadership changes was not a set of rules but a shared orientation—an understanding of what was being built and why it mattered that was specific enough to guide daily decisions and resilient enough to survive the deaths of the people who first articulated it.

When vision is clear and genuinely shared—not posted on a wall but embedded in how decisions get made, how conflicts get resolved, how new people are welcomed into the work—teams retain direction even through leadership transitions. They don't need to be told what to do because they understand what they're building. When vision is absent or ambiguous, every leadership change becomes a reset, and the organization spends enormous energy re-establishing basic orientation rather than advancing the work.

In multicultural organizations, vision that actually functions this way is harder to build—because the same words do not always carry the same meaning across cultural frameworks. What "excellence" means, what "community" means, what "service" means—these are not universal. Vision that is specific enough to be actionable but culturally flexible enough to genuinely include different backgrounds requires the kind of collective construction that most organizations skip.

The Work Could Not Stop Because One Trade Was Missing

Here is something cathedral builders understood practically that organizational leaders often miss theoretically: interdependence is not optional. If the glaziers went on strike, the stonecutters could not finish the windows. If the ironworkers were absent, the wooden scaffolding could not be secured. Each trade depended on the others completing their work adequately for their own work to proceed.

The organizational equivalent is the relationship between the conditions that make learning possible. Learning cannot be systematized in environments where trust is absent—because people will not surface what they actually know. Systems for capturing knowledge cannot function where psychological safety is low—because the learning that most needs to be captured (what went wrong and why) is also the most dangerous to admit. Cultural intelligence cannot be developed in organizations where the people with the most relevant experience are structurally excluded from contributing to the conversation.

These are not separate programs to run in sequence. They are trades that must work together. You cannot build the vault until the walls are ready to carry it. You cannot build genuine organizational learning until the conditions for honest contribution are in place.

The Cathedral Was Built for Someone Who Was Not Yet Born

This is perhaps the most countercultural aspect of the cathedral metaphor for contemporary organizations: the work was explicitly oriented toward people who were not yet present. Decisions about what to build and how to build it were shaped by the understanding that this structure would be used and inhabited by generations the builders would never meet.

Organizational learning, at its deepest level, is this kind of work. Documentation is not paperwork—it is a gift to your successor. After-action reviews are not administrative burden—they are letters to the people who will face similar situations after you are gone. The knowledge transfer systems that feel inefficient in the moment are the mechanisms by which the organization becomes more capable over time rather than merely recycling the same capabilities in new people.

Leaders and staff who think of their work as contribution to something larger than their own tenure—who document what they know, who invest in developing the people who will eventually replace them, who design systems with an eye toward sustainability rather than personal control—create organizations that compound their learning. Those who treat their knowledge as personal equity, hoarding it consciously or unconsciously, create the cycle the opening scene describes: the same failures, the same lost lessons, the same expensive re-learning.

Single-Loop, Double-Loop, and Cultural Loop Learning

Two organizational theorists, Chris Argyris and Donald Schön, gave leaders a valuable framework for understanding why some problems keep recurring no matter how many solutions are applied. Their distinction between two types of learning remains one of the most practically useful ideas in organizational life.

Single-Loop Learning detects and corrects errors within existing assumptions and goals. Think of a thermostat: when the temperature drops, it triggers the heat, returns to the set point, and asks no further questions. The goal is never examined. Only the method adjusts.

Example: Program enrollment is declining, so the organization increases marketing. The assumption that marketing drives enrollment goes unquestioned. The goal of maintaining enrollment stays fixed. Only the tactic changes.

Double-Loop Learning goes further, questioning whether the thermostat is set to the right temperature at all. It examines not just what we are doing but why—whether our goals and underlying assumptions still make sense.

Example: Program enrollment is declining. Instead of immediately increasing marketing, leaders ask: Should we even run this program? Is it meeting a real need? Are we the right organization to deliver it? What assumptions led us to create it? The inquiry turns from method to purpose.

Most organizations excel at single-loop learning and struggle with double-loop learning—and for understandable reasons. Questioning assumptions threatens existing power arrangements, challenges organizational identity, and requires a degree of psychological safety that many environments do not sustain.

Drawing on this framework and extending it into multicultural contexts, there is a third dimension worth naming: Cultural Loop Learning asks not just what we are doing and whether we should do it, but whose understanding of the world has shaped the very framework we are operating within—and whether that framework is genuinely accessible to everyone it claims to include.

In multicultural organizations, many of the assumptions being protected are not merely strategic—they are cultural. And when that is the case, neither single-loop nor double-loop learning is sufficient, because the framework being optimized or even questioned was built by and for a particular cultural worldview. The people with the most insight into this are often those with the least structural safety to say so.

Why Cultural Loop Learning Is Harder Than the Others

Single-loop problems feel technical. Double-loop problems feel strategic. Cultural loop problems feel personal—because they are. When you question an organizational strategy, you question a decision. When you question a cultural assumption embedded in how the organization operates, you are questioning a way of being in the world that belongs to real people, often the people who hold the most influence.

This creates a specific dynamic in multicultural organizations: the people who most clearly see what is not working are frequently least positioned to say so. High power distance, language barriers, minority status, or accumulated risk-consciousness keep the most valuable observations from reaching the surface. Meanwhile, leaders who could act on cultural assumptions are often least able to see them, because those assumptions form the water they swim in.

Cultural loop learning does not require dismantling what has been built. It requires the honesty to ask who built it, whose experience it reflects, and whether the framework is as hospitable in practice as it claims to be in vision.

Four Practices of Cultural Loop Learning

Cultural loop learning is not a retreat or an annual exercise. It is a set of habits embedded into ordinary organizational life.

1. **Cultural Assumption Mapping**: Examine recurring practices for cultural defaults. When a meeting format, a communication expectation, or a decision process causes friction for some people but not others, ask: Where did this come from? Whose preferences does it reflect? Who does it require the most adaptation from?

2. **Distributed Voice Audit**: Notice who is and is not contributing to decisions and learning. Whose concerns surface early and whose surface late or not at all? Are patterns of voice and silence tracking along cultural or positional lines?

3. **Assumption Interruption**: Build regular moments into team life where the normal flow is paused to ask whether a different cultural framework might illuminate something being missed. A simple practice: before moving to solutions, ask, "Whose perspective might we be missing?"

4. **Equitable Adaptation**: If some team members are doing most of the work of cultural adaptation while others rarely adjust at all, that asymmetry needs to be named and redistributed—not

just acknowledged.

Trust, voice, and cultural intelligence—explored throughout this book—are the infrastructure on which all three loops depend. You cannot practice cultural loop learning without psychological safety. You cannot have psychological safety without trust. You cannot build trust across difference without cultural intelligence. These are not separate topics; they are layers of the same foundation.

After-Action Reviews: Systematic Learning from Experience

The U.S. Army developed After-Action Reviews as a systematic method for learning from experience. The process is simple but powerful, built around four questions:

1. What was supposed to happen? (Intent and plan)

2. What actually happened? (Observed results)

3. Why was there a difference? (Analysis of gap)

4. What will we do next time? (Lessons learned)

What makes them work is less the questions than the culture that surrounds them. The principles matter:

- **Everyone Participates**: Hierarchical rank doesn't determine whose input matters. Junior participants often see things senior leaders miss.

- **No Blame**: Focus is on learning, not punishment. This requires genuine psychological safety—people won't speak honestly if they fear consequences.

- **Focus on Facts**: "What happened?" not "Whose fault was it?"

Data matters more than opinions about character or competence.

- **Discuss Immediately**: While memory is fresh and before narrative consolidates into a protective story.

- **Capture Lessons**: Document insights so organizational memory develops, not just individual learning.

- **Apply Learning**: An AAR without implementation is just conversation. Learning requires changed behavior.

In multicultural contexts, AAR processes need thoughtful adaptation. Some cultures find public performance review uncomfortable and prefer written input or small group discussion. Direct feedback feels different across cultural frameworks. Time orientation varies—some want immediate debrief; others need processing time before they can reflect honestly. Power distance affects who feels free to speak openly, making multiple participation pathways essential.

The key is After-Action Reviews as systematic practice, not occasional event. Organizations that debrief every significant initiative build collective intelligence over time. Organizations that debrief only when things go badly miss half of what matters—because successes contain lessons too, and understanding why something worked is as valuable as understanding why something failed.

Positive Deviance: Learning from What's Already Working

One of the most underused sources of organizational learning sits in plain sight: the people in your own organization who are already doing something better than everyone else, often with the same or fewer resources. This phenomenon—where certain individuals or small groups achieve exceptional outcomes despite facing the same constraints as their peers—is called positive deviance. The term was coined in nutrition research when scientists studying malnutrition noticed that in severely impoverished communities, a handful of families had unusually healthy children. They weren't working with different resources. They were doing something different with the same resources. And once researchers identified and spread those behaviors, child malnutrition in targeted communities dropped dramatically.

The application to organizational learning is direct. In virtually every organization, some people handle difficult cross-cultural conversations gracefully while their colleagues avoid or mishandle them. Some teams maintain high trust and low turnover while neighboring teams cycle through conflict. Some leaders develop people while others extract from them. The question is not whether these positive deviants exist in your organization—they almost certainly do. The question is whether your organization has systems to find them, learn from them, and spread what they know.

Most organizations don't. They look for problems to solve rather than for existing solutions to amplify. They bring in external consultants to teach practices that are already being demonstrated internally, unrecognized. They assume that if something is working, everyone must already know about it—when in reality, effective practices often remain as invisible as ineffective ones.

How to Find Positive Deviance in Your Organization

Positive deviance inquiry starts with two questions: Who in this organization is achieving unusually good outcomes in this area? And what are they doing that others aren't?

The process matters as much as the questions. Standard performance review focuses on individuals who are below expectations. Positive deviance inquiry focuses on individuals who are above them—not to create heroes but to identify transferable practices. The goal is not to celebrate certain people but to extract what they know and make it available to everyone.

In multicultural organizations, positive deviance often concentrates in unexpected places. The practices that work best for building cross-cultural trust are frequently demonstrated by people with minority cultural backgrounds who have had to develop sophisticated cultural navigation skills simply to function. The people most effective at reading across cultural differences in communication are often those who grew up code-switching. The leaders most skilled at building psychological safety across high power-distance and low power-distance staff are often those who have themselves experienced both sides of that dynamic.

Ignoring these sources of expertise while importing external solutions is one of the most common and costly errors in organizational learning. It signals to the people who have the relevant knowledge that their experience doesn't count—which is both untrue and damaging to the trust and voice that all learning depends on.

The Historical View

History offers compelling examples of how systematic organizational learning creates enduring advantage—and how its absence leads to repeated failure.

The House of Wisdom: Organizational Learning Across Cultures

In eighth-century Baghdad, the Abbasid caliph Harun al-Rashid established an institution that would, over the following century, become history's most ambitious organizational learning system. The Bayt al-Hikma—the House of Wisdom—was not simply a library. It was a deliberate infrastructure for capturing, translating, synthesizing, and transmitting knowledge across cultural and personnel boundaries.

What made it organizational learning rather than individual learning was precisely its architecture. Scholars were dispatched to Constantinople, Alexandria, Persia, and India with a specific mandate: find knowledge worth preserving and bring it back for translation. Greek medical texts, Persian astronomical tables, Indian mathematical systems, and Syriac philosophical works were all brought into a common institutional repository. The goal wasn't to honor any single tradition but to ask what was true and useful—and then make it accessible to everyone.

The House of Wisdom deliberately recruited scholars across religious and ethnic lines. Christians, Jews, Zoroastrians, and Muslims worked alongside Arab, Persian, Greek, and Indian scholars. This wasn't idealistic multiculturalism—it was epistemological strategy. Leaders understood that knowledge fragmented by cultural silos was knowledge wasted. Synthesis required encounter. The institution's diversity was a feature of its learning design, not incidental to it.

The critical test of organizational learning is what survives when people leave. At the House of Wisdom, when a scholar died or departed, their translations, commentaries, and discoveries remained in the institutional archive—accessible and available to the next generation of scholars who built on rather than repeated their predecessors' work. Al-Khwarizmi's mathematical work gave the world algebra and the algorithm. Ibn Sina's medical encyclopedias shaped medicine for five centuries. These contributions compounded because they were institutionalized, not just personally remembered.

The House of Wisdom thrived for nearly five centuries—surviving the deaths of countless individual scholars, multiple caliphates, and significant political turbulence—because its learning was structural rather than personal. When skilled individuals departed, the organization didn't lose their contribution. When new scholars arrived, they inherited centuries of accumulated institutional intelligence rather than starting from scratch.

The lesson for multicultural organizations is doubly relevant: the House of Wisdom's exceptional productivity was inseparable from its cultural breadth. Mono-cultural knowledge systems produced predictable knowledge. The encounter of diverse traditions—each with different methods, questions, and frameworks—generated insights that none could have produced alone. Diversity was not the price of inclusion. It was the source of the breakthrough.

Florence Nightingale: Data as Organizational Memory

Florence Nightingale arrived at Scutari military hospital in 1854 to find catastrophic death rates—not primarily from battlefield wounds, but from preventable infections and poor sanitation. What distinguished her response wasn't only compassion but systematic knowledge management.

She understood that individual nurses could observe problems and individual doctors could diagnose patients, but without systematic data collection, those observations would never become organizational learning. Her pioneering use of statistical graphics—the now-famous polar area diagrams that visualized mortality causes over time—transformed raw data into a compelling argument for systemic reform. The death rate from disease fell from 42.7% to 2.2% within six months of implemented reforms.

But the deeper achievement was what happened after. The learning became organizational: documented, shared with the War Office, and eventually institutionalized into British Army medical practice. Nightingale didn't just solve a problem at one hospital. She created the systems that prevented the same problem from recurring in other hospitals, under other administrators, with other staff. That is the difference between individual problem-solving and organizational learning.

The lesson for contemporary leaders: intuitions about what's going wrong are not enough. Organizational learning requires capturing observations in forms that persist and compel action. Documentation is not bureaucracy—it is the mechanism by which experience becomes wisdom. Nightingale's charts were not primarily about the past. They were insurance that the future would be different.

Kodak: The Failure of Organizational Learning

Kodak engineers invented the digital camera in 1975 and understood that digital photography would eventually replace film. But the organization didn't learn. Kodak's organizational identity as a "film company" meant information that challenged that model was discounted. When film sales declined, leadership optimized film products without questioning whether film should remain the core business. Insights from engineers didn't reach senior leadership. Those who benefited from the film business resisted changes that would diminish their importance.

The result: a company with remarkable individual talent and cutting-edge technical knowledge failed to adapt because organizational learning systems were absent. They had the information they needed. They just couldn't act on it organizationally. Kodak is not a story about ignorance. It's a story about what happens when individual learning and organizational learning are completely disconnected—and when power protects existing arrangements rather than enabling honest examination of them.

Every organization has its version of the film business: the product, program, or approach whose continued existence benefits those in power, whose questioning feels threatening rather than helpful, whose decline is explained as a temporary problem requiring more effort rather than a signal requiring honest examination. Cultural loop learning is what makes it possible to see those sacred cows clearly enough to ask whether they should still be there.

The Biblical View

Scripture emphasizes both individual wisdom and collective learning, with particular attention to passing knowledge across generations and creating systems that ensure critical understanding doesn't die with any one person.

Deuteronomy's Teaching Mandate

"Hear, O Israel: The LORD our God, the LORD is one. Love the LORD your God with all your heart and with all your soul and with all your strength. These commandments that I give you today are to be on your hearts. Impress them on your children. Talk about them when you sit at home and when you walk along the road, when you lie down and when you get up" (Deuteronomy 6:4–7, NIV).

This isn't occasional instruction—it's systematic integration of learning into daily rhythm. Knowledge transfer happens continually, not just in formal settings. The community creates shared understanding through persistent, embodied teaching. The command extends even to physical reminders: "Write them on the doorframes of your houses and on your gates" (6:9). The ancient equivalent of making knowledge visible in the environment—not stored somewhere inaccessible but present in the spaces people inhabit.

What makes this instructive for organizational learning is the combination of intensity and distribution. The teaching mandate didn't live in a priest class alone. It was distributed to parents, embedded in daily conversation, woven into domestic architecture. When any individual teacher died, the knowledge didn't die with them. It had been transmitted too widely, through too many channels, to be lost.

Josiah's Discovery of the Law: Recovering Lost Knowledge

When workers were repairing the temple during Josiah's reign, the high priest Hilkiah discovered the Book of the Law—a foundational document apparently lost, forgotten, or suppressed for decades. Josiah's response was immediate and visceral: he tore his robes in grief, recognizing how far the nation had drifted from knowledge it should have possessed all along (2 Kings 22:1–13).

What followed is one of Scripture's most striking examples of organizational learning in action. Josiah didn't treat the discovery as personal conviction alone. He gathered all the people—from the greatest to the least—and read the entire Book of the Law aloud in their hearing

(2 Kings 23:1–3). He made the recovered knowledge communal. He then systematically acted on what was learned, ending practices that violated the covenant and reinstating the Passover that "had not been observed since the days of the judges" (23:22). Individual discovery became organizational transformation.

The lesson is pointed: how much institutional knowledge currently sits unread in your organization's files? How many lessons from past failures are documented somewhere but never consulted? How many after-action reviews were filed and forgotten? Josiah's response—treat recovered knowledge as urgent, share it broadly, act on it systematically—is precisely what distinguishes organizations that learn from those that repeat the same mistakes across generations.

The Bereans: Rigorous Collective Verification

When Paul and Silas arrived in Berea, Luke records a telling detail: "Now the Berean Jews were of more noble character than those in Thessalonica, for they received the message with great eagerness and examined the Scriptures every day to see if what Paul said was true" (Acts 17:11, NIV).

The Bereans model a specific discipline of organizational learning: they didn't simply accept teaching on authority, nor did they reflexively reject it. They examined claims against existing knowledge, daily, collectively. Note the combination of those three words: daily (systematic habit, not occasional practice), examined (active inquiry, not passive reception), and collectively (organizational learning, not individual evaluation). Their noble character was not skepticism for its own sake; it was disciplined, eager, daily engagement with what was true.

That same rigor transforms passive compliance into genuine collective intelligence. Organizations that encourage people to bring their full intellectual engagement to the work—that create space for honest examination of what is and isn't working, that welcome challenge as a form of contribution rather than treating it as disloyalty—build the kind of organizational intelligence the Bereans demonstrated. They don't just have dedicated people. They have people who think carefully about what they are doing and why.

The Early Church: Distributed Knowledge and Adaptive Learning

The Acts narrative is, among other things, a story of how a small group of frightened disciples became a movement that outlasted the Roman Empire—and did so without any of the institutional advantages that normally enable organizational continuity.

What they had instead was a learning system built into community life. Problems surfaced and were addressed collectively—the dispute about neglected Greek-speaking widows in Acts 6 produced not defensive denial but structural adaptation: the creation of deacons. Conflicts over cultural practice (circumcision requirements, food offered to idols) were brought to a gathered community for deliberation rather than resolved unilaterally by whoever had the most authority. The Jerusalem Council in Acts 15 is essentially an organizational after-action review—a systematic effort to examine what was working, what wasn't, and what principles should guide future decisions.

Letters circulated between communities shared learning across geographic and cultural distance. When Paul wrote to the church in Corinth about problems in that community, those letters became organizational learning for communities Paul had never visited—accessible to people who hadn't experienced the original problem. The knowledge transferred across boundaries because someone thought to capture it and share it widely.

The early church grew not because it was uniform but because it was adaptive—willing to examine its practices in light of new contexts, willing to challenge assumptions (including deeply held ones about who the gospel was for), willing to distribute learning across a network rather than hoarding it in a center. That combination of shared conviction and adaptive practice is a picture of organizational learning working the way it should.

Nuances and Blind Spots

Organizational learning is not the same as training. Training develops individual capability. Organizational learning creates collective knowledge that persists across personnel changes. An organization can run excellent training programs while failing completely at learning as a system — because the moment trained individuals leave, everything they learned leaves with them. Documentation isn't bureaucracy; it's memory. Organizations that don't build it have organizational amnesia, condemned to relearn the same lessons every time the people who learned them walk out the door.

Repeated mistakes are a systems failure, not a personnel failure. When the same errors recur in different locations or across different time periods, the problem isn't the individuals involved — it's that learning isn't being systematized and shared. The initiative graveyard compounds this: programs launched with enthusiasm, quietly abandoned, never analyzed. New initiatives proposed without anyone asking what the last three attempts revealed. Without deliberate reflection infrastructure — debriefs, documentation, shared review — organizations don't accumulate wisdom. They just accumulate history.

Blame culture drives errors underground, where they compound. When mistakes trigger a search for who's at fault rather than what can be learned, people stop surfacing errors. They hide problems, work around failures quietly, and protect themselves — which means the organization loses access to precisely the information it most needs. Learning from failure requires genuine psychological safety: the credible assurance that honest disclosure leads to learning, not punishment. Organizations that perform openness while punishing candor don't learn from mistakes. They just get better at concealing them.

Power dynamics shape what gets learned — and what doesn't. Learning that challenges existing power structures tends to get suppressed, consciously or not. Sacred cows don't get examined. Cultural loop blindness is a particularly persistent version of this: the same practices causing friction for certain cultural groups get adjusted and readjusted at the surface without anyone ever asking whose assumptions originally shaped them, or whether those assumptions should be revisited entirely. Genuine organizational learning requires safety to question things that currently benefit those in a position to block the questions.

Cultural frameworks determine what counts as knowledge. Some cultures value explicit, documented, transferable knowledge. Others value tacit, relational knowledge passed through apprenticeship and proximity. Organizational learning systems built entirely around documentation and formal processes will capture knowledge from some people while systematically missing what others carry. Honoring multiple ways of knowing isn't just culturally sensitive — it's epistemically honest about where real organizational wisdom actually lives.

The best learning happens closest to the work. Front-line staff encounter real problems, develop real solutions, and accumulate real insight that leadership rarely sees. Siloed learning — different teams solving identical problems independently, unaware others have already figured it out — wastes that distributed knowledge. Organizational learning systems must be designed to capture and circulate insight from all levels, not just aggregate what leadership already knows and distribute it downward.

Speed and learning are in genuine tension — and speed usually wins. Reflection takes time. Organizations that treat any pause as inefficiency will keep repeating mistakes, reinventing wheels, and missing the compounding returns that accumulated knowledge could provide. Quick fixes — single-loop adjustments that solve the immediate problem without examining the underlying assumptions causing it — feel faster and often are, until the problem recurs in a slightly different form and the cycle begins again. The investment in slowing down to actually learn is one of the most consistently undervalued choices available to any organization.

***

Try This Week

Choose ONE practice to build organizational learning capacity:

Practice 1: Conduct One After-Action Review

Pick one recent completed project or significant event. Gather key participants. Use the four AAR questions: (1) What was supposed to happen? (2) What actually happened? (3) Why was there a difference? (4) What will we do next time? Focus on learning, not blame. Document insights. Share with others who could benefit.

Practice 2: Create a Knowledge Transfer System

Identify three critical roles where knowledge loss would be catastrophic. For each, start building a knowledge repository: What does this person know that isn't documented? What relationships do they maintain? What would a successor need? Schedule monthly 30-minute sessions to capture their knowledge systematically before departure becomes a crisis.

Practice 3: Document One Lesson Learned

Think about something significant your organization learned recently — success or failure. Write a brief document: (1) What happened? (2) What did we learn? (3) What should we do differently? (4) Who else could benefit from this? Share it. Create an accessible folder for lessons learned so organizational memory develops systematically.

Practice 4: Practice Cultural Loop Learning

Pick one recurring organizational problem or friction point. Before jumping to solutions, ask deeper questions: What assumptions are underneath this? Whose cultural framework shaped the expectation that isn't being met? Who in the room might experience this situation differently — and are they being asked? Allow thirty minutes for questioning before proposing solutions.

Reflection Questions

Quick Check (1–2 minutes)

- When someone leaves your organization, how much critical knowledge leaves with them?

- Can you name three significant lessons your organization has learned in the past year? Are they documented anywhere accessible?

Deeper Reflection (5–10 minutes)

- What mistakes has your organization made repeatedly? Why don't you learn from them permanently? What would need to change?

- Where does learning happen in your organization? If it's only in individuals' heads, what happens when they leave?

- If your organization were truly a learning organization, what would be different about how you handle failures, successes, and knowledge transfer?

- What "sacred cows" in your organization are protected from examination? What would it take to create safety for questioning them?

- Who in your organization is doing most of the work of cultural adaptation? Is that distribution fair? What would equitable adaptation look like?

Team Discussion (15–30 minutes)

- As a leadership team, identify three initiatives from the past three years: one success, one failure, one mixed. For each, ask: What did we learn? Is that learning documented anywhere? Has it influenced subsequent decisions? Who knows about it besides those directly involved? Create a plan to systematically capture and share these lessons — and commit to regular After-Action Reviews going forward.

Moving Forward

The opening scene revealed an organization making the same mistake in two different offices because learning stayed trapped in one location. The East Coast office learned. The organization didn't. When the West Coast office launched a similar program, they had no access to lessons already paid for in failure.

The cathedral was not built in a generation, and it was not built by any one kind of worker. Its endurance depended on systems that carried knowledge forward past the deaths of the people who first held it, on the willingness of each trade to honor what the others knew, and on a vision capacious enough to guide the work long after the original builders were gone.

The British Admiralty built systematic learning through captain's logs, knowledge sharing, formalized signals, and gunnery schools. Florence Nightingale demonstrated that individual observations, when systematically documented and analyzed, become the collective knowledge that transforms entire institutions. Kodak had individual learning but failed at organizational learning — their engineers knew digital photography was coming, but the organization couldn't act on that knowledge.

The biblical pattern is clear: systematic knowledge transfer embedded in daily rhythm (Deuteronomy 6), the urgent obligation to recover lost institutional knowledge and act on it broadly (Josiah, 2 Kings 22–23), rigorous daily collective examination of what is true (the Bereans, Acts 17:11).

Argyris and Schön gave us the tools to distinguish between adjusting methods and questioning assumptions. In multicultural organizations, that framework needs one further extension — the willingness to ask whose assumptions have shaped the framework itself. Not as an accusation, but as an act of organizational integrity. Organizations formed by difference have unusual access to this kind of wisdom. The friction, the misunderstanding, the moment when something doesn't translate — these are not failures. They are invitations to learn something the organization could not have learned any other way. Build as if you will not be present to see it finished. It is the most faithful thing you can do.

The Final Caveat

Opening Scene

The leadership retreat had been productive. Two days of frameworks, tools, and strategies. Systems for building trust across cultural difference. Methods for creating voice pathways. Approaches to distributing leadership and navigating scarcity. The executive director felt equipped—finally, practical handles for the complex challenges she faced daily.

On the drive home, her mind wandered to the deeper questions the retreat hadn't addressed. The frameworks were helpful. But something felt incomplete. She knew leaders who had mastered every technique, read every book, implemented every system—and still led organizations marked by manipulation, self-protection, and quiet despair. She knew others with fewer tools who somehow created environments of genuine flourishing.

What made the difference?

She thought about her own leadership journey. The seasons when she'd used good frameworks in service of her own image. The times when "servant leadership" language had masked her need for control. The moments when "empowerment" had really been delegation of tasks she didn't want, not genuine sharing of authority.

The tools mattered. But tools in service of what? Leadership for what end? All the frameworks in this book—and every leadership book—could be used for flourishing or for extraction, for genuine service or for sophisticated self-interest. The techniques were morally neutral. The leader using them was not.

She arrived home with a question she couldn't shake: What keeps leadership from drifting toward self-protection, image management, and outcomes detached from love—even when leaders have the best frameworks and finest intentions?

The Limits of Techniques and Frameworks

This book has offered many practical tools: frameworks for understanding cultural difference, methods for building trust, approaches to creating voice, strategies for distributing leadership, rhythms for sustainable practice. These tools are genuinely useful. Research supports their effectiveness. Organizations that implement them well outperform those that don't.

But tools have limits.

Systems, strategies, and skills matter deeply. They shape environments, create structures, and enable practices that would otherwise be impossible. Without good systems, even well-intentioned leaders create chaos. Without effective strategies, genuine care produces little lasting impact. Without developed skills, noble motives remain frustrated.

Yet systems, strategies, and skills cannot, on their own, heal the human heart or align motives perfectly with what is good. Every framework in this book can be corrupted:

- Trust-building can become manipulation—creating the appearance of trustworthiness to serve hidden agendas

- Voice pathways can become theater—soliciting input with no intention of being influenced

- Cultural intelligence can become exploitation—understanding cultural frameworks to manipulate more effectively

- Distributed leadership can become abdication—using empowerment language to avoid responsibility

- Vision can become propaganda—inspiring words that mask self-serving reality

The problem isn't the tools. The problem is what happens when tools serve ends other than genuine human flourishing. And that problem is ultimately a problem of the heart—the center from which leadership flows.

This is not merely a spiritual observation. It maps onto something that behavioral research has documented with striking precision. Leaders who use influence primarily to benefit themselves—taking undue credit, exerting quiet pressure, under-challenging followers, operating from an ego-driven rather than mission-driven foundation—produce organizations that show surface signs of productivity while quietly eroding from within. The behaviors look like leadership. The vocabulary often sounds like it. But the motivational center has shifted, and over time, teams feel the difference even when they cannot name it.

What research consistently shows is that the distinction between empowering leadership and its shadow version—exploitative leadership—is not primarily a skill distinction. It is a motivational and identity distinction. Empowering leaders share authority because they genuinely trust others and are invested in others' growth. Exploitative leaders deploy the language of empowerment while the actual weight of decisions, credit, and authority quietly flows upward. The outward behaviors can look similar for a season. The outcomes diverge predictably and significantly over time.

The question, then, is not simply "Do you have the right tools?" but "What is the actual center from which you lead?" That question is not one any framework can answer on its own. It is a question of formation—of who the leader is becoming, not merely what techniques the leader is deploying.

Christ at the Center

The author writes as a Christian, convinced that leadership ultimately cannot be separated from the question of who sits at the center. From this perspective, the values woven throughout this book—integrity, service, justice, humility, hope—find their fullest meaning and coherence in the person of Jesus Christ. These aren't arbitrary preferences or culturally constructed ideals. They reflect the character of God revealed in Christ, who "did not come to be served, but to serve, and to give his life as a ransom for many" (Mark 10:45).

Without Christ at the center, even well-intentioned efforts can drift toward self-protection, image management, or the pursuit of outcomes detached from love. The drift is often subtle—justified by results, rationalized by circumstances, invisible to the drifting leader. Good frameworks deployed in service of ego, fear, or control produce organizations that may succeed by worldly metrics while failing by eternal ones.

With Christ at the center, leadership becomes an arena of worship, repentance, and Spirit-enabled service, where even weaknesses can become places of grace. The leader remains accountable not just to boards, stakeholders, and results—but to the One who sees the heart and calls leaders to faithfulness, not just effectiveness.

This doesn't mean Christian leaders are automatically better leaders. History and experience demonstrate otherwise—Christians have led organizations with the same dysfunction, manipulation, and harm as anyone else. Christ at the center is not a guarantee of competence or an excuse for poor practice. It's an orientation that, when genuinely embraced, creates accountability beyond what any human system can provide.

Leadership as Discipleship

From a Christian perspective, leadership is not only a set of skills or frameworks but a form of discipleship. The daily practice of leading—making decisions, navigating conflict, building trust, developing people—becomes a context for spiritual formation. Every chapter of this book addresses challenges that are also spiritual:

- Trust requires vulnerability, which requires security in something deeper than organizational position

- Voice requires humility—genuinely believing others have insights you lack

- Cultural intelligence requires dying to the assumption that your way is the right way

- Distributed leadership requires releasing control and trusting God's work through others

- Navigating scarcity requires faith that God provides, even when resources feel insufficient

- Sustained faithfulness requires hope grounded in something beyond visible results

These aren't just leadership competencies. They're spiritual disciplines. The leader who practices them is being formed—becoming someone different through the practice itself.

What makes this more than spiritual sentiment is that the formation and the effectiveness are not parallel tracks running separately. They converge. The leader who cultivates genuine humility—dying to the need to have all the answers—creates the conditions under which others feel genuinely empowered to contribute. The leader who practices actual self-awareness—not as a performance technique but as a spiritual discipline—is far more likely to notice the gap between stated values and actual practice before it widens into a chasm. The leader whose identity is grounded in something deeper than organizational outcomes is more able to bear the slow work of trust-building without hijacking the process for short-term results.

This is why research into what makes teams genuinely thrive keeps surfacing the same cluster of characteristics: people who feel psychologically safe, genuinely valued, invested in rather than merely utilized, and connected to a purpose larger than the tasks in front of them. These aren't outcomes that can be engineered from the outside in. They emerge from leadership that flows from a formed interior life. From the Christian perspective, that interior life finds its source and its accountability in Christ.

The disciplines reinforce each other. A leader shaped by daily examination—honest self-inventory before God—is practicing the same attentiveness that good feedback systems require. A leader shaped by genuine sabbath rest—trusting that the work does not depend on their constant vigilance—is practicing the same releasing of control that empowering leadership requires. The spiritual formation and the organizational competencies point the same direction, because both are oriented toward the same fundamental question: is this leader genuinely for others, or for self?

For Christian leaders, this means organizational challenges are also spiritual opportunities. The difficult colleague is an occasion for patience. The budget crisis is a context for faith. The cross-cultural conflict is an invitation to humility. The long season without visible results is training in hope. This reframing doesn't make leadership easier. It makes it meaningful in ways that transcend organizational success. The leader whose identity is grounded in Christ can face failure, criticism, and disappointment without being destroyed—because ultimate worth doesn't depend on leadership outcomes.

The Historical View

History offers examples of leaders whose Christ-centered orientation shaped their leadership in distinctive ways—and cautionary tales of Christian leaders whose practice contradicted their profession.

William Wilberforce: Sustained Faithfulness Against Every Incentive to Quit

William Wilberforce spent nearly five decades working to abolish the slave trade and slavery in the British Empire. He introduced his first abolition bill in 1789; slavery wasn't fully abolished until 1833—the year he died.

What makes Wilberforce instructive for this chapter is not simply that he persisted, but what his persistence reveals about the relationship between interior formation and exterior effectiveness. The slave trade was enormously profitable; the forces arrayed against abolition had every structural and financial advantage. Wilberforce faced repeated defeat, mockery, and political marginalization. His abolition bills failed year after year.

He was also—and this is worth noting—a man with considerable natural gifts and political skill. He understood power. He knew how to build coalitions, frame arguments, and use the tools of political persuasion. But those tools, deployed by dozens of equally capable people, had not produced the result. What made Wilberforce different was not superior technique. It was the center from which his effort flowed.

His conversion experience in 1785 transformed his understanding of public life. He came to see political leadership as stewardship—using influence not for personal advancement but for justice aligned with God's character. He wrote in his diary: "God Almighty has set before me two great objects: the suppression of the slave trade and the reformation of manners." The mission was larger than his reputation, larger than his political career, larger than any single parliamentary session. Because it was held in trust before God rather than measured against personal success, he could return to it year after year, bill after bill, decade after decade.

This is the organizational pattern that formation produces: intrinsic motivation—the deep drive that comes from identity and conviction rather than from external reward—sustains effort far beyond what strategic calculation or self-interest can maintain. Wilberforce demonstrates what Christ-centered leadership can sustain across seasons of failure that would extinguish any motivation rooted in outcome alone.

Dietrich Bonhoeffer: Formation That Made Resistance Possible

Dietrich Bonhoeffer, German theologian and pastor, led an underground seminary during the Nazi era and eventually participated in active resistance that led to his execution in 1945. His leadership is studied primarily for its courage and theological depth. But there is an organizational dimension that deserves attention here.

Bonhoeffer understood that the crisis his generation faced was not fundamentally political. It was a formation failure. The German church had not developed leaders whose identity was anchored deeply enough in Christ to resist the social pressure of National Socialism. The institutions were there. The theological training was there. The organizational structures were there. What was missing was the interior formation that would hold when everything external was aligned against faithfulness.

His response was to build a community at Finkenwalde organized around deep spiritual practice—shared prayer, confession, mutual accountability, service. He was not simply training pastors in doctrine. He was forming people whose identity in Christ would be stable enough to hold under pressure that would expose every lesser anchor.

The parallel for organizational leadership is direct. Leaders who invest heavily in skills while neglecting their own formation eventually hollow out. The soul shapes the leader; the leader shapes the organization. An organization whose leaders have developed strong technical competency without equally strong interior formation is building on a foundation that will crack under sustained pressure—not because the skills are wrong but because skills without formation leave the deepest motivational questions unanswered. When circumstances make self-protection look reasonable, only formation that has answered the question "for whom do I lead?" can hold the line.

Bonhoeffer coined the term "cheap grace"—the assumption that God's forgiveness requires nothing of us. Against this, he proclaimed "costly grace"—grace that calls us to follow Christ, which may cost everything. His own leadership journey embodied this: from pacifism to active resistance, a trajectory he understood as following Christ into costly places. He wrote from prison: "When Christ calls a man, he bids him come and die." By organizational metrics, his Finkenwalde community was shut down and he was executed. By eternal metrics, his witness continues to form leaders more than eighty years later.

The Failures of Christian Leadership

History also offers abundant examples of leaders who professed Christ while practicing exploitation, manipulation, and abuse. The Crusades, the Inquisition, colonial missions that served imperial interests, and countless contemporary scandals remind us that Christian profession doesn't guarantee Christ-like practice. These failures share common patterns:

- Using spiritual language to serve institutional or personal power

- Prioritizing organizational success over human dignity

- Creating cultures where challenge to leadership was framed as spiritual rebellion

- Separating public profession from private practice

What research into organizational health consistently surfaces is that these patterns are not unique to Christian organizations—but they may be uniquely dangerous within them, precisely because spiritual language provides such effective cover for the drift. When "trust God" becomes a substitute for transparent communication, when "submit to leadership" becomes a mechanism for silencing legitimate concern, when organizational success is narrated as divine blessing in ways that make questioning it feel like faithlessness—the very vocabulary of faith has become a tool of extraction. The framework has been corrupted, and the corruption is harder to see because it is dressed in the most sacred language available.

The failures are a warning: Christ at the center is not automatic protection against leadership dysfunction. It must be genuine—examined, accountable, and expressed in actual practice, not just language. Christian leaders are not immune to the drift toward self-protection; they may be especially vulnerable because spiritual language can mask that drift so effectively.

The Biblical View

Scripture provides both the model for Christ-centered leadership and honest acknowledgment of how leaders fail.

Jesus: The Model of Servant Leadership

The night before his crucifixion, Jesus took a towel and washed his disciples' feet—work reserved for the lowest servants. Then he said: "Do you understand what I have done for you? You call me 'Teacher' and 'Lord,' and rightly so, for that is what I am. Now that I, your Lord and Teacher, have washed your feet, you also should wash one another's feet. I have set you an example that you should do as I have done for you" (John 13:12–15).

This is the ultimate model: the one with all authority using it for service. Leadership not as position to be protected but as opportunity to serve. Power deployed for the flourishing of others, not the aggrandizement of self. What Jesus modeled that evening was not a technique. It was an identity. He was not performing servant leadership—he was demonstrating, in the starkest possible terms, what genuine authority looks like when it flows from a secured rather than a threatened self.

This matters enormously for what research consistently identifies as the difference between empowering and exploitative leadership. Empowering leaders—those who genuinely share authority, develop others, and create conditions where people feel psychologically safe and intrinsically motivated—do so from a posture of security. They are not threatened by others' growth or contributions. They do not experience others' competence as a challenge to their own standing. Jesus's leadership consistently inverted worldly patterns:

- He touched the untouchable (lepers, the bleeding woman, the dead)

- He elevated the marginalized (women, children, Samaritans, sinners)

- He challenged the powerful (religious leaders, Roman authority)

- He served rather than being served

- He gave his life rather than taking others'

None of this was strategic positioning. It was the overflow of an identity so anchored in the Father's love that status, reputation, and survival were not the currency being protected. Christ-centered leadership takes this model seriously—not as nice aspiration but as actual pattern, and as the only secure foundation from which genuinely empowering leadership can sustainably flow.

Jonah: The Right Tools, the Wrong Direction

Jonah is one of Scripture's most honest portraits of a leader who ran from his calling. God commissioned him to go to Nineveh; Jonah boarded a ship heading the opposite direction. His flight didn't just fail—it endangered everyone around him. Exposed in the storm, he admitted his responsibility. Swallowed, humbled, and redirected, he eventually obeyed.

What Jonah's story reveals for this chapter is something more specific than simple disobedience. Jonah had the ability—he was a prophet with genuine gifting. He had the opportunity—God commissioned him directly. He eventually had the behavioral compliance—he preached in Nineveh. And the results were extraordinary: the city repented, one of the most sweeping responses to prophetic ministry in all of Scripture.

By every external metric, Jonah's Nineveh campaign was a success. And then Jonah sat down outside the city and was angry about it. He had done the work but never aligned his heart with the mission. He wanted the task accomplished on his terms, for ends he controlled. The ability, the opportunity, and the compliance were all present. The motivational center was not.

This is why Jonah's story is so specifically instructive for leaders. It is possible to have genuine gifts, clear opportunities, and even compliant behavior while the actual center of motivation is running the wrong direction. Organizations can be built. Results can be produced. Tools can be correctly deployed. And the heart can remain fundamentally oriented toward self—toward vindication, toward control, toward outcomes that satisfy the leader's needs rather than the mission's demands.

God's response to Jonah's sulking is one of Scripture's most tender cross-examinations of a leader's motives: "Is it right for you to be angry?" The question doesn't challenge Jonah's competence. It goes directly to the center. The warning is clear: tools and techniques can be deployed even by a leader whose heart is running the wrong direction. The invitation is equally clear: God can redirect, restore, and use even the most reluctant leader—if that leader is willing to keep showing up and let God deal with the condition of their heart.

Paul: Power in Weakness

Paul's leadership philosophy inverted worldly assumptions about strength: "But he said to me, 'My grace is sufficient for you, for my power is made perfect in weakness.' Therefore I will boast all the more gladly about my weaknesses, so that Christ's power may rest on me. That is why, for Christ's sake, I delight in weaknesses, in insults, in hardships, in persecutions, in difficulties. For when I am weak, then I am strong" (2 Corinthians 12:9–10).

Paul was criticized for his speaking ability, faced constant opposition, and struggled with a "thorn in the flesh" he couldn't remove. Yet through this weakness, Christ's power was displayed. What Paul's example reveals—and what research into sustainable leadership confirms from a different direction—is that the leaders most likely to maintain genuinely empowering rather than extractive practices over time are those who are honest about their own limitations and dependent on something beyond their personal competence.

Leaders who operate from a self-sufficient posture—who must appear strong, competent, and certain—create organizational cultures that mirror those requirements. Followers learn not to surface problems that might expose leadership weakness. Voice is constrained not by formal policy but by the implicit understanding that the leader needs to appear to have answers. Innovation slows, because genuine empowerment requires admitting that the leader does not have all the solutions.

Paul's model—strength through weakness, power through surrender, effectiveness through dependence on Christ rather than self-sufficiency—is not merely theological. It produces the organizational conditions under which others can genuinely contribute, take risks, grow, and thrive. Christ-centered leadership doesn't require leaders to be strong in themselves. It invites leaders to be honest about weakness, dependent on grace, and confident that Christ's power works through human limitations in ways that self-sufficiency consistently forecloses.

Nuances and Blind Spots

Spiritual language can mask drift rather than prevent it. The warning signs of Christ-centered leadership failure rarely announce themselves clearly. They arrive dressed in familiar vocabulary—mission, calling, grace, kingdom—while the actual center of gravity quietly shifts from service toward self-protection, image management, or organizational survival. Leaders who use faith language fluently are not thereby insulated from this drift; they may simply be better equipped to narrate it spiritually while it happens.

Organizations whose stated values are loudest are not automatically those whose actual practices most closely reflect those values. The gap between espoused values and enacted values is common in every kind of organization—but in faith-based organizations, the espoused values carry such authority that the gap can persist longer before being named, precisely because naming it feels like a spiritual accusation rather than an honest observation. The spiritual vocabulary raises the stakes for honest assessment in ways that make the drift harder to catch and correct.

Christ-centered leadership is not softer leadership. Some assume that servant leadership means avoiding difficult decisions, conflict, or accountability. But Jesus drove money-changers from the temple, rebuked Peter sharply, and told truths that drove followers away. Framing honest feedback or disagreement as spiritual attack rather than potential gift is one of the more subtle distortions of this—it uses spiritual authority to justify the very isolation that makes accountability impossible. Grace without accountability isn't biblical generosity; it's dysfunction with theological cover.

Spiritual formation and leadership development are inseparable. Leaders who invest heavily in skills while neglecting their own formation eventually hollow out. The soul shapes the leader; the leader shapes the organization. Burnout worn as a badge of commitment, spiritual bypass substituted for actual action, ends-justify-means rationalization in service of good goals—these aren't primarily strategic failures. They are formation failures, and no amount of technique repairs them.

Organizational success can be a spiritual danger. Growth, influence, and acclaim can subtly shift the center from Christ to self in ways that are nearly invisible during the shift itself. Leaders who remained faithful in obscurity sometimes drift precisely when success arrives—because the very fruit of faithful leadership can become occasion for the pride that undermines it. Failure, by contrast, may be more spiritually formative than success. Seasons of genuine struggle often produce a depth of dependence on God that sustained abundance simply doesn't require.

Leaders whose sense of worth, competence, and belonging depends primarily on organizational outcomes—on results, on being seen as effective, on the approval of stakeholders—are more likely to unconsciously distort empowerment in ways that serve those needs. Research into why some leaders sustain empowering practices over time and others drift toward extraction consistently surfaces the question of what the leader's identity is grounded in. They delegate tasks they don't want; they withhold authority that might make them look less central; they build voice pathways that feel participatory while the actual decisions remain upstream. The outward form of empowering leadership is present. The motivational center is not. Scripture names this—"doing your acts of righteousness before other people, in order to be seen by them" (Matthew 6:1)—and the antidote it prescribes is the same one that research on sustainable motivation confirms: practices oriented toward an audience of one, not toward external validation.

The leader's private practice is the actual measure. Image over integrity—maintaining the appearance of spiritual leadership while private practice contradicts public profession—is not merely hypocrisy. It's a leading indicator of what is coming. The gap between public spiritual language and private reality doesn't stay stable; it widens. Evaluating leadership primarily by organizational metrics—growth, revenue, influence—rather than by faithfulness, character, and genuine human flourishing trains leaders to manage the appearance while the substance erodes.

Christian community is not optional for Christ-centered leaders. Leaders who operate outside genuine community—where they can be known, challenged, and held accountable by people who aren't dependent on them—are uniquely vulnerable to the drift that isolated leadership cannot self-correct. When leaders are surrounded only by people whose livelihood depends on the leader's approval, honest feedback becomes structurally nearly impossible. The body of Christ isn't a resource for leaders to deploy; it's the accountability structure without which no leader remains healthy for long.

Leader isolation is one of the most reliable predictors of leadership drift. The leader who has no one to whom they are genuinely accountable—not just performatively, but actually, with the real power to challenge and be heard—gradually loses the external reference points that make self-correction possible. The spiritual community functions as that reference point for the Christian leader, and its absence, regardless of how busy or productive the leader's organizational life appears, is a significant vulnerability.

Honest acknowledgment is part of faithful witness. Christian leaders bear responsibility for the historical and contemporary failures of those who professed Christ while practicing oppression. Defensive minimization of those failures—in the church, in organizations, in leadership history—is not faithfulness. It is the same ends-justifying-means reasoning that produces the failures in the first place. Honest acknowledgment, without deflection, is itself a form of integrity.

Every leader needs the gospel every day. Christ-centered leadership isn't achieved once and maintained automatically. It requires daily return—acknowledging sin, receiving grace, renewing dependence. This is not only a spiritual prescription; it maps onto what we understand about how habits and identity are actually formed. Research into sustainable behavior change consistently shows that identity—"I am the kind of leader who..."—shapes practice more reliably than willpower or intention. But identity itself must be continually renewed, anchored, and returned to. The daily practices of prayer, examination, confession, and Scripture are not merely devotional. They are the repetitive loops by which a leader's identity in Christ is reinforced, clarified, and kept from drifting toward the identities that organizational culture will otherwise supply. Leaders who believe they've arrived spiritually are not at the summit. They are at the point of greatest vulnerability, where the drift is most likely to begin and least likely to be noticed.

Try This Week

Choose ONE practice to center your leadership in Christ:

Practice 1: Daily Examination

Before ending your day, reflect: Where did I lead from fear rather than faith today? Where did I serve my own image rather than others' flourishing? Where did I experience God's grace? Confess what needs confessing. Receive forgiveness. Ask for tomorrow's grace. This rhythm keeps the center from drifting—and it builds the kind of self-awareness that makes genuine empowerment of others possible. Leaders who cannot see their own fear are most likely to create organizations organized around it.

Practice 2: Seek Honest Feedback

Ask someone who knows you well and will tell you truth: "Where do you see gap between my stated values and my actual practice? Where might I be drifting without realizing it?" Receive their observations without defending. Thank them. Take what they say to God in prayer. This practice is not merely strategic accountability—it is an act of humility that both your relationship and your soul require.

Practice 3: Sabbath Practice

Take genuine sabbath—not just time off but intentional rest that acknowledges God is God and you are not. Let the organization function without you for a day. Notice what anxieties arise. Bring them to God. Practice trust that doesn't depend on your constant effort. The leader who cannot rest is the leader who has quietly made the organization's survival dependent on their own centrality—which is empowerment's opposite and a form of control that exhausts everyone involved.

Practice 4: Serve Anonymously

Do something that serves another person with no possibility of recognition, credit, or return. Not leadership service that builds your reputation—hidden service that only God sees. Notice how it feels. What does it reveal about your motivations? This practice cuts directly at the performance dimension of leadership—the tendency to do the right things for the visibility they provide. Service that cannot be seen strips away every motivation except the one that matters.

Reflection Questions

Quick Check (1–2 minutes)

- If your leadership practices were examined by someone who didn't know your stated beliefs, would they conclude Christ is at the center?

- What would change about your leadership if organizational success became impossible but faithfulness remained available?

Deeper Reflection (5–10 minutes)

- Where has leadership success become subtly more important to you than faithfulness to Christ? What would it look like to reorder those priorities?

- What fears drive your leadership decisions? What would it mean to lead from trust in God rather than those fears?

- Who provides genuine accountability for your spiritual life, not just your leadership performance? If no one, why not?

- If you faced significant leadership failure tomorrow, where would your identity rest? What does your answer reveal about what's actually at the center?

Team Discussion (15–30 minutes)

- As a leadership team, discuss honestly: "What would it look like for Christ to be genuinely at the center of how we lead—not just in our language but in our actual practices, decisions, and priorities?" Identify one area where your practice doesn't match your profession. Commit to specific change. Create accountability for following through.

—◦—

Moving Forward

Eugene Peterson's concept "long obedience in the same direction" very much applies to the concepts within this book. This book has offered many tools: frameworks for cultural intelligence, methods for building trust, approaches to voice and fairness, strategies for distributed leadership, practices for navigating scarcity and change. These tools are genuinely useful. Leaders who implement them well create healthier organizations than those who don't. But tools serve ends. The question is: what ends?

Wilberforce used political tools in service of a conviction that human dignity, grounded in the image of God, demanded nothing less than total abolition—and sustained that conviction across five decades of defeat. The sustainability of his effort was inseparable from its center. His motivation was intrinsic in the deepest possible sense: grounded not in outcome or reputation but in identity before God and conviction about what God cared about. When the external rewards were absent—and they were absent for most of his career—the center held.

Bonhoeffer deployed every theological and pastoral skill he possessed in service of costly discipleship that eventually led to his death. His lasting influence came not from his organizational success—the seminary was shut down, the resistance failed, he was executed—but from the quality of formation he embodied and reproduced. Leaders shaped by Finkenwalde continued to hold under pressure because the formation had gone deeper than technique.

Jonah is the sobering reminder that even genuine gifts, clear opportunities, and compliant behavior can mask a heart running the wrong direction—and that God's patience with reluctant, self-serving leaders is an invitation to deeper surrender, not just better performance. The question God asked Jonah outside Nineveh—"Is it right for you to be angry?"—is the question every leader must be willing to receive, about the actual center from which their leadership flows.

The final caveat is simple: use whatever is helpful here, but know that the deepest hope behind these pages is that leaders will not only implement better practices but also be drawn nearer to the One who defines what it means to lead, to serve, and to lay down one's life for others.

For readers who share this faith, the hope is that the tools and stories not only improve leadership practice but draw you closer to

Christ's heart for people from every culture and background. May your leadership be not just effective but faithful. May your organizations not just succeed but flourish. May Christ be not just acknowledged but actually at the center—shaping every decision, redeeming every failure, empowering every act of genuine service.

For readers from other backgrounds, take whatever is helpful. The practical insights don't require Christian faith to apply. But know that for the author, these insights aren't spiritually neutral—they emerge from and point toward a larger story of redemption in which every act of leadership, every moment of service, and every effort toward human flourishing finds its ultimate meaning in the God who made us, loves us, and calls us to reflect his character in how we lead.

"Whatever you do, work at it with all your heart, as working for the Lord, not for human masters, since you know that you will receive an inheritance from the Lord as a reward. It is the Lord Christ you are serving" (Colossians 3:23–24). **May it be so.**

Conclusion

Leadership across cultures is not a technique to be mastered. It is a posture to be cultivated.

When I first began wrestling with the realities of multicultural leadership, I was looking for clarity. I wanted categories, clean frameworks, something that would remove ambiguity. What I discovered instead was something both more demanding and more beautiful: the work is not primarily about managing difference. It is about being formed through it.

If you have read this far, you already understand that leading across cultures is rarely neat. It exposes assumptions you did not know you carried. It reveals blind spots that feel uncomfortable. It forces conversations you might prefer to postpone. It stretches patience, demands humility, and yet—it also enlarges the soul.

Throughout this book, we have explored pillars, practices, tensions, and tools. We have examined systems and stories. We have considered both the structural and the spiritual dimensions of leadership. But none of these exist to create a polished organization that looks diverse from a distance. They exist to help build communities where people genuinely belong, where voices are not merely included but valued, and where vision is shared rather than imposed.

If there is one truth I hope you carry forward, it is this: multicultural leadership is not sustained by charisma or strategy alone. It is sustained by character. The frameworks matter, the assessments matter, and te practices matter. But they only bear fruit when leaders are willing to be shaped—again and again—by the very diversity they steward.

You will make mistakes. You will misread a moment. You will underestimate cultural weight. You will discover that good intentions are not the same as good outcomes. This does not disqualify you. It invites you deeper. The goal is not perfection. The goal is faithfulness. Faithfulness to listen before speaking, to examine power rather than protect it, to create pathways for ownership rather than control, to hold vision in a way that transcends personal preference. Faithfulness to align practice with conviction.

Over time, these small acts of faithfulness accumulate. They form cultures and establish trust. They create organizations that do not fracture under pressure but grow stronger because they are rooted in something deeper than personality or popularity. The work is slow. There are seasons when progress feels invisible and conversations seem repetitive. When tensions resurface in new forms and when scarcity tempts you to retreat into what feels familiar and manageable. In those moments, remember: health is rarely dramatic; it is consistent.

Healthy multicultural organizations are not built through grand gestures. They are built through steady habits—clear communication, shared ownership, honest reflection, and a commitment to personal and professional integrity that anchors everything else.

If you are leading in a context marked by cultural complexity, you are stewarding something sacred. You are shaping not only strategy, but experience. Not only outcomes, but belonging. Not only productivity, but people. That responsibility can feel heavy, and it should. But it is also hopeful. Because when leaders approach this work with humility and courage, something remarkable happens. Diversity stops feeling like a problem to solve and becomes a gift to receive. Differences stop being obstacles and begin to function as teachers. Vision expands. Creativity deepens. Trust grows. And perhaps most importantly, leadership itself becomes less about being the central voice and more about cultivating a chorus.

As you move forward, do not attempt to implement everything at once. Choose one pillar. One practice. One conversation. Start there. Allow consistency to do what intensity never can. Return to the tools when needed. Revisit the assessments when tension rises. Invite feedback before it is demanded. ***Pause before reacting. Pray before deciding. <u>Above all, remain teachable.</u>*** The organizations that flourish across cultures are led by men and women who never graduate from learning.

This journey will not end with the final page of this book. In many ways, it begins here. Each context will present new nuances and each team will surface new questions. Each season will require renewed discernment. That is not failure; it is leadership.

If you continue with humility, courage, and faithfulness, you will build more than a functioning multicultural organization. You will build a community where people experience dignity, voice, and shared purpose. You will model leadership that resists fragmentation and embodies **<u>unity without uniformity</u>**. And in a world increasingly divided by difference or that demonizes difference, that witness matters. We are stronger for our differing views and voices, more capable for our unique strengths and talents, and leaders who steward this well will find themselves humbled by the positive change in their organization and in their own hearts.

Full Companion Toolkit Available

The frameworks, templates, and tools referenced throughout this book are available as a comprehensive companion toolkit. This free resource includes assessment templates and implementation guides to help you apply these principles in your organization.

Access the full toolkit at: https://fordmountainpublishing.com/for

med_by_difference_toolkit/

Acknowledgements

To the leaders and staff members in multicultural organizations who graciously opened their lives and shared their stories: Your honesty about both struggles and growth made this research possible. May these insights serve others facing similar journeys.

To the mentors who shaped my understanding of leadership: Your investment in my development models what this book advocates.

To my spouse and loved ones, who bore the cost of this work with patience and encouragement: Your support made the journey sustainable. You remind me daily that leadership begins at home.

Multicultural Organizational Health Check

A comprehensive self-assessment for leaders of multicultural teams,

How to use this tool: Work through each domain honestly. Rate 1 (**significant concern**) to 5 (**genuine strength**). Use real evidence, not impressions. The goal is honest diagnosis, not a good score.

Best used: Annually by a leadership team, or quarterly for a specific domain under pressure. Complete independently first, then compare scores to surface perception gaps.

How to Score and Interpret

Score – What It Means – Leader's Posture

- 5 Genuine strength with consistent evidence — ask 'how do we sustain and spread this?' – Celebrate. Protect. Replicate elsewhere.

- 4 Mostly present – occasional gaps, ask 'what specific condition causes this to dip? – Maintain and strengthen the weak spots.

- 3 Mixed — present some of the time, absent other times; inconsistency is the problem – Diagnose which conditions produce the 3 and address those.

- 2 Significantly underdeveloped; more absent than present; needs deliberate attention – Prioritize. Set a 90-day target. Name who owns it.

- 1 Serious concern; this domain is fragile or broken; urgent attention needed – Stop and address before other priorities compound the damage.

Overall Score Interpretation (out of 350)

Total Score: *Health Profile—>*<u>Recommended Response</u>

- **280–350:** *Strong multicultural health — most domains functioning well—>*<u>Sustain. Deepen. Focus on the 1–2 lowest domains. Celebrate progress.</u>

- **210–279:** *Solid foundation with real gaps — 3–5 domains needing focused attention—>*<u>Name the priority domains. 90-day action plans for each.</u> Revisit quarterly.

- **140–209:** *Fragile — more gaps than foundations; risk of compounding problems—>*<u>Don't try to fix everything. Choose 2–3 highest-leverage domains. Address them before others.</u>

- **Below 140:** *Organizational crisis — multiple domains weak; passive cold war likely—>*<u>Bring in outside support. Candid assessment with the whole leadership team. Start with trust.</u>

Critical Rule: The Floor Principle

Any single domain scoring 8 or below (average 1.6 per question) is a floor — it limits the impact of every other domain, regardless of how high other scores are. A team can have excellent vision (25/25) but if psychological safety is broken (6/25), people cannot act on what they see. Address floors before celebrating ceilings.

Score Summary — All 14 Domains

Complete this page after scoring all 14 domains. Transfer your domain totals here.

Domain Chapter Score (out of 25) Priority? (Y/N) 90-Day Action
1 Cross-Cultural Reality ___/25
2 Cultural Intelligence ___/25
3 Human Performance ___/25
4 Trust & Safety ___/25
5 Voice & Fairness ___/25
6 Shared Leadership ___/25
7 Vision ___/25
8 Faith & Values Culture ___/25
9 Scarcity Mindset ___/25
10 Turnover & Transitions ___/25
11 Personal Development ___/25
12 Growing People ___/25
13 Learning Organization ___/25
14 Faithfulness & Formation ___/25
OVERALL ORGANIZATIONAL HEALTH SCORE ___/350

After completing the summary, ask your leadership team:
   1. Which domain score surprised us most — and why?

2. Are there domains where different team members scored very differently? What does that gap tell us?

3. Which 1–2 domains, if improved, would most benefit the people we serve?

4. Is any domain below 10? If so — what do we do this week?

Perception Gap Check: Did leaders and team members complete this separately and compare? The gap between how leaders rate organizational health and how staff rate it is often more diagnostic than either score alone.

Best practice: Have 3–5 staff from different cultural backgrounds and roles complete this assessment independently. Aggregate their scores. Compare to leadership scores. Where the gap is widest — that is where to start.

PART ONE

Seeing What's Really Happening

Chapters 1–3 | Domains 1–3

Chapter 1 – Cross-Cultural Work in Practice

- Leaders regularly address all three layers (Task, Relational, Cultural) — not only task-level challenges ___/5

- Cultural 'unspoken rules' are surfaced and discussed openly rather than left to newcomers to discover alone ___/5

- Staff who navigate multiple cultural registers are recognized and valued, not just expected to adapt silently ___/5

- The 'translation tax' — energy spent interpreting meaning across cultures — is acknowledged and reduced ___/5

DOMAIN TOTAL ___/25

Chapter 2 – Cultural Intelligence for Everyone

- Leaders approach cultural difference with curiosity rather than labeling or judgment ___/5

- Communication is offered in multiple formats and styles — not one-size-fits-all ___/5

- Differences in communication style (direct vs. indirect, high-context vs. low-context) are understood and bridged, not penalized ___/5

- Cultural tensions are diagnosed accurately — distinguishing cultural patterns from individual personality ___/5

- People from all cultural backgrounds feel their style of contributing is genuinely honored ___/5

DOMAIN TOTAL ___/25

Chapter 3 – What High Performance Means

Assessment Question Score (1–5)
- Clarity: people know what success looks like, why it matters, and how their specific role contributes ___/5

- Consistency: leaders do what they say; policies apply equitably across all cultures and roles ___/5

- Contribution: people see how their work creates value; voice genuinely shapes decisions ___/5

- Care: people are treated as whole persons with lives beyond their job function ___/5

- The Five Forces (Consistency, Communication, Vision, Growth, Inclusion) are all present and reinforcing each other ___/5

DOMAIN TOTAL ___/25

PART TWO

Building the Foundation

Chapters 4–6 | Domains 4–6

Chapter 4 – Trust and Safety in Diverse Teams

- Predictability: staff can roughly anticipate how leadership will respond — decisions follow a recognizable pattern ___/5

- Transparency: decisions are explained at the right depth; the logic and values behind choices are visible ___/5

- Proximity: leadership is relationally close enough that people feel safe raising real concerns ___/5

- Psychological safety: staff believe they can speak honestly without punishment — including across cultural lines ___/5

- Trust is equitably distributed — it does not thin out along cultural, role, or language lines ___/5

DOMAIN TOTAL ___/25

Chapter 5 – Voice, Feedback, and Fairness

- Multiple voice pathways exist (public, private, participatory design) — not only group meetings ___/5

- The feedback loop is complete: input is invited, received, considered, and visibly acted on ___/5

- Distributive fairness: resources, recognition, and development are allocated equitably across roles and cultures ___/5

- Procedural fairness: decision-making processes are consistent, clear, and applied without favoritism ___/5

- Interactional fairness: every person is treated with dignity in every interaction — not only in formal settings ___/5

DOMAIN TOTAL ___/25

Chapter 6 – Shared Vision and Leadership

- Decision authority is explicit — staff know which level applies to which decisions (Inform / Consult / Recommend / Decide / Own) ___/5

- Authority is matched to competence and preparation — empowerment does not outpace support   ___/5

- Empowerment is equitably distributed — it does not favor certain roles, cultures, or personalities   ___/5

- Initiative is celebrated, not punished — people who take appropriate ownership are recognized   ___/5

- Leadership is being reproduced — others are growing into broader responsibility through deliberate investment   ___/5

DOMAIN TOTAL ___/25

PART THREE

Leading for the Long Haul

Chapters 7–10 | Domains 7–10

Chapter 7 – Vision That Transcends Backgrounds

- The vision is articulated in diverse voices' own words — not only recited; people own it, not just know it   ___/5

- Vision is referenced in actual decisions, not confined to documents, posters, or retreats   ___/5

- Staff from all cultural backgrounds can locate themselves in the vision — it transcends majority-culture assumptions ___/5

- Vision communication intensifies (not goes silent) during transitions and organizational change ___/5

- Resources — budget, time, leadership attention — demonstrably reflect the stated vision priorities ___/5

DOMAIN TOTAL ___/25

Chapter 8 – Faith, Values, and Workplace Spirituality

- Integrity: words and actions align — especially under pressure and in costly decisions ___/5

- Spiritual language is not used to silence disagreement, avoid conflict, or substitute for accountability ___/5

- Diverse expressions of faith and values are honored — not ranked by cultural or theological similarity to leadership ___/5

- There is a shared moral vocabulary that bridges different traditions without requiring theological uniformity ___/5

- The gap between professed values and lived practices is named honestly — not spiritualized away ___/5

DOMAIN TOTAL ___/25

Chapter 9 – Practices to Offset Scarcity Mindset

- Resource constraints are met with strategic choice-making — not panic, paralysis, or information-hoarding ___/5

- The 'grief arc' of organizational change is understood — leaders respond to where people actually are, not where they wish they were ___/5

- Change is communicated clearly: what is changing, what is not, what is known, what is not yet known ___/5

- The burden of scarcity is distributed equitably — it does not fall disproportionately on the least powerful ___/5

- Knowledge is shared proactively rather than hoarded as job security ___/5

DOMAIN TOTAL ___/25

Chapter 10 – Managing Turnover and Transitions

- Transition seasons (ending, in-between, new beginning) are named and led appropriately — not skipped or rushed ___/5

- Handover systems exist: knowledge, relationships, and process documentation transfer when people leave ___/5

- Remaining staff are supported through the fatigue of repeated relational loss from turnover cycles ___/5

- The three change response groups (Active Fighters, Accepters/Adapters, Faith-Reliers) are all engaged — not just the compliant ___/5

- New arrivals receive genuine onboarding investment — not 'figure it out alone' ___/5

DOMAIN TOTAL ___/25

PART FOUR

Sustainable Transformation

Chapters 11–14 | Domains 11–14

Chapter 11 – Personal Development

- Leaders are actively engaged in their own growth — emotional, managerial, intellectual, and spiritual   ___/5

- Micro-practices and deliberate habits are embedded in daily and weekly rhythms — not only in crisis response   ___/5

- Personal development is supported with time, accountability, and reflection — not just encouraged in speeches   ___/5

- Leaders can name specific ways they have grown in cultural intelligence in the past year   ___/5

- Formation and character development are treated as leadership priorities, not soft options   ___/5

DOMAIN TOTAL ___/25

Chapter 12 – Growing People, Not Just Results

- People are being developed intentionally: strengths affirmed, growth edges named, opportunities provided   ___/5

- The 70-20-10 principle operates in practice: experience, relationships, and formal training all develop people ___/5
- Development is equitably distributed — investment does not follow demographic or role-based favoritism ___/5
- Feedback is developmental (growth-focused) not only evaluative (performance-focused) ___/5
- There is a visible pathway — people can see how they might grow into more responsibility over time ___/5

DOMAIN TOTAL ___/25

Chapter 13 – Building Learning Organizations

Assessment Question Score (1–5)

- After-Action Reviews or equivalent structured reflection happen routinely — not only after failures ___/5
- When things go wrong, 'what happened?' is asked before 'whose fault?' — analysis before blame ___/5
- Institutional knowledge is documented and shared so it doesn't walk out the door with people ___/5
- People from minority cultural backgrounds actively shape how organizational events are interpreted ___/5
- Positive deviants — people already solving hard problems well — are identified and learned from ___/5

DOMAIN TOTAL ___/25

Chapter 14 – The Final Caveat

- Leaders track faithfulness markers (integrity, humility, justice, service, courage) not only performance outcomes   ___/5

- There is a culture of honest self-examination — leaders can name where they are out of alignment   ___/5

- Long-view thinking governs decisions — the organization is building for the next decade, not only the next quarter   ___/5

- Leaders are sustained by community, purpose, and spiritual practice — not only by willpower and urgency   ___/5

- The organization is becoming a place where people are formed — character and culture growing together over time   ___/5

DOMAIN TOTAL ___/25

Integrated Analysis & Action Planning

Pattern Analysis: What the Scores Reveal Together

Before identifying actions, look at your scores as a system, not a list. These domains are interdependent.

Pattern to Look For: *What It Means*

- **HIGH trust (D4) but LOW voice (D5):** *People trust leadership enough to feel safe, but the systems for speaking don't actually exist or work. Build the pathways.*

- **HIGH vision (D7) but LOW trust (D4) or LOW voice (D5):** *Vision without foundation becomes pressure. The vision is good; the soil it needs to grow in isn't ready yet.*

- **HIGH CQ (D2) but LOW cultural reality (D1):** *Cultural intelligence knowledge exists but isn't changing the lived experience. Skills haven't changed the system.*

- **HIGH performance (D3) but LOW care (D3 sub) or LOW fairness (D5):** *The organization is getting results by consuming people. Sustainable performance requires both.*

- **HIGH faith/values (D8) but LOW integrity patterns (D14):** *Professed values exceed lived reality. Spiritual language may be substituting for operational accountability.*

- **HIGH growing people (D12) but LOW equity (D12 sub):** *Development exists, but who gets it is patterned. Check whether investment follows cultural or role bias.*

- **LOW across Part Three (D7–D10):** *The organization is running on legacy — it built something, but isn't sustaining or renewing it. Urgent.*

- **LOW across Part Four (D11–D14):** *Leaders are not investing in themselves or the long game. Short-term extraction. Risk of burnout and fragility.*

⸺◈⸺

Equity Check: The Invisible Scorecard

The most important question this assessment cannot ask itself: <u>do different groups experience this organization differently?</u>

Group: Estimated Score (if they completed this)—>Biggest Gap from Leadership Score Action Implied

- Staff from majority culture

- Staff from minority cultures

- Support/administrative roles

- Teaching/program roles

- Long-tenured staff

- New staff (under 2 years)

If you cannot estimate these scores with confidence — that itself is a finding. You don't have enough cross-cultural relational access yet.

—◆○◆—

90-Day Priority Action Plan

Create a chart and choose no more than 3 domains to prioritize. More than 3 diffuses focus. For each, identify one concrete action with a specific owner and date. Sections for the chart could be titled: Priority Domain—>Why This One?—>One Concrete Action—>Owner—>Target Date—>Review Date

—◆○◆—

Before You Close This Assessment

- Ask: Who else should see these scores — and who helped generate them?

- Ask: Are the people most affected by these domains represented in the discussion?

- Ask: What one thing would change most visibly for staff if we addressed our lowest-scoring domain?

- Ask: Who is already doing this well in our organization — and can we learn from them first?

This tool does not produce a grade. It produces a conversation. The honest conversation it generates is the work.

Warning Signs: The Passive Cold War Checklist

These patterns — drawn from all 14 chapters — signal when organizational health is deteriorating beneath the surface, often before scores have moved. Check any you recognize.

Part One — Cross-Cultural Reality, CQ, Performance

☐ The same few voices dominate every meeting; others stay consistently silent across all settings

☐ Cultural differences are addressed only when they cause conflict, not proactively

☐ Staff from minority cultures describe constant code-switching and the 'translation tax' of daily work

☐ High performers from non-dominant cultures are leaving faster than others

☐ 'Personality clash' conflicts consistently fall along cultural lines — but are treated as individual issues

Part Two — Trust, Voice, Leadership

☐ Job security anxiety exists among staff who have no objective cause to fear — the perception gap is the problem

☐ Surprise resignations — leadership was genuinely surprised, meaning people stopped telling them real concerns long ago

☐ Whisper networks are faster and more trusted than official communication channels

☐ Exit interviews reveal cultural pain that was never mentioned while people were employed

☐ Feedback is collected but loops are not closed — people stop offering input because nothing visibly changes

☐ Initiative is punished (explicitly or implicitly) — people learn that speaking up or acting carries cost

☐ Decision authority is either over-concentrated (everything needs approval) or undefined (nobody knows who decides what)

Part Three — Vision, Values, Scarcity, Transition

☐ Vision lives on walls and documents but is not referenced in actual decisions

☐ Different groups interpret the same value or event in completely contradictory ways — story fragmentation

☐ Spiritual or values language is used to avoid conflict, accountability, or difficult operational conversations

☐ Scarcity is used as a chronic explanation rather than a context for strategic choice

☐ Knowledge hoarding — people protecting information as job security rather than sharing for organizational health

☐ Transition seasons are rushed past — endings not honored, grief not named, 'we just need to move forward'

☐ New arrivals receive minimal handover and must self-teach critical processes and relationships

Part Four — Development, Learning, Formation

☐ Development is celebrated in speeches but not protected in budgets or calendars

☐ Development investment follows clear patterns — certain roles or cultural groups receive significantly more

☐ After difficult events, the organization moves on without structured reflection — learning by accident only

☐ Leaders cannot name specific ways they have grown in the past year

☐ Long-term building is consistently sacrificed for short-term urgency — nothing is being built for the next decade

☐ Cynicism is increasing — people losing hope that things will change, seeing only problems, forgetting progress

If you checked more than 5 items: Do not address them all. Choose the one that, if improved, would most visibly change the experience of the people most affected. Start there. Do it well. Then continue.

You are being formed by difference. The work is long. It is worth it. You do not do it alone.

References

Abacioglu, C. S., Volman, M., & Fischer, A. H. (2020). Teachers' multicultural attitudes and perspective taking abilities as factors in culturally responsive teaching. *British Journal of Educational Psychology, 90*(3), 736-752. https://doi.org/10.1111/bjep.12328

Addo, J. K. J., & Dube, Z. (2020). Interactional leadership: Jesus' model of leadership – A case of mark 7:25–29. *Hervormde Teologiese Studies, 76*(4), 1-7. https://doi.org/10.4102/hts.v76i4.5554

Aflaki, I. & Lindh, M. (2021). Empowering first-line managers as change leaders towards co-creation culture: the role of facilitated sensemaking. *Public Money & Management.* DOI: 10.1080/09540962.2021.2007636

Afsar, B., & Waheed, A. U. (2020). Transformational leadership and innovative work behavior: The role of motivation to learn, task complexity and innovation climate. *European Journal of Innovation Management, 23*(3): 402-428. http://dx.doi.org.ezproxy.liberty.edu/10.1108/EJIM-12-2018-0257

Aguas, P. (2022). Fusing approaches in educational research: Data collection and data analysis in phenomenological research. *Qualitative Report, 27*(1), 1-20. https://doi.org/10.46743/2160-3715/2022.5027

Akemu, A., & Abdelnour, S. (2020). Confronting the digital: Doing ethnography in modern organizational settings. *Organizational Re-*

search Methods, 23(2), 296-321. https://doi.org/10.1177/1094428118791 018

Åkerblad, L., Seppänen-Järvelä, R., & Haapakoski, K. (2021). Integrative strategies in mixed methods research. *Journal of Mixed Methods Research, 15*(2), 152-170. https://doi.org/10.1177/1558689820957125

Ali, Z., Fazal, u. R., Imran, M., Ali, M., & Rawdha, G. A. (2020). Authentic leadership traits, high-performance human resource practices and job performance in Pakistan. [Authentic leadership traits and job performance] *International Journal of Public Leadership, 16*(3), 299-317. https://doi.org/10.1108/IJPL-02-2020-0011

Alnaimi, A. M. M., & Rjoub, H. (2021). Perceived organizational support, psychological entitlement, and extra-role behavior: The mediating role of knowledge hiding behavior. *Journal of Management & Organization, 27*(3), 507-522. https://doi.org/10.1017/jmo.2019.1

Ameyaw, M. A., Sun, B., Antwi, S., Bentum-Micah, G., & Ameyaw, J. E. (2022). Relationship beyond the workplace: Impact of guanxi GRX scale on employee engagement and performance. *Sustainability (Basel, Switzerland), 14*(12), 7364. https://doi.org/10.3390/su14127364

Ahmed, F. (2018). Leadership and management influences on personal and professional development and group dynamics: a student's experience. *Nursing Children and Young People, 30*(2): 40. http://dx.doi.org.ezproxy.liberty.edu/10.7748/ncyp.2018.e1027

Ali, M., Qu, Y., Shafique, S., Pham, N. T., & Usman, M. (2022). The role of ethical leadership in enhancing exploitative and explorative learning simultaneously: What does it matter if employees view work as central? *Personnel Review, 51*(2): 787-804. https://doi.org/10.1108/PR-12-2019-0708

An, C. H., West, A. D., Sandage, S. J., & Bell, C. A. (2019). Relational spirituality, mature alterity, and spiritual service among ministry leaders: An empirical study. *Pastoral Psychology, 68*(2), 127-143. https://doi.org/10.1007/s11089-018-0846-9

Anthony, E. L. (2017). The impact of leadership coaching on leadership behaviors. *The Journal of Management Development, 36*(7):

930-939. http://dx.doi.org/10.1108/JMD-06-2016-0092

Arefin, M. S., Alam, M. S., Islam, M. R., & Rahaman, M. (2019). High-performance work systems and job engagement: The mediating role of psychological empowerment. *Cogent Business & Management, 6*(1). https://doi.org/10.1080/23311975.2019.1664204

Armstrong, J. P. (2020;2019;). Assessing intercultural competence in international leadership courses: Developing the global leader. *Journal of Leadership Education, 19*(4), 1. https://doi.org/10.12806/V19/I4/R1

Arshad, M., Qasim, N., Farooq, O., & Rice, J. (2022). Empowering leadership and employees' work engagement: A social identity theory perspective. *Management Decision, 60*(5), 1218-1236. https://doi.org/10.1108/MD-11-2020-1485

Arthur, J. B., Herdman, A. O., & Yang, J. (2021). Which way to high performance? comparing performance effects of high-performance work system components in small- to medium-sized establishments. *Industrial & Labor Relations Review. 74*(2). 352-387. https://doi.org/10.1177/0019793919893668

Atwater, L., Yu, J., Tawse, A., Fields, L. H., McFarren, J. A., & Nae, E. Y. (2021;2019;). Relevance of culture in studies of leadership: Ignored or dismissed? *Asia Pacific Journal of Management, 38*(2), 687-708. https://doi.org/10.1007/s10490-019-09678-w

Baker, C. & Power, M. (2018) Ghosts in the machine: beliefs, values and worldviews in the workplace and business environment. *Journal of Beliefs & Values, 39*(4): 474-489. DOI: 10.1080/13617672.2018.1477705

Baker, E. L., Dunne-Moses, A., Calarco, A. J., & Gilkey, R. (2019). Listening to understand: A core leadership skill. *Journal of Public Health Management and Practice, 25*(5), 508-510. https://doi.org/10.1097/PHH.0000000000001051

Bakhuys Roozeboom, M. C., Schelvis, R. M. C., Houtman, I. L. D., Wiezer, N. M., & Bongers, P. M. (2020). Decreasing employees' work stress by a participatory, organizational level work stress prevention approach: a multiple-case study in primary education. *BMC Public Health, 20*(1): 676. https://doi-org.ezproxy.liberty.edu/10.1186/s12889

-020-08698-2

Barak, M., & Green, G. (2021). Applying a social constructivist approach to an online course on ethics of research. *Science and Engineering Ethics, 27*(1), 8-8. https://doi.org/10.1007/s11948-021-00280-2

Baron, P. (2020). Owning one's epistemology in religious studies research methodology. *Kybernetes, 49*(8), 2057-2071. https://doi-org.ezproxy.liberty.edu/10.1108/K-03-2019-0159

Bartram, T., Cooper, B., Cooke, F. L., & Wang, J. (2021). High-performance work systems and job performance: The mediating role of social identity, social climate and empowerment in Chinese banks. *Personnel Review, 50*(1): 285-302. https://doi.org/10.1108/PR-08-2019-0425

Bell, E., Winchester, N., & Wray-Bliss, E. (2021). Enchantment in business ethics research. *Journal of Business Ethics, 174*(2), 251-262. https://doi.org/10.1007/s10551-020-04592-4

Bell, S., Choi, G., Patterson, S., & Penno, D. (2020). A call to relational leadership arising from a shared eschatological vision. *The Journal of Applied Christian Leadership, 14*(1), 26-41. https://www.proquest.com/docview/2539313589

Belwalkar, S., Vohra, V., & Pandey, A. (2018). The relationship between workplace spirituality, job satisfaction and organizational citizenship behaviors – an empirical study. *Social Responsibility Journal, 14*(2), 410-430. http://dx.doi.org.ezproxy.liberty.edu/10.1108/SRJ-05-2016-0096

Blackburn, B. R, and Williamson, R. (2018). Leading change in your school: A sustainable process. *Australian Educational Leader, 40*(1). 8-12. https://search-informit-com-au.ezproxy.liberty.edu/documentSummary;dn=478468826974780;res=IELHSS

Blanche, C., & Dupuis, J. P. (2019). From the Hague to Paris to Montréal: Knowledge transfer and cultural synergy in a multicultural organization. *International Journal of Cross Cultural Management, 19*(1), 27–46. https://doi.org/10.1177/1470595819839756

Bogna, F., Raineri, A., & Dell, G. (2020). Critical realism and constructivism: Merging research paradigms for a deeper qualitative study. *Qualitative Research in Organizations and Management. 15*(4). 461-484. https://doi.org/10.1108/QROM-06-2019-1778

Bonache, J. & Festing, M. (2020). Research paradigms in international human resource management: An epistemological systematisation of the field. *German Journal of Human Resource Management. 34*(2). 99–123. https://doi-org.ezproxy.liberty.edu/10.1177/2397002220909780

Bragger, J. D., Alonso, N. A., D'Ambrosio, K., & Williams, N. (2021). Developing leaders to serve and servants to lead. *Human Resource Development Review, 20*(1), 9-45. https://doi.org/10.1177/1534484320981198

Breevaart, K. & Zacher, H. (2019). Main and interactive effects of weekly transformational and laissez-faire leadership on followers' trust in the leader and leader effectiveness. *Journal of Occupational and Organizational Psychology, 92*: 384-409. doi:10.1111/joop.12253

Brenkert, G.G. (2019). Mind the Gap! The challenges and limits of (Global) business ethics. *J Bus Ethics.* 155: 917–930. https://doi-org.ezproxy.liberty.edu/10.1007/s10551-018-3902-6

Brooks, A. W., Hammons, J., Nolan, J., Dufek, S., & Wynn, M. (2019). The purpose of research: What undergraduate students say. *Scholarship and Practice of Undergraduate Research, 3*(1), 39-47. https://doi.org/10.18833/spur/3/1/7

Campos-Moreira, L., Marlon I. Cummings, M., Grumbach, G., Williams, H. & Hooks, K. (2020). Making a case for culturally humble leadership practices through a culturally responsive leadership framework. *Human Service Organizations: Management, Leadership & Governance, 44*(5): 407-414. DOI: 10.1080/23303131.2020.1822974

Cao, M., Zhao, S., & Xu, Y. (2022). How HR systems are implemented matters: High-performance work systems and employees' thriving at work. *Asia Pacific Journal of Human Resources, 60*(4), 880-899. https://doi.org/10.1111/1744-7941.12307

Candela,   A.   (2019).   Exploring   the   function of member checking. *Qualitative Report, 24*(3), 619-628. https://doi.org/10.46743/2160-3715/2019.3726

Cantarero, K., Szarota, P., Stamkou, E., Navas, M., & Alejandra del Carmen, D. E. (2018). The effects of culture and moral foundations on moral judgments: The ethics of authority mediates the relationship between power distance and attitude towards lying to one's supervisor: Research and Reviews. *Current Psychology:* 1-9. http://dx.doi.org.ezp roxy.liberty.edu/10.1007/s12144-018-9945-0

Casteel, A., & Bridier, N. L. (2021). Describing populations and samples in doctoral student research. *International Journal of Doctoral Studies, 16*, 339-362. https://doi.org/10.28945/4766

Castillo, C, Vicenc Fernandez, V. & Sallan, J. M. (2018). The six emotional stages of organizational change. *Journal of Organizational Change Management, 31*(3): 468-493. DOI 10.1108/JOCM-05-2016-0084

Chapman, A. (2021). Resolving conflict: Superordinate goals and careful communication. *BMJ (Online), 372,* n785-n785 https://doi.or g/10.1136/bmj.n785

Chen, G., Smith, T. A., Kirkman, B. L., Zhang, P., Lemoine, G. J., & Farh, J.-L. (2019). Multiple team membership and em-powerment spillover effects: Can empowerment processes cross team boundaries? *Journal of Applied Psychology, 104*(3): 321–340. https://doi.org/10.1037/apl0000336.supp

Chen, M., & Bedford, O. (2022). Measuring guanxi quali-ty in the workplace. *Journal of Business and Psychology, 37*(3), 581-599. https://doi.org/10.1007/s10869-021-09762-3

Chen, M. S. & Eweje, G. (2020). Establishing ethical guanxi (inter-personal relationships) through Confucian virtues of xinyong (trust), lijie (empathy) and ren (humanity). *Corporate Governance, 20*(1): 1-15. DOI: http://dx.doi.org/10.1108/CG-01-2019-0015

Chen, S., Fan, Y., Zhang, G., & Zhang, Y. (2019). Collectivism-ori-ented human resource management on team creativity: effects of interpersonal harmony and human resource management strength. *The International Journal of Human Resource Management:* 1-29.

DOI: 10.1080/09585192.2019.1640765

Chen, Y., & Chen, S. (2021). Looking at both sides of high-performance work systems and individual performance: A job demands–resources model. *Journal of Management & Organization:* 1-21. https://doi.org/10.1017/jmo.2021.4

Cho, Y. J., & Song, H. J. (2021). How to facilitate innovative behavior and organizational citizenship behavior: Evidence from public employees in Korea. *Public Personnel Management, 50*(4), 509-537. https://doi.org/10.1177/0091026020977571

Chughtai, A. (2019). Servant leadership and perceived employability: Proactive career behaviours as mediators. *Leadership & Organization Development Journal, 40*(2), 213-229. https://doi.org/10.1108/LODJ-07-2018-0281

Chung Y. W. (2020). The relationship between workplace ostracism, TMX, task interdependence, and task performance: A moderated mediation model. *International journal of environmental research and public health, 17*(12): 4432. https://doi.org/10.3390/ijerph17124432

Cole, E. (2018). Building strength: Unlocking the potential of a multicultural team: How Sandra Bennett's leadership transformed a demoralised workforce, empowered staff to enhance their skills and improved patient care. *Nursing Standard (2014+), 33*(7), 30. http://dx.doi.org/10.7748/ns.33.7.30.s15

Collins, C. S., & Stockton, C. (2022). The theater of qualitative research: The role of the researcher/actor. *International Journal of Qualitative Methods, 21.* https://doi.org/10.1177/16094069221103109

Cooke, F. L., Cooper, B., Bartram, T., Wang, J., & Mei, H. (2019). Mapping the relationships between high-performance work systems, employee resilience and engagement: A study of the banking industry in china. *International Journal of Human Resource Management, 30*(8), 1239-1260. https://doi.org/10.1080/09585192.2015.1137618

Cook, I. (2021). *Who is driving the Great Resignation?* Harvard Business Review. https://hbr.org/2021/09/who-is-driving-the-great-resignation

Coun, M. J. H., Peters, P., & Blomme, R. J. (2019). 'Let's share!' the mediating role of employees' self-determination in the relationship between transformational and shared leadership and perceived knowledge sharing among peers. *European Management Journal, 37*(4), 481-491. https://doi.org/10.1016/j.emj.2018.12.001

Cornelius, E. M. (2019). The obsession with greatness leads to power abuse : Is spiritual intelligence an appropriate response? *In Die Skriflig : Tydskrif Van Die Gereformeerde Teologiese Vereniging, 53*(2), 1-7. https://doi.org/10.4102/ids.v53i2.2463

Crede, M., Jong, J., & Harms, P. (2019). The generalizability of transformational leadership across cultures: a meta-analysis. *Journal of Managerial Psychology, 34*(3), 139-155. http://dx.doi.org.ezproxy.liberty.edu/10.1108/JMP-11-2018-0506

Cronje, J. C. (2020). Designing questions for research design and design research in e-Learning. *Electronic Journal of e-Learning, 18*(1), 13-24. https://doi.org/10.34190/EJEL.20.18.1.002

de Peralta, A. M., Gillispie, M., Mobley, C., & Gibson, L. M. (2019). It's all about trust and respect: Cultural competence and cultural humility in mobile health clinic services for underserved minority populations. *Journal of Health Care for the Poor and Underserved, 30*(3), 1103-1118. https://doi.org/10.1353/hpu.2019.0076

de Reuver, R., Van de Voorde, K., & Kilroy, S. (2021). When do bundles of high performance work systems reduce employee absenteeism? the moderating role of workload. *International Journal of Human Resource Management, 32*(13), 2889-2909. https://doi.org/10.1080/09585192.2019.1616594

Dietl, E., & Reb, J. (2021). A self-regulation model of leader authenticity based on mindful self-regulated attention and political skill. *Human Relations (New York), 74*(4), 473-501. https://doi.org/10.1177/0018726719888260

Dirani, K. M., Abadi, M., Alizadeh, A., Barhate, B., Garza, R. C., Gunasekara, N., Ibrahim, G., & Majzun, Z. (2020). Leadership competencies and the essential role of human resource development in times of crisis: A response to covid-19 pandemic. *Human Resource Development International, 23*(4), 380-394. https://doi.org/10.1080/1 3678868.2020.1780078

Dörfler, V., & Stierand, M. (2021). Bracketing: A phenomenological theory applied through transpersonal reflexivity. *Journal of Organizational Change Management, 34*(4), 778-793. https://doi.org/10.1108/J OCM-12-2019-0393

Egwuonwu, A., Sarpong, D., & Mordi, C. (2022). Cultural intelligence and managerial relational performance: A resource advantage perspective. *Journal of Intellectual Capital, 23*(3), 617-638. https://doi. org/10.1108/JIC-07-2020-0243

Ehrnrooth, M., Barner-Rasmussen, W., Koveshnikov, A., & Törnroos, M. (2021). A new look at the relationships between transformational leadership and employee attitudes—Does a high-performance work system substitute and/or enhance these relationships? *Human Resource Management, 60*(3): 377-398. https://doi.org/10.1002/hrm.22024

Eldor, L. (2020). How collective engagement creates competitive advantage for organizations: A Business-Level model of shared vision, competitive intensity, and service performance. *Journal of Management Studies, 57*(2): 177-209. https://doi.org/10.1111/joms.12438

Erfani, G. (2021). Visualising urban redevelopment: Photovoice as a narrative research method for investigating redevelopment processes and outcomes. *Geoforum, 126,* 80-90. https://doi.org/10.1016/j.geoforum.2021.07.021

Erkutlu, H., & Chafra, J. (2019). Leader Machiavellianism and follower silence: The mediating role of relational identification and the moderating role of psychological distance. *European Journal of Management and Business Economics, 28*(3), 323-342. https://doi.org/10.11 08/EJMBE-09-2018-0097

Et. al, Mohammed Wamique Hisam. (2021). Impact of workplace spirituality on organizational commitment – A study in an emerging economy. *Turkish Journal of Computer and Mathematics Educa-*

tion, 12(4), 984-1000. https://doi.org/10.17762/turcomat.v12i4.589

Evans, K., Sanner, B., & Chiu, C. (2021). Shared leadership, unshared burdens: How shared leadership structure schema lowers individual enjoyment without increasing performance. *Group & Organization Management, 46*(6). 1027-1072. https://doi.org/10.1177/1059601121997225

Farrugia, B. (2019). WASP (write a scientific paper): Sampling in qualitative research. *Early Human Development, 133,* 69-71. https://doi.org/10.1016/j.earlhumdev.2019.03.016

Farquhar, J., Michels, N., & Robson, J. (2020). Triangulation in industrial qualitative case study research: Widening the scope. *Industrial Marketing Management, 87,* 160-170. https://doi.org/10.1016/j.indmarman.2020.02.001

Felfe, J. (2017). The interplay of team and organizational commitment in motivating employees' interteam conflict handling. *The Academy of Management Journal., 60*(4): 1554–1581. https://doi.org/10.5465/amj.2014.0718

Ferguson, A. J., Ormiston, M. E., & Wong, E. M. (2019). The effects of cohesion and structural position on the top management team boundary spanning–firm performance relationship. *Group & Organization Management, 44*(6): 1099–1135. https://doi.org/10.1177/1059601119840941

Fischer, D. (2020). Group-level integrative complexity: Enhancing differentiation and integration in group decision-making. *Group Processes & Intergroup Relations.* https://doi.org/10.1177/1368430219892698

Framp, C., A., McAllister, M., & Dwyer, T. (2019). Narrative research methods with vulnerable people: Sharing insights. *Nurse Researcher, 27*(4), 42-47. https://doi.org/10.7748/nr.2019.e1671

Friedman, H. H., & Friedman, L. W. (2019). What Went Wrong? Lessons in leadership from Solomon, the Bible's wisest and worst ruler. *The Journal of Values-Based Leadership, 12*(1), 21. https://bi-gale-com.ezproxy.liberty.edu/global/article/GALE%7C

A581864344?u=vic_liberty&sid=summon

Friedman, H. H., & Herskovitz, P. J. (2019). Rebuilding of the temple and renewal of hope: Leadership lessons from Zerubbabel, Ezra, and Nehemiah. *The Journal of Values Based Leadership, 12*(2), 23. https://doi.org/10.22543/0733.122.1271

Fu, Y., Liu, J., Wang, Z., & Zhang, Y. (2019). Feeling energized: A multilevel model of Spiritual leadership, leader integrity, relational energy, and job performance. *Journal of Business Ethics, 158*(4), 983-997. http://dx.doi.org.ezproxy.liberty.edu/10.1007/s10551-017-3713-1

Gao, Y., & He, W. (2017). Corporate social responsibility and employee organizational citizenship behavior: The pivotal roles of ethical leadership and organizational justice. *Management Decision, 55*(2): 294-309. http://dx.doi.org.ezproxy.liberty.edu/10.1108/MD-05-2016-0284

Gafni Lachter, L. R., & Ruland, J. P. (2018). Enhancing leadership and relationships by implementing a peer mentoring program. *Australian Occupational Therapy Journal, 65*(4): 276-284. https://doi.org/10.1111/1440-1630.12471

Gerpott, F. H., Niels, V. Q., Schlamp, S., & Voelpel, S. C. (2019). An identity perspective on Ethical Leadership to explain organizational citizenship behavior: The interplay of follower moral identity and leader group prototypicality. *Journal of Business Ethics, 156*(4): 1063-1078. http://dx.doi.org.ezproxy.liberty.edu/10.1007/s10551-017-3625-0

Gobbens, R. J., & Uchmanowicz, I. (2021). Assessing frailty with the Tilburg Frailty Indicator (TFI): A review of reliability and validity. *Clinical Interventions in Aging, 16*, 863-875 https://doi.org/10.2147/CIA.S298191

Gong, T., Sun, P., & Kang, M. J. (2022). Customer-oriented constructive deviance as a reaction to organizational injustice toward customers. *Cornell Hospitality Quarterly, 63*(1), 119-135. https://doi.org/10.1177/1938965521101232327

Gu, Q., Liang, B., & Cooke, F. L. (2022). How does shared leadership affect creativity in teams? A multilevel motivational investigation in the

Chinese context. *International Journal of Human Resource Management, 33*(8), 1641-1669. https://doi.org/10.1080/09585192.2020.1783345

Guan, S., & Ploner, J. (2020). The influence of cultural capital and mianzi (face) on mature students' orientation towards higher education in China. *Compare, 50*(1), 1-17. https://doi.org/10.1080/03057925.2018.1490999

Gregory, K. (2019). Lessons of a failed Study: lone research, media analysis, and the limitations of bracketing. *International Journal of Qualitative Methods, 18.* https://doi.org/10.1177/1609406919842450

Haans, R.F.J. (2018). What's the value of being different when everyone is? The effects of distinctiveness on performance in homogeneous versus heterogeneous categories. *Strategic Management Journal, 40*: 3– 27. https://doi-org.ezproxy.liberty.edu/10.1002/smj.2978

Hagues, R. (2021). Conducting critical ethnography: Personal reflections on the role of the researcher. *International Social Work, 64*(3), 438-443. https://doi.org/10.1177/0020872818819731

Hah, S. M. (2019). Intercultural missional leadership: Theological foundation and biblical narratives. *Hervormde Teologiese Studies, 75*(1). http://dx.doi.org.ezproxy.liberty.edu/10.4102/hts.v75i1.5211

Ha-Vikström, T. & Takala, J. (2018). Do cultures, genders, education, working experience or financial status influence the effectiveness of transformational leaders? *Theoretical Issues in Ergonomics Science,* 19(1): 21-41. DOI: 10.1080/1463922X.2016.1243275

Han, J., Yoon, J., Choi, W., & Hong, G. (2021). The effects of shared leadership on team performance. [Shared leadership and team performance]. *Leadership & Organization Development Journal, 42*(4), 593-605. https://doi.org/10.1108/LODJ-01-2020-0023

Hancock, B. H., Sykes, B. L., & Verma, A. (2018). The problem of "cameo appearances" in mixed-methods research: Implications for twenty-first-century ethnography. *Sociological Perspectives, 61*(2), 314-334. https://doi.org/10.1177/0731121418756045

Hansen, N., & Heu, L. (2020). All human, yet different: An emic-etic approach to cross-cultural replication in social psychology. *Social Psy-*

chology,51(6): 361-369. https://doi.org/10.1027/1864-9335/a000436

Hassi, A. (2019). Empowering leadership and management innovation in the hospitality industry context The mediating role of climate for creativity. *International Journal of Contemporary Hospitality Management. 31*(4): 1785-1800. DOI 10.1108/IJCHM-01-2018-0003

Haynes-Brown, T. K. (2023). Using theoretical models in mixed methods research: An example from an explanatory sequential mixed methods study exploring teachers' beliefs and use of technology. *Journal of Mixed Methods Research, 17*(3), 243-263. https://doi.org/10.1177/15586898221094970

Hendryadi, S., Suryani, & Purwanto, B. (2019). Bureaucratic culture, empowering leadership, affective commitment, and knowledge sharing behavior in Indonesian government public services. *Cogent Business & Management, 6*(1): 1-12. http://dx.doi.org.ezproxy.liberty.edu/10.1080/23311975.2019.1680099

Hester, J. P. (2021). Building relationships and resolving conflicts: Infusing critical thinking into workplace practices. *The Journal of Values Based Leadership, 14*(1), 70. https://doi.org/10.22543/0733.141.1353

Hirschi, A., Shockley, K. M., & Zacher, H. (2019). Achieving work-family balance: An action regulation model. *The Academy of Management Review, 44*(1), 150-171. https://doi.org/10.5465/amr.2016.0409

Hoch, J. E., Bommer, W. H., Dulebohn, J. H., & Wu, D. (2018). Do ethical, authentic, and servant leadership explain variance above and beyond transformational leadership? A meta-analysis. *Journal of Management, 44*(2), 501-529. https://doi.org/10.1177/0149206316665461

Holland, P. (2019). The impact of a dysfunctional leader on the workplace: a new challenge for HRM. *Personnel Review, 49* (4): 1039-1052. DOI 10.1108/PR-03-2019-0134

Holmes, C., & Lindsay, D. (2018). In search of Christian theological research methodology. *SAGE Open, 8*(4). https://doi.org/10.1177/2158244018809214

Horila, T., & Siitonen, M. (2020). A time to lead: changes in relational team leadership processes over time. *Management Communication Quarterly, 34*(4), 558–584. https://doi.org/10.1177/0893318920949700

Howard, C. & Irving, J. (2021). A cross-cultural study of the role of obstacles on resilience in leadership formation. *Management Research Review. 44*(4): 533-546. DOI 10.1108/MRR-02-2020-0067

Huang, L, Krasikova, DV, Harms, PD. (2020). Avoiding or embracing social relationships? A conservation of resources perspective of leader narcissism, leader–member exchange differentiation, and follower voice. *Journal of Organization Behavior, 41*: 77–92. https://doi-org.ezproxy.liberty.edu/10.1002/job.2423

Hughes, R., Ginnett, R., & Curphy, G. (2019). *Leadership: Enhancing the Lessons of Experience*. McGraw-Hill Higher Education.

Hunsaker, W. D. (2019). Spiritual leadership and job burnout: Mediating effects of employee well-being and life satisfaction. *Management Science Letters:* 1257-1268. doi:10.5267/j.msl.2019.4.016

Hutt, C. & Gopalakrishnan, S. (2020). Leadership humility and managing a multicultural workforce. *South Asian Journal of Business Studies. 9*(2): 251-260. DOI 10.1108/SAJBS-08-2019-014

Ibidunni, A. S., Olokundun, M. A., Ibidunni, O. M., Osibanjo, A. O., & Uchendu, J. O. (2018). Enhancing employees' perceived ethical working conditions through a task-trait approach to strategic leadership. *Journal of Legal, Ethical and Regulatory Issues, 21*(3): 1-8. http://ezproxy.liberty.edu/login?qurl=https%3A%2F%2Fwww.proqu est.com%2Fscholarly-journals%2Fenhancing-employees-perceived-ethi cal-working%2Fdocview%2F2177046678%2Fse-2%3Faccountid%3D12 085

Intezari, A, & Pauleen, D. J. (2018). Conceptualizing wise management decision-making: A grounded theory approach. *Decision Sciences, 49* (2): 335-400). https://doi.org/10.1111/deci.12267

Invernizzi, D.C., Locatelli, G., & Brookes, N. J. (2018). The need to improve communication about scope changes: frustration as an indicator of operational inefficiencies. *Production Planning & Control, 2*(9):729-742. DOI: 10.1080/09537287.2018.1461949

Iofrida, N., De Luca, A. I., Strano, A., & Gulisano, G. (2018). Can social research paradigms justify the diversity of approaches to social life cycle assessment? *The International Journal of Life Cycle Assessment. 23*(3). 464-480. https://doi.org/10.1007/s11367-016-1206-6

Iqbal, A., Ahmad, I., & Latif, K. F. (2021). Servant leadership and organizational deviant behaviour: Interpreting some contradictory results from public sector of Pakistan. *Leadership & Organization Development Journal, 42*(7), 1136-1152. https://doi.org/10.1108/LODJ-07-2020-0305

Ivey, G. (2023). Interpreting hidden meaning in qualitative research interview data: Opportunities and challenges. *Qualitative Research in Psychology, 20*(1), 21-51. https://doi.org/10.1080/14780887.2022.2067509

Jackson, E. A. (2018). Triangulation. *African Journal of Economic and Management Studies, 9*(2), 266-271. https://doi.org/10.1108/AJEMS-01-2018-0034

Jacobsen, C.B., Andersen, L.B., Bøllingtoft, A. and Eriksen, T. L.M. (2022), Can leadership training improve organizational effectiveness? Evidence from a randomized field experiment on transformational and transactional leadership. *Public Admin Rev, 82*: 117-131. https://doi-org.ezproxy.liberty.edu/10.1111/puar.13356

Janak, E. (2018). Bracketing and bridling: Using narrative reflexivity to confront researcher bias and the impact of social identity in a historical study. *Philanthropy & Education, 1*(2), 82-93. https://doi.org/10.2979/phileduc.1.2.04

Javed, B., Sayyed Muhammad Mehdi, R. N., Abdul, K. K., Arjoon, S., & Hafiz, H. T. (2019). Impact of inclusive leadership on innovative work behavior: The role of psychological safety. *Journal of Management and Organization, 25*(1): 117-136. :http://dx.doi.org.ezproxy.liberty.edu/10.1017/jmo.2017.3

Javidan, M., Waldman, D. A., & Wang, D. (2021). How life experiences and cultural context matter: A multilevel framework of global leader effectiveness. *Journal of Management Studies, 58*(5),

1331-1362. https://doi.org/10.1111/joms.12662

Jennings, K. &Stahl-Wert, J. (2003). *The Serving Leader.* Berrett-Koehler Publishers.

Johnson, C. E. (2018). *Organizational Ethics.* SAGE Publications.

Johnsson, L. (2021). Multidimensional property supplementation: A method for discovering and describing emergent qualities of concepts in grounded theory research. *Qualitative Health Research, 31*(1). 184-200. https://doi.org/10.1177/1049732320970488

Jones, G., Bernardita, C. C., & Wright, J. (2020). Cultural diversity drives innovation: empowering teams for success. *International Journal of Innovation Science, 12*(3), 323-343. http://dx.doi.org/10.1108/IJIS-0 4-2020-0042

Jopke, N., & Gerrits, L. (2019). Constructing cases and conditions in QCA - lessons from grounded theory. *International Journal of Social Research Methodology, 22*(6), 599-610. https://doi.org/10.1080/13645 579.2019.1625236

Kankam, P. K. (2019). The use of paradigms in information research. *Library & Information Science Research. 41*(2). 85-92. https://doi.org /10.1016/j.lisr.2019.04.003.

Kalemci, R.A., Kalemci-Tuzun, I., & Ozkan-Conbolat, E. (2019). Employee deviant behavior: role of culture and organizational relevant support. *European Journal of Management and Business Economics, 28* (2): 126-141. DOI 10.1108/EJMBE-11-2018-0125

Kaushik, V., & Walsh, C. A. (2019). Pragmatism as a research paradigm and its implications for social work research. *Social Sciences (Basel). 8*(9). 255. https://doi.org/10.3390/socsci8090255

Kelly, D. P., Weigard, A., & Beltz, A. M. (2021). Directions of relations and idiographic-nomothetic continua in psychosomatic research: Reflections on Groen et al. (2021). *Journal of Psychosomatic Research, 146*: 110428-110428. https://doi.org/10.1016/j.jpsychores.2021.110428

Kelle, B. E. (2021). Moral injury and biblical studies: An early sampling of research and emerging trends. *Currents in Biblical Research, 19*(2), 121-144. https://doi.org/10.1177/1476993X20942383

Khan, A. K., Quratulain, S., & Crawshaw, J. R. (2017). Double Jeopardy: subordinates' worldviews and poor performance as predictors of abusive supervision. *Journal of Business and Psychology, 32*(2): 165-178. http://dx.doi.org.ezproxy.liberty.edu/10.1007/s10869-016-9442-0

Khan, M. R., & Wajidi, A. (2019). Role of leadership and team building in employee motivation at workplace. *Global Management Journal for Academic & Corporate Studies, 9*(1), 39-49. http://ezproxy.liberty.edu/login?qurl=https%3A%2F%2Fwww.proquest.com%2Fscholarly-journals%2Frole-leadership-team-building-employee-motivation%2Fdocview%2F2264569963%2Fse-2%3Faccountid%3D12085

Khari, C., & Sinha, S. (2020). Organizational Spirituality and Employee Volunteering: A Study of Mediating Variables. *Vision, 24*(4): 460–470. https://doi.org/10.1177/0972262920946146

Kılıçoğlu, G. & Kılıçoğlu, D. Y. (2021). Understanding organizational hypocrisy in schools: the relationships between organizational legitimacy, ethical leadership, organizational hypocrisy and work-related outcomes. *International Journal of Leadership in Education,* 24(1): 24-56, DOI: 10.1080/13603124.2019.1623924

Kim, M., & Beehr, T. A. (2020). Empowering leadership: Leading people to be present through affective organizational commitment? *International Journal of Human Resource Management, 31*(16), 2017-2044. https://doi.org/10.1080/09585192.2018.1424017

Kim, M. J., & Choi, J. N. (2018). Group identity and positive deviance in work groups. *The Journal of Social Psychology, 158*(6), 730-743. https://doi.org/10.1080/00224545.2017.1412931

Kim, Y. J., & Toh, S. M. (2019). Stuck in the past? the influence of a Leader's past cultural experience on group culture and positive and negative group deviance. *Academy of Management Journal, 62*(3), 944-969. https://doi.org/10.5465/amj.2016.1322

Kim, K. Y., Shen, W., Evans, R., & Mu, F. (2022). Granting leadership to Asian Americans: The activation of ideal leader and ideal follower traits on observers' leadership perceptions. *Journal of Business and Psy-*

chology, 37(6), 1157-1180. https://doi.org/10.1007/s10869-022-09794-3

Kimura, T. & Nishikawa, M. (2018). Ethical Leadership and its cultural and institutional context: An empirical study in Japan. *J Bus Ethics. 151:* 707–724. https://doi-org.ezproxy.liberty.edu/10.1007/s105 51-016-3268-6

King James Bible. (2017). King James Bible Online. https://www.kingjamesbibleonline.org/ (Original work published 1769).

Kloutsiniotis, P. V., & Mihail, D. M. (2020). Is it worth it? linking perceived high-performance work systems and emotional exhaustion: The mediating role of job demands and job resources. *European Management Journal, 38*(4): 565-579. https://doi.org/10.1016/j.emj.2019.12. 012

Knotts, K. G., & Houghton, J. D. (2021). You can't make me! the role of self-leadership in enhancing organizational commitment and work engagement. *Leadership & Organization Development Journal, 42*(5): 748-762. https://doi.org/10.1108/LODJ-10-2020-0436

Koo, H., & Park, C. (2018). Foundation of leadership in Asia: Leader characteristics and leadership styles review and research agenda. *Asia Pacific Journal of Management, 35*(3), 697-718. http://dx.doi.org.ezpr oxy.liberty.edu/10.1007/s10490-017-9548-6

Korzynski, P., Kozminski, A., Baczynska, A., Haenlein, M. (2021). Bounded leadership: An empirical study of leadership competencies, constraints, and effectiveness. *European Management Journal. 39*(2): 226-235. https://doi.org/10.1016/j.emj.2020.07.009.

Kouzes, J. M. & Posner, B. Z. (2017). *The Leadership Challenge.* Wiley.

Krispin, K. R. (2020). Christian leader development: An outcomes framework. *Christian Education Journal, 17*(1), 18-37. https://doi.org/10.1177/0739891319869697

Krystin, Z., Héliot YingFei, & Le, G. A. (2021). Analyzing leadership attributes in faith-based organizations: Idealism versus reality. *Journal of Business Ethics, 170*(4): 743-757. http://dx.doi.org.ezproxy.liberty.e

du/10.1007/s10551-019-04358-7

Kucharska, W. (2021). Wisdom from experience paradox: Organizational learning, mistakes, hierarchy and maturity issues. *Electronic Journal of Knowledge Management: EJKM, 19*(2): 105-117. https://doi.org/10.34190/ejkm.19.2.2370

Kucharska, W. & Bedford, D. (2020). Love your mistakes!—they help you adapt to change. How do knowledge, collaboration and learning cultures foster organizational intelligence? *Journal of Organizational Change Management, 33*(7): 1329-1354. DOI 10.1108/JOCM-02-2020-0052

Kuenzi, M., Mayer, D., & Greenbaum, R. (2018). Creating an ethical organizational environment: The relationship between ethical leadership, ethical organizational climate, and unethical behavior. *Personal Psychology, 73*: 43-71. https://doi-org.ezproxy.liberty.edu/10.1111/peps.12356

Kumar, S., Sahoo, S., Lim, W. M., & Dana, L. (2022). Religion as a social shaping force in entrepreneurship and business: Insights from a technology-empowered systematic literature review. *Technological Forecasting & Social Change, 175*, 121393. https://doi.org/10.1016/j.techfore.2021.121393

Kumari, G., & Eguruze, E. S. (2022). Positive deviance traits and social entrepreneurship for women empowerment amid COVID-19. *IIM Kozhikode Society & Management Review, 11*(1), 109-125. https://doi.org/10.1177/22779752211030697

Kuo, M., Zhu, D., & White, L. P. (2020). An integrated B2B guanxi model: A Taiwan perspective. *Journal of Relationship Marketing (Binghamton, N.Y.), 19*(4), 309-328. https://doi.org/10.1080/15332667.2019.1705743

Lasu, S., & Biaggi, C. E. (2021). A theory of virtuous leadership and its influence on organizational performance in Christian organizations: A classic grounded theory study. *The Journal of Applied Christian Leadership, 15*(1), 54-79.

Lavefjord, A., Sundström, F. T. A., Buhrman, M., & McCracken,

L. M. (2021). Assessment methods in single case design studies of psychological treatments for chronic pain: A scoping review. *Journal of Contextual Behavioral Science, 21:* 121-135. https://doi.org/10.1016/j.jcbs.2021.05.005

Lavee, E., & Itzchakov, G. (2021). Good listening: A key element in establishing quality in qualitative research. *Qualitative Research: QR.* 14687941211039402. https://doi.org/10.1177/14687941211039402

Lavefjord, A., Sundström, F. T. A., Buhrman, M., & McCracken, L. M. (2021). Assessment methods in single case design studies of psychological treatments for chronic pain: A scoping review. *Journal of Contextual Behavioral Science, 21:* 121-135. https://doi.org/10.1016/j.jcbs.2021.05.005

Lee, A, Willis, S, Tian, AW. (2018). Empowering leadership: A meta-analytic examination of incremental contribution, mediation, and moderation. *J Organ Behav. 39*: 306–325. https://doi-org.ezproxy.liberty.edu/10.1002/job.2220206314546193

Lee, J. D., & Kolodge, K. (2018). Understanding attitudes towards self-driving vehicles: Quantitative analysis of qualitative data. *Proceedings of the Human Factors and Ergonomics Society Annual Meeting, 62*(1), 1399-1403. https://doi.org/10.1177/1541931218621319

Levine, E., Roberts, A., & Cohen, T. (2020). Difficult conversations: navigating the tension between honesty and benevolence. *Current Opinion in Psychology, 31:* 38-43. https://doi.org/10.1016/j.copsyc.2019.07.034

Li, C., Wu, C., Brown, M. & Dong, Y. (2021). How a grateful leader trait can cultivate creative employees: A dual-level leadership process model. *The Journal of Positive Psychology.* DOI: 10.1080/17439760.2021.1871941

Li, H. (2020). Towards an emic understanding of mianzi giving in the Chinese context. *Journal of Politeness Research: Language, Behaviour, Culture, 16*(2), 281-303. https://doi.org/10.1515/pr-2017-0052

Li, H., Jin, H., & Chen, T. (2020). Linking proactive personality to creative performance: The role of job crafting and High-

-Involvement work systems. *The Journal of Creative Behavior, 54*(1): 196-210. https://doi.org/10.1002/jocb.355

Li, N., Chiaburu, D. S., & Kirkman, B. L. (2017). Cross-level influences of empowering leadership on citizenship behavior: organizational support climate as a double-edged sword. *Journal of Management, 43*(4), 1076–1102. https://doi.org/10.1177/0149

Li, P. P., Zhou, S. S., Zhou, A. J., & Yang, Z. (2019). Reconceptualizing and redirecting research on guanxi: 'Guan-xi' interaction to form a multicolored Chinese knot. *Management and Organization Review, 15*(3): 643-677. https://doi.org/10.1017/mor.2019.36

Li, Y., Li, X., & Liu, Y. (2021). How does a high-performance work system prompt job crafting through autonomous motivation: the moderating role of initiative climate. *International Journal of Environmental Research and Public Health, 18*(2): 384. https://doi.org/10.3390/ijerph18020384

Lin, C. (2019) Modeling corporate citizenship and turnover intention: Social identity and expectancy theories. *Review of Managerial Science,13,* 823–840. https://doi-org.ezproxy.liberty.edu/10.1007/s11846-017-0275-7

Lin, X., Chen, Z. X., Tse, H. H. M., Wei, W., & Ma, C. (2019). Why and when employees like to speak up more under humble leaders? the roles of personal sense of power and power distance. *Journal of Business Ethics, 158*(4): 937-950. https://doi.org/10.1007/s10551-017-3704-2

Lisak, A., & Harush, R. (2021). Global and local identities on the balance scale: Predicting transformational leadership and effectiveness in multicultural teams. *PLoS One, 16*(7). http://dx.doi.org/10.1371/journal.pone.0254656

Liu, Y., Fuller, B., Hester, K., Bennett, R. J., & Dickerson, M. S. (2018). Linking authentic leadership to subordinate behaviors. *Leadership & Organization Development Journal, 39*(2): 218-233. https://doi.org/10.1108/LODJ-12-2016-0327

Liu, Y., Wang, S. and Yao, X. (2019), Individual Goal Orientations, Team Empowerment, and Employee Creative Performance: A Case of Cross-level Interactions. *J Creat Behav, 53*: 443-456. https://doi-org.ezproxy.liberty.edu/10.1002/jocb.220

Liu, W. & Xiang, S. (2020). The Effect of Leaders' Coaching Behaviors on Employee Learning Orientation: A Regulatory Focus Perspective. *Frontiers in Psychology. 11.* DOI=10.3389/fpsyg.2020.543282

Liu, T., Chen, Y., Hu, C., Yuan, X., Liu, C., & He, W. (2020). The paradox of group citizenship and constructive deviance: A resolution of environmental dynamism and moral justification. *International Journal of Environmental Research and Public Health, 17*(22), 8371. https://doi.org/10.3390/ijerph17228371

Lorinkova, N. M., & Bartol, K. M. (2021). Shared leadership development and team performance: A new look at the dynamics of shared leadership. *Personnel Psychology, 74*(1), 77-107. https://doi.org/10.1111/peps.12409

Luciano, M. M., Nahrgang, J. D., & Shropshire, C. (2020). Strategic Leadership Systems: Viewing Top Management Teams and Boards of Directors from A Multiteam Systems Perspective. *Academy of Management Review, 45*(3): 675–701. https://doi.org/10.5465/amr.2017.0485

Lu, J., Zhang, Z., & Jia, M. (2021). Servant leadership effectiveness: Do religious atmosphere and housing price matter? social information-processing perspective. *Current Psychology (New Brunswick, N.J.), 40*(8), 3944-3957. https://doi.org/10.1007/s12144-019-00337-3

Lusiana, M. & Langley, A. (2019). The social construction of strategic coherence: Practices of enabling leadership. *Long Range Planning, 52*(5): 1-23. https://doi.org/10.1016/j.lrp.2018.05.006

Ma, Z., Gong, Y., Long, L., & Zhang, Y. (2021). Team-level high-performance work systems, self-efficacy and creativity: Differential moderating roles of person-job fit and goal difficulty. *International Journal of Human Resource Management, 32*(2): 478-511. https://doi.org/10.1080/09585192.2020.1854816

Mahipalan, M., & Muhammed, S. (2019). Examining the Role of Workplace Spirituality and Teacher Self-efficacy on Organizational Citizenship Behaviour of Secondary School Teachers: An Indian Scenario.

Vision, 23(1), 80–90. https://doi.org/10.1177/0972262918821241

Main, L. F., Delcourt, M. A. B., & Treffinger, D. J. (2019). Effects of group training in Problem-Solving style on future Problem-Solving performance. *The Journal of Creative Behavior, 53*(3), 274-285. https://doi.org/10.1002/jocb.176

Malik, P., & Lenka, U. (2019). Exploring the impact of perceived AMO framework on constructive and destructive deviance: Mediating role of employee engagement. *International Journal of Manpower, 40*(5), 994-1011. https://doi.org/10.1108/IJM-05-2018-0164

Martono, S., Wulansari, N. A., & Khoiruddin, M. (2020). The role of empowering leadership in creating employee creativity: moderation – mediation mechanism. *IOP Conference Series.Earth and Environmental Science, 485*(1). http://dx.doi.org/10.1088/1755-1315/485/1/012060

Martínez-Corcoles, M., Tomas, I., Gracia, F. & Peiro, J. (2021). The power of empowering team leadership over time: A multi-wave longitudinal study in nuclear power plants. *Safety Science. 133:* 105015. https://doi.org/10.1016/j.ssci.2020.105015 R

Matić, D., Cabrilo, S., Grubić-Nešić, L., & Milić, B. (2017). Investigating the impact of organizational climate, motivational drivers, and empowering leadership on knowledge sharing. *Knowledge Management Research & Practice, 15*(3): 431-446. http://dx.doi.org/10.1057/s41275-017-0063-9

McCarthy, L., Imboden, R., Shdaimah, C. & Forrester, P. (2020) 'Ethics Are Messy': Supervision as a tool to help social workers manage ethical challenges. *Ethics and Social Welfare.* 14(1): 118-134. DOI: 10.1080/17496535.2020.1720265

McLeod, J., & O'Connor, K. (2020). Ethics, archives and data sharing in qualitative research. *Educational Philosophy and Theory, 53*(5), 523-535. https://doi.org/10.1080/00131857.2020.1805310

McNarry, G., Allen-Collinson, J., & Evans, A. B. (2019). Reflexivity and bracketing in sociological phenomenological research: Researching the competitive swimming lifeworld. *Qualitative Research in Sport, Exercise and Health, 11*(1), 138-151. https://doi.org/10.1080/2159676X.2

018.1506498

Mehta, J., Yurkofsky, M., & Frumin, K. (2022). Linking continuous improvement and adaptive leadership. *Educational Leadership, 79*(6), 36-41.

Mersid, P., Mekić, E., Hadžiahmetović, N., & Budur, T. (2020). Effectiveness of transformational leadership among different cultures. *International Journal of Social Sciences & Educational Studies, 7*(3), 119-129. https://doi.org/10.23918/ijsses.v7i3p119

Meskelis, S. & Whittington, J. (2020). Driving employee engagement: how personality trait and leadership style impact the process. *Journal of Business & Industrial Marketing, 35*(10): 1457–1473. DOI 10.1108/JBIM-11-2019-0477

Metwally, D., Ruiz-Palomino, P., Mewally, M. & Gartzia, L. (2019). How Ethical Leadership shapes employees' readiness to change: The mediating role of an organizational culture of effectiveness. *Frontiers in Psychology.*1-18. https://doi.org/10.3389/fpsyg.2019.02493

Misra, S., Roberts, P., & Rhodes, M. (2020). Information overload, stress, and emergency managerial thinking. *International Journal of Disaster Risk Reduction, 51*: 1-11. https://doi.org/10.1016/j.ijdrr.2020.101762

Mishra, S., & Dey, A. K. (2022). Understanding and Identifying 'Themes' in Qualitative Case Study Research. *South Asian Journal of Business and Management Cases, 11*(3), 187–192. https://doi.org/10.1177/22779779221134659

Monzani, L., Seijts, G. H., & Crossan, M. M. (2021). Character matters: The network structure of leader character and its relation to follower positive outcomes. *PLoS One, 16*(9). http://dx.doi.org.ezproxy.liberty.edu/10.1371/journal.pone.0255940

Moore, C., Mayer, D., Chiang, F., Crossley, C., Karlesky, M., & Birtch, T. (2019). Leaders Matter Morally: The Role of Ethical Leadership in Shaping Employee Moral Cognition and Misconduct. *Journal of Applied Psychology., 104*(1): 123–145. https://doi.org/10.1037/apl0000341

Muchiri, M., Shahid, S., & Ayoko, O. (2019). And now for something completely different: Reframing social processes of leadership theory using positive organisational behaviour. *Journal of Management and Organization, 25*(3), 370-373. http://dx.doi.org.ezproxy.liberty.edu/10.1017/jmo.2019.33

Muff, K., Delacoste, C., & Dyllick, T. (2022). Responsible leadership competencies in leaders around the world: Assessing stakeholder engagement, ethics and values, systems thinking and innovation competencies in leaders around the world. *Corporate Social-Responsibility and Environmental Management, 29*(1), 273-292. https://doi.org/10.1002/csr.2216

Murillo, F. J. & Hidalgo, N. (2020). Fair student assessment: A phenomenographic study on teachers' conceptions. *Studies in Educational Evaluation, 65*: 100860. https://doi.org/10.1016/j.stueduc.2020.100860.

Naim, M. F., & Lenka, U. (2020). Organizational learning and gen Y employees' affective commitment: The mediating role of competency development and moderating role of strategic leadership. *Journal of Management & Organization, 26*(5), 815-831. https://doi.org/10.1017/jmo.2018.19

Najam, U., & Mustamil, N. B. M. (2022). Does proactive personality moderate the relationship between servant leadership and psychological ownership and resilience? *SAGE Open, 12*(2), 215824402210872. https://doi.org/10.1177/21582440221087273

Nell, I. A. (2020). Competency-based theological education in a postcolonial context: Towards a transformed competency framework. *Transformation in Higher Education, 5*(1), 1-9. https://doi.org/10.4102/the.v5i0.74

Nghe, M., Hart, J., Ferry, S., Hutchins, L. & Lebet, R. (2020). Developing Leadership Competencies in Midlevel Nurse Leaders. JONA: The Journal of Nursing Administration, 50 (9), 481-488. doi: 10.1097/NNA.0000000000000920.

Novosel, L. M. (2022). Understanding the Evidence: Purpose Statement, Research Questions, and Hypotheses. *Urologic*

Nursing, 42(5), 249-251,257. https://go.openathens.net/redirector/liberty.edu?url=https://www.proquest.com/scholarly-journals/understanding-evidence-purpose-statement-research/docview/2729114942/se-2

O'Donoghue, D., & van der Werff, L. (2022). Empowering leadership: Balancing self-determination and accountability for motivation. *Personnel Review, 51*(4), 1205-1220. https://doi.org/10.1108/PR-11-2019-0619

Ou, A. Y., Seo, J., Choi, D., & Hom, P. W. (2017). When can humble top executives retain middle managers? the moderating role of top management team faultlines. *Academy of Management Journal, 60*(5): 1915-1931. https://doi.org/10.5465/amj.2015.1072

Page, N. C., Nimon-Peters, A. J., & Urquhart, A. (2021). Big Need Not Be Bad: A Case Study of Experiential Leadership Development in Different-Sized Classes. *Journal of Management Education, 45*(3), 360–386. https://doi.org/10.1177/1052562920948921

Paiuc, D. (2021). Cultural intelligence as a core competence of inclusive leadership. *Management Dynamics in the Knowledge Economy, 9*(3), 363-378. https://doi.org/10.2478/mdke-2021-0024

Pan, W., Sun, L., Sun, L., Li, C., & Leung, A. S. M. (2018). Abusive supervision and job-oriented constructive deviance in the hotel industry. *International Journal of Contemporary Hospitality Management, 30*(5), 2249-2267. https://doi.org/10.1108/IJCHM-04-2017-0212

Pasricha, P., Singh, B., & Verma, P. (2018). Ethical Leadership, Organic Organizational Cultures and Corporate Social Responsibility: An Empirical Study in Social Enterprises: *Journal of Business Ethics, 151*(4), 941-958. http://dx.doi.org.ezproxy.liberty.edu/10.1007/s10551-017-3568-5

Patton, C. (2017). What made Nehemiah an effective leader? *The Journal of Applied Christian Leadership, 11*(1), 8-14. http://ezproxy.liberty.edu/login?qurl=https%3A%2F%2Fwww.proquest.com%2Fscholarly-journals%2Fwhat-made-nehemiah-effective-leader%2Fdocview%2F2093222634%2Fse-2%3Faccountid%3D12085

Peng, S., Liao, Y., & Sun, R. (2020). The influence of transformational leadership on employees' affective organizational commitment in public and nonprofit organizations: A moderated mediation model. *Public Personnel Management, 49*(1), 29-56. https://doi.org/10.117 7/0091026019835233

Peralta, C. F., Saldanha, M. F., Lopes, P. N., Lourenço, P. R., & Leonor, P. (2021). Does supervisor's moral courage to go beyond compliance have a role in the relationships between teamwork quality, team creativity, and team idea implementation?: *Journal of Business Ethics, 168*(4): 677-696. http://dx.doi.org.ezproxy.liberty.edu/10.1007 /s10551-019-04175-y

Petzold, M. B., Bendau, A., Plag, J., Pyrkosch, L., Mascarell Maricic, L., Betzler, F., Rogoll, J., Große, J., & Ströhle, A. (2020). Risk, resilience, psychological distress, and anxiety at the beginning of the COVID-19 pandemic in Germany. *Brain and Behavior, 10*(9), e01745-n/a. https://doi.org/10.1002/brb3.1745

Podgórska, M., & Pichlak, M. (2019). Analysis of project managers' leadership competencies: Project success relation: What are the competencies of Polish project leaders? *International Journal of Managing Projects in Business, 12*(4), 869-887. https://doi.org/10.1108/IJMPB-0 8-2018-0149

Prabowo, R., Mustika, M., & Sjabadhyni, B. (2018). How a leader transforms employees' psychological empowerment into innovative work behavior. *Psychological Research on Urban Society, 1*(2): 90-99. doi:https://doi.org/10.7454/proust.v1i2.32

Priyadarshi, P., & Premchandran, R. (2019). Millennials and political savvy – the mediating role of political skill linking core self-evaluation, emotional intelligence and knowledge sharing behaviour. *VINE Journal of Information and Knowledge Management Systems, 49*(1), 95-114. https://doi.org/10.1108/VJIKMS-06-2018-0046

Quintao, C., Andrade, P., & Almeida, F. (2020). How to improve the validity and reliability of a case study approach. *Journal of Interdisciplinary Studies in Education, 9*(2), 264. https://doi.org/10.32674/jise.

v9i2.2026

Raza, I. & Awang, Z. (2020). Knowledge sharing in multicultural organizations: evidence from Pakistan. *Higher Education, Skills and Work-Based Learning.10*(3): 497-517. DOI 10.1108/HESWBL-09-2019-0114

Remišová, A., Lašáková, A. & Kirchmayer, Z. (2019). Influence of formal ethics program components on managerial ethical behavior. *J Bus Ethics, 160*: 151–166. https://doi-org.ezproxy.liberty.edu/10.1007/s10551-018-3832-3

Ren, S., & Zhu, Y. (2017). Context, self-regulation and developmental foci: A mixed-method study analyzing self-development of leadership competencies in China. *Personnel Review, 46*(8), 1977-1996. http://dx.doi.org/10.1108/PR-10-2015-0273

Riasudeen, S., & Singh, P. (2021). Leadership effectiveness and psychological well-being: The role of workplace spirituality. *Journal of Human Values, 27*(2), 109-125. https://doi.org/10.1177/0971685820947334

Ribeiro, N., Duarte, A. P., Filipe, R., & Torres de Oliveira, R. (2020). How Authentic Leadership Promotes Individual Creativity: The Mediating Role of Affective Commitment. *Journal of Leadership & Organizational Studies, 27*(2): 189–202. https://doi.org/10.1177/1548051819842796

Roberts, R. (2020). Qualitative interview questions: Guidance for novice researchers. *Qualitative Report, 25*(9), 3185-3203. https://doi.org/10.46743/2160-3715/2020.4640

Robinson, V., Meyer, F., Le Fevre, D., & Sinnema, C. (2021). The quality of leaders' problem-solving conversations: Truth-seeking or truth-claiming? *Leadership and Policy in Schools, 20*(4), 650-671. https://doi.org/10.1080/15700763.2020.1734627

Rose, J., & Johnson, C. W. (2020). Contextualizing reliability and validity in qualitative research: Toward more rigorous and trustworthy qualitative social science in leisure research. *Journal of Leisure Research, 51*(4), 432-451. https://doi.org/10.1080/00222216.2020.1722042

Rowley, C., Oh, I. & Jang, W. (2019). New perspectives on East Asian leadership in the age of globalization: local grounding and historical comparisons in the Asia Pacific region. *Asia Pacific Business Review,* 25(2): 307-315. DOI: 10.1080/13602381.2018.1557424

Saad, G. B., Al Altheeb, S., & Abbas, M. (2020). Knowledge Management Practices and Transformational Leadership Traits: Predicting Process Innovation in FMCG Industry. [Prácticas de gestión del conocimiento y rasgos de liderazgo transformacional: predicción de la innovación de procesos en la industria de bienes de consumo] *Propositos y Representaciones, 8,* 1-16. https://doi.org/10.20511/pyr2020.v8nS PE2.662

Sahakyan, T. (2023). Member-Checking through diagrammatic elicitation: Constructing meaning with participants. *TESOL Quarterly, 57*(2), 686-701. https://doi.org/10.1002/tesq.3210

Saidur Rahaman, H. M, Camps, J., Decoster, S., & Stouten, J. (2020). Ethical leadership in times of change: the role of change commitment and change information for employees' dysfunctional resistance. *Personnel Review:* 1-18. DOI 10.1108/PR-03-2019-0122

Salas-Vallina, A. (2020). Towards a sustainable leader-follower relationship: Constructive dissensus, organizational virtuousness and happiness at work (HAW). *Sustainability, 12*(17): 7087. http://dx.doi.org /10.3390/su12177087

Sánchez, I. D., Ospina, S. M., & Salgado, E. (2020). Advancing constructionist leadership research through paradigm interplay: An application in the leadership–trust domain. *Leadership, 16*(6): 683–711. https://doi.org/10.1177/1742715020919226

Sanfilippo, M. (2021, December). *Shared Leadership: How Modern Businesses Run Themselves.* Business News Daily. https://www.businessnewsdaily.com/135-shared-leadership-social -media-fuel-business-growth.html

Sanou, B. (2021). Leadership development and succession: A review of best practices with insights for mission leadership. *The Journal of Applied Christian Leadership, 15*(1), 28-53.

https://go.openathens.net/redirector/liberty.edu?url=https://www.proquest.com/scholarly-journals/leadership-development-succession-review-best/docview/2812787721/se-2

Sellberg, M. M, Ryan, P., Borgstrom, S.T., Norstrom, A.V., & Peterson, G.D. (2018). From resilience thinking to resilience planning: lessons from practice. *Journal of Environmental Management. 217*: 906-918. https://doi.org/10.1016/j.jenvman.2018.04.012

Scheibe, S., Yeung, D. & Doerwald, F. (2019). Age-Related Differences in Levels and Dynamics of Workplace Affect. *Psychology and aging. 34*(1):106–123. DOI: 10.1037/pag0000305

Shahriari, M., & Allameh, S. M. (2020). Organizational culture and organizational learning: Does high performance work systems mediate? *The Journal of Workplace Learning, 32*(8): 583-597. https://doi.org/10.1108/JWL-03-2020-0047

Shan, J., Konishi, M., Pullin, P., & Lupina-Wegener, A. (2021). Effects of cultural intelligence on multicultural team effectiveness: The chain mediation role of common ingroup identity and communication quality. *Journal of Theoretical Social Psychology, 5*(4), 519-529. https://doi.org/10.1002/jts5.115

Sharma, N. (2022). Using positive deviance to enhance employee engagement: An interpretive structural modelling approach. *International Journal of Organizational Analysis (2005), 30*(1), 84-98. https://doi.org/10.1108/IJOA-07-2020-2341

Sharma, P. & Kumra, R. (2020). Relationship between workplace spirituality, organizational justice and mental health: mediation role of employee engagement. *Journal of Advances in Management Research, 17*(5): 627-650. DOI 10.1108/JAMR-01-2020-0007

Shelton, C., Hein, S. & Phipps, K. (2021). Positive and proactive leadership: disentangling the relationships between stress, resilience, leadership style and leader satisfaction/well-being. *International Journal of Organizational Analysis.* 1-22. DOI 10.1108/IJOA-05-2020-2221

Shen, Y. & Lei, X. (2022). Exploring the Impact of Leadership Characteristics on Subordinates' Counterproductive Work Behavior:

From the Organizational Cultural Psychology Perspective. *Frontiers in Psychology. 13.* DOI=10.3389/fpsyg.2022.818509.

Shukla, S. (2020). Concept of Population and Sample. *Indian Institute of Teacher Education.* https://www.researchgate.net/publication/346426707

Singletary, J. (2020). Head, heart, and hand: Understanding enneagram centers for leadership development. *Social Work and Christianity, 47*(4), 3-18. https://doi.org/10.34043/swc.v47i3.126

Slade, K. (2020). Innovation Management in a Multicultural Context. *Research-Technology Management. 63*:6, 31-40. DOI: 10.1080/08956308.2020.1813495

Slater, J. (2020). The first shall be last... A biblical inversion of leadership traps and pressure-cooker appetites for ambitious statuses. *Hervormde Teologiese Studies, 76*(2). http://dx.doi.org.ezproxy.liberty.edu/10.4102/hts.v76i2.5963

Snyder, H. (2019). Literature review as a research methodology: An overview and guidelines. *Journal of Business Research, 104*: 333-339. https://doi.org/10.1016/j.jbusres.2019.07.039.

Sobral, F., Furtado, L., & Islam, G. (2019). Humor as Catalyst and Neutralizer of Leadership Effectiveness. *Revista De Administração De Empresas, 59*(5): 313-326. http://dx.doi.org.ezproxy.liberty.edu/10.1590/S0034-759020190502

Soule, K., & Freeman, M. (2019). So you want to do post-intentional phenomenological research? *Qualitative Report, 24*(4), 857-872. https://doi.org/10.46743/2160-3715/2019.3305

Sowicz, T. J., Sefcik, J. S., Teng, H. L., Irani, E., Kelly, T., & Bradway, C. (2019). The use of closing questions in qualitative research: Results of a web-based survey. *Nursing Research (New York), 68*(6), E8-E12. https://doi.org/10.1097/NNR.0000000000000380

Stahl, G. K., & Maznevski, M. L. (2021). Unraveling the effects of cultural diversity in teams: A retrospective of research on multicultural work groups and an agenda for future research. *Journal of International Business Studies, 52*(1), 4-22. https://doi.org/10.1057/s41267-020-0038

9-9

Stijn, D., Jeroen, S., & Tripp, T. M. (2021). When Employees Retaliate Against Self-Serving Leaders: The Influence of the Ethical Climate: JBE. *Journal of Business Ethics, 168*(1): 195-213. http://dx.doi.org.ezproxy.liberty.edu/10.1007/s10551-019-04218-4

Stratton, S. J. (2021). Population research: Convenience sampling strategies. *Prehospital and Disaster Medicine, 36*(4), 373-374. https://doi.org/10.1017/S1049023X21000649

Strom, T. (2020). Authentic leadership and relational power increasing employee performance: A systematic review of "leadership and power" as a positive dyadic relationship. *Journal of Small Business Strategy, 30*(3), 86-101. https://libjournals.mtsu.edu/index.php/jsbs/article/view/1315

Stuckey, S. M., Collins, B. T., Patrick, S., Grove, K. S., & Ward, E. (2019). Thriving vs surviving: benefits of formal mentoring program on faculty well-being. *International Journal of Mentoring and Coaching in Education, 8*(4): 378-396. http://dx.doi.org/10.1108/IJMCE-02-2019-0024

Suleman, Q., Makhdoom, A. S., Shehzad, S., Hussain, I., Alam, Z. K., Khan, I. U., Amjid, M., & Khan, I. (2021). Leadership empowering behaviour as a predictor of employees' psychological wellbeing: Evidence from a cross-sectional study among secondary school teachers in Kohat Division, Pakistan. *PLoS One, 16*(7). http://dx.doi.org/10.1371/journal.pone.0254576

Sungu, L. J., Weng, Q., & Kitule, J. A. (2019). When organizational support yields both performance and satisfaction: The role of performance ability in the lens of social exchange theory. *Personnel Review, 48*(6), 1410-1428. https://doi.org/10.1108/PR-10-2018-0402

Szymanski, M. & Kalra, K. (2021). Performance effects of interaction between multicultural managers and multicultural team members: Evidence from elite football competitions. *Thunderbird Int. Bus. Rev. 63*: 235– 251. https://doi-org.ezproxy.liberty.edu/10.1002/tie.22175

Tabea Franziska Hirth-Goebel, & Weißenberger, B.,E. (2019). Management accountants and ethical dilemmas: How to promote ethical intention? *Journal of Management Control, 30*(3), 287-322. http://dx.doi.org.ezproxy.liberty.edu/10.1007/s00187-019-00288-7

Tang, G., Yu, B., Cooke, F. L., & Chen, Y. (2017). High-performance work system and employee creativity: The roles of perceived organisational support and devolved management. *Personnel Review, 46*(7): 1318-1334. https://doi.org/10.1108/PR-09-2016-0235

Tang, L. (2021). Burning out in emotional capitalism: Appropriation of ganqing and renqing in the Chinese platform economy. *Journal of Sociology (Melbourne, Vic.).* 14407833211044s. https://doi.org/10.1177/14407833211044568

Tang, G., Chen, Y., Knippenberg, D., & Yu, B. (2020). Antecedents and consequences of empowering leadership: Leader power distance, leader perception of team capability, and team innovation. *Journal of Organizational Behavior, 41*(6), 551-566. https://doi.org/10.1002/job.2449

Taquette, S. R., & Borges da Matta Souza, Luciana Maria. (2022). Ethical dilemmas in qualitative research: A critical literature review. *International Journal of Qualitative Methods, 21,* 16094069221078731. https://doi.org/10.1177/16094069221078731

Thacker, L. (2020). What is the big deal about populations in research? *Progress in Transplantation, 30*(1)3. DOI:10.1177/1526924819893795

Thi, H. N., & Le, A. N. (2019). Promoting creativity and innovation: expected and unexpected consequences. *Asia Pacific Journal of Innovation and Entrepreneurship, 13*(3): 296-310. http://dx.doi.org.ezproxy.liberty.edu/10.1108/APJIE-03-2019-0008

Thille, P., Chartrand, L., & Brown, C. (2022). Diary-interview studies: Longitudinal, flexible qualitative research design. *Family Practice.* https://doi.org/10.1093/fampra/cmac039

Thomas, M. (2018). The indispensable mark of Christian leadership: Implications from Christ's methods of leadership development in Mark's gospel. *Perichoresis (Oradea), 16*(3): 107-117. https://doi.org/10

.2478/perc-2018-0019

Tian, S. L., I-Hsiung, C., Tsz, C. M., Lie, P. Z., & Kai, C. C. (2019). Influences of transformational leadership, transactional leadership, and patriarchal leadership on job satisfaction of cram school faculty members. *Sustainability, 11*(12): 1-13. http://dx.doi.org.ezproxy.liberty.edu/10.3390/su11123465

Toby, N., Dawkins, S., Macklin, R., & Martin, A. (2020). The Virtues Project: An Approach to Developing oRW1S34RfeSDcfkexdo9rT2Good1RW1S34RfeSDcfkexdo9rT2 Leaders: *Journal of Business Ethics, 167*(4), 605-622. http://dx.doi.org.ezproxy.liberty.edu/10.1007/s10551-019-04163-2

Tran, L. T., & Nghia Tran, L. H. (2020). Leadership in international education: leaders' professional development needs and tensions. *Higher Education, 80*(3), 479-495. http://dx.doi.org.ezproxy.liberty.edu/10.1007/s10734-019-00494-1

Tsai, C., Carr, C., Qiao, K. & Supprakit, S. (2019) Modes of cross-cultural leadership adjustment: adapting leadership to meet local conditions and/or changing followers to match personal requirements? *The International Journal of Human Resource Management, 30*(9), 1477-1504. DOI: 10.1080/09585192.2017.1289549

Tseng, S. & Levy, P. (2019). A multilevel leadership process framework of performance management. *Human Resource Management Review. 29*(4): 100668. https://doi.org/10.1016/j.hrmr.2018.10.001.

Tuin, L., Schaufeli, W. B., & Van den Broeck, A. (2021). Engaging leadership: Enhancing work engagement through intrinsic values and need satisfaction. *Human Resource Development Quarterly, 32*(4): 483-505. https://doi.org/10.1002/hrdq.21430

Tremblay, M., Gaudet, M.-C., & Parent-Rocheleau, X. (2018). Good Things Are Not Eternal: How Consideration Leadership and Initiating Structure Influence the Dynamic Nature of Organizational Justice and Extra-Role Behaviors at the Collective Level. *Journal of Leadership & Organizational Studies, 25*(2): 211–232. https://doi.org/10.1177/1548051817738941

Turyahikayo, E. (2021). Philosophical paradigms as the bases for knowledge management research and practice. *Knowledge Management & E-Learning. 13*(2). 209-224. https://go.openathens.net/redirector/liberty.edu?url=https://www.proquest.com/scholarly-journals/philosophical-paradigms-as-bases-knowledge/docview/2559469688/se-2

Umans, T., Smith, E., Andersson, W., & Planken, W. (2020). Top management teams' shared leadership and ambidexterity: the role of management control systems. *International Review of Administrative Sciences, 86*(3): 444–462. https://doi.org/10.1177/0020852318783539

Ünal, A.,F., Chen, C. C., & Xin, K. R. (2017). Justice climates and management team effectiveness: The central role of group harmony. *Management and Organization Review, 13*(4): 821-849. http://dx.doi.org.ezproxy.liberty.edu/10.1017/mor.2017.54

Usman, M, Ali, M, Yousaf, Z, Anwar, F, Waqas, M, Khan, M.A.S. (2020). The relationship between laissez-faire leadership and burnout: Mediation through work alienation and the moderating role of political skill. *Can J Adm Sci*:1– 12. https://doi-org.ezproxy.liberty.edu/10.1002/cjas.1568

Van Den Berg, M. J., Signal, T. L., & Gander, P. H. (2020). Fatigue risk management for cabin crew: the importance of company support and sufficient rest for work-life balance-a qualitative study. *Industrial health, 58*(1): 2–14. https://doi.org/10.2486/indhealth.2018-0233

Van der Wal, Z. & Demircioglu, M.A. (2020). More ethical, more innovative? The effects of ethical culture and ethical leadership on realized innovation. *Aust J Publ Admin. 79*: 386– 404. https://doi-org.ezproxy.liberty.edu/10.1111/1467-8500.12423

Vila Porras, C., & Toro-Jaramillo, I. (2020). The ethical and spiritual considerations of Matthew's Beatitudes: Configuration of the human being in companies. *Verbum Et Ecclesia, 41*(1): 1-8. http://dx.doi.org.ezproxy.liberty.edu/10.4102/ve.v41i1.2090

Vlajčić, D., Caputo, A., Marzi, G., & Dabić, M. (2019). Expatriates managers' cultural intelligence as promoter of knowledge transfer in multinational companies. *Journal of Business Research, 94,* 367-377. https://doi.org/10.1016/j.jbusres.2018.01.033

Wakelin, K. J., McAra-Couper, J., Fleming, T., & Erlam, G. D. (2023). A process for assessing the reliability and validity of questions for use in online surveys: Exploring how communication technology is used between lead maternity carer midwives and pregnant people in Aatearoa New Zealand. *Methodological Innovations, 16*(1), 91-101. https://doi.org/10.1177/20597991221148401

Wang, I., Lin, H., Lin, S., & Chen, P. (2022). Are employee assistance programs helpful? A look at the consequences of abusive supervision on employee affective organizational commitment and general health. *International Journal of Contemporary Hospitality Management, 34*(4), 1543-1565. https://doi.org/10.1108/IJCHM-06-2021-0765

Wang, W., Fu, Y., Qiu, H., Moore, J. H., Wang, Z. (2017). Corporate social responsibility and employee outcomes: A moderated mediation model of organizational identification and moral identity. *Frontiers in Psychology, 8:* 1-19. https://doi.org/10.3389/fpsyg.2017.01906

Wang, Z., Lu, X., Haoying, X., & Hannah, S. T. (2021). Not all followers socially learn from ethical leaders: The roles of followers' moral identity and leader identification in the Ethical Leadership Process. *Journal of Business Ethics, 170*(3), 449-469. http://dx.doi.org/10.1007/s10551-019-04353-y

Wang, Z., Sun, C., & Cai, S. (2021). How exploitative leadership influences employee innovative behavior: the mediating role of relational attachment and moderating role of high-performance work systems. [Exploitative leadership and employee innovation] *Leadership & Organization Development Journal, 42*(2), 233-248. https://doi.org/10.1108/LODJ-05-2020-0203

Wang, Z., & Xu, H. (2019). When and for whom Ethical Leadership is more effective in eliciting work meaningfulness and positive attitudes: The moderating roles of core self-evaluation and perceived organizational support. *Journal of Business Ethics, 156*(4): 919-940. http://dx.

doi.org.ezproxy.liberty.edu/10.1007/s10551-017-3563-x

Wang, R., & Xu, X. (2021). A bayesian-motivated test for high-dimensional linear regression models with fixed design matrix. *Statistical Papers (Berlin, Germany), 62*(4), 1821-1852. https://doi.org/10.1007/s00362-020-01157-5

Wang, Z., Xing, L., & Zhang, Y. (2021). Do high-performance work systems harm employees' health? an investigation of service-oriented HPWS in the Chinese healthcare sector. *International Journal of Human Resource Management, 32*(10), 2264-2297. https://doi.org/10.1080/09585192.2019.1579254

Wang, S., De Pater, I. E., Yi, M., Zhang, Y., & Yang, T. (2022). Empowering leadership: Employee-related antecedents and consequences. *Asia Pacific Journal of Management, 39*(2), 457-481. https://doi.org/10.1007/s10490-020-09734-w

Waring, J., Bishop, S., Clarke, J., Exworthy, M., Fulop, N. J., Hartley, J., & Ramsay, A. I. G. (2018). Healthcare leadership with political astuteness (HeLPA): A qualitative study of how service leaders understand and mediate the informal 'power and politics' of major health system change. *BMC Health Services Research, 18*(1), 918-918. https://doi.org/10.1186/s12913-018-3728-z

Wattoo, M. A., Zhao, S., & Xi, M. (2020). High-performance work systems and work–family interface: Job autonomy and self-efficacy as mediators. *Asia Pacific Journal of Human Resources, 58*(1): 128-148. https://doi.org/10.1111/1744-7941.12231

Wee, E. X. M., Liao, H., Liu, D., & Liu, J. (2017). Moving from abuse to reconciliation: A power-dependence perspective on when and how a follower can break the spiral of abuse. *Academy of Management Journal, 60*(6), 2352-2380. https://doi.org/10.5465/amj.2015.0866

Weckesser, A., & Denny, E. (2022). BJOG perspectives – qualitative research: Role of theory and ethics. *BJOG : An International Journal of Obstetrics and Gynaecology, 129*(9), 1608-1609. https://doi.org/10.1111/1471-0528.17147

Welch, J. & Hodge, M. (2018). Assessing impact: the

role of leadership competency models in developing effective school leaders. *School Leadership & Management, 38*(4): 355-377. DOI: 10.1080/13632434.2017.1411900

Wells, T., Chimka, M., & Kaur, S. (2021). Rural Principal Perspectives of Leadership Development Needs. *The Rural Educator, 42*(3),   45-55. http://ezproxy.liberty.edu/login?qurl=https%3A%2F%2Fwww.proqu est.com%2Fscholarly-journals%2Frural-principal-perspectives-leadershi p%2Fdocview%2F2618171201%2Fse-2%3Faccountid%3D12085

Wendler, D. (2020). Minimizing Risks Is Not Enough: The Relevance of Benefits to Protecting Research Participants. *Perspectives in Biology and Medicine, 63*(2), 346-358. https://doi.org/10.1353/pbm.20 20.0023

Wheelan, S. A., Åkerlund, M., & Jacobsson, C. (2020). *Creating Effective Teams (6th Edition).* SAGE Publications, Inc.

White, E. G. (2022). *Education.* https://m.egwwritings.org/en/boo k/29.29 (Original work published in 1903).

Wilkins, C. H., Mapes, B. M., Jerome, R. N., Villalta-Gil, V., Pulley, J. M., & Harris, P. A. (2019). Understanding what information is valued by research participants, and why. *Health Affairs, 38*(3), 399-407. https://doi.org/10.1377/hlthaff.2018.05046

Williams, H. (2021). The meaning of "Phenomenology": Qualitative and philosophical phenomenological research methods. *Qualitative Report, 26*(2), 366-385. https://doi.org/10.46743/2160-3715/2021.4 587

Wilson, A. (2019). Crucibles of Christian leadership: an exploration of Bennis's and Thomas's 'Crucible' concept as it relates to Christian leaders. *The Journal of Applied Christian Leadership, 13*(1): 40-54. https://go.openathens.net/redirector/liberty.edu?url=https://www.pr oquest.com/scholarly-journals/crucibles-christian-leadership-explorati on/docview/2514743745/se-2

Wolinetz, C. D., & Collins, F. S. (2020). Recognition of research participants' need for autonomy: Remembering the legacy of Henrietta Lacks. *JAMA : The Journal of the American Medical Association, 324*(11), 1027-1028. https://doi.org/10.1001/jama.2020.15936

Wu, X, Lyu, Y, Kwan, HK, Zhai, H. (2019). The impact of mentoring quality on protégés' organization-based self-esteem and proactive behavior: The moderating role of traditionality. *Hum Resource Manage. 58*: 417–430. https://doi-org.ezproxy.liberty.edu/10.1002/hrm.21968

Xu, N., Chiu, C.-Y., & Treadway, D. C. (2019). Tensions Between Diversity and Shared Leadership: The Role of Team Political Skill. *Small Group Research, 50*(4): 507–538. https://doi.org/10.1177/10464 96419840432

Yang, K, Zhou, L, Wang, Z, Lin, C, Luo, Z. (2019). Humble leadership and innovative behaviour among Chinese nurses: The mediating role of work engagement. *J Nurs Manag. 27*: 1801– 1808. https://doi-org.ezproxy.liberty.edu/10.1111/jonm.12879

Yang, F., Liu, J., Wang, Z., & Zhang, Y. (2019). Feeling energized: A multilevel model of spiritual leadership, leader integrity, relational energy, and job performance. *Journal of Business Ethics, 158*(4), 983-997. https://doi.org/10.1007/s10551-017-3713-1

Yang, I., Seong, J. Y., & Hong, D. (2020). The Indirect Effects of Ethical Leadership and High Performance Work System on Task Performance through Creativity: Exploring a Moderated Mediation Model *. *Journal of Asian Sociology, 49*(3), 351-370. https://doi.org/10.21588/ dns.2020.49.3.004

Yang, H., van Rijn, M. B., & Sanders, K. (2020). Perceived organizational support and knowledge sharing: Employees' self-construal matters. *International Journal of Human Resource Management,31*(17), 2217-2237. https://doi.org/10.1080/09585192.2018.1443956

Yen, D., Abosag, I., Huang, Y., Nguyen, B. (2017). Guanxi GRX (ganqing, renqing, xinren) and conflict management in Sino-US business relationships. *Industrial Marketing Management, 66.* 103-114. https://doi.org/10.1016/j.indmarman.2017.07.011.

Yu, L.T., Chen, M.C., Chiu, C.W., Hsu, C.C., Yuan, Y.P. (2022) Examining English Ability-Grouping Practices by Aligning CEFR Levels with University-Level General English Courses in Taiwan. *Sustainability. 14*(8):4629. https://doi.org/10.3390/su14084629

Yuan, L. & Zhang, L. (2018). When a leader is seen as too humble A curvilinear mediation model linking leader humility to employee creative process engagement. *Leadership & Organization Development Journal. 39*(4): 468-481. DOI 10.1108/LODJ-03-2017-0056

Yue, C., Fong, P. S. W., & Li, T. (2019). Meeting the challenge of workplace change: Team cooperation outperforms team competition. *Social Behavior and Personality, 47*(7): 1-15. http://dx.doi.org/10 .2224/sbp.7997

Zagenczyk, T. J., Purvis, R. L., Cruz, K. S., Thoroughgood, C. N., & Sawyer, K. B. (2021). Context and social exchange: Perceived ethical climate strengthens the relationships between perceived organizational support and organizational identification and commitment. *International Journal of Human Resource Management, 32*(22), 4752-4771. https://doi.org/10.1080/09585192.2019.1706618

Zhang, G., & Inness, M. (2019). Transformational leadership and employee voice: A model of proactive motivation. *Leadership & Organization Development Journal, 40*(7), 777-790. https://doi.org/10.1 108/LODJ-01-2019-0017

Zhang, H., Ou, A. Y., Tsui, A. S., & Wang, H. (2017). CEO humility, narcissism and firm innovation: A paradox perspective on CEO traits. *The Leadership Quarterly, 28*(5): 585-604. https://doi.org/10.10 16/j.leaqua.2017.01.003

Zhang, J. & Gill, C. (2019), Leader–follower guanxi: an invisible hand of cronyism in Chinese management. *Asia Pac J Hum Resource, 57*: 322-344. https://doi-org.ezproxy.liberty.edu/10.1111/1744-7941.12191

Zhang, S. (2020). Workplace Spirituality and Unethical Pro-organizational Behavior: The Mediating Effect of Job Satisfaction. *Journal of Business Ethics, 161*(3): 687-705. http://dx.doi.org.ezproxy.liberty.edu /10.1007/s10551-018-3966-3

Kwan, H. K., Chen, H., & Chiu, R. K. (2022). Effects of empowering leadership on followers' work-family interface. *International Journal of Human Resource Management, 33*(7), 1403-1436. https://doi.org/10.1080/09585192.2020.1762701

Zhuo, F., & Yuan, L. (2022). The impact of knowledge distance on turnover intention of millennial employees: From the perspective of mianzi. *Journal of Knowledge Management, 26*(10), 2558-2578. https://doi.org/10.1108/JKM-07-2021-0542